ATROPOS PRESS
new york • dresden

Bruce Barber

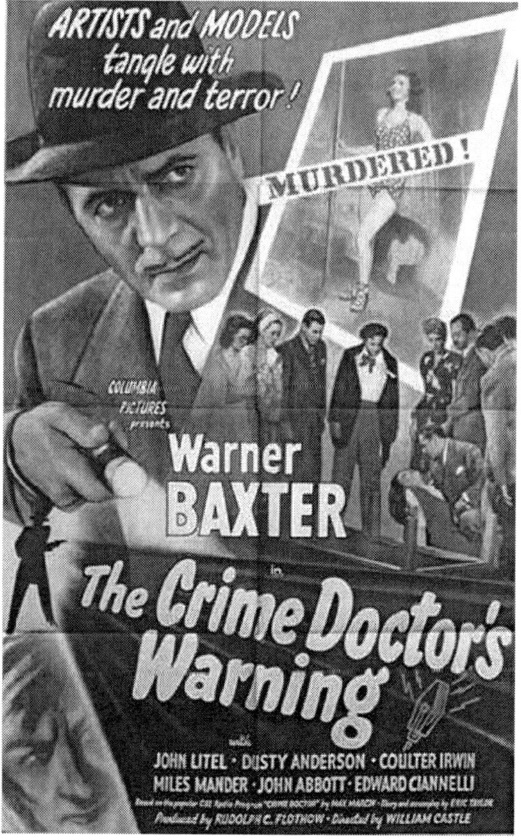

William Castle Crime Doctors Warning poster (1945)

Think Media EGS Series is supported by the European Graduate School

ATROPOS PRESS
New York • Dresden

US: 151 First Avenue # 14, New York, N.Y. 10003
Germany: Mockritzer Str. 6, D-01219 Dresden

cover design: Hannes Charen

ISBN 978-0-9748534-3-7

Acknowledgements

It is perhaps a truism that no author writes alone. Any book is arguably the result of the intellectual and creative efforts of many besides the author whose name graces the cover and title page. This author wishes to acknowledge many individuals whose work contributed directly and indirectly to *Trans/actions, Art Film and Death*: among them many film makers, philosophers and artists whose work is discussed in these pages: Special thanks to Peter Greenaway, Giorgio Agamben, Alain Badiou, Slavoj Žižek, Avital Ronell and Wolfgang Schirmacher who have influenced the direction of some of my thinking on the topic of art and death. Thanks also to Yve-Alain Bois, Agnes Varda, Hubertus von Amelunxen, Lewis Baltz, Siegfried Zielinski, Diane Davis, Victor Vitanza, Joan Grossman, and Alena Alexandrova. I have benefited from learned lectures presented by Pierre Aubenque, Christopher Fynsk, Samuel Weber, Claude Lanzmann and the writings of Jean Francois Lyotard, Jacques Derrida, Judith Butler and Jean-Luc Nancy.

Acknowledgement is also due to those colleagues with whom I have participated in conversation on related topics: Hadley Howes and Maxwell Stephens, Harlan Levey, Michael Anker, Ray Kalas, Sarah Wild, Alejo Duques, Diana Dilworth, Mahmoud Hojeij, Sherrien Rieder, Kiri Chamberlain, Juling Huang. Special thanks also to Sigrid Hackenberg, Serena Hashimoto, Johannes Heide, Simon Glass, Mark Daniel Cohen, Alexander Klemm, and Mark Reilly. My art history and film studies colleagues of UAAC (Universities Art Association of Canada), FSAC (the Film Studies Association of Canada), the Cinema Studies Association and the EPTC (Existentialism, Phenomenology, Theory, Culture, Society), also deserve acknowledgement in this context for their perceptive responses to my papers delivered at conferences.

In Australia where I spent a three month period as a visiting research fellow in the School of Fine Arts and the School of Humanities at the University of Newcastle, I would like to express my thanks to the following individuals: Anne Graham, Allan Chawner, Miranda Lawry, Lyndall Ryan of The University of Newcastle; Brad Buckley, Sydney College of Art, my faculty colleagues at NSCAD University, University Kings College and Dalhousie University especially Dorota Glowacka, Len Diepeveen and University of Kings College students who ii

encouraged me in my research endeavour. I have especially enjoyed the support and encouragement of graduate students at NSCAD University and students in classes that I taught: "The Films of Peter Greenaway"; "Hitchcock's Films"; "Reading Theory through Hitchcock", "The Pictorial Turn", and "Cyclops: Vision and Visuality in Late Twentieth Century Thought" (University of Kings College). Also special thanks are due to Mark Cheetham, Michael Ann Holly and Keith Moxey for publishing a version of the first chapter of this book which began this Odyssey; Vivien Cameron, William Clark for critical advice on the book's title and chapter headings and Photofest in New York, especially Brent Nicholson for help with the research and provision of images.

I also wish to acknowledge the Social Science and Humanities Research Council of Canada (SSHRC) that provided me with a three year Standard Research Grant enabling me to undertake research on the relationships between art, crime and cinema, and to attend several academic conferences in Canada, the United States, England, Ireland and Australia. Special thanks to Wolfgang Schirmacher, Virginia Cutrufelli, Hannes Charen and Jake Reeder of Atropos Press for their professional expertise in bringing this book to publication. And last but certainly not least, I wish to express thanks to my family in Halifax, Nova Scotia, for their forbearance to my work, Pauline Gardiner Barber, Claire and Lachlan Barber and two dogs, Abby (1990-2004) and Bella (2005-) who express a better understanding of being "thrown into life" than any human animals I have yet to meet.

Illustrations

Contents

Introduction: Marking the Limit

> Practice and theory must advance *pari passu*. People begin to see that something more goes to the composition of a fine murder than two blockheads to kill and be killed – a knife – a purse – and a dark lane. Design, gentleman, grouping, light and shade, poetry, sentiment, are now deemed indispensable to attempts of this nature. (Thomas De Quincey, 1827)[1]

> There is no essential incongruity between crime and culture. We cannot re-write the whole of history for the purpose of gratifying our moral sense of what should be. (Oscar Wilde, 1891)[2]

Crewe the artist in Alfred Hitchcock's film *Blackmail* (1929) is killed by Alice White, a young *ingénue* he attempted to rape after inviting her to his studio to view his paintings.[3] Doctor Orday the psychiatrist sleuth in William Castle's film *The Crime Doctor's Warning* (1945), cares for a patient, an artist from New York's art world who suffers from mental blackouts and cannot remember a thing from these episodes.[4] He is accused of murdering his girlfriend and several models during these episodes and Dr. Orday's task is to solve these crimes. Christopher Cross (Edward G. Robinson), a shy cashier in *Scarlet Street* (1945), an important example of film noir directed by Fritz Lang, is caught up in a relationship with Kitty March (Joan Bennett), a street wise *femme fatale* who he finally kills in a rage because she is two-timing him and presenting his paintings to the New York art world as her own.[5] In *House of Wax* (1953), the classic horror film directed by Andre de Toth, a psychotic artist murderer (Vincent Price), constructs museum exhibits of wax figures who were previously very much alive.[6] Walter Paisley (Dick Miller), the shy restaurant busboy and amateur artist in Roger Corman's *Bucket of Blood* (1962), accidentally kills his cat, then has the creative idea of covering it with plaster and exhibiting it as *Dead Cat*, a sculpture that is subsequently valorized by a local art critic who encourages the artist to produce more work for exhibition. Walter follows this suggestion with the production of several figurative sculptures and is finally honored with a solo gallery exhibition where his naturalistic works are found to contain real dead bodies. The psychotic wife of the blind sculptor (Boris Karloff), in *Cauldron of Blood* (1967), directed by Edward Andrews, provides him with human skeletons as the raw material for the production of his figurative sculpture. In the film *Colour Me Blood Red* (1969), directed by Eddie Davis, a painter decides that the red colour he desires for his paintings is best rendered in real human blood, and the mad genius artist in director Ted Hooker's *Crucible of Terror* (1972), covers his beautiful models with hot wax and then imprisons them in a bronze mold. The Joker (Jack Nicholson), in Tim Burton's *Batman* (1989), proclaims himself as "the world's first fully functioning homicidal artist," trashes key works from the historical canon in the collection of the Gotham City Art Museum and squirts acid over the faces of beautiful models as a feature of his innovative art practice. In *Backtrack* (1990), a film directed by Dennis Hopper, a multimedia artist (Jodie Foster), witnesses a mob killing and is subsequently tracked by a killer, and in *Just Cause* (1995), directed by Arne Glimcher, a serial killer in jail paints his cell in an obsessive compulsive parody of the creative magus/ mad genius archetype. *Still Life* (1994), a slasher film directed by Graeme Campbell introduces a scary performance artist with the initials AK (Art Killer), who engages in serial killing as a major feature of his progressive art practice. And in Jonathan Demme's academy award winning *Silence of the Lambs* (1991), two psychopathic serial killers display their creative talents as visual artists. The cell containing Dr. Hannibal - 'the Cannibal' - Lecter (Anthony Hopkins) is decorated with drawings of cityscapes and at one point in the narrative he produces an accomplished conté crayon drawing of FBI agent Clarice Starling (Jodie Foster), as the Virgin Mary carrying a lamb in her arms. Buffalo Bill, the transvestite serial killer sought by the FBI creatively skins his female victims to stitch them together into a woman's suit for himself. John Doe (Kevin Spacey), an equally creative serial killer in the film *Seven* (1995), directed by David Fincher is compared in one key scene to a contemporary performance artist producing a *magnum opus* by executing his murders according to the pattern provided by the seven deadly sins

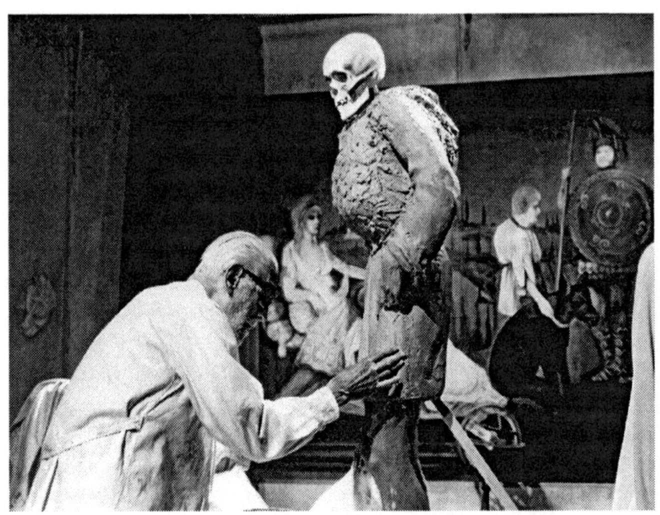
Andre de Toth   *House of Wax* (1953)

These films are among scores of others (see appendix I), that conflate art with crime, representing artists as homicidal and/or suicidal figures, criminals as artists and the perfect crime, usually murder, reconstituted as a work of art. This book explores how film participates in both the construction and undermining of our understanding of the value of both historical and contemporary art, how it reinforces stereotypical perceptions of artists as "other" in our society and the work of the avant-garde in particular, as a shocking intrusion – "the shock of the new" – into the life world that is to be resisted and rejected.[7]

Trans/actions, Art, Film and Death subscribes the notion that certain antagonisms exist within society over the value of art and culture, a thesis advanced by French sociologist Pierre Bourdieu, (1977, 1994), who empirically determined how specific social groups -- classes and class fractions -- are engaged in a largely symbolic struggle over the meaning and value of art, especially the innovative and challenging work of the avant-garde, and through this struggle configuring a world that conforms largely to their interests. This book also demonstrates how cinematic parodies and satires of modernist and postmodernist art can assist those in subordinate or marginal social positions to contest and subvert, but also, paradoxically, accommodate themselves to the ideological power(s) of the dominant culture. The principal objective of this examination of the representation of art, artists and art history in film is to complement and extend the cultural territory explored in *Popular Modernisms: Art, Cartoons, Comics and Cultural In/subordination,* an earlier book project that sought to demonstrate how graphic parodies and satires of art function become a means through which those in subordinate or marginal social positions are able to contest, subvert, and also accommodate themselves to the hegemony of the cultural dominant.[8] *Popular Modernisms* discussed mass and popular culture critiques -- in/subordinations -- of historical and contemporary art located in various media sources: *Punch* and *The New Yorker* magazines, Walt Disney comics, syndicated newspaper comic strips and cartoons, *MAD* magazine and *The National Lampoon*, comparing the political economy of these graphic satires to critiques circulating within the domain of the art world, for example the comic and cartoon satires of the art world produced by Honoré Daumier, Max Lieberman and Ad Reinhardt.[9] The research undertaken for *Trans/actions: Art, Film and Death* negotiates a similar yet somewhat larger number of questions concerning the conflation of art and crime, for instance the cinematic representation of the artist/criminal and the criminal/artist, artists as murderers, the failed artist - artist *manqué* [10]- turned murderer;[11] the artist who commits suicide, and the sites of 'perfect' crimes constituted as works of art worthy of aesthetic appreciation and veneration.[12] A preliminary question subtending this research is why there is such a prevalence of representations within mass culture of stereotypical artists; that is neurotic, melancholic, licentious, alcoholic, mad geniuses, and especially for this context, psychopathic serial killer artists, when within the history of art, there are so few clearly documented cases of artists who were indicted in a court of law for acts of murder.[13] This may be compared to a slightly higher number of artists, for which statistics are available, who committed suicide. As the art historians Rudolf and Margot Wittkower observed from their historical research into the incidence of suicide by artists over the course of several centuries:

> If the image of the mad artist as it developed over a long period of time were based on objective facts, artists should be particularly prone to suicide. The opposite, however, seems to be the case. Our search....lead to the discovery of a remarkably small number of self-inflicted deaths among artists.[14]

Since the foundation of art history as a relatively autonomous discipline area or 'discursive formation' -- to adopt a Foucauldian perspective -- a relatively small number of artists, approximately twenty, have been indicted for murder. This is a surprisingly low number given the tens of thousands of artists who were working professionally in Europe from the early Renaissance through to the inception of modernity. Among the twenty artists historically recorded who committed acts of homicide, the best known is probably the Italian painter Michelangelo Merisi - Il Caravaggio (1573-1610), who killed a man in a gambling dispute, followed by Benvenuto Cellini, the sculptor and jeweler, who killed a rival as a result of professional jealousy.[15] Lesser known artist murderers during the seventeenth century include men from three generations of the violence prone Leoni family: Leone Leoni, his son Pompeo and grandson Miguel Angel, each of whom at different times was charged with murdering someone. The historical record also includes Tommaso Luini, called Caravaggino (1600-35), described by the early art historian Giovanni Baglioni as a "furious and crazy killer," Agostino Tassi, the teacher and rapist of the painter Artemesia Gentillischi who was accused of murdering a rival, and Marco Ricci who murdered a Venetian gondoliere who had offended him, then a decade later took his own life by apparently substituting a doctor's prescription for poison.[16]

In the nineteenth century, several Northern European artists were added to the list: Jacques Van Loo (1614-70), became involved in a brawl with a wine merchant who he then stabbed to death; Pieter Mulier (c.1637-1701), killed his first wife in order to marry a second, and painter Richard Dadd, who killed his father in an apparent fit of madness.[17] There are also references in the literature to a number of suspected artist murderers. Charles Le Brun was suspected of killing rival painter Eustache Le Sueur thus echoing the famous murder committed by Cellini. And the English painter Walter Sickert (1860-1942), was indicted posthumously by crime novelist Patricia Cornwell and other writers for the infamous unsolved serial killings of Jack the Ripper. Neither artist however, was ever charged with murder or prosecuted in a court of law. In a more recent case that occurred in New York City on the 8th September 1985, Carl Andre, the international artist celebrated for his minimal sculpture and conceptual art was accused of killing Ana Mendiata, his Cuban-American wife, by pushing her out the window of their thirty-second floor apartment. The prosecution argued that the motive for the murder was Andre's jealousy towards his younger and increasingly more successful partner, who was also a well known artist, but after a nine-day trial that included testimony from many luminaries within the New York art world, Andre was acquitted.[18]

Beyond the small sampling represented above from the annals of art history; in film history there are scores, probably hundreds of artist killers, and in literature, for example in the novels of Patricia Highsmith, Minette Walters and other writers, there are equally as many, if not more.[19] These homicidal artists, their capital crimes valorized as works of art, keep company with murderers whose homicidal actions are framed as art worthy of aesthetic contemplation and veneration. A recent literary example, Jonathan Santlofer's *The Death Artist: A Novel of Suspense* (2002), somewhat unusual for having been written by a visual artist, is literally that, a serial killer who stages his murders after great paintings by famous artists. Unfortunately for the victims, the paintings selected for murderous simulation allow for some of the most gruesome and horrific killings possible -- including in one case, the skinning of a victim, thus echoing the creative actions of Buffalo Bill in the film *Silence of the Lambs*.[20]

On the world wide web there are also a few fictitious artist serial killers created by enterprising artists and writers, for example the figure of Philip LeMarchand (1717-?), French sculptor, painter and architect, the fictitious producer of dozens of exquisite puzzle boxes, architectural projects and paintings (purportedly executed with human fat), posthumously credited with being one of the most prolific mass murderers in history with over 200 murders accomplished before he magically disappeared. [21] The producers of LeMarchand's identity on the web have even provided him with an extensive gallery of work for sale consisting of puzzle box facsimiles, drawings, paintings and a fake bibliography; books with titles, and in one case, a few pages, none of which can be found in the catalogue systems of the Library of Congress or any of the New York University or Columbia University library data bases. [22] There are only two LeMarchand entries listed in standard French dictionaries of artists and engravers, both with slightly different spellings of the name, David Le Marchand (1674-1726), an ivory carver and Louis-Edouard Lemarchand (1795-1872), a cabinetmaker. And to this author's knowledge, neither artist murdered anyone.

Many of the films discussed in the following chapters reinforce the otherness (alterity) of the artist, thus encouraging the reproduction of several long-standing stereotypes of artists as dangerous individuals, whose neurotic, psychopathic, sexually avaricious and criminal behaviors threaten the social order. On a psychoanalytic level the research also explores contemporary "*phantasmatic*" reversals of the Greek myth of Pygmalion in which the artist takes a live subject, kills it and thereby turns it into a fetish object worthy of disinterested aesthetic contemplation in the Kantian sense theorised in *The Critique of Judgement* (1790). [23] The philosophical coordinates attending/extending this research encompass the discursive territories linking fetishism, creativity and death, as well as ethics and aesthetics from Plato to Kant, Spinoza, Schopenhauer, Nietzsche, Freud, Heidegger, Derrida, Nancy, Žižek, Agamben, Badiou, Schirmacher and others. *Trans/actions* also negotiates various theoretical debates about culture, class, ideology, power, with special attention accorded the political and psychical economies of the subaltern and alterity as these have been variously discussed in the writings of Raymond Williams, Michel Foucault, Franz Fanon, Edward Said, Stuart Hall, Homi Bhabha, Chantal Mouffe, Levinas, and Badiou among others.

Tracing the Limit:

> I try to keep myself at the limit of philosophical discourse. I say limit and not death, for I do not at all believe in what today is so easily called the death of philosophy, nor, moreover, in the simple death of whatever - the book, man, or god, especially since, what is dead wields a specific power.[24]

Jacques Derrida argued famously that the truth (the *trait*)[25] in painting lies outside the frame, and that in order to understand painting one must "travel four times around it." This he says, is the whole story -- "all that is needed to know" -- (that) which is "contained in *surrounds* or *approaches* (emphasis added), to the work, frame, *passe partout*, title, signature, museum, archive, discourse, marketplace -- in short, wherever there is legislation by *marking of the limit.*"[26]

I believe that we may often lose sight of the fact that the 'truth,' such as it is, in film also resides outside, around and between the marking of the limit. Too often our focus may be concentrated upon the minutiae of signification: bars, triangles, blots and stains, the rhetoric in the projected frame(s), or the syntagmatic chains that result from their concatenation and suturing. This attention I characterize as the *microscopy* of the 'perfect instant' of Diderot and Barthes, and those imperfect instants that promise, but only occasionally deliver the return of the viewer's gaze, in those writers, from Raymond Bellour to Slavoj Žižek who have variously endorsed the psychoanalytic project of Jacques Lacan.

It is perhaps a truism that no artist, certainly no film maker works alone, and yet many film critics and historians have blithely built a whole edifice on the reductive principles of auteurship. Thus for example, the personal signature of Alfred Hitchcock in his films supplants other less exalted but nonetheless, in my view, legitimate claims to authorship provided by his partners in crime, the producers, novelists, screenplay writers, the art directors, set designers, decorators *et al*, whose work is subordinated in the drive to construct and maintain that provocative word, Hitchcockian, the adjectival ascription that we reserve for the geniuses of Western civilization (Shakespearean, Joycean, Steinian, Picassoesque, Duchampian), who become like Joseph Knecht in Herman Hesse's novel, *ipso facto* authors, rule makers and breakers -- *magisters ludi* -- of their own game.[27]

What and who should we privilege in the film study project? The author: work, narrative, actors, spectator, audience, the apparatus, or the institution cinema itself? And how appropriate are our discursive practices, theoretical positions and interpretive strategies? How important is it to submit to a trend or dominant ideology and/or methodology in any film research project? And should we confirm the omnipotence of this or that discursive regime, or perhaps take the ripest fruits from each of them for our own endorsement?[28] This is not to suggest here that the abundant varieties of overlapping discursivities under the umbrella of cinema studies are inappropriate or inadequate to the tasks at hand. Rather, I will flag the super-ordinate capacities of certain interpretive and quasi analytical practices that reduce the possibility for a perspicacious understanding of the film artifact in *all* of its discursive contexts, with all that this phrase can denote and connote with respect to cultural expression, socio-economic, political and institutional realities. Too often the privileged object of the study becomes the complex ensemble of signs within the frame(s) with some observations about subjecthood and identity according to a prescriptive model read off on the side. In Hitchcock studies for example, the discussion that follows the microscopy of the frame often becomes how this and that ensemble of details lend themselves to the reinforcement of the specific genius characteristics of the Master. Ripped out of its production, distribution and reception sites that will allow the researcher to understand the object of study more fully in its dynamic, shifting and changing social contexts, the cultural artifact submits to the exemplary, if potentially myopic reading faculties of the researcher armed with his or her favorite academic paradigm who engages in the mechanics of a barely disguised connoisseurship, and hagiography is often the unanticipated result. Auteurship therefore becomes the privileged domain of research almost by default.

I believe that the primary theoretical tasks for film researchers in this new millennium should coincide with Derrida's; that is, writing four times *around* (the) work, a process that necessitates the "apperception and negotiation of the spaces *in between*, and those *transitional* encounters along the way." For Derrida the task of writing (four times) *around* painting assumed the following circular (periscopic, perambulatory), and deconstructive (folding and interventionist) forms: "The first time (around), I am occupied with folding the great philosophical question of the tradition." He writes of inducing a disturbance (an intervention) in the philosophy that still dominates the discourse on painting: Plato, Kant, Hegel, and Heidegger. "All that Kant glimpsed under the name *parergon* (for example, the frame) is neither in the work (*ergon*) nor outside it."[29] For film studies the task is similar, with the addition of some of this discipline's *Ur* figures: arguably, Marx, Freud, Foucault and Lacan. The second time around, Derrida describes as an attempt to "decrypt or unseal a singular contract, one that links the phonic trait, even before the word (GI, Tr., +R), to the so-called graphic *trait*."[30] The implication this time around for film studies is that the researcher proceeds to negotiate, interpret (read) or otherwise engage the work in formal terms. This entails assessing its imminent meaning structures yet postponing indefinitely the quest for analytical or interpretive wholeness or closure. This aspect of the project necessitates a discussion of tailoring techniques: For example the analysis of shot language, suturing, and the rhetoric of the image -- the diegetic and enunciative codes -- but *not* in the absence of other information that may disrupt the coherence of the schema. The third time around the work is in order to analyse what Derrida terms the *ductus* (idiom of the *trait/* trace as the draftsman's signature), and the system of *duction* (production, reproduction, reduction, *etc.*). This, he argues, concerns "the letter and proper name in painting" (read film), "with narration, technical reproduction, ideology, the phoneme, the biographeme, and politics among other things." For film studies this engages the authorship question, properly situated in its socio-historical, political and economic contexts. The fourth time around Derrida weaves all these threads through a polylogue of N + 1 voices which happens to be that of a woman." He revisits the famous correspondence between Heidegger and Schapiro in order to find out to whom in truth, are the unlaced shoes of Vincent van Gogh's painting addressed? This time around, the researcher has to engage in some cross-dressing, assuming or performing the identity of the classed, raced, gendered, queer other, to slip out of a mind (and body) set in order to access the interpretative capacities of the 'not me.'

The common feature of the four times is the *trait* / trace a word that Derrida employs to engage a number of meanings including to draw (-ing), to pull (-ing), and in phrases such as *trait d'esprit* (flash of wit), and *trait de genie* (stroke of genius). Derrida's *passe partout* is not simply a master key but a matt and matrix for the cultural artifact in its entirety. This he suggests, "would be almost the place for a preface or a foreword between, on the one hand, the cover that bears the names (author and publisher) and the titles (work and series or field), the copyright, the flyleaf and on the other hand the first word of the book, here the first line of the lemmata, with which one ought to begin." He concludes with the implicit understanding, and perhaps warning, that the "internal edges of a *passe-partout* are often beveled."[31]

Derrida's project is at once philosophical, historical, sociological, interpretive, analytical, and deconstructive. There is no privileged reductive semiotic here and no attachment to the power dynamics of the gaze, transcendental reflection of the mirror stage, interpellation of the subject, the competent viewer's awareness of the stain (Bonitzer), absorptive characteristics of the *punctum* (Barthes), or the anamorphism of "the blot" (Žižek).[32] Has Derrida posed an impossible task? I do not believe so. Difficult? Yes. Does this mean that the film studies project must become more philosophical, sociological and ethnographic? And should we follow his other prescriptions for the deconstructive project and submit our own findings to the imprimatur of his *sur/sous rature* (parenthetical suspension and possible erasure)? Yes, I also believe this to be the case. The old assumptions simply will not do.

In keeping with the implicit critical self-reflexivity of this project, it is perhaps time at this juncture to reveal how my own research has been challenged and at times both guided and limited by Derrida's intervention(s). I have attempted throughout this book to be directed by his periscopic, circumambulatory (four times around) methodology albeit not in any specific order, occasionally privileging one 'go round' in favour of another; the circumcircle (touching all the vertices of a triangle or polygon), as opposed to circumvention, if only as Alain Badiou has insisted, "to force some truths" about the condition of art and the status of the artist in contemporary society.[33] But I also recognize the warnings about truth seeking posted by Lyotard, Bourdieu, Derrida, Deleuze and Wolfgang Schirmacher, for example, who has argued that "the disclosure of truth is never overt but, rather, an indirect communication and a complex happening in life that needs concealing as much as revealing. Difference results from the power that lies in the unknown, in the not-yet known or never-known."[34]

There exists already a rich corpus of material on the theoretical relationships between the arts, and although I believe that the weaving of the history of visual art with that of cinema can sustain further explication in historical, critical and theoretical terms, the principal aim of the research for *Trans/actions* has been to explore the underside (or dark side), of this rich discursive territory; principally the representation of artists, art and art history - "the institution art" in film.[35] My preliminary research for this project resulted in the production and presentation of six conference papers, each in various ways, arguing that this discursive process engaged a very different set of relationships, marked less by similarities of discourse, hybridity and consonance, than dissonance and differ/ance. For all of those films that reproduce modernist technical innovations, or faithfully represent and simulate the projects of modernist art, there are as many that repudiate, reject and disavow art and artists, playing out familiar popular resistance, rejection and negation strategies employing irony, satire, parody, burlesque, in a manner reminiscent of cartoons, comics and other forms of mass and popular culture.[36] A few art and film historians have engaged in research of the cinematic representation of art, artists and art history in film, without however, specifically exploring the conflation of art and crime, or the aesthetics of murder. John Berger (1959), Peter Wollen (1973), Stephen Heath (1976), Griselda Pollock (1980), Diane Waldman (1981), Brigitte Peucker (1995), Angela Della Vacche (1996), and Susan Felleman (1997), have each discussed various aspects of the representation of art and artists in film, Della Vacche more specifically between painting and cinema. John Walker's *Art and Artists on Screen* (1993), and the Montreal Museum of Fine Arts exhibition catalogue *Alfred Hitchcock and Art* (1999), represent other contributions to the field, albeit without the specific philosophical, theoretical and implicit sociological foci of this research. Joel Black's *The Aesthetics of*

Murder: A Study in Romantic Literature and Contemporary Culture (1991) is an excellent discussion of Thomas De Quincey's famous "Murder" essays configured as a satire of Kant's aesthetic philosophy. Although Black primarily focuses his discussion on literature, he also discusses a few art works by Rauh, Rops, Cézanne, Magritte, and films, Brian De Palma's *Dressed to Kill*, Martin Scorsese's *Taxi Driver* and Alfred Hitchcock's *Rope*. Black does not however, place much emphasis upon either the sociological significance or the political economy of the conflation of art/crime or recognize this as a phantasmatic process with specific historical origins.

Trans/actions: Art, Film and Death represents an attempt to understand the political, libidinal and psychic economies of culture criticism, specifically cultural in/subordination as this represents the symbolic contest of power between various classes and class fractions over the meaning and value of art (and crime). It can be argued that *in/subordination* is always the basis of criticism.[37] The critical act, whatever that may be - an ironic aside, performed parody, a graphic satire, subversive or transgressive broadside, engages, both the subject's will *to resist,* and the will *to overcome* its dominating object. This is the philosophical character of in/subordination, which is to be distinguished somewhat from its more restrictive familial and military definitions of disobedience and rebelliousness. In/subordination represents an urge to disavow or refuse an extant cultural 'law' or legitimation in progress. Practices of in/subordination, subversion or denunciation are also characteristic behaviors of the avant-garde, a usually self-marginalized, and therefore subordinate, sub-group within the dominant culture. Pierre Bourdieu has described the process of subordination somewhat differently as a political game with certain stakes where culture itself is the ultimate fetish and the operational axes of differentiation and competition are dependent upon the original investment that operationalises the stakes under which it is played.

> Culture is a stake which like all social stakes,
> simultaneously presupposes and demands that
> one take part in the game and be taken in by it;
> and interest in culture without which there is no

> race, no competition, is produced by the very
> race and competition which it produces. [38]

The game is ultimately tied to the reproduction of ideologically inflected class interests, ordinate and subordinate positions on the 'board' that both maintains and reproduces cultural hegemony. In the same passage Bourdieu outlines the function of the avant-garde with respect to the "genuine (social) objectification" of the cultural game and correlates the power dynamic operating within the counter culture with the sub-cultural avant-garde(s).

> Nothing is further from such objectification that the artistic denunciation of the art which some artists go in for, or the activities grouped under the term counter- culture. The latter merely contest one culture in the name of another, counterposing a culture dominated within the relatively autonomous field of cultural production and distribution (which does not make it the culture of the dominated) to a dominant culture; in so doing they fulfill the traditional role of a cultural avant-garde, which by its very existence helps to keep the cultural game going. [39]

Bourdieu's argument is very similar to that proposed by art historian Thomas Crow who has argued that "the avant-garde serves as a kind of research and development arm of the culture industry" a process of appropriation and incorporation from mass culture that serves to revitalize the dominant culture, and indeed, keep 'the game' going. [40]

The term *in/subordination* invokes a comparison with the use of the term *subaltern* in post-colonial discourse in for example the writings of Said (1978, 1984), Spivak (1988), Guha 1989, and Bhabha, (1994). [41] In this context however, the use of the term in/subordination should not be confused with the use of *subalternity* which has greater currency in the debates around identity and subject politics rather than class, witness Homi Bhabha's (1994) claim that:

> The move away from the singularities of 'class' or 'gender' as primary conceptual and organizational categories, has resulted in an awareness of the subject positions - of race, gender, generation, institutional

location, geopolitical locale, sexual orientation - that inhabit any claim to identity in the modern world.[42]

Bhabha goes on to argue the need to think beyond foundational categories to explore sites of confluence - in between spaces-between subjectivity, identity formation and sites for redefining the idea of society itself. Like Derrida, Bhahba is concerned about ascertaining the limits of discourse, albeit around identity politics.

> What is theoretically innovative, and politically crucial, is the need to think beyond narratives of originary and initial subjectivities and to focus on those moments or processes that are produced in the articulation of cultural differences. These 'in-between' spaces provide the terrain for elaborating strategies of self-hood - singular or communal - that initiate new signs of identity, and innovative sites of collaboration and contestation, in the act of defining the idea of society itself.[43]

Acknowledging Bhabha's cautionary criticism, I suggest here that the littoral spaces between class and subject/identity/other must be negotiated before any "innovative sites for collaboration and/or contestation" can actually occur. The English historian E.P.Thompson's definition of class as "lived experience" one moreover -- that constructs itself as much as it is made -- finds acceptance in the work of many contemporary writers on class and identity politics. Stanley Aronowitz for example suggests that:

> What has occurred in the last quarter century is that, on the assumption that the working class shares in the general level of material culture, class has been removed ideologically and politically from the politics of subalternity, at least in late capital societies, and has been replaced by new identities or by conceptions according to which the 'new' middle classes - hardly oppressed social categories - have emerged as political agents, but in their own behalf.[44]

I concur with many aspects of the post-structural critique of restrictive foundational categories particularly where these reproduce extant power relations and prohibit the defining (and changing) of society, but like Aronowitz, I have difficulty with the elimination of class as a useful category distinction as has been suggested by some theoreticians. For example Giorgio Agamben in *The Coming Community* (1993) collapses -- he uses the term "dissolves" -- social classes into "just a single planetary *petty bourgeoisie* (emphasis added), which has taken over the aptitude of the proletariat to refuse any recognizable identity" a being-thus -- to be the thus -- singularity without identity therefore fit subjects for entering a community without presuppositioned and without subjects, into a communication without the incommunicable." In another section of his book Agamben prophesies that the "planetary petty bourgeoisie is probably the form in which humanity is moving towards its own destruction."[45] Recognizing social deprivation, power differentials and struggles raging between groups in multiple discursive and social contexts -- think of the struggles that take place within the still rigid caste system in India of the 160 million Dalits or so-called "Untouchables" (1 in 6 of the total population), the ethnic, religious and class rivalries in Britain, any country in Africa, Europe, Asia and even in North America -- I have some difficulty endorsing Agamben's somewhat quixotic argumentation in this context but I do however recognize it as a warning to continue questioning the viability of class as a foundational concept upon which to structure difference and struggle.[46]

A principal aim of the research for this book in the first 'go-round' is to place the category [class] under erasure with the hope of resuscitating it; that is without delivering it into the postmodern hopper and relativising it out of existence. There are, I believe, many social and political confluences that intersect with the symbolic construction, interpretation and criticism of culture. As Bourdieu's work readily demonstrates, culture criticism represented symbolically between class fractions can be identified as ideological conflict.[47] For example, he writes: Different classes (and social fractions) are engaged in a specifically symbolic struggle to impose the definition of the social world most in conformity with their interests. The field of ideological positions reproduces in transfigured form the field of social positions.[48] He follows this subsequently with a more comprehensive statement about the symbolic representation of power differentials within culture and class struggle: "The field of symbolic production is a microcosm of the struggle between the classes." [49] The focus upon film in these chapters represents an attempt to provide some practical explication of the symbolic contest of power as this process represents the struggle to achieve and maintain cultural hegemony. I argue that this contest of power can be read as ideological conflict (in/subordination), between various dominant and subordinate groups, classes and class fractions and that this moreover, has important consequences for the reception of contemporary art in the public sphere.

Chapter I, "Art History's Significant Other...Film Studies" explores the inter-discursive relationships between film studies, art history and the philosophy of art, as these pertain to the research of cultural critiques of modernist art and the "agonist, antagonist and activist," work of the sub-cultural avant-gardes.[50] The chapter introduces preliminary readings of three films, two that feature homicidal artists, Fritz Lang's *Scarlet Street* (1945) and Tim Burton's *Batman* (1989), and Iain Softley's film *Backbeat* (1994), in which art, love and death intersect. The second chapter "Alterity, Sovereign Consciousness and Cultural In/subordination" explores and discusses the compatibility of various theoretical approaches to social conflict, ideology and cultural hegemony in the writings of: Voloshinov, Bahktin, Gramsci, E.P.Thompson, Bourdieu, Williams, Laclau, Mouffe, Žižek and Butler. Other writers are explored with respect to their positions on ethics, alterity, cultural sovereignty and in/subordination including: Derrida, Foucault, Bataille, Deleuze, Levinas, Agamben and Bhahba. Chapter 3, "The Artist *Manqué* as *Alter Deus*" explores the artist as outsider/other God figure. In this chapter special attention is accorded the construction and cinematic reproduction of the psychopathic artist and the failed artist (*l'artiste manqué*) stereotypes. This chapter contains an overview of literature discussing the image of the artist, specifically the mad genius archetype, from the Renaissance to the twentieth century: Marcilio Ficino, Sigmund Freud, Ernst Gombrich, Ernst Kris, Rudolf and Margot Wittkower and Geraldine Pelles. Chapter 4, "Murder as One of the Fine Arts" negotiates the critical neo-Kantian philosophical position on the aesthetic sublime adopted by Thomas De Quincey in his famous essay "On Consideration of

Murder as One of the Fine Arts" (1822), and discusses Oscar Wilde's *The Picture of Dorian Gray* (1890), arguing that both these texts have provided extremely influential models for the conflation of art and crime in film. Chapter 5, "The Pygmalion Effect" discusses several reversals of the Pygmalion myth with a special focus upon the ethics and aesthetics of terror. Close readings are undertaken of Roger Corman's film *Bucket of Blood* (1959), Michael Powell's *Peeping Tom* (1960), Martin Scorsese's film *After Hours* (1985), and Graeme Campbell's *Still Life* (1992). The Pygmalion effect is discussed in terms of disavowal (*verleugneung*) in the sense discussed by Giorgio Agamben (1974, 1993), in which the melancholic fetishist simultaneously affirms and denies his object of desire. Chapter 6, "The Art Crimes of Alfred Hitchcock" provides a deconstructive reading of the role of artists, art works and art tropes in the work of Alfred Hitchcock with special attention paid to the films: *The Lodger* (1927), *Easy Virtue* (1927), *Blackmail* (1929), *The Trouble with Harry* (*1955*), and *Frenzy* (1972). Chapter 7, "A Perfect Murder " contains a reading of Hitchcock's *Dial M for Murder* (1954), and its remake *A Perfect Murder* (1999), directed by Andrew Davis. This chapter explores the resilience through time of the art/murder model of perfection.

Chapter 8, "Art and Death in the Films of Peter Greenaway" and Chapter 9, "The Belly of an Artist" discuss phantasmatic themes in the films of Peter Greenaway with readings of: *The Falls* (1980), *The Draughtsman's Contract* (1982), *Zed and Two Noughts* (1985), *The Belly of an Architect* (1986), and *The Cook, The Thief, His Wife and Her Lover* (1989). Chapter 10, "The Death of Film," the vertex of this book -- where the axis meets the curve -- discusses the killing of cinema itself, through a reading of the International Situationist's critique of the "society of the spectacle" and the situationist films of Guy Debord, focusing upon *Hurlements en Faveur de Sade* (*Screams on Behalf of de Sade*, 1952), and the palindrome title *In girum imus nocte et consumimur igni* (*We turn in the night consumed by fire* (1978). This chapter argues that the obverse of the art crime conflation is naturally the crime of art itself, an obsession of the necrophiliacal historical avant-garde movements of the modernist era, that have initiated and engaged in the usurping of the authority of previous vanguards, a type of Oedipal ritualistic killing of the father in order to secure the identity of the son. The concluding postscript reviews the basic arguments articulated in the previous chapters, reinforcing the need to recognize the art/crime, art/death conflation as phantasms of Eros and Thanatos, ideologised products of the Oedipal, Trinitarian and dialectical foundations of Western epistemology.

---

[1] De Quincey, T. "On Consideration of Murder as one of the Fine Arts" in *The English Mail Coach and other Writings* Edinburgh Adam and Charles Black 1893 p. 4. See also *The Collected Writings of Thomas De Quincey* ed David Masson Edinburgh Adam and Charles Black 1890 13.12

[2] Wilde, O. *The Artist as Critic : Critical Writings of Oscar Wilde* ed Richard Ellmann New York Vintage Books 1969: 339

[3] Crewe the artist character is played by Cyril Ritchard and Alice White, by the Czech actress Anny Ondra. Alice's lines were spoken off camera by Joan Barry.

[4] Castle was later known as the shock horror showman of Hollywood cinema, best known for the film *The Tingler* for which he rigged special seats for his viewers that gave them a mild electric shock during moments of high suspense.

[5] A remake of Jean Renoir's film *La Chienne* (1931).

[6] *House of Wax* is a remake of the earlier horror film *Mystery of the Wax Museum* (1933) about a disfigured
wax dummy maker who turns to murder to populate his museum with sculpture. *Video Hounds Golden Movie Retriever* 2005:571

[7] Dunlap, I. *The Shock of the New*. St. Louis, San Francisco, American Heritage Press 1972:1

[8] See also Barber, B. Guilbaut, S and O'Brian J., (eds) *Voices of Fire: Art, Rage, Power and the State* Toronto, University of Toronto Press 1996

[9] See Barber, B., *Popular Modernisms: Art, Cartoons, Comics and Cultural In/Subordination..* (forthcoming)

[10] See also Barber, B. Guilbaut, S and O'Brian J., (eds) *Voices of Fire: Art, Rage, Power and the State* Toronto, University of Toronto Press 1996

[11] Here the signal example is provided by Adolf Hitler who author J.P. Stern describes as "an artist manqué." See Stern, J.P. *Hitler: The Fuhrer and the People* Berkeley and Los Angeles: University of California Press. 1975:45 fn and Spotts, Frederic, *Hitler and the Power of Aesthetics* Overlook Press, 2003.

[12] A note about what this study does not explore. Any web search using the keywords, artist and murder will turn up dozens of web pages for the rap band *The Murderers* (artist page). This study also does not discuss recent murders by popularly designated con artists, previously called confidence tricksters or confidence men, for example the mother and son team, Sante and Kenny Kime, *con artists* who murdered Irene Silverman.

[13] A similar question could be posed with respect to the mad scientist, nutty professor and mad doctor stereotypes that have also generated scores of representations within popular culture.

---

[14]Wittkower, R. and M. Born Under Saturn: The Character and Conduct of Artists: A Documented History from Antiquity to the French Revolution New York, Norton Random House 1963:133

[15] Both artists have been the subjects of films: *The Affairs of Cellini* aka *The Firebrand* (1934) directed by Gregory La Cava and Derek Jarman's *Caravaggio* (1986)

[15]Wittkowers, p.308

[16] Wittkowers, p.308

[17] Black, J., The Aesthetics of Murder: A Study in Romantic Literature and Contemporary Culture Baltimore, The John Hopkins University Press 1991:37

[18] The Mystery of the Carl Andre Murder Case" <u>Village Voice</u> (March 29, 1988 25:32, and also Robert Katz *Naked by the Window: The Fatal Marriage of Carl Andre and Ana Mendieta*" New York Atlantic Monthly Press, 1990

[19]Patricia Highsmith's novel *Ripley Under Ground* (1970), in which Ripley masquerades as a dead painter and kills an art collector. The plot of Minette Walter's novel *The Sculptress* introduces author Rosalind Leigh who has been commissioned to write a book about Olive Martin, an obese young woman, known as The Sculptress after hacking up her mother and sister with an axe and rearranging the pieces as a work of art. In her prison cell she carves small wax figurines including, after their first interview, one of Rosalind Leigh.

[20] On line reviewer Roberta O'Hara describes *The Death Artist* as "a taut, riveting thriller set in the New York art world. Jonathan Santlofer, the author, brings to the book a lifetime in the creative and exclusive circle of buyers, curators, experts, and artists. He is the winner of two National Endowment for the Arts painting grants, several Visiting Artist residencies at The Vermont Studio Center, and a variety of other honors. Santlofer knows art --- the classic and the contemporary --- and he puts this knowledge to good use in his first novel, at once educating and entertaining us."

[21] For example Holt, Laura *The Art Legend and Evil of Philip LeMarchand* Prentice-Abbott 1966 and Isadora Klauski *Architecture and Madness* Bell Publishing 1924.

[22] As far as I have been able to deduce from the available evidence the creators of LeMarchand's fantastic 'life' are New York based artist/designers Daniel W. Holland and Dan McNeil.

[23] Phantasmatic refers to the specific "technically precise" uses of this and related terms, phantasm, phantasy, phantastic employed by Giorgio Agamben in his *Stanzas: Word and Phantasm in Western Culture*. Ronald L. Martinez (Translation) Theory and History of Literature, Vol. 69. Minneapolis, University of Minnesota Press. 1993

[24] Derrida, J. *The Truth in Painting* Bennington, G. and McLeod, I.,Trans Chicago, University of Chicago Press, 1987:6

[25] Derrida uses *trait* in many senses: trace, distinguishing attribute, inherent characteristic, including rhyming with *vrai* and *vérité* to signal tracing as a truth function. *Trait* means drawing or pulling and in phrases such as *trait d'esprit* (flash of wit), and *trait de genie* (stroke of genius).

[26] Derrida, 1987:9

[27] "Joseph [Knecht] devoted his free time during that year chiefly to the Glass Bead Game, which enthralled him more and more. A notebook of jottings from that period, dealing with the meaning and theory of the Game, begins with the sentence "The whole of both physical and mental life is a dynamic phenomenon, of which the Glass Bead Game basically comprehends only the aesthetic side, and does so predominantly as an image of rhythmic processes." Hesse, H. *Magister Ludi* (*The Glass Bead Game*) New York, Bantam Books 1970:95; originally published in 1943 under the title *Das*

Glasperlenspiel Fretz &Wesmuth Ag Zurich.

[28] This point will discussed further in Chapter 1

[29] Derrida, p 9

[30] Ibid, p.10

[31] Ibid pp. 12-13

[32] See Barthes. R. *Image Music Text* translation Stephen Heath New York, Hill and Wang. Žižek S "The Hitchcockian Blot" pp 123-140 and Bellour, R. "Hitchcock-Endgame", pp179-187 in Allen R. and Gonzales S. Ishi. *Alfred Hitchcock: Centenary Essays* London, British Film Institute 1999; and Žižek, S., (ed) *Everything You Always Wanted to Know About Lacan (But were Afraid to ask Hitchcock)* London, Verso 1992

[33] Badiou, Alain (EGS Lecture notes 2002). See also Badiou, Alain; Barbara P. Fulks (Translation). 'The Political as a Procedure of Truth.'" *Lacanian ink* 19. The Wooster Press. Fall 2001

[34] Schirmacher, W. "Homo Generator: Media and Postmodern Technology" In Bender, G and Druckery, T *Culture on the Brink*: *Ideologies of Technology* Seattle, Bay Press , 1994:73

[35] Bürger, P. *Theory of the Avant-Garde*, Minneapolis, University of Minnesota, Theory and History of Literature Vol 4 1984:2

[36] B. Barber *Popular Modernisms: Art, Cartoons, Comics and Cultural In/Subordination* (forthcoming)

[37] The / backslash represents a subordinating and linking feature analogous to the backslash in cyber culture discourse.

[38] Bourdieu, P. *Distinction: A Social Critique of the Judgement of Taste* Translated by Richard Nice, Cambridge Mass. Harvard University Press 1984 p 250

[39] Ibid 251 see also Bourdieu, P. "The Social Conditions of the International Circulation of Ideas" in Shusterman, R. (ed) *Bourdieu: A Critical Reader* Oxford Blackwell Publishers 1999 pp 220-228

[40] Buchloh, B., Guilbaut, S., and Solkind, D., *Modernism and Modernity: The Proceedings from The Vancouver Conference.* Halifax, NSCAD and NYU Press 1983, 2004: 253 Crow, T., *Modern Art in the Common Culture* New Haven and London, Yale University Press 1996

[41] The problems of political agency in the colonial subject are discussed at length in the volumes 1-6 (1983-1990) of *Subaltern Studies* New Dehli: Oxford University Press edited by Ranajiit Ruha. See also Ashcroft, Griffiths, G. and Tiffin, H. *The Post-Colonial Reader*, London and New York, Routledge 1995.

[42] Bhabha, H.K., 1994:1-2

[43] Ibid

[44] Aronowitz, S. *How Class Works: Power and Social Movements* New Haven, Yale University Press 2003 ix)

[45] See Agamben, Giorgio, Georgia Albert (Translation). *The Man Without Content.* Stanford University Press. Stanford, 1999 and also Agamben, Giorgio, Michael Hardt (Translation). *The Coming Community.* Minneapolis, Theory Out of Bounds, Vol. 1. University of Minnesota Press, 1993.

[46] A recent Italian Study indicated that more than a third of the 20.7 million inhabitants in southern Italy are poor, earning less that 521 or 637 euros per month and two thirds of this number are extremely poor. The authors of the study Maurizio Bonati and Rita Campi of Milan's Mario Negri Institute of Pharmacological research concluded that if

southern Italy were an independent country it would have the highest poverty rate in Europe. They highlighted the "constellation of risks" to children living there as a result of such dire poverty. Reuters Report International Herald Tribune Wednesday August 24th 2005.

[47] Class *fraction* describes a social grouping within a class. The identity of sub-group categories has been employed usefully by many cultural studies theorists and researchers: Stuart Hall, Dick Hebdige, Colin Mercer, Janet Woollacott *et al*. The most useful definition of *class fraction* based upon the acquisition of cultural capital is Bourdieu's (1977, 1984, 1990). "The hostility of the working class and of the middle class fractions least rich in cultural capital [*knowledge and experience*] towards every kind of formal experimentation asserts itself both in the theatre and in painting, or still more clearly, because they have less legitimacy, in photography and the cinema." (Bourdieu, P. *Distinction: A Social Critique of the Judgement of Taste* Translated by Richard Nice, Cambridge Mass. Harvard University Press 1984:32) see also this author's *"Table* 9 Social origin of members of the dominant class, by class fraction" (121).

[48]Bourdieu, P. *Outline of a Theory of Practice* Cambridge, Trans R. Nice, London, New York, Cambridge University Press 1977: 112

[49] Ibid

[50] Poggioli, R. *The Theory of the Avant-Garde* Cambridge, University of Cambridge, 1968

Chapter 1

Art History's Significant Other...Film Studies [1]

The still is the major artifact of the projected film.
(Roland Barthes)[2]

In a number of important respects, modern art history has been a supremely cinematic practice, concerned with the orchestration of historical narratives and the display of genealogy by filmic means. In short the modern discipline has been grounded in metaphors of cinematic practice to the extent that in nearly all of its facets, art history could be said to continually refer to and to implicate the discursive logic of realist cinema. The art history slide is always orchestrated as a still in a historical movie.   (Donald Preziosi) [3]

In the introduction to their provocative anthology *The New Art History* (1986), A.L. Rees and Frances Borzello wrote that the next stage of art history "is anyone's guess." [4] They suggested however, that a possible direction could be supplied by film studies, a field that had influenced the direction of the so-called 'new' art history. Nodding appreciatively in the direction of David Bordwell, Janet Staiger and Kristin Thompson's socio-historical study, *The Classical Hollywood Cinema* (1985), Borzello and Rees argued that the uniting of *Screen*-style theoretical explorations with traditional historical research could pave the way to a more progressive model of art history for the future.[5] This introductory chapter of *Trans/Actions, Art, Film and Death* will reflect upon comments that construct art history as a "cinematic practice," born as they are of the putative crisis in art history established with the publication of several key texts in the 1970s[6] and early 1980s.[7] I will trace in the first section, aspects of the discursive relationship between the new art history and film studies explicitly acknowledged by several art historians (Rees, Borzello, Preziosi, Clark, Pollock, Tagg, Burgin, Wollen, Bois), and implicitly by many others (Fried, Krauss, Pollock, Frascina, Guilbaut and Crow).[8] This will be followed by a preliminary reading of four films that ironise, parody, or satirize art, artists and art history through their conflation of art and crime. I argue that the relationship between cinema, film studies and the "institution art" (Bürger, 1984) has been far from innocent, and that as much as art history has provided a fertile ground for the germination of various discursive hybrids and tropes, such as Preziosi's above, and nurtured the work of scores of film makers, among them: Alfred Hitchcock, Peter Greenaway, Tim Burton, Martin Scorsese, Roger Corman and others discussed in this book, who have borrowed directly and indirectly from art history for their productions; it has also powerfully signified difference, in the oppositional sense of this keyword and *différance* [9] in the sense invoked by Jacques Derrida, that conflates difference/deference (differ/defer), enabling the implicit binary to be eclipsed and multiple differentials of meaning and power to be affirmed.[10] There is some legitimacy to Preziosi's cinematic paradigm for art history; Roland Barthes (1977) and Michael Fried (1989), both taking their cues from Denis Diderot, have promoted similar conflations with regard to the 'organon of representation' figured in the perfect instants of canvas, cinema and theatre. But when art history is actually represented in film, it often reveals less the "discursive logic of realist cinema" argued by Preziosi than examples of popular antagonism towards high culture and modernist art that exist within classed society. In films such as: *Blackmail* (1929), *Suspicion* (1941), *Scarlet Street* (1945), *Crime Doctor's Warning* (1945), *The Party* (1957), *Vertigo* (1958), *Bucket of Blood* (1960), *The Rebel* (1960), *The Moderns* (1988), *After Hours* (1985), *Still Life* (1989), *Batman* (1992), and *Just Cause* (1995), (see Appendix I), the institution art is subjected to the critical machinations of popular culture, becoming in the process, a site for the symbolic contestation of meaning and a "nodal point" in the continuing struggle for cultural power.[11]

The postmodern era did not inaugurate the traffic in ideas, theories and methodologies between disciplines, but it did in an important sense legitimize - *legislate* - the overlaying of one discipline's discursive practices (or regimes) upon another. The traveling metaphors associated with this littoral process: cross roads, intersections, boundaries, borders through which one, with intellectual baggage in hand, transports oneself; territory over which one crosses, hops, glides and elides, in many ways affirm the correspondences between relatively homogenous textual practices (discipline grounded discourse), that have been in evidence since the inauguration of modernism. Many researchers have identified the postmodern theoretical free market as a battleground of competing theories, methodologies, ideologies, discursive practices,[12] and names.[13] Others (Laclau and Mouffe, 1985; Thompson, 1990; Norris, 1990; Laclau, Butler and Žižek, 2000), have explored these discursive regions of inter-textuality and found them to be bounded/bonded territories that privilege specific theoretical (ideological) positions and interpretive strategies, which become, as Laclau and Mouffe argued, nodal points for continuing discursive struggles.

> Every nodal point is constituted with an intertextuality that overflows it. The practice of articulation, therefore consists in the construction of nodal points which partially fix meaning; and the partial character of this fixation proceeds from the openness of the social, a result, in its turn, of the constant overflowing of every discourse by the infinitude of the field of discursivity.[14]

Viewed from within the sub-sets of historiographic discourse constituted as art history and film studies, these nodal points have had an interesting evolution, particularly since the early 1960s, a period identified by many film scholars as the origin point for the instutionalisation and academicisation of the film or cinema studies discipline.[15] Sklar, for instance, underlines film studies "coming of age" at a time "when its most closely aligned fields, such as philosophy, literary studies and art history, fell deeply under the thrall of European theories, Marxist and non-Marxist."[16] While it could be stated, somewhat generously, that the study of cinema, like art history, traverses the time of its origins to the present - which for film is the last century [17] - cinema studies actual existence as an independent study area has been quite recent, spanning the post World War II period - yet coinciding in a fascinating way with the development and critique of structuralism, the formations of post-structuralism, the introduction of both feminism, post-colonialism and queer studies into cultural and socio-political debates, and the constitution of a new non-generic discursive territory, loosely titled cultural studies, now itself subdivided into visual (culture) studies.[18] It could be argued, in fact, that film studies is one of the few academic disciplines to owe it's very existence to the challenging debates accompanying the so-called 'paradigm shifts' from modernism to postmodernism.

Where the names of Saussure, Althusser, Benjamin, Brecht, Jakobsen and Barthes figure prominently in the early film studies texts, these are followed subsequently by Foucault, Eco, Todorov, Lacan, Derrida, Kristeva and Said. And the names shadowing these European ones, for much of film studies early history (in Britain at least) - are English - those of the labour historian E.P. Thompson and the literary historian, critic and novelist, Raymond Williams. Each of these intellectuals provided a rich mix of theoretical material and practical examples of socio-cultural interpretation for film studies researchers of the past four decades. Examining the film studies texts of the foundational period can provide a good vantage point from which to review the shifting sediment of late modernist discourse. Such a purview reveals that the "overflowing of discourse by the infinitude of field(s) of discursivity" identified by Laclau and Mouffe developed in film studies as a result of theoretical competition between several generic discourses associated with more firmly established academic disciplines: history, art history, philosophy, sociology, anthropology, political science and English literature (literary studies). It is somewhat ironic that academics working within some of these disciplines now attribute film studies as an influence on the rejuvenation of their own fields. Rees and Borzello note that Bordwell, Staiger and Thompson (1985) cite the venerable art historian Ernst Gombrich as a major influence on their work, in company with E.P. Thompson, Raymond Williams, and the labour historian Harry Braverman.

Screen Education

Reviewing issues of the British film journal *Screen* from the 1970s provides a window to the various shifts of attention in the theoretical discourse that have largely determined the shape of the English-language film studies field and subsequently the new art history. While this is properly the scope of a separate study or book, I will briefly trace some aspects of the intellectual provenance of *Screen* discourse over a five year period, which have enabled art historians like Rees and Borzello to promote the appropriateness, indeed the *naturalness*, of the marriage of "*Screen*-like theoretical research with more conventional historical work," and to project this as a model for the future practice of art history.[19]

During its early years *Screen* published formalist criticism and promotional reviews on various aspects of the revitalized British film and developing television industries. With the editorship of Sam Rhodie in the spring of 1971 however, *Screen* began to turn its editorial policy away from this indigenous practice and direct it more firmly towards contemporary theory and film in an international context. This shift led to a privileging of the semiotic analysis of ideology and the practical negotiation of engaged politics in filmmaking and cultural criticism. The reorientation began with the translation and publication of work by writers associated with the influential French film journals *Cahiers du Cinéma, Cinétique,* and the theoretical journal *Tel Quel* who were responding to the volatile political situation in France precipitated by the student and worker demonstrations in Nanterre and Paris of May/ June 1968. *Screen*'s new identity was established with the introduction of the provocative ideas of the writers Jean-Louis Comolli, Jean Narboni, and later Marcelin Pleynet and Pierre Braudy.[20] The importation of structuralist discourse encouraged the *Screen* writers to join their continental cousins in producing Saussurean based semiotic analyses of the classical narrative forms of the bourgeois realist cinema. They attempted also to initiate a radical praxis through the formation of educational discussion groups, mandated in part by their association with the Society for Education in Film and Television. While less privileged than it was in the early years, this attention to praxis has remained an aspect of *Screen*'s engaged politics to the present. In keeping with their somewhat idealistic interest in political education - conscientization - the *Screen* constituency engaged in extensive discussions on the history of the modernist avant-garde cinema and forms of documentary practice. A few writers, for example Laura Mulvey and Peter Wollen, directors of the film *Riddles of the Sphinx* (1977), also attempted to put their newly adopted theories into practice by becoming film makers themselves. Unlike many of its sister film journals, *Screen* frequently accommodated writers and theorists from fields outside of its domain, including individuals whose discipline bases were in literary theory, history, art history, sociology and philosophy, such as Raymond Williams, Colin McCabe, Terry Eagleton, T.J. Clark and Griselda Pollock.

In part as a result of the influence of the French writers, the contributors to *Screen* of the early 1970s endorsed and promoted the revision of traditional Marxist concepts in Althusser's influential books *Reading Capital* (1970), *Lenin, Philosophy and Other Essays*

(1971) and later *For Marx* (1977).[21] Althusser's strategic revision of the conventional Marxian base/ superstructure model, his privileging of ideology rather than economy in his critique of capitalism, as well as his introduction of the concept of the state and institutional apparatuses was enormously influential in film studies literature of the early 1970s and remained so to a somewhat lesser degree throughout the decade.[22] Another key text *Screen*writers of this period responded was from one of their own, Peter Wollen's *Signs and Meanings in the Cinema* (1972). Wollen re-examined the film aesthetics and politics of the revolutionary Soviet cinema and argued for a revision of conventional critical concepts based on semiotic analysis. The work of Christian Metz, translated somewhat later into English, was based upon Saussurean, Barthesian semiotics, and Lacanian psychoanalytic models, that subsequently became the most influential branch of theory for *Screen* and subsequent researchers, Wollen's semiological model was based upon American C.S. Peirce's theory of indexicality, employing his triad of index, icon and symbol.[23]

John Ellis, a member of the editorial board and editor of *Screen Reader I* (1977), an important collection of essays from this period, wrote that early on the *Screen* projects were quite varied and involved:

> A critique of established critical concepts, such as auteurism, content analysis; an examination of the theory and practice of realism, seen as the dominant aesthetic of bourgeois cinema and television; work on the nature of the institution of cinema and on technological determinations; work on the theorisation of the articulation cinema/ ideology/politics: the criticism and rewriting of the 'history of the cinema'; the re-examination of the Russian cinema of the 1920s regarded as the major historical attempt to construct a revolutionary cinema; the examination of British cinema and television practices and histories.[24]

It was this openness and attention to the institution of the cinema in *all* of its aspects: aesthetics, technology, the industry, marketing, spectatorship, cinema/ideology/ politics, that proved to be so attractive to the new art historians of the 1980's, whose training had most probably excluded most of the items listed by Ellis to focus upon more conventional staples of art history such as iconography, style, attribution, dating, and the inspired life of the artist.

Screen's critical work of the early to mid 1970s involved the total revision of stock-in-trade formalist methods, particularly psychologisms that aimed at disclosing the imminent meanings residing within film through various Freudian reductions of the psychology of either the author or characters represented in the film's narrative. Many of the essays repudiated the authority of the author in favour of a shot by shot analysis (decoding) of film sequences in order to render ideology more visible. *Screen*'s Althusserianism remained relatively constant throughout the early 1970s. There were however, some major shifts in mid-decade as a result of the introduction of feminist discourse and psychoanalytic theory, which resulted in a foregrounding of sexual politics (gendered power relations), textuality, subjectivity, and spectatorship. Under the sway of several key post-structuralist texts by Michel Foucault, Roland Barthes, Jacques Lacan, Jacques Derrida, Julia Kristeva and Christian Metz, attention was now accorded subjectivity, processes of reading, language and power.[25]

There was much hybridity between art history and film studies in the early 1970's issues of *Screen*, which evidenced some extensive discussions of the aesthetico-political theories of Benjamin, Brecht and Lukacs, as well as the theories of the avant-garde and the Soviet art of the revolutionary period. It was not until 1975 however, that a firm opening for a fully-fledged relationship between film studies and the new art history appeared. And although many artists and art historians in that decade were subscribers or regular readers of the journal, a number felt excluded from the theoretical and technical debates about film itself. But with the publication of some important feminist texts and a few others with specific art historical content, this attitude began to change. For example, Laura Mulvey's famous essay "Visual pleasure and narrative cinema" (*Screen* 16, no. 2 Summer 1975), is often cited as a major influence on the course of discussions within the film studies, feminist, art and art history communities about the nature of spectatorship within patriarchal society. Mulvey argued that the classical narrative cinema reinforces a specific kind of looking, a fetishistic form of spectatorship that is phallocentric and patriarchal, subjugating women to the sexual pleasure seeking and controlling gaze of the male voyeur.[26]

As far as the development of the new art history is concerned the crucial period of *Screen*'s influence occurred between the spring of 1975 and the winter of 1980.[27] In this period several influential articles appeared that began to shift the terms of discourse away from a mechanical structuralism with its analytical emphasis upon the decoding of ideology, toward discussions about forms of spectatorship, film language, intertextuality, reading, interpretation, class and gender politics, and relations of power. Discussions subsequently revolved around the importance of context and the authority of the author versus that of the reader. If the psychoanalytic theories of subjectivity initiated through the importation of Barthes, Foucault, Lacan and Kristeva were dominant at this time, they began to be challenged around mid-decade by the critical Derridian strategy of deconstruction imbricated with a more conventional brand of historical materialism. The key debates of the late 1970's concerned realism, the existence of the real, reading, suture, ideology, with labour process, class, culture and society fighting for visibility.[28] A further curb upon the prevailing influence of Althusserian theory and the entrance of deconstructive criticism occurred with the publication in winter of 1978 (*Screen* vol. 18, no. 4) of a debate on the topic Marxism and Culture with a response by Rosalind Coward. The debaters: Stuart Hall, Ian Connell, Lidia Curti, Iain Chambers, Tony Jefferson, and John Clarke, were members of an increasingly influential Cultural Studies constituency associated with the Birmingham Centre for Contemporary Cultural Studies and the Open University. This Winter issue also included a section (pp 23-48), with three articles on the topic of Suture - Jacques-Iain Miller's "Suture (elements of the logic of the signifier)", Jean-Pierre Oudart's article "Cinema and Suture", and Stephen Heath's "Notes on Suture", still revealing a strong adherence to French post-structuralism.

A major sign of a shift in theoretical orientation, that I will suggest cemented the relationship between film studies and the developing new art history, occurred over the next three years, culminating with the Spring 1980 publication of T.J. Clark's article "Preliminaries to a possible treatment of *Olympia* in 1865."[29] Clark introduced his essay as a practical response to some theoretical questions posed with the publication of Colin MacCabe's essay "The Discursive and the Ideological in Film: Notes on the Conditions of Political Intervention" (*Screen* vol. 19, no. 4, 1978), which was itself a politically strategic response to several earlier articles that addressed the topic of spectatorship in a rather narrow, theory bound and depoliticized manner. Clark's essay focused upon Paul Willemen's "Notes on Subjectivity" (*Screen* vol. 19, no. 1), that was a response to some earlier formalist essays engaging the topics of film signifying practices, POV (point of view), framing, the positioning of the subject, ideology, reading and the practice of meaning production. Two of these articles were written by Edward Branigan – "Subjectivity under Siege - From Fellini's *8 ½ to* Oshima's *The Story of a Man Who Left his Will on Film*" (that appeared in the same issue as Willemen's essay) and "Formal Permutations of the POV Shot" (*Screen* Vol 16 no 3 1975). The third article in this issue, which is somewhat ironic, given Rees and Borzello's 1986 promotion of these authors' texts as a model for the anti-formalist post-new art history, was written by Kristin Thompson and David Bordwell and titled: "Space and narration in the films of Ozu" (*Screen* Vol 17, no.2, 1976).

T.J. Clark wrote that his study of Manet was an attempt "to raise some theoretical questions which relate to *Screen*'s recent concerns" and to provide, with his examples (he quotes from MacCabe's essay), "a materialist reading [specifying] articulations within the [picture] on determining grounds" (1978:36). And not content with providing MacCabe merely with a practical (materialist) response to his theoretical questions, Clark's introduction shifts to Paul Willemen's essay "Notes on subjectivity - On reading: subjectivity under siege" (*Screen* Vol. 19, no.1) and by extension, the aforementioned texts from the previous three years. Clark writes of his concern about recent movements in *Screen*'s discourse: "There has been an impatience lately in the pages of *Screen* with the idea that texts construct spectators, and an awareness that" (he incorporates a quotation from Willemen's text),

> The activity of the text must be thought in terms of which set of discourses it encounters in any particular set of circumstances, and how this encounter may restructure both the productivity of the text and the discourses with which it combines to form an intertextual field which is *always in ideology, always in history*. Some texts can be more or less recalcitrant if *pulled into* a [my emphasis] particular field, while others can be fitted comfortably into it.[30]

These essays, in the company of other publications outside of the *Screen* context, reveal an important indication of the shift in attention away from a formalist and ahistorical reading of a work of art, grounded in a programmatic communication system and seamless semiotic, to one that fore grounded the *instability* of meaning. They also acknowledge the implicit power relations between texts and readers within a dynamic social, political and historical context. In this context, the location of the (classed) subject is always at issue.

As Willemen announced in his provocative introduction, he wished to attend to the problem of

> Enunciation and subjectivity, to mark a possible site of an exit from *formal semiotics and mechanical structuralism* [my emphasis] both of which tend to locate films as messages circulated between 'inscribed' or abstractly conceived addressers and addressees, the a-historical `persons' put into place by conventional information theory.[31]

Later he engages "the possibility of thinking discursive practices as constructing subjectivity in social formations, in/for ideology."[32]

The key theoretical issues to which T.J. Clark responded in these essays, some of which he subordinated in his books on Courbet, involved the visual representation of ideology, the position of the author, the status of the reader - both author and reader's discursive relationships to the artifact - as well as the historical relationship of the cultural product to a labour process, a system of production and a socio-political reality. These became, a few years later - almost by default - the bread and butter issues of the 'new' art history.
As Willemen wrote:

> The process of meaning production can no longer be thought of as the effectivity of a system of representation, but rather as a production of and by subjects already in social practices; a production not dependent upon any single 'system of representation,' but determined by the relations of force, the conjunction of discursive, economic and political practices which produces subjects in history.[33]

Willemen's gloss of the socio-political context and his emphasis upon history and power relations are key indicators of the shift in attitude away from coded representations that demand an exemplary reader/ analyst (or historian) who seeks in the signifying practice some (Althusserian) vestige of state and/or institutional power, to one in which the political subject and his/her potential agency is predominant. Willemen assumed the reader to be a political subject (or agent), who is firmly planted – not simply *interpellated* as Althusser argued – within ideology, part of a social formation (class) and embedded in history. Willemen invoked the theoretical positions of Pierre Macherey, Tzvetan Todorov and Umberto Eco on the stochastic nature of language and the 'political projects' with respect to language and relations of power articulated by Antonio Gramsci, Michel Foucault and Jacques Derrida. The various rhetorical accents of Willemen's essay provide cues to his move away from theoretical positions that emphasize structure to those that privilege agency. However, his use of competing theoretical points of view forced him into the somewhat anomalous position of arguing that while "real readers are subjects in history" (classed subjects), "the real is never in its place" and, moreover, "it is only grasped through discourse" revealing his privileging emphasis on the psychoanalytic theories of Jacques Lacan, for whom 'the real' is always beyond the reach of the symbolic.[34]

Willemen's essay is one of a small number of *Screen* essays that mark a major shift in the intellectual provenance of the journal, abridging or transgressing some of the discursive nodal points evident previously in the work of other *Screen* writers, among them: Wollen, Heath, and Mulvey.[35] In this particular essay his theoretical elisions and political 'transgressions' encouraged Ben Brewster and Elizabeth Cowie, then members of the Editorial Board, to make the uncharacteristic move of adding a critical addendum to the essay. In particular, they expressed some reservations regarding Willemen's Lacanian distinction between the real and reality. Willemen, they wrote:

> Employs the psychoanalytic distinction between the 'real' and 'reality', which has been expounded in *Screen* by Stephen Heath in "Anata Mo" (vol.17 no.4), but links it to the question of the relations between discursive formations and the relations of production. The danger is that reality will be assigned to the former and the real to the latter, reproducing the now surely discredited notion of ideology as the

> misleading phenomenal form of the real movement of the
> relations of production. The problem is not just that this
> position is difficult to sustain theoretically, but also in so far as
> it answers a demand - for the reconciliation of two discourses:
> that of psychoanalysis and that of historical materialism - it
> does so in such a way that each reduces the effectivity of the
> other rather than the combination being productive of either.

This major editorial intervention prevented Willemen's discursive
shift from becoming mired in a form of postmodern relativism and
reaffirmed the engaged politics and historical materialism long
associated with the *Screen* project. MacCabe's essay also reinforced
the in-house critique of this relativism by focusing the reader's
attention upon *Screen*'s contradictory use of the Foucauldian term,
discourse. He persuasively presented a materialist point of view,
arguing that: the appeal to the economic is necessary to anchor the
ideological struggle in definite political terms. Without reference to
the economic, ideological struggle would be given no political
content. MacCabe argues that while theoretical considerations allow
us to "appreciate the conditions for political intervention...they do not
enable us provide any immediate solution into any specific debate or
struggle."(42) Affirming that *Screen*'s success in transforming the
critical discourse of cinema and television was limited to the
professional world and academia, MacCabe promoted the useful
political work of film critics and other writers working for the popular
London magazine *Time Out*, cautioning however, that while *Time
Out*'s work regularly reached a larger audience, it was still too
journalistic, impressionistic and reactionary to provide a model for
resisting the hegemonic power of the ideologically dominant
culture.[36]

Clark's response to both Willemen and MacCabe subscribes the
reemerging (reconstituted) Marxism of some members of the *Screen*
Editorial Board while implicitly endorsing the post-structuralist
concerns with the relativity of meaning. The bulk of his "Olympia"
essay is based on his reading of sixty popular reviews (in the late 19th
century French versions of *Time Out*) of the Salon of 1865, and three
cartoon satires of Manet's *Olympia* published that year. He considers
this to be a practical response to Willemen's theoretical point that
"the activity of the text must be thought in terms of which set of
discourses it encounters in any set of circumstances." Clark questions

which discourses Olympia encountered in 1865 and concludes that there were two:

> A discourse in which the relations and disjunctions of the terms Woman/ Nude/Prostitute were obsessively rehearsed (which I shall call, clumsily, the discourse on Woman in the 1860's), and the complex but deeply repetitive discourse of aesthetic judgement in the second empire.[37]

Any new art historian would now add another set of discourses to Clark's two: editorial policies of the media, the politics of humour (satire, parody, irony), race, gender, sexuality, the roles of the artist and the critic, all of which would now have to be integrated. The clarity of Clark's argument in this essay, his exemplary interpretation of examples, a rich extended corpus - beyond the painted artifact - provided an *ex cathedra* example of the concentration he sought in the social historical project. Clark's intervention reveals that while Rees and Bordello can claim a conjugal relationship with film studies, film studies can certainly claim the same of art history, and cultural studies/visual culture can do so with both.

Art, Artists and Art History in Film

Many film history texts argue the close formal relationships between theatre, literature, visual arts and film. Without I hope, belaboring the point, we should acknowledge that there is also much interchange, appropriation, quoting and borrowing - both formally and theoretically - from within the discursive fields of art history, film and literary studies, and between the rival arts of theatre, literature, visual arts and film. In the work of hundreds of filmmakers who have borrowed strategies from the historical avant-gardes, the formal innovations presented by modernist art have been very productive for the development of cinema as an art form. Similarly, the theoretical and methodological innovations within the history of art have been conducive to the development of critical and theoretical discourse on cinema and film historiography, participating in the construction of historical periodisation and stylistic registers, genre typology, and for demonstrating the importance (or lack thereof), of national identities in the production of culture. The selection of exemplary authors/auteurs – canon building – as well as the sharing of technological language, has all presented opportunities for shared discourses, some productive and useful for enriching film studies discourse, some not.

Film historians and film theorists, among them: Eisenstein, Kracauer, Bazin, Sadoul, Mast, Rhode, Bordwell, Thompson, Metz, Kaplan, Wollen, Sklar, Williams and Naremore, have each acknowledged in various ways the important influences on the development of cinema of modernist avant-garde strategies in theatre, literature and visual art. Other texts that examine the close formal relationships between film and the other arts include: Timothy Murray's *Like a Film: Ideological Fantasy on Screen, Camera and Canvas* (1993), Brigitte Peucker's *Incorporating Images: Film and the Rival Arts* (1995), and Angela Della Vacche's *Cinema and Painting: How Art is used in Film* (1996), each book providing useful examples of the co-optation and/or conflation of theories and forms. And inspired by Lacan's psychoanalytic models, Barthes' *Camera Lucida*, and Jacques Derrida's *The Truth in Painting*, among other theoretical texts, the relationships between visual art and film have also registered in the work of Slavoj Žižek, Jacqueline Rose, Kaja Silverman, Raymond Bellour, Constance Penley, Pascal Bonitzer and Jacques Aumont, continuing the important work of *Cahiers du Cinéma*, *Cinétique*, *Screen* and other film studies journals with theoretical perspectives on criticism and film history.

The connection between the history of visual art and film history does not require rewriting here; but what of the representation of art and art history – the institution art – in film? This has been a very different relationship; one marked less by discourse conflation, utility, hybridity, similarity, and consonance than of dissonance, *difference/différance*. For all of those films that reproduce modernist technical innovations, or faithfully represent and pay homage to the masters and works of modernist art, there are as many that repudiate, reject and disavow art, artists and art history, playing out familiar popular rejection and negation strategies (irony, satire, parody, burlesque) in a manner reminiscent of cartoons, comics and other forms of popular culture.

In an essay published in *Screen* Stephen Heath discusses the relationship between modernist art and narrative. He cites the example of the Alfred Hitchcock film *Suspicion* (1941), in which a character, Lina (née McLaidlaw) Aysgarth, played by Joan Fontaine in an Oscar award winning performance, is questioned by police detectives about her rakish husband Johnnie (Cary Grant). Before and after their interrogation of Aysgarth, one of the detectives, Benson, pauses on his way into the living room of the Aysgarth residence to inspect a Picassoesque cubist painting. Heath argues that this gesture provides a rupture in the film's diegesis, thus presenting "a problem of point of view, different framing, disturbance of the law and its inspectoring eye, interruption of homogeneity of the narrative economy, it is somewhere else again, another scene, another story, another space."[38]

I will add that the insertion of this gesture also represents an interruption of homogeneity in the film's *political economy* by reinforcing the popular hostility between the 1940's public and the project(s) of modernist art. Moreover, the insertion of this scene may also reveal Hitchcock's own somewhat ambivalent opinion at that time, certainly not uncommon among members of the general public, including film directors during the 1940's, about the value of modernist art. This view is reinforced in *Suspicion* by the introduction early on in the film of another painting, a conventional three-quarter length military style naturalistic portrait of Lina's father, the imperious General McLaidlaw (Sir Cedric Hardwicke). This gilt framed painting conveniently falls down off its pride of place above a mantle when the rakish suitor Johnnie asks it in jest for Lina's "hand in marriage." This situation is pre-figured in an earlier paternalistic comment from the General that is overheard by Lina standing outside the living room window of her parents' home - "Lina will never marry, she's not the marrying sort.... Lina has intellect and a fine solid character." The painting appears in other significant sequences in the film, usually animated by the framing eye of the camera or the point of view shots of the protagonists. In a crucial sense, Hitchcock anthropomorphizes this painting, using it to simulate the imperious presence of the absent father. After the somewhat hasty marriage of Lina and Johnnie, it begins to cast the General's disapproving eye upon their increasingly tense relationship.

In the scene that contains the police questioning of Lina, Benson's rapt yet distracted attention toward the modernist painting is contrasted with the very alive naturalistically painted portrait of the General. This tension between the vital animated representation and the 'inert' modernist abstract appears in many Hitchcock films and has its origins in his early reading of Oscar Wilde's *The Picture of*

Dorian Gray (1890), a Faustian tale that figures an animated portrait, a doppelganger that also inhabits many of Hitchcock's films.[39]

Hitchcock's films are riddled with subtle references to art, less, I believe, a result of the scripts he worked on than his own somewhat conservative introduction to art at London University, and his typically ironic sense of humour. In many of his films, most of which conform to conventional Hollywood genres, art and art history often become vehicles for providing suspense-filled dramas with some light relief, and more often, some dark necromantic significance, yet the underlying discursive motifs, I believe register both Hitchcock and his viewers resistance to the work of the modernist avant-garde, particularly abstraction in painting, which challenged the dominant aesthetic ideology on representation. The origins of this resistance can be traced to the so-called *fin de siecle* 'crisis of representation' stimulated by the introduction of photography.

Brigitte Peucker has discussed the shock of contrast between the representation of art and the public apperception in Hitchcock's *Vertigo* (1958). She describes the scene that contains a painting by Midge the fashion designer/artist character in the film, a simulacrum of the Madeleine Elster/ Judy Barton (Kim Novak) character who throughout the film is the 'object' of desire of Scottie Ferguson (James Stewart). In order to convince him that she is an available substitute, Midge imbricated her own image upon Judy's portrait body, creating a kind of surrealist palimpsest of Scottie's obsession. Peucker suggests that the shock value of Midge's painting is difficult to assess, particularly for contemporary audiences exposed to modern art. But located back into its time of reception in the late 1950=s, Midge's studio is full of examples of abstract art that she argues would have been recognized by many viewers as shockingly avant-garde. Midge's entry into Hitchcock's sardonic discourse on the relationship between art and death is signaled in a conversation between her and Scottie. When she tells him that she "has gone back to her first love, painting," he asks whether it is a "still life?" "Not exactly," she replies, a comment that Peucker interprets as a further indication of the "unnaturalness" of her portrait palimpsest, which is "not even *like* nature and hence doubly lifeless."[40]   She goes on to suggest that this scene with

> Its flaunting of fragmented and modernist works of art
> figures the hesitation created in the film by its multiplicity

of perspectives, the splitting of point of view that finds its visual analogue in the fragmentation of the female body, displayed not only in the doubled portrait, but in the freestanding sculpture of the breast. [41]

Diane Waldman argued that the 1940s woman's Gothic film conventionally casts suspicion on the husband's sanity by associating him with the distorted style of modern art.[42] Peucker's examples reveal that this is not specific necessarily to the husband, and I would suggest that this critical use for modernism may have as much to do with the public [mis]perception of the modernist project as the exigencies of the film's diegesis. In the hundreds of films throughout the history of the cinema that critically represent the institution art, the political and libidinal economy of such representations is always at stake. And in many films, the work of modernist art, like Manet's *Olympia,* discussed by T.J. Clark, is situated at the confluence of several (competing) discourses, the body/ the idea of woman, art, technical competency, the role of the artist, the psychology of the artist, architecture, art history, criticism, the museum, capital/the art market, crime and genius.   The film frames become sites for questioning and contesting the meanings and value of modern art and culture, both generally and also in more specific senses. [43]

Pierre Bourdieu (1977, 1984) demonstrated that the aesthetic tastes of members of various classes and class fractions are strongly tied to the accumulation of cultural capital provided by an individual's education and class background. The sociological research into the art institution undertaken by Bourdieu and his colleagues reveal that a high level of "cultural competency" is required in order to understand and appreciate (consume), the products of high culture including the discursive fields in which they are located as he writes: "A work of art has meaning and interest only for someone who possesses the cultural competence, that is the code, into which it is encoded."[44] He goes on the elaborate that "the hostility of the working class and of the middle-class fractions least rich in cultural capital towards every kind of formal experimentation asserts itself both in theatre and in painting, or still more clearly, because they have less legitimacy, in photography and cinema."[45] The representation of modernist art in film often confirms the lack of such competency on the part of the viewing public, as well as the producers of the film. As much as the classical Hollywood cinema confirms popular expectations and attitudes, "a system of norms operating at different levels of generality,"[46] the art framed within this system provides an affirmation of conservative ideologies generally understood and upheld by the culture consuming and producing public.

3. & 4 Edward .G. Robinson as Chris Cross and Joan Bennett as Kitty March in Fritz Lang's *Scarlet Street* (1945)

The institution art also figures prominently in *Scarlet Street* (1945), an important example of film noir directed by Fritz Lang. Like Hitchcock, Lang had some training in art before he immersed himself in film and this education is evident in many of his films. In Lang's film, based on *La Chienne* (1931) by Jean Renoir, Edward G. Robinson plays the part of Christopher Cross, a shy, sensitive and honest office clerk with a domineering wife, who spends his leisure hours painting naive modernist works, a cross between the work of modernist neo-primitive Henri 'Le Douanier' Rousseau and Jean Dubuffet. On a typically noirish rainy night after a work celebration for his boss J.J., he intervenes in a struggle between Kitty March a beautiful vamp, and her rakish beau Johnnie Prince. Not realizing the relationship between them, he falls helplessly in love with Kitty and over the course of a few days is drawn unwittingly into a 'sugar daddy' relationship, providing her with money for a studio apartment, clothes, cosmetics and food. In order to accede to her and boyfriend Johnnie's escalating demands, Chris steals money from the company till. And to placate his philistine wife Adele who abhors his art, he removes his "dreadful paintings" to Kitty's studio apartment. Grasping for more money to satisfy his desires, Johnnie decides to try and sell several of Chris' paintings. He finds an interested curbside art dealer who offers to exhibit the paintings among his other works for sale. The painting soon commands the attention of a famous art critic who is excited by what he perceives to be a rare talent. He demands to know who painted them and requests a meeting with the artist. Johnnie passes Kitty off as the artist and with some positive attention from the critic and another art dealer, her first solo exhibition is completely sold out and her success in the art world assured.

Meanwhile Adele has discovered that a painting similar to one of her husband's works is showing in an uptown gallery and convinced that this is the original, she accuses her husband of producing fakes of this famous artist's work. This leads to Chris' discovery of the relationship between Kitty and Johnny and the revelation that both he and his art have been taken for a proverbial ride. In a blind rage about Kitty's two-timing and her belittling of him as a man, not about her success with his art, he kills her. The crime is pinned on the protesting Johnnie who is prosecuted for murder and sent to the electric chair. At the conclusion of the film it appears that Chris may have gotten away with his crime, an ending that was considered a breach of the Production Code Administration rules of the day, but this was overruled because the artist was finally driven mad by his acute remorse and thus effectively punished by a higher power.

The film's narrative and characters represent several negative stereotypes of the artist's role and the conditions of creativity. Adele is the domineering philistine severely lacking in cultural competency who absolutely detests modern art. Her stereotypical counterparts appear in hundreds of cartoons in the pages of *The New Yorker* and other magazines from the 1930s through to the 1960s, often reinforcing the opinions of their sexist male companions. The film's narrative also underlines the popular perception that the art world is fickle, that reputations are made on very little evidence of talent and that the value of art can be easily inflated by the system. Another stereotypical position for the consideration of viewers is that artists are fakes, fools or misunderstood geniuses and that critics make arbitrary and quite often wrong judgments of excellence. *Scarlet Street* provides a context for the contestation of several aesthetic discourses and a site for questioning over the terms and conditions of the entry of modernist art into popular culture. It encounters resistance all the way and finally falls into the abyss of cultural disenfranchisement, alienation, criminality and death.

With its extraordinary Gotham City scenes inspired by Fritz Lang's *Metropolis* (1926), director Tim Burton's *Batman* (1989) fully deserved its Academy Award for best Art Direction. However, art and art history figure in a very different way to the Academy's Direction in a crucial scene from the film. In company with the Hitchcock and Lang films discussed previously, discourses of death, crime and art are conflated to provide an engaging and educative burlesque on the value and meaning of art in society. When Bruce Wayne does his research on Jack Napier a.k.a. the Joker, surely one of the most loveable if diabolical characters in any film of the past few decades, he finds that his high school aptitudes were listed as "Science, Chemistry and Art", those of a stereotypical Renaissance man. The Joker's hideout features on the wall a huge Playboy Varga-type mural of a 1930's 'vamp', his ideal of womanhood. The Joker's status as a contemporary artist is further confirmed when we see him working on a huge montage of magazine and newspaper photograph cutouts. And when the Joker takes a liking to an image he finds in his pile that has been photographed by Vicky Vale (Kim Bassinger), he decides to arrange a meeting with her in the Gotham City Museum, a generic composite of New York's Frick, Metropolitan, Whitney and the Museum of Modern Art. Using his superior chemistry skills he injects the museum space with a purple gas that anaesthetizes everybody in sight, with the exception of Miss Vale to whom he has sent a protective facemask in a gift box.

After the gas has filled the space and to the accompaniment of a bouncy Joker raps song, Jack intones his pack with "Gentlemen... Let's broaden our minds," while they move from art work to art work, altering, plastering, painting, cutting, destroying famous works from the art historical canon. The desecration of culture is accompanied throughout by a bizarre rap by Jack, directing his band with a choreographed point here, a point there, ten major works of art are "creatively altered" Shafrazi-style, including a late self-portrait by Rembrandt, a Degas *Dancer*, a Renoir, a Monet, until he stops one of his men from defacing an expressionist Francis Bacon painting saying "Hold it! I rather like that one." [47]

The Joker then alights next to the astounded Vicki Vale, who is sitting in the museum restaurant. He demands to see her portfolio and quickly flicks through the pages of glossy coloured advertising photographs saying "no good, no good, no good, no good" (in an earlier pre-sanitized version of the film, the Joker says "crap, crap, crap"), until he arrives at some black and white documentary photographs of social commentary, victims of flood, war and famine.

"Ah, now that's good work... the body... skulls... you give it so much of a glow," he says, followed by the phrase of popular appraisal "I don't know whether it's art…but I like it!" He then announces to Vale that he, Jack Napier, is also an artist: "I make art.... I am the world's first fully functioning homicidal artist!" and announces that she will "join him in his avant-garde - a new aesthetic!" Ordering Alicia, one of his companions to unmask, the Joker reveals one of his masterpieces, a once beautiful model with an acid-scarred face. "I'm no Picasso," he says, "but do you like it?" He then presses a pocket bulb in his pocket to propel some acid from a joke flower in his lapel, as Batman, crashing through a skylight, arrives on the scene to rescue this damsel in distress. High drama, comic book style, but the political messages are similar to those discussed earlier. The Joker's satirical burlesque of the art institution encourages the audience to do the same. The conflation of the separate discourses of art, crime, death would be humorous, if it were not for the fact that these represent powerful ideological positions that are commonly voiced and represented in other contexts.

5. Tim Burton *Batman* 1989

Backbeat (1993) Ian Softley's film about the Beatles early days in Liverpool and Hamburg, provides another example of the institution art in film. This film's narrative revolves around the relationship between the fifth Beatle, Stuart Sutcliffe, Astrid his German girlfriend an artist and photographer and John Lennon,. Art is introduced early on in the film when art students John and Stuart are shown drunkenly parodying the woman singing on a Liverpool pub stage. Their singing performance engages the ire of the woman's boyfriend and he and his mates make their way menacingly to John and Stu's table to make trouble. The boyfriend points accusingly at the sketchpad image of a nude that Stu is drawing of his girl on stage. "What's that?" he says menacingly at this representation of his naked girlfriend. "That's art," offers John, with feigned innocence. "I call it filth!" retorts the boyfriend. A chase and fight ensues, that result in Stuart being smashed up in a lane outside and John screaming after the attackers, "I'll kill yer... I'll kill the fucking lot of yer!" Apart from the sexual politics involved here, this scene implicitly reveals the philistinism of tough working class males towards the art project, as well as reinforcing the stereotypical role of the romantic artist/creative magus figure who reveals his creativity wherever he travels.[48]

Another scene shows Sutcliffe in a studio with a nude model, engaged in painting an abstract portrait to the diegetic accompaniment of the blues standard *I've Got a Woman* on the phonograph. At the conclusion of the sitting, the model gets up to look at Stu's painting of her and exclaims loudly in a Liverpudlian accent "Yer call that art?" to which Stu protests, "It's not finished". "It doesn't look like anything," says the model, wincing away as Stu tries to placate her by nuzzling his muse's neck with a kiss. At this point in the scene, John Lennon enters the studio and the model, still stuck on her first question says to Stu: "Ask 'im what he thinks." Stu mocks her in a serious comic fashion and puts the question to his band mate - "what do you think John?" The model completes the question in an incriminating tone of voice - "does that look like me? Does it?" she implores, to which John replies to Stu - "well... you got the tits right." Stu, in mock protest asks, "What do you think?" John replies "Do you want the truth?" Stu replies - "Sure." To which John retorts "Hanging is too good for it!"

This scene strategically introduces several themes for the film, again becoming nodal sites for several discursive struggles over the classed antagonistic relationships between visual art, music, sexuality, desire, femininity, masculinity, love and death. Throughout the film we witness struggles between men over women, vanguard youth culture versus tradition, photography and painting, struggles between the band members, especially Stu Sutcliffe and Paul McCartney and last, but not least, between the two childhood friends Stu and Lennon - John who gives up visual art to pursue a life as a rock musician and Stu who forsakes rock for visual art and (what he believes) is true love.

These film examples reveal the symbolic contest of power, as this is representative of the struggle between various groups and constituencies over the social relevance and use, or lack thereof, of art and art history. They confirm that art's otherness is significant, and moreover, that specific classes and class fractions are engaged in a specifically symbolic struggle to impose the definition of the social world most in conformity with their interests. The field of ideological positions encrypted in language and performance reproduces in transfigured form, the field of social positions.[49]

---

[1]An earlier version of this chapter was published in Cheetham, M., Holly, M.A. and Moxey, K (eds.) *The Subjects of Art History: Historical Objects in Contemporary Perspectives* Cambridge and New York, Cambridge University Press, 1998.

[2] Barthes R. *Image Music Text* trans Stephen Heath New York, Hill and Wang 1985:61

[3] Preziosi, D. *Rethinking Art History: Meditations on a Coy Science* New Haven Yale University Press 1989:72-3

[4] Rees, A.L. and Borzello, F. *The New Art History* London, Camden Press 1986

[5] Bordwell, D., Staiger, J., and Thompson, K., *The Classical Hollywood Cinema: Film, Style and Mode of Production to 1960* New   York, Columbia University Press 1985:9

[6] The indications of a crisis can be traced to T.J. Clark's famous *Time Literary Supplement* essay of May 24, 1974, in which he stated, "It ought to be clear by now that I'm not interested in the social history of art as part of a cheerful diversification of the subject, taking its place alongside the other varieties - formalist, modernist, sub-Freudian, filmic, feminist, radical. For diversification read disintegration. And what we need is the opposite: concentration, the possibility of argument instead of this deadly co-existence, a means to the old debates. This is what the social history of art has to offer: it is the place where the questions have to be asked, but where they can't be asked in the old way." Rees and Borzello (1986) cite the importance for the development of the new art history of the publication in 1973 of T.J. Clark's *The Absolute Bourgeois: Artists and Politics in France 1988-51* and *The Image of the people: Gustave Courbet and the 1848 Revolution*, as well as the institution in 1975 of the MA course in the social history of art at Leeds University.

[7] The winter 1982 issue of *Art Journal* (42,4) was partially responsible for introducing the crisis into the North American context. Guest-edited by H. Zerner, the issue included contributions by O. Grabar, O.K. Werkmeister, J. Hart, D. Summers, R. Krauss, and D. Preziosi. In Britain the Middlesex Polytechnic and *Block*, a magazine devoted to the publication of progressive art history, held a conference called "The New Art History?" Preziosi suggested that there "both is and is not a crisis in art history at the present time" (1982:2), and distinguishes between a crisis *in* the discipline" and a "crisis *of* the discipline" - the latter a constituent and ongoing feature "that antedates the instutionalisation of the discipline and has been built into it from it's academic beginnings (p.19), and the former (crisis *in* the discipline) a feature that questions the accommodation of theories and methodologies that disavow the

foundational historicism of art history which Preziosi suggests has more serious implications.

[8] The terms discourse and discursive are used throughout this dissertation in the senses articulated by Michel Foucault in *The Archeology of Knowledge* translation, A.M. Sheridan-Smith New York, Harper and Row (1972) to signal institutional discourses that enable certain truths to prevail through the exercise of a professional authority, for example through the public statements and texts of art historians. "Whenever one can describe, between a number of statements, such a system of dispersion, whenever, between objects, types of statement, concepts or thematic choices, one can define a regularity (an order, correlations, positions and functioning's, transformations) we will say, for the sake of convenience that we are dealing with a *discursive formation.*" Foucault, 1972:38

[9] I am employing Derrida in this context to distinguish between two discursive fields.

[10] See Derrida, J. *Writing and Difference* translation A Bass, London Routledge Kegan Paul 1978

[11] This is similar to the horticultural metaphor "rhizome" and "rhizomatic" developed by Deleuze and Guatarri (1987, 1994)

[12] Formalism, connoisseurship, feminism, Marxism, neo-Marxism, social history, phenomenology, structuralism, post-structuralism, discourse analysis, reception aesthetics, deconstruction.

[13] Althusser, Bakhtin, Barthes , Bataille, Baudrillard, Coward, Cixoux, Derrida, Deleuze, Eco, Foucault, Greimas, Jameson, Kristeva, Lacan, Levi-Strauss, Marx, Said, Spivak, Thompson, and Williams - to list a few of the more prominent ones.

[14] Laclau, E and Mouffe, C. *Hegemony and Socialist Strategy* London, Verso 1985:113

[15] Many texts within the film studies field appeared well before this time; e.g. Hugo Munsterberg's *The Film: A Psychological Study* (1916) and Siegfried Kracauer's classic *From Caligari to Hitler; A Psychological study of the German Film* (1947). The introduction of film studies to the academic curriculum with the concomitant development of films studies programs and degrees did not occur until the early 1960s. See Robert Sklar, "Oh! Althusser: Historiography and the Rise of Cinema Studies," in *Resisting Images: Essays on Cinema and History*, ed Robert Sklar and Charles Musser Philadelphia: Temple University Press, 1990

[16] Sklar, 1988:11

[17] John Tagg argues that *Screen*'s sister journal *Screen Education*, which later merged with *Screen*, "had an idea of cultural history and cultural theory that was, by then (1980) much broader that the journal *Screen*'s idea of finding a methodology and a text to apply it to- a can opener to open the text. The Board of *Screen Education* had tried to develop a notion of cultural politics that carried over into the journal's specific involvement with teaching and pedagogy" (Tagg, 1992: 78-9). John Tagg's view can be considered somewhat biased given his place on the Editorial Board of *Screen Education* at that time.

[18] A similar process could be undertaken with a large number of journals (*October, Parachute, New Literary History, Jumpcut, Social Text, Yale French Studies, Camera Obscura,* etc.). each of which would emphasize different aspects of the structuralist, post-structural and postmodern debates.

[19] *Screen* has been the subject of a number of essays, and it figures prominently in several texts examining film theory of the 1970s and 1980s. See Anthony Easthope, "The Trajectory of *Screen*," in *The Politics of Theory*, ed. Francis Barker, Colchester: University of Essex Press, 1983); and Robert Lapsley and Michael Westlake (eds.) *Film Theory: An Introduction* Manchester, Manchester University Press, 1988

[20]The late 1960s and early 1970s saw the translation and publication of several influential books on film theory and criticism, among them Andre Bazin's *What is Cinema?* Hugh Gray, translation and editing. 2 Vols. Berkeley and Los Angeles, University of California Press 1967-71; Noel Burch, *Theory of Film Practice*, Helen R. Lane translation New York: Praeger, 1973; and J-P. Lebel, *Cinema et idéologie* Paris: Editions Sociales, 1971

[21] Translated by Ben Brewster, who subsequently became an important member of *Screen*'s editorial board,. Brewster's translations, along with those of Stephen Heath (Roland Barthes *Image-Music-Text* (1977), helped facilitate the smooth entry of French theory into the English intellectual milieu.

[22] In contrast to *Screen*'s appropriation of French theory, other journals were attempting to revisit some of the implications of Marxist discourse in the western European context. Throughout the 1970s the *New Left Review* remained an important forum for discussions among Williams, Thompson, Terry Eagleton, Perry Anderson et about the changing relationships among theory, politics, social and cultural practice Anderson's book *Considerations on Western Marxism* appeared in 1974 as a result of some of the important debates which had occurred in the NLR in the preceding three years.

[23] Ferdinand de Saussure's *semiotics* became the preferred term over Charles Sanders Peirce's *semiology*. According to its supporters, "semiotics connotes a discipline less static and taxonomic than semiology" Stam, R. Burgoyne, R and Flitterman-Lewis, S., *New Vocabularies in Film Semiotics: Structuralism Post-Structuralism and Beyond* London New York Routledge 1992:4

[24] Ellis, 1977: ii

[25] Christian Metz, *Film Language* New York: Oxford Univesrity Press, 1974, and *Language and Cinema* D. Umikerseboek translation The Hague: Mouton, 1974; Julia Kristeva "The System and the Speaking Subject", *Times Literary Supplement* October 12, 1973, as well as R. Coward and J. Ellis *Language and Materialism: Developments in Semiology and the Theory of the Signifier* London, Routledge & Kegan Paul, 1975

[26] This model was present in John Berger's famous book *Ways of Seeing* (1973), from the successful television series with the same title.

[27] I do not wish to isolate *Screen* in this development. Many other journals were active participants in the revisionist process, among them: *October, Parachute, New German Critique, Telos, Art Journal, Art History, Camera Obscura, Art Forum, Yale French Studies, Semiotica, Critical Enquiry, Representations, Social Text, Semiotexte*

[28] The year 1980 witnessed the publication of a very influential group of essays under the title *The Cinematic Apparatus*, (ed.) Teresa de Lauretis and Stephen Heath London, St. Martins Press 1980

[29] A number of writers (Tagg: 1992:104) have identified the coincidence of a more politicized orientation in the late 1970's and early 1980's with the first election victory of Margaret Thatcher in 1979.

[30] *Screen* Vol 19. No. 1

[31] *Screen* Vol. 19 No. 1:41

[32] Ibid p43

[33] Ibid 4

[34] Lacan, J. *Ecrits: A   Selection* Trans. A Sheridan-Smith London, Tavistock 1977 and Lacan, J. *The Four Fundamental Concepts of Psycho-Analysis* edited Miller Trans. A Sheridan New York W. Norton 1977

[35] From 1973 to 1983, the list of *Screen*'s contributors reads like a "who's who" of the developing film, literary, and cultural studies fields: Terry Eagleton, Stuart Hall, Rosalind Coward, Ian Chambers, Stephen Heath, Laura Mulvey, Colin MacCabe,

Geoffrey Nowell-Smith, Peter Wollen, T.J Clark, Edward Branigan, Ben Brewster, Constance Penley, Kristin Thompson, David Bordwell, Paul Willemen, and last but not least, Raymond Williams.

[36] I have previously explored the negotiation of meaning and the symbolic contest of power with respect to the representation of modernist art in cartoons and comics. See B. Barber *Popular Modernisms: Art, Cartoons, Comics and Cultural In/Subordination* (forthcoming).

[37] Clark, p.23

[38] Heath, Stephen, "Narrative Space" Screen 17:3 Autumn 1976:71

[39] Hitchcock was trained as an engineer at a school of engineering and navigation, where he studied mechanics, electricity, acoustics and navigation. After graduating he took employment with Henley's Telegraphy company and studied part time at the University of London. As a result of his art training, Henley's transferred him to the advertising department where he worked on promotion for electric cables.

[40] Peucker, B. *Incorporating Images: Film and the Rival Arts* Princeton, Princeton University Press1995: 66

[41] Ibid.

[42] Waldman, D. "Horror and Domesticity: The Modern Gothic Romance Film of the 1940's," unpub. PhD Thesis University of Wisconsin 1981, pp.164-93 Cited in Bordwell, Staiger and Thompson, 1985

[43] Bordwell, D., Staiger, J., and Thompson, K., *The Classical Hollywood Cinema: Film, Style and Mode of Production to 1960* New York, Columbia University Press 1985: 7

[44] Bourdieu, P. *Distinction: A Social Critique of the Judgment of Taste*, trans. Richard Nice Cambridge: Harvard University Press 1984 and Bourdieu, P and Passeron J.C. *Reproduction in Education and Culture* trans Richard Nice Beverley Hills Calif., Sage, 1977:112

[45] Ibid

[46]Ibid.

[47] This is a reference to Tony Shrafazi an Iranian American artist and now a gallery owner and art dealer in NYC who became famous for defacing Picasso's Guernica in 1974 with the painted slogan "Kill Lies All" as a protest against the Vietnam war.

[48] See Pelles, G. *Art Artists and Society: Origins of a Modern Dilemma: Painting in France and England* 1750-1850 New Jersey, Englewood Cliffs, Prentice Hall 1963 Wittkower, R. & M. *Born Under Saturn, The Character and Conduct of Artists. A Documented History from Antiquity to the French Revolution* New York, Norton Random House 1963,

[49] Bourdieu, P. and Passeron, J.C. *Reproduction in Education, Society and Culture* Trans. Richard Nice London, Beverly Hills, Sage Publications 1977:112

Chapter 2

Alterity, Sovereign Consciousness and In/subordination

> What is the destiny of the universal in our societies? Is it a proliferation of particularisms ...or their correlative side: authoritarian unification - the only alternative in a world in which dreams of global human emancipation are fading away? (Ernesto Laclau)[1]

Slavoj Žižek's essay "Class Struggle or Postmodernism? Yes please!" opens with an anecdote about a well known Marx Brothers' joke in which Groucho answers the question "Tea or Coffee?" with "Yes, please!" which Žižek suggests is "a refusal of choice." He chooses to read Groucho's reply positively as a rhetorical question: moreover as an accommodation between two opposing positions representing two critical paradigms constituted within modernism and postmodernism that he frames with apostrophes (scare quotes) -- contains within parentheses -- and elaborates upon in the following terms: "either 'class struggle' (the outdated universal problematic of class antagonism, commodity production, *etc.*,) or 'postmodernism' (the new world of dispersed multiple identities, of radical contingency, of an irreducible ludic plurality of struggles).[2] But this "refusal of choice" that Žižek indicates is present in Groucho Marx's response to the tea or coffee question may also be read in other ways: As a performative speech act "Yes, please!" may be read in its context more perversely as "I'll take both", "I didn't hear you" or, "I didn't understand what you said" and perhaps a substitute for "you choose", "I don't know", "I don't care", or "whatever [you choose] is good for me", or simply a "whatever." In other words without the *performative* dimension to Groucho's words, his reply to Harpo may, and perhaps should be read ironically, satirically, perhaps as a negation of a negation, or an horizon of choice. And the danger always of "having one's cake and eating it too," is that indigestion may well be the result.

This chapter revisits some of the classical antinomies and conundrums with respect to the spectral keywords, ideology, class and hegemony, principally to determine their limits of intelligibility and use value within contemporary critical theory and cultural studies. In the first section of this chapter I will review some of the changing definitions of these terms and locate their relevance for my research. Following this I will attempt to breathe some life into the perennial question of the subject [Other] whom Claude Levi-Strauss once anointed as "the spoilt brat" of philosophical discourse. The purpose of this chapter is to confirm the compatibility of various theoretical approaches to social conflict and cultural hegemony, alterity and cultural in/subordination in the writings of several theoreticians: Marx, Voloshinov, Bahktin, Gramsci, E.P.Thompson, Bourdieu, Williams, Laclau, Mouffe, Žižek and Butler. In the second section of this chapter a number of positions on alterity, cultural sovereignty, in/subordination and ethics will be explored in the writings of Derrida, Levinas, Agamben, Badiou and Bhahba, followed by a discussion of the applicability of these terms to the discussion of art, film and death.

Revisiting Ideology, Class and Hegemony

> In considering such transformations a distinction should always be made between the material transformation of the economic conditions of production, which can be determined with the precision of a natural science, and the legal, political, religious, aesthetic or philosophic - short *ideological forms* in which men become conscious of this conflict and fight it out.[3]

Ideology has had an extraordinarily rich yet often problematic existence as a concept within class and culture studies, primarily because it is either conflated with or used as a descriptive or synonym for other key concepts, as in the famous passage from Marx cited above. Among these concepts are philosophy, ethos, worldview, political beliefs, common sense, consciousness, the unconscious, representation, and misrepresentation. And even as

Patrick Brantlinger (1990) has identified with respect to much cultural studies literature, even *culture* as a whole.

Ideology has been defined as everything from false consciousness -- a distorted or upside-down-view of reality -- to a set of philosophical beliefs, positioning and political posturing. In most instances however, the term ideology has been accorded a certain instrumental, determining power or sociological effect, one that has been frequently overemphasized and misunderstood. The German Marxist philosopher Wolfgang Fritz Haug has written: "Ideology - one word and so many meanings," as he reflects upon the important question, "are ideologies on ideologies our fate?"[4] Haug and other members of the Project Ideology Theory (PIT) group struggled to separate the denotative ideology from the highly connotative ideological. Other writers, Roland Barthes for example, tended to privilege the connotative aspects of ideology at the expense of the denotative. Shifts in semiotic emphasis from the denotative to the connotative have caused as many problems as they have attempted to solve. At this time under the power of postmodern discourse it appears that the relativising tendencies contained within the connotative approach to ideology and its effects/affects have centre stage. As far as visual representation is concerned, this connotative approach has resulted methodologically in a postmodern emphasis upon fluid processes of reading and interpretation as opposed to structural analysis.

Within the Marxist canon ideology has had a much contested existence. Perhaps, given its early origin in post-enlightenment discourse as "the science of ideas" this should be so.[5] Ideology has been discussed generally as an instrumental component of culture and specifically as a principal agent upon the individual formation of consciousness. Marxists discuss the ideological in various ways: in terms of its forms and powers on social life in general (Marx and Engels, 1885-6); as a network of struggles (Lenin, 1902); visual ideology (Hadjinicolaou, 1973), compromise formations (Haug, 1982), multiple force relations (Foucault; 1990), and legitimating discourses (Bourdieu 1994). Althusser's concept of the "ideological subject effect" defines the human subject as the *'animal ideologique,'* who in his/her daily life acts within a complex matrix of ideologies that bonds/binds (interpellates), her/him to the social order. He argued provocatively that the ideological apparatuses of the State: education, the legal system and the police, military and in some cases the media, as well as the governing institutions themselves, are the powerful instruments of domination, subordination and control. Althusser shifted the emphasis away from Marx's model of a determining economic base, a compliant ideological superstructure and with it, the dominance of the social economic over the cultural. He theorised not only that the ideological apparatuses of the State are as determining as the economic base, but also that, as ideological agents, human subjects are themselves implicated in the reproduction of the State's structured agenda. Althusser was among the first theorists to recognize the importance of the special dialectical relationships between institutional structures and human agency with respect to the role that ideology plays in the maintenance, and therefore reproduction of the hegemony of the dominant culture. If *structure* was privileged by many of the early theorists of ideology, now under the influence of postmodern discourse, *agency* has acquired greater currency. The truth probably lies somewhere in between, that is in the liminal modalities of both structure and agency. In this book, I have employed a practical model of structure with respect to class working in tandem with individual agency. This model can provide some explanation as to why minority elite cultures can exercise their ideological hegemony over popular culture, which are often economically dominant; and moreover, why those in subordinate positions accept the naturalness of their fate.

Since Marx's invocation of ideology as false consciousness, the role of ideology in the formation of group psychology and social behaviour has waxed and waned. In the early work of the Birmingham cultural studies researchers, the editors and writers for the film journals *Screen, Block, Cahiers du Cinéma, Cinétique*, the reconciliation of the separate discourses of Marxism and psychoanalysis in the work of Althusser and Lacan seemed complete. The conflation of social and psychological discourses permitted researchers to argue that while individuals may believe that they speak freely, ideology actually speaks through them. For many writers this helped explain why individual members of subordinate groups – classes and class fractions – often act less in their own best interests than in the interests of their class. This model provided an understanding of how an individual subject's consciousness of their subordination may change, yet in most external respects their social position remains the same as other members of their class. For sociologist Paul Willis, this explained how class-consciousness is reproduced and "why working class kids get working class jobs."[6] The Italian Marxist Antonio Gramsci argued that there is a material or common sense basis to ideology; a lived comprehension or understanding that further naturalizes the power relations subsumed under the mantle of hegemony. For Gramsci ideology is not simply a set of ideas or beliefs, but has a material and specific sense. Employing one sense of ideology adopted from the early writings of Marx argued that consciousness itself is structured as ideological. If this is true, the question of how a subject articulates, acts out, or symbolically represents their commonsense lived relationships within ideology becomes a key to understanding its social and cultural affects. If common sense is, as Gramsci suggests, the "sub-stratum of ideology," then these lived ideas, many of which are unconsciously held, yet consciously acted upon, become the key to understanding class-consciousness and class relations. His articulation of hegemony explained why class divisions and class antagonisms are reproduced through time.

Pierre Bourdieu argued that ideologies are "legitimating discourses" that operate with a great deal of complexity and contrariness. He acknowledged moreover, that these discourses and the institutions from which they emanate provide the sites within which our understanding of ideological effects influences and power must be located.

> The most successful ideological effects are the ones
> that have no need of words, but only of *laissez faire*
> and complicitous silence.[7]

The difficulties of both defining ideology and explaining both its effects and affects have not deterred the maintenance of its status as a keyword within critical and cultural studies. If anything, it has encouraged its continued use. Under the influence of feminism, postmodernist and post-colonial discourse the work of a number of writers demonstrates however that there have been some shifts in the strategies and methods used to address the representation of ideology and its effects/affects. These range from quasi-scientific forms of sociological analysis, to forms of reading and textual interpretation within various interpretive communities (Nelson and Grossberg (1988); Grossberg, Nelson, and Treichler (1992), Gibson-Graham, Resnick and Wolff (2000). This shift in attention occurred without lessening ideology's value as an explanatory concept, but rather lending it greater use value by contextualising it within discursive fields marked by their interdisciplinary and theoretical heterogeneity. This makes the business of class ascription a more difficult, if nonetheless, interesting proposition.

From a conventional Marxist perspective social classes are defined in relation to other classes within a given system of production, their formation the consequence of property ownership, labour and wealth accumulation. For many sociologists class, like ideology, is one-dimensional: that is one's class is objectively located and established on the basis of certain discrete criteria and relatively autonomous categories such as education, occupation and income. For example Paul Fussell who divides class in America into eight registers provides an extreme and somewhat risible version of this.

"Top out-of-sight: the super-rich, heirs to huge fortunes
Upper Class: rich celebrities and people who can afford full-time domestic staff
Upper-Middle Class: self-made well-educated professionals
Middle Class: office workers
High Prole: skilled blue-collar workers
Mid Prole: workers in factories and the service industry
Low Prole: manual laborers
Destitute: the homeless Bottom out-of-sight: those incarcerated in prisons and institutions"[8]

For some researchers within the culture studies orbit (Frith, 1986), class is a relatively autonomous category. For others however, class is contextual, dynamic and "resonates with political meaning."[9] Since E.P. Thompson's landmark study *The Making of the English Working Class* (1963), much has been done to try and establish bases for understanding the dynamics of class structures, as well as the modes and manners by which class is expressed and reproduced. Bourdieu for example, has discussed this typical class conundrum, as an attempt to locate the objectivity of the subjective.

Bourdieu writes.

> The objectivist vision [of social class] is able to extract the `objective' truth of class relations as power relations, only by destroying everything that helps to

> give domination the appearance of legitimacy. But it falls short of objectivity by failing to write into its theory of social classes the primary truth *against* which it is constructed, in particular the veil of symbolic relations without which, in many cases, class relations would not be able to function in their 'objective' truth as relations of exploitation.[10]

E.P. Thompson has also critiqued the seeking of objective truth in autonomous class categories, arriving at the matter-of-fact explanation, that a class may participate in its own making as much as it is made, a commonsense notion that has become (almost by default), the stock-and-trade of much of the best cultural studies and new sociological research. Thompson's position suggests that it is important to consider class as relational as distinct from oppositional, although the differences between the two are often difficult to locate. In their reading of Marx, Resnick and Wolff (1987), declared that class "is an adjective not a noun" a comfortable postmodern declaration that enables contemporary researchers to bypass the problems of reification inherent in the conventional nominalization of class and it's a/effects. For the purposes of my research I have endorsed the notion of class, after Bourdieu, as a symbolic *process*, and in so doing, have recognized the descriptive [class] to be multi-dimensional and somewhat less homogeneous than many cultural researchers would admit. I have also resisted the urge to homogenize social reality into a classless *lebenswelt* populated by apolitical agents and actors, either reduced to individualized identity politics or heterogeneous taste cultures. I wish to emphasize that the objective categorizations of class grounded in education, occupation, income, and what Bourdieu has termed 'symbolic' or 'cultural capital,' must also be subjectively understood and confirmed by the classed subject. In these terms class may be less objective or subjective, than *contingent*, its boundaries shifting constantly, but not yet boundary-less (permeable) or worse invisible and therefore, as a consequence, unable to be read.

Ideology enters significantly into the formation of classes, through the manner in which the lived experiences of individuals are represented, reconstituted and communicated. Communication occurs through various forms of discourse: speech, stories, visualizations (film and television), performances, dress codes, eating habits and consumer preferences. As Eric Hobsbawm argued class "is ideology as well as structure" and class 'consciousness' is articulated "as a group's awareness and understanding of itself that grows out of opposition to other groups."[11] In other words, the individual classed subject comes to know and understand his/her class position *only* in terms of their opposition to others, and this is signified (represented), through various symbolic/performative means as relations of power. This dynamic provides the basis for understanding how dominant/subordinate relationships can develop in a wide variety of social circumstances that are not necessarily the result of institutional or 'classed' structures. But this inevitably leads to a conundrum with respect to the negotiation of the other, as Judith Butler has described this in her response to Žižek's model of "radical contingency" a position he upholds from his reading of Lacan.

> This happens when we think we have found a point of opposition to domination, and then realize that the very point of opposition is the instrument through which domination works, and that we have unwittingly enforced the powers of domination through our participation in its opposition. Dominance appears most precisely as its Other.[12]

It should be apparent from this brief discussion of ideology and class that class divisions and class-consciousness are extremely difficult to isolate and identify. Sociological models do not always provide adequate criteria for the correct placement of individuals within social and/or cultural hierarchies, and in many instances prove too restrictive. A traditional class indicator such as education may be less useful than it at first appears, even when Bourdieu, whose models of symbolic and cultural capital accumulation have considerably enriched this important category for class ascription, employs it. No simple correlation or equation such as social class = cultural class can be made with any degree of certainty as to its general applicability to patterns of cultural consumption or production, or even to the description, analysis and determinations thereof. The phenomenon dubbed in the literature as 'cultural straddling' by various class fractions,[13] is accompanied in the domains of production and consumption by another: borrowing and 'trafficking.'[14] The appropriation or expropriation of the products of one group by another, a process, tied ultimately to market conditions, is one of the most salient characteristics of social relations at all levels within capitalist society. Class mobility and trans-cultural mobility, whether actual or perceived on the part of any group studied, are also important in any study that attempts to link cultural (ideological) distinctiveness to socio-economic (class) difference. More comprehensive sets of class indicators have to be employed for adequate methodologies to be developed. And where these criteria are developed, they must be used with some caution; that is, with the realization that both the subjects of this process, and the process of class ascription itself, is complex, dynamic rather than static, and moreover, exists within highly matrixed discursive fields of interpretability that tend to undermine differentiation, which is one of the principle goals of sociological inquiry itself.

Hegemony has also had a somewhat contested existence as a keyword within critical and visual studies. In many ways however, using the term hegemony obviates the necessity for providing reductive definitions and assigning specific instrumentalities for the previous keywords, ideology and class, which is therefore useful in this respect. Since its emergence in the early writings of the Russian political strategists Plekhanov (1895), and Lenin (1902), and subsequent elaboration in the prison notebooks of Gramsci (1920), the term hegemony has obtained major currency in the work of many culture researchers and critical theorists. [15] It has been especially relevant for those investigating the representation and contestation of cultural, as well as political and economic power both locally and globally (Hardt and Negri, 2000). Most importantly, the keywords embraced, if not subsumed by hegemony – culture, ideology and class – have been permitted to transcend the more mechanical, econometric and 'fatal' aspects [16]of historical materialism, becoming in the process, much more useful tools with which to negotiate (interpret and analyse), social/cultural relations within the modern and postmodern eras.[17]

According to many of his interpreters, Gramsci viewed hegemony as both the process and the evidence of relations of power, particularly the power that the dominant classes exercise through various means – culture, education, law – over subordinate and marginal groups. The evidence is not only reflective of the imposition of power in a mechanical and authoritarian fashion; that is through coercion or direct enforcement through the policing apparatuses of the State. It is also presented in cultural terms that appear and moreover, are acknowledged as being totally natural, legitimate, and in some crucial senses, inviolable. This naturalness is underscored by the distinction first advanced by Lenin, and elaborated by Gramsci, between political and civil society.[18] Where political society and its institutional forms of governance allow for, and in fact encourage various forms of coercion in the maintenance of control - civil society is composed of those non-coercive and seemingly non-political (cultural) elements of society.[19] According to Gramsci, hegemony cannot be defined strictly in economic terms, hence its relevancy for those researchers interested in moving beyond econometric models that emphasize causality and determination without devolving into extreme forms of postmodern relativism.

Hegemony is not *a priori* and universal – an *ur* phenomenon – rather, it is reproduced and sustained, according to Gramsci, as a 'moving equilibrium' containing relations of force favourable to this or that tendency.[20] It is in the cracks and fissures that one recognises the normalizing tendencies, and in stronger terms, the institutionalization, or cementing of hegemonic relations of power. This is where control is being contested and resisted. Just as the dominant class is recognized in the forms of its subordinates, so too is hegemony recognized for what it effects/affects, produces and reproduces within its domain. Gramsci's work demonstrates how ideology and culture generally, can exert a powerful hegemonic influence on the production and reproduction of structural inequalities within a society. Within classed society, hegemonic conflict, or better, the struggle to achieve hegemony, can occur anywhere: within government, business, within various institutes of education, religious and other community groups, private and public sector unions, but especially the media and as I argue in this book, in cinema and other forms of visual representation. These struggles may take place on a large scale: in institutions of government, at public meetings, television debates, in the print media and on the Web. Alternately, they can exist at the micro-level that is at the level of the ideological signification of the sign, and within ensembles of signs.

In the context of the research for this book the macro level is film in its philosophical, social and historical context. These become sites for Derrida's first and second "go around." The micro level is present in the details of a sequence, a single shot, a dialogue, a phrase or word; Derrida's third "go around." Film, static images, written texts, speech and performed actions are important vehicles for both the contestation and cementing of hegemony and are therefore useful sites for research.

It is important to recognize the compatibility of various theoretical approaches to the key concepts discussed above. Like Ludwig Wittgenstein and Raymond Williams, Gramsci had a deep appreciation for the philosophical character of ordinary language. He also recognized language itself as the site of power differentials, the potential ground for the contest of meaning to erupt, always signifying ideological if not class difference. His understanding of language is compatible with earlier theoretical positions on the importance of language in class ascription elaborated by the Russian formalists Voloshinov and Bahktin. For Voloshinov:

> Class does not coincide with the sign community, i.e. with the community, which is the totality of users of the same set of signs of ideological communication. Thus various different classes will use one and the same language. As a result, differently oriented accents intersect in every ideological sign. *Sign becomes the arena of class struggle.*[21]

On one important level this study of the proliferation of cinematic satires and parodies of the '-isms' of modernist art, and the status of avant-garde artists associated with these; reveal the social and cultural significance of the struggle to resist the hegemony of the cultural dominant. This book also affirms the recognition of this as a political process; a struggle to achieve and maintain hegemony. In a somewhat more limited sense the discussion of these popular critiques of art can promote an understanding of the contestation over the meaning of the sign(s) of modern (and postmodern) art; and in the senses articulated by Bourdieu and Voloshinov, through the intersection of "differently oriented accents" of the sign(s). The discussion of art, film and death in the following chapters also reveal how trans/actional processes of reading and interpretation encourage comprehension and valuation to occur. In linguistic terms, it is not the structure of the units of language that is analysed, or the syntactical variations within this structure, but the manner in which these units may be accented and trans/acted in a variety of ways by their users and therefore subjected to differing ideological inflections as they are read. This remains a principally symbolic contest of meaning. Another fundamental aspect of this study reveals how these accents can be used to either reinforce a particular set of resistant social practices, or allow subjects to accommodate themselves to the social order.

> All processes of socialization and all social struggles or political articulations inevitably connect themselves with ideological powers. At the core of concrete historical studies must be placed (the dimension of) hegemony.[22]

Films that ironise parody or satirize art are important vehicles for negotiating and contesting the terms of value for modernist culture as a whole, as well as determining the role and status of the artist in society. Culture is the privileged terrain of investigation in this book and yet my discussions are not limited to this; I stress throughout the existence of power relations and social conflicts within modernist (and postmodern) culture. I will attempt to reveal that the symbolic representation of these contests of power are not neutral in character, but instead, represent historically entrenched antagonisms between various social groups and constituencies – classes and class fractions – about the meaning and value of the institution art itself.

Thus far the discussion has merely revisited the difficulties and complexities attaching to class and moreover, of establishing its very legitimacy as a mode of social and cultural enquiry. One crucial means of perceiving and interpreting cultural and class difference, is to examine the ways in which one constituency, class, or class fraction responds to, represents, and through its cultural representations, criticizes another class or class fraction. My claim here is that the examination of these critical representations reveals hegemonic and counter-hegemonic tendencies, which if not determined *in extenso,* are certainly influenced in a dialogical fashion by those conflicts occurring in the social/economic arena, or to employ Bourdieu's trope, this sector of the game board. The struggles, conflicts and points of resistance within the domains of cultural production (and consumption) are as significant as those that occur elsewhere; far from being separate from class conflict as a whole, are wedded to it.

Within contemporary society, the contestation of ideological dominance and *sovereign power* occurs at *all* social and cultural levels, often representing patterns of accommodation to the prevailing order – subordination -- but more often than not, providing the evidence of contestation and resistance, a counter hegemony, or what I prefer to call *in/subordination*. The task will be to practically elucidate these claims in the following chapters but before this may be undertaken I must take the opportunity to explore the status of 'the other' without which an understanding of class processes, power relations, subordination and in/subordination have little meaning. In this second section of this chapter I explore the extremes of otherness (alterity) – racism and murder – with reference to the writings of Emmanuel Levinas, Giorgio Agamben, Homi Bhabha , Alain Badiou and Jacques Derrida.

The Status of the Other

> No difference without alterity, no alterity without singularity; no singularity without here now. (Jacques Derrida, 1994)

Emmanuel Levinas, philosopher of ethics argued that "To kill is not to dominate but to annihilate; it is to renounce comprehension absolutely."[23] Giorgio Agamben in his books *Homo Sacer: Sovereign Power and Bare Life* (1998); *Means Without Ends* (2000), and *Remnant's of Auschwitz: The Witness and the Archive* (Homo Sacer III, 2002),[24] also negotiates the problem of death, killing, annihilation, mass murder, evil, witnessing and ethics, from a somewhat different position; one in which the question and indeed status of 'the other' is always a parenthetical (?) in the process of becoming, or as he would say echoing Heidegger's *dasein* – in *potentia* –as is the human subject him/herself. In *Homo Sacer 1* Agamben discusses that "special obscurity" embedded in early Roman law that declared the one who was condemned to death as sacred could therefore be killed with impunity.[25] In *Remnants of Auschwitz* Agamben provides a more contemporary model of *homo sacer* in his extensive discussion of the figure in Auschwitz "to which

(sic) no one has borne witness but who has a name --*Muselmann*--
literally "The Muslim."[26] In Auschwitz the Muselmänner were the
incarnation of the living dead (*unter/unter mensch*), for whom no one
felt compassion or sympathy; figures who no one acknowledged; that
even "the other inmates did not even judge worthy of being looked
at…and who to the SS Guards were (considered) merely useless
garbage."[27]

It is perhaps necessary at this juncture to reiterate that a primary
fulcrum of Agamben's view of modernity is his discursive
negotiation of "the camp"; nominally the concentration camp, and
"the state of exception" both physical and psychical, that the camp
induces in its inmates and overseers, who become at times, (perhaps
ultimately), indistinguishable. He argues that the camp was/is the
space where a state of exception occurs; where the exceptional could
and indeed does take place.[28] The camp is also the territory in which
Agamben's theories of biopolitics come in to play; more specifically
where the antagonism between *zoe* and *bios* become evident. Under
Agamben's "state of exception" the human subject is not only
stripped of *bios* (bare naked life), but also exposed as *zoe* (politically
qualified life), such that anything, including the unspeakable can be
done to the inmate – and here is the important qualifier – since
nothing can be considered a *criminal act*. Moreover the Camp,
according to Agamben, is "the space that opens up when the state of
exception starts to become the rule." He argues that the camp is the
new bio-political *Nomos* of the world today, which arguably has its
most contemporary manifestations in the detainment camps in
Afghanistan, Iraq, and Guantanamo Bay, the Palestinian camps in
Israel, those in Nigeria, the Sudan, exile internment camps in
Australia and elsewhere throughout the world.[29] The relationship
between what Agamben terms bare life and the *polis* is one of
inclusive exclusion – ultimately a "such as it is" – *a quodlibet en sets
unum* (whatever entity in one).[30] His important rumination on the
state of exception enables us to understand the camp beyond its
archetypes in refugee camps, prisons and gated communities; where
the pursuit of the good (sovereign) life is compromised by the
prospect of an ignoble death, to a imagine a permanent political
ecology of the mind which is one of incarceration.[31] In *Remnants of
Auschwitz*, arguably one of his most challenging books, Agamben
discusses these issues in intimate detail. He explores the

origin and definition of the name *Muselmann* and the association of this figure with the Arab term Muslim/Moslem "the one who submits unconditionally to the will of God [Allah]." In this naming, the typical repetitive movements of the Muselmänner, that is "the swaying motions of the upper part of the body" are associated with genuflected "Islamic prayer rituals," yet not, interestingly, with similar prayer rituals of Orthodox Jews, Buddhists or any other religious group. Agamben negotiates the representation of the "M" figure through a range of texts including those of Primo Levi (1989, 1986), Ryn and Klodzinski (1987), Bruno Bettelheim (1967, 1979), Sofsky (1997), among others, reinterpreting and affirming this figure in Auschwitz and other Nazi concentration camps as a modern(ist) variant of *homo sacer*. The book's appendix also contains several extraordinary testimonies from survivor Muselmänner themselves; men (and women) who somehow managed to cheat the death for which they had been destined. Agamben offers the "ferocious irony" that "in any case, it is certain that, the Jews knew that they would not die at Auschwitz *as* Jews."[32] But at no point in his text does he really attempt to negotiate - broach- what it means to nominate the Jew as Muslim! Nor obviously, does Agamben invoke the common terminology of post-colonial discourse: alterity, subaltern, xenophobe, xenophobia, misanthropy, or the keyword "racism" from which they all derive. We must then pose the question: what is it to call a Jew a Muslim in that context (the Nazi concentration camps), or for that matter, any context?[33]

French philosopher Alain Badiou, posits an answer to this primary "othering" question that is invested in the identification, he would say "production" of evil. This is both a question of ethics and the problem of evil about which he has written extensively.[34] Badiou declares in the preface to the Verso edition of *Ethics* that it was originally written as an introductory text for secondary and post-secondary students. He wrote it in the countryside in the space of two weeks in 1993. It has since enjoyed several editions and translations and has been widely read. Without the lengthy introduction by Peter Hallward, Badiou's translator, and the interview between him and Hallward in the appendix, the book is a long essay less than a hundred pages long, divided into five chapters, the first two posed as questions 1) Does Man exist? And 2) Does the Other Exist? The remaining three chapters explore ethics, the truth process and the problem of Evil.

What does Badiou have to say about the Other and how does this intersect with Agamben's position in Homo Sacer III? Badiou's first two chapters are essentially a response to Levinas' position on the other, upon which his own provocative position on ethics is based. He begins by critically analyzing the ethical position proposed by Levinas before presenting his own. Levinas argues that it is impossible to arrive at an ethics in relation to the other because of the "despotism of the same, which is an incapability of recognizing this other."[35] Same and other conceived ontologically under the dominance of self-identity ensures the absence of the other in effective thought which he (Levinas) argues suppresses all *genuine encounters* with the other.... thus barring an ethical opening to alterity itself! This conundrum, Levinas argues, is the problem of western metaphysics and an undesirable remnant of its Greek origins. According to Badiou's reading of Levinas, the antidote to this problem is to shift the implicit same/other dialectic to a different foundation or origin point, one not tainted by metaphysical thinking, specifically the subject/object, reality/appearance oppositions; and in so doing Levinas "proposes a radical, primary opening to the other conceived as ontologically anterior to the construction of identity." For Levinas everything is grounded in the immediacy of an opening to the other that disarms the reflexive subject. The "thou" [*tu*] therefore as a result, prevails over the "I". This, Badiou asserts, has the status of Law in Jewish thought. For Badiou, the ineffable authority of the altogether Other- that is God - implicit in Levinas' enterprise makes his ethics "essentially a category of pious discourse" with its own rules and regulations, hence upholding and reproducing the omnipotence of religious dogma.[36] Moreover, with this parasitical or symbiotic attachment between religion and ethics, if we remove one from the Other, if would result, according to Badiou, "in a dog's breakfast!" He writes, "Our suspicions are aroused when the self-declared apostles of ethics and of the right to difference are clearly horrified by a vigorously sustained difference... For them African customs are barbaric, Muslims are dreadful, the Chinese are totalitarian." In fact, he argues, "these others are only acceptable if they become *good* others, which is to say *they should be the same as us* which serves to evacuate the use value of difference and otherness as a political and/or ethical category.[37]

I will draw attention at this point to Badiou's useful discussion with Peter Hallward who asks rhetorically: "Where do you stand in relation to the contemporary obsession with the other, with the valorization of difference as such?" And "how", he adds, "do you avoid this question once it's been admitted that it is not a matter of claiming a particular essence (sexual, racial or religious), but of developing a critical position that takes account of the fact that where people are oppressed, they are oppressed as women, as black, as Jewish or Arab?[38] Badiou has characteristically interesting and provocative responses to these questions. "When" he says, "I hear people say we are oppressed as blacks, as women, I have only one problem: what exactly is meant by 'black' or 'women'?" Badiou is not being facetious. He follows this with: "if this or that particular identity is put into play in the struggle against oppression, against the state, my only problem is with the *exact political meaning* of the identity being promoted. Can this identity, in itself, function in a progressive fashion – that is *other than a property invented by the oppressors themselves?*" And with this powerful comment, Badiou goes on to discuss Jean Genet, an important writer for both post-colonial and queer studies. "In his preface to *Les Negres* Jean Genet said that everything turns around the question: what/who are black people, and for starters, what colour are they?" You can then answer, says Badiou, "That black people are black. But what does black mean to those who in the name of the oppression they suffer, and make it a political category? I understand very well what black means for those who use the *predicate in a logic of differentiation, oppression and separation*" (my emphasis). "Just as I understand very well what French means when Le Pen (the extreme right wing politician) uses the word. When Le Pen champions national preference, France for the French, [he means] the exclusion [of immigrants], the Arabs and so on." [39]

Badiou suggests that in the context of (philosophical) thought that is "genuinely contemporary and a-religious," the whole ethical predication based upon recognition of the other "should be purely and simply abandoned."[40] That is, the privileging of a binary concept of otherness (I/you) complicates not only political agency but also what he terms the truth process; the production of truths. Badiou's philosophical propositions/ axioms are not only based upon those advanced by Heidegger, Spinoza and others, but also mathematics, specifically set theory proposed in 1873 by Georg Cantor, with important subsequent developments by Godel and Cohen. Set theory proposes the multiple 'without one' – every multiple being in its turn nothing other than a multiple of multiples – which is the law of being, with the only stopping point infinity: the void. Thus *the infinite is the reality of every situation, not the predicate of transcendence* (emphasis added). For Cantor, the infinite is actually only the most general form of multiple being. And with this as his *a priori* foundation, Badiou asserts that every situation, in as much as it *is*, is a multiple.

To shift register here somewhat, I will take this opportunity to briefly explore the history of set theory as it pertains to Badiou's deconstruction of the other before I return to assign its relevance to Agamben's work. In his paper the Russian born Cantor considered at least two different kinds of infinity. Before his intervention into classical mathematics, infinite collections of numbers were considered the same size; that is, orders of infinity did not exist. The language of set theory is based upon a fundamental relation termed *membership*. A is a member of B (A *E* B) or that B contains A as its element. The understanding promoted in this construct, is that each set is determined by its elements; it follows that two sets are equal if they have exactly the same element, sets of numbers, sets of points, sets of functions, sets of sets *etc.* In theory it is not necessary to distinguish between objects that are members and objects that contain members – the only objects one needs for the theory are sets. Unambiguously then, the object of study of set theory is sets, and as sets are fundamental objects that can be used to define all other concepts in mathematics, they are not defined reductively in terms of more fundamental or foundational concepts. Introduced informally they become self-evident. After Cohen's subsequent work in the field, the study of the role of sets in mathematics became understood *axiomatically*, this is why it this takes on some importance with respect to contemporary philosophy and any theory of subjecthood, alterity and class.

For both Badiou and Agamben, the philosophical lessons of set theory are clear. There is no God…meaning that the One is not. And if *infinite alterity is just (quite simply) what there is*, the question of other/same does not therefore present a problem. The issue then is that any experience one has --as a Lacanian divided subject -- *is the infinite deployment of infinite differences*. Even the self-reflexive term *myself*, that would have been considered solecistic in Locke's time, is not the intuition of a fundamental unity of the one but *a labyrinth of differentials* – a truly divided – fractured / subject. Again, within the terms he has established, Badiou's examples are clear: Rimbaud's "*I am another*...." as he writes, "the understanding that there are as many differences between a Chinese peasant and a young Norwegian professional and between himself (Badiou), and for that matter, anybody at all ..." followed here, with a beautifully axiomatic phrase: "[there are] as many differences but also neither more nor less."[41] *Quel Différance!*

In other words through their deconstruction of the status of the other, Badiou and Agamben indict *both* objectivist and relativist conceptions of ethics. Badiou for example, rejects both the implicit use of the altogether other implicit in Levinas' conception of the Other, and what he terms the vulgar sociology of culturalism, the "result of noble savagery directly inherited from the "astonishment of the colonial encounter with savages...as a foundation for contemporary ethics." Differences are what [that is all] there is! And with this in mind, the one/other; same/ other dialectics don't have any explanatory and hence, as he argues, ethical use value. The only genuine ethic is of truths in the plural, or better, the only ethics is of processes of truth. Badiou affirms that the thinking/labour that brings (his term *forces*), some truths into the world... are worth pursuing. He pits Lacan against Kant's ethics based upon a general morality, proposing that ethics (plural), do not exist; that there is only a (singular) ethic of: politics, love, art, and science. For Badiou truths are political, scientific, artistic, amorous (love), and every human is inscribed in these four subjective categories/ vehicles for (the construction/creation) procedures/ processes of truths in the making. The truth process *induces* a subject.[42] As Badiou proposes, "a philosophy (not philosophy in general), sets out to construct a space of thought in which the different subjective types, expressed by the singular truths of its time, co-exist.... But this co-existence is not a unification - that is why it is impossible to speak of *one* ethics." [43]

Badiou is rhetorically assertive when he contrasts the Evil considered as simply "lies, ignorance and deadly stupidity." But for the philosopher, the condition of EVIL (capitalized) is much rather, "the process of a truth." He concludes that "there is Evil only insofar as there is an axiom of truth at the point of the undecidable, a path of truth at the point of the indiscernible, an anticipation of being for the generic, and the forcing of a nomination (a naming) at the point of the unnamable." "EVIL is the will to name at any price." Badiou insists that a specific philosophy - again, not philosophy in general - sets out "to construct a space of thought in which the different subjective types, expressed by the singular truths of its time, co-exist.... But this co-existence is not a unification - that is why it is impossible to speak of *one* ethics.[44] For Agamben, similarly, Ethics has "no room for repentance; this is why the only ethical experience (which, as such, cannot be a task or a subjective decision) is the experience of (being one's own) potentiality, of being (one's own) possibility."[45] An ethics predicated simply upon recognition of the other cannot be sustained.[46]

Is that all there is? [47]

Badiou and Agamben's conclusions are useful for sharpening the terms of debate with respect to the holy trinity of race, class and gender but their deconstruction of the other runs the risk of throwing the proverbial "baby out with the bath water." If difference is but a horizon of opportunity (potential) then what do structural (systemic) inequalities and deprivations in Africa, the Middle East, Asia, Europe, North and South America signify? Perhaps it is appropriate to return to Derrida at this point to invoke the fourth of his go-rounds to weave "all these threads through a polylogue of N + 1 voices which happens to be that of a (black) woman" and to engage in some cross-dressing and performing the identity of the classed, raced, gendered, queer other, to slip out of a mind (and body) set in order to access the interpretative capacities of the 'not me.'

Deriving his precepts on otherness from Franz Fanon, particularly this author's *Black Skin, White Masks* (1952), and *The Wretched of the Earth* (1961), works that have made Fanon a prominent foundational contributor to post-colonial studies, the prominent post-colonial theorist, Homi Bhabha has argued that one's "otherness" is articulated *stereotypically* "at once (as) an object of desire and derision, an articulation of fantasy of origin and identity."[48] The "other" stereotype, in other words (if you will excuse the pun), is a combination of both fear and fetish to which he gives a Lacanian twist; there is, writes Bhahba, "both a structural and functional suggestion for reading the racial stereotype of colonial discourse in terms of fetishism. Fetishism, as the disavowal of difference, is that repetitious scene around the problem of castration. The recognition of difference – as the precondition for the circulation of the chain of absence and presence in the realm of the Symbolic – is disavowed by the fixation on an object that masks the difference and restores an original presence."[49] A *functional* link between the fixation of the fetish and the stereotype (or the stereotype as fetish), is perhaps even more relevant here. Bhahba posits "fetishism is always a 'play' or vacillation between the archaic affirmations of wholeness/similarity; that is 'all men have the same skin/race/culture', and the anxiety associated with absence, lack and difference - that is 'some men *do not* have the same skin/race/culture.' He goes on to explain another feature of othering and stereotypy that I suggest has relevance in this context. "The scene of fetishism is [also] the scene of reactivation and repetition of the primal fantasy - *the subject's desire for a pure origin* that is always threatened by its division, for the subject must be gendered to be engendered, to be spoken." For both colonized and colonizer (the inmates and the overseers of the camp), the stereotype *is* the "primary point of subjectification."[50] In another sense articulated by Cornelius Castoriadis the self is actually unable to be constituted without the painful reality of the confrontation with the other. "The apparent incapacity to constitute oneself as oneself without excluding the other.... coupled with an apparent inability to exclude others without devaluing and, ultimately hating them."[51]

Transposed to the concentration camp, if we return now to Agamben; in order to be rendered invisible and therefore, if you will excuse the vulgar phrase 'fit for death,' the Muselmänner had to be denied at the "primary point of their subjectification." In effect, this became a xenophobic process of *negative* fetishization, that enabled them to be to turned from human into less than human, and therefore, from subjects into objects.[52] The Muslim term for the Jew in this context actually becomes (to use Badiou's phrase here) "a predicate (a force) in the nominal logic of differentiation, oppression and separation." Given the generic subsets of stereotypical belief within Nazi (National Socialist) ideology; for example: the mythically superior Aryan origins of the pure German *volk*, the sacrificial importance of blood and soil; the reinforcement of the Jews as the killers of Christ and exploiters of the German working class; the miscegenation of German society through association and inter-marriage, this was – given the ideological blinkers of the Nazi propaganda machine – almost too easily accomplished. It was not then, simply a matter of Muselmann demeanor, the repetitive rocking of the upper torso and subordinate genuflection that lead him to be associated and therefore identified with Muslims. The Muselmänner were doubly negated through a transgressive fetishization of race and religion; the erasure of one hated name and the supplanting with an/other that is *equally* a product of xenophobic disavowal -- a double condemnation -- hence Agamben's "ferocious ironisation of the name."

Julia Kristeva also invokes the good name of Rimbaud, acknowledging that the stranger resides within us as the hidden (unconscious) component of our identity. "It is not simply - humanistically - a matter of our being able to accept the other, but of being in his place, and this means being able to imagine and make oneself other for oneself."[53] Perhaps the last words of this chapter section should mirror, Janus like, the first words of Jacques Derrida. "No here without singularity; no singularity without alterity, no alterity without difference no." [54]

---

[1] Laclau, E.Butler, Judith, Ernesto Laclau and Slavoj Žižek. *Contingency, Hegemony, Universality: Contemporary Dialogues on the Left*. London, New York, Verso Books 2000:86

[2] Ibid. Žižek, S. p.90

[3] Marx, K., *Preface to a Contribution to a Critique of Political Economy in Karl Marx and Frederick Engels*, Selected Works London, Lawrence and Wishart 1968:182

[4] Haug, W.F. in Hänninen, S and Paldan, L *Rethinking Ideology: A Marxist Debate* NY and Bagnolet International General 1982:9. See also *Commodity Aesthetics, Ideology and Culture*. N Y
and Bagnolet International General 1987

[5] Kennedy, E. *A Philosophe in the Age of Revolution: Destutt de Tracy and the Origins of Ideology* Philadelphia, The American Philosophical Society 1978:215

[6] Willis, P. *Learning to Labour*, London, Gower 1977:1

[7] Bourdieu, P. *The Logic of Practice* Stanford, Stanford University Press 1990:133, original Paris, Les Editions de Miniut 1980.

[8] Paul Fussell *Class: a Guide through the American status system* NY Touchstone 1983

[9] McNall, S., Levine, R., and Fantasia, R. (eds) *Bringing Class Back In Contemporary and Historical Perspectives Boulder*, San Francisco, Oxford Westview 1991:3

[10] Bourdieu, 1990:136

[11] Hobsbawm, E. 1984:8

[12] Butler, 2000:28

[13] Gans, H. *Popular Culture and High Culture* New York, Basic Books 1974:109. There are some problems with Gan's use of this term. The notions of *taste cultures*

with which he underlines the concept of 'straddling', raise the problem of the determining power of 'false consciousness'. How is it that those whose taste is governed by certain class interests and training, consume the products of other (competing classes)? Bourdieu's concept of cultural capital does much to explain the straddling issue without resorting to the negativism within the term false consciousness. Bourdieu argues that *class* cannot be reduced simply, to *taste*.

[14] This rich concept, itself the product of popular cultural discourse (traffic - trade in commodity literally and figuratively) has recently become useful in the broader context of discussions attending the politics of representation. In the company of related terms in recent theoretical discourse "appropriation" and "expropriation", "trafficking" lends some material and economic substance to the trans-valuative terms "representation" and "appropriation". See Sekula, A. "The Traffic in Photographs" in Buchloh, B., Guilbaut, S., and Solkind, D., *Modernism and Modernity: The Proceedings from the Vancouver Conference.* Halifax: NSCAD and NYU Press 1983

[15] Gramsci, A. *Selections From the Prison Notebooks of Antonio Gramsci* edited and trans. Q. Hoare and G. Nowell Smith, London, Lawrence and Wishart 1971 a selection from the original Italian Edition: A. Gramsci *Quaderni del Carere (1928-1935)* (ed) V. Gerratana, Turin, Einaudi, 1948-51; Gramsci, A. *Selections from Political Writings Vol I 1910-1920* and *1921-1926* Vol II edited and translations by Hoare, Q. and Mathews London: Lawrence and Wishart 1977, 1978

[16] For Gramsci historical materialism is too deterministic and therefore capitulates to some form of teleological position with respect to history. He called this resignation to history a form of "fatalism". Aspects of Gramsci's of critique of historical materialism occurs in *Selections from the Prison Notebooks* (eds. and translation) Hoare, Q. and Nowell Smith, G., London: Lawrence and Wishart (1978: 419-472).

[17] For a useful study of developments in contemporary Marxism see Anderson, Perry *Considerations on Western Marxism* London: NLR (1976) "Hegemony" (78-81), and *passim*. Also Gurevitch, M., Bennett, T., Curran J. and Woollacott, J., *Culture, Ideology and Social Process: A Reader* London: Open University Press (eds) *Culture, Society and the Media* London: Methuen (1982), and Bennett, Woollacott *et al.* (eds) University Press (1981), particularly Section 4"Class Culture and Hegemony" (185-251). See especially, Chantal Mouffe's contribution in this collection: "Hegemony and Ideology in Gramsci" (219-235).

[18] See Williams, Gwyn A., "Gramsci's Concept of Egemonia" *Journal of the History of Ideas_*21:4 (586-99), republished in Hymes, Del, *Reinventing Anthropology.* See also Bocock (1986: 21-37).

[19] Ibid 591

[20] Ibid 589

[21] V.N. Voloshinov, 1986: 23

[22] Hanninen & Paldan 1982:13

[23] Levinas, Emmanuel, *Totality and Infinity* translated by Alphonso Lingus, Duquesne University Press 1969:198

[24] Throughout this chapter I will use the primary title *Remnants of Auschwitz* or *Homo Sacer 111.* In the Zone edition (2002) *HOMO SACER 111* is capitalized in italics on the verso of the inside cover.

[25] This is similar to the edict within Muslim Sharia (law) that allows an individual who kills an enemy of Islam to be considered sacred and therefore immune from prosecution. The case of Salmon Rushdie is instructive here.

[26] Agamben, *Remnants of Auschwitz* p. 41

[27]Agamben, 43, quoting Ryn and Klodzinski, 1987:127

[28]Agamben, G. *State of Exception* translation, Kevin Attell, Chicago, University of Chicago Press, 2005

[29]*Nomos,* plural *nomoi,* a norm in the sense of both custom and law. In 5th century Athenian thought *Nomos* is contrasted with *phusis* (nature); the later represents underlying reality and the former denotes the patterns by which men try to shape this. In this sense Nomos is normally translated as norm or convention. In Agamben's sense this is also the new order, or extant hegemony.

[30] Agamben, G. *The Coming Community.* Minneapolis, Theory Out of Bounds, Vol. 1. University of Minnesota Press. 1993:2.1

[31]The phrase "ecology of the mind" derives from anthropologist Gregory Bateson's book *Steps to an Ecology of the Mind* originally published in 1971. A new edition has recently been published by the Press of the University of Chicago, 2000

[32] Agamben, 2000:45

[33] A related question concerns the animalization of humans which had its recent outrageous expression in media photographs from a U.S. controlled prison in Baghdad that revealed a female prison guard leading a naked and blindfolded prisoner around as a dog with collar and leash.

[34] Badiou is chair of the philosophy department at the École Normal Superiere and teaches at the College Internationale de Philosophie in Paris. It is not well known in North America and Australasia that he also has taught philosophy in marginal sites such as migrants' hostels and factories. He trained as a mathematician and philosopher and is a published playwright and novelist. Badiou is a long standing member of L'organisation Politique (party without party), a group of political activists founded in May 1968. His major publications include: *Theory of the Subject* (1982); *Deleuze: The Clamour of Being*; (1999); *Manifesto for Philosophy* (1999); *Ethics an Essay on the Understanding of Evil* (2001).

[35] Badiou, A., *Ethics: An Essay on the Understanding of Evil* New York, Verso Books. 2001:18

[36] Ibid p.23

[37] Ibid p.24

[38] Ibid p. 107

[39] Ibid p.108-9

[40] Ibid p. 25

[41] Ibid p. 26

[42] Notes taken at a lecture presented by Badiou to EGS faculty and students in Saas-Fee, Switzerland, August 2003

[43] Badiou 2001:28

[44] Ibid p.28

[45] Agamben *The Coming Community* 1993:44.4

[46]Agamben's discussion of homonyms and non-predicative properties of objects in *The Coming Community* Section XVII 72.1-7 is relevant in this context.

[47] *Is that All There Is?* (1966). Words by Jerry Leiber, music by Mike Stoller. Spoken: "I remember when I was a very little boy, our house caught on fire. I'll never forget the look on my father's face as he gathered me up in his arms and raced through the burning building out to the pavement. I stood there shivering in my pajamas and watched the whole world go up in flames. And when it was all over I said to myself, "Is that all there is to a fire?" Refrain Sung: "Is that all there is?, is that all there is? If that's all there is my friends, then let's keep dancing. let's break out the booze and have a ball if that's all there is."

[48]Bhabha, H.K., *The Location of Culture* New York Routledge 1994:67

[49] Ibid p.67

[50] Ibid p.75

[51]Castoriadis, C. *World in Fragments: Writings on Politics, Society, Psychoanalysis, and the Imagination* Stanford, California Stanford University Press 1997

[52]The Muselmänner were also called *figuren*, the German word for doll.

[53]Kristeva, J. *Strangers to Ourselves* New York, Harvester Wheatsheaf 1991:13

[54]"No Difference without alterity, no alterity without singularity; no singularity without here now."

Chapter 3

The Artist Manqué as *Alter Deus*.

When one has dealings with scholars and artists it is easy to miscalculate in opposite directions: behind a remarkable scholar one not infrequently finds a mediocre man, and behind a mediocre artist, often a very remarkable man. (Friedrich Nietzsche, 1886)[1]

Adj. manquéé: meaning unfulfilled or frustrated in the realization of one's ambitions or capabilities: *artist manquéé*; *writer manquéé*. Etymology: Old French from past participle *manquer*, to fail, Italian *mancare,* from *manco,* lacking from the Latin *mancus,* maimed, infirm (Larousse Dictionary)

Etymologically the term *manqué* (L. *mancus,* maimed), engages the notion of physiological maiming or infirmity, a condition for which today we would assign the euphemism 'physically challenged.' The Latin word *manco* is also defined as "a lack" and its importation into the Old French verb form *manquer* (to be missing, to give out; *manquer à,* to fail, to lack), provides the additional meaning of *failure,* with which today we associate the notion *manqué, ée* as an adjective meaning missed, unsuccessful, as in *un coup manquéé*; an abortive attempt; *marriage manqué,* a broken engagement, *un objet de manqué* and figuratively in the phrase *c'est un danseur manqué* – he ought to have been a dancer (Dictionnaire Larousse). In English, *manqué* (appropriated from French), placed after a noun: artist, dancer, musician, poet, filmmaker, conveys the meaning: that might have been but is not, and the condition of being unfulfilled (Concise Oxford Dictionary). In casual conversation between individuals the term can often politely convey the judgement of failure as in the (interrogative) phrase "perhaps you're a musician (or a filmmaker) manqué." Individuals rarely identify their own *manqué* status as such but they may indicate that they are "a frustrated musician" or "a frustrated artist," conveys a similar meaning, and depending upon how empathetic their listeners, this too may be interpreted as a sign of failure.

A recent media report indicated that a British Association of Teachers was considering a motion at its annual meeting in July 2005 to replace the grade 'Fail' on a report card with 'Suspended Success.'[2] A follow-up interview with members of this association said that the motion was unlikely to pass, i.e. fail, but the fact that the motion was even raised speaks to the deep cultural ambivalence we harbour particularly, in the school system, against failure. It can be said that failure, like otherness and stupidity (Ronell, 2003), is a feature of our socialized identity as human subjects and perhaps a true measure of its presence in our lives is only available to us when we negotiate a culturally constructed 'normative' plateau and approach or achieve the plenitude of success. Of course otherness and stupidity have differing ideological coordinates that secure their legitimacy as cultural discursives, hence, as was argued in the previous chapter, otherness can be constituted within and of itself - I am an/other -, but to obtain a measure of its e/affects in the social arena we must acknowledge /inscribe a concept of difference and recognize the *conditio sine qua non* of Derrida's "no singularity without alterity, no alterity without difference, no!"   But as Avital Ronell has argued, stupidity presents altogether another set of options and opportunities that exclude lack as a founding principle.

> Unlike truth, or the history of its inscription, stupidity does not suffer from its own lack, however, because in a sense it has arrived without diversion or delay. Stupidity can be situated in terms of its own satiety, as the experience of being full, fulfilled, accomplished: *le bonheur bête*. Protected from any alterity, making sense to and of itself, enveloped by a narcissistic certitude that rhymes internally – being, in sum, without a care – stupidity may well approximate a plenitude. It may be as close as we mortals come to plenitude."[3]

Unlike stupidity, failure *is* usually constituted in terms of its other. Without a concept of failure we would not have a concept of success and *vice versa*, but the criteria by which we measure success or failure and different gradations thereof, for example in the realm of art, are at best questionable. The status of failure in *manquéhood* is therefore worthy of discussion, particularly in the context of the arguments presented thus far in this study that link inter-class criticism and alterity with the conflation of art/crime in film.[4]

Is merely being frustrated in realizing one's ambition(s) to be considered a measure of failure, when failure can have so many different mitigating circumstances, for example, illness, poverty, the pursuit of a different career path, a difficult marriage? At what point does frustration in one's desires and ambition degenerate into the (absolute) negative value judgement of failure? The cynics will say failure always has its excuses but few will view failure, however it is constituted or framed, as necessarily a cause for celebration, or even success.[5] What is failure? The arch response to this question is that failure is the 'flipside' or negative of success. In the dictionary sense failure is defined in terms of a lack. A lack (an absence or deficit) of success, a lack of desire for success, non-performance, non-occurrence, inactivity; physiologically, in the sense of an organ ceasing to function, heart or kidney failure, and mechanically as in engine failure. Economically the lack is expressed in terms of indebtedness, loss of capital gains and bankruptcy, *etc*. Failure in love can have innumerable consequences but usually means alienation from and/or rejection by the subject of one's affection. In the practice of daily life failure can embrace many situations; some for example, such as the preparation of a family meal can be recognized as a successful exercise by father the chef, but be considered an abject failure by the family members who would probably not feel the desire to overtly express their dissatisfaction. Similarly a college teacher or university professor may have judged their most recent lecture to be a resounding success but the obverse may be the opinion of his or her students who may make their judgement known during class evaluation time.

The phrase "nothing succeeds like success," also has its counterpart in the more rarely heard "nothing fails like failure." It is often remarked that one's success is tantamount to another's failure – "your loss is my gain"— and this is usually perceived to be the fundamental (Darwinian) 'survival of the fittest' character of the worlds of commerce and sport. A "win, win" situation is a popular speech performative for plenitude in certain situations where the evacuation of the potential for loss, defeat and failure is required. But are examples of failure the lacunae of defeat or retreat? When does the lack of achieving success (achievement) – a no win situation – acquire a negative value judgement? Can we question after Derrida, whether this lack itself is the frame of the theory of failure? "What does the lack depend on? What lack is it? And what if it were the frame? What if the lack formed the frame of the theory? Not its accident but its frame. More or less still: what if the lack were not only the lack of theory of the frame but the place of the lack in a theory of the frame."[6]

And what of success? Etymologically *succeed* stems from the ME and OF *succeder* which derives from Latin *succedere* as sub-, *cedere, cess*, meaning to go [forward]; success is from the Latin *successus* as succeed – a pass go. The synonyms for success indicate the accomplishing of a purpose, favourable outcomes, the accomplishment of a goal or aim, betterment of one's position, progress, the accumulation of wealth, property and status (Concise Oxford Dictionary). Within capitalist society conventional indicators of artistic success are readily indicated by the accumulation of material and symbolic capital: awards, certificates, diplomas, prizes, profitable sales, goods and property – distinction and status. The artist and her/his work become the subject/object of critical legitimation and valorisation in newspaper, magazine reviews, journal essays, catalogues and books. S/he may also be offered honorary appointments and awards, etc. But these evaluations are *intrinsic* to success. The *succès de scandale* that with *épater le bourgeois* was a key objective of the historical avant-gardes, may be the only example of a success that includes in its very definition a measure of failure (provocation and scandal) that is also *ipso facto* perceived as success. The value of success, however, like the value of beauty, the sublime and pleasure, which we know from Kant, is necessarily a question of judgement, and about which Derrida has posted a few warnings.

> Now you have to know what you are talking about, what *intrinsically* concerns the value of 'beauty' and what remains external to your immanent sense of beauty. This permanent requirement - to distinguish between the internal or proper sense and the circumstance of the *objet* being talked about - organizes all philosophical discourse on art, the meaning of art as such from Plato to Hegel, Husserl and Heidegger. This requirement presupposes a discourse on the limit between the inside and the outside of the art object, here a discourse on the frame. Where is it to be found?[7]

This then, appears to be a/the question. Where indeed, is it to be found? Where is the limit between the inside and outside of failure? How for example, are success and the failure 'to pass go' signified in films that represent art, artists and art history? Christopher Cross the 'Sunday painter' in Fritz Lang's *Scarlet Street* discussed in the first chapter is a classic artist manqué. Although he treats his painting as a hobby, he recognises the particular power of modernist art and the celebrated high place – the pantheon of the great – that the successful artist may occupy within culture and society. "Cézanne...he was a great painter," he tells Kitty March during their 'courtship/ entrapment' scene, expressing the desire that some day he too would like to be an artist of distinction. Painting in his spare time enables Chris to avoid Adele his demanding wife who berates him at every given opportunity for any perceived infractions against her domestic rule. As a classic pre-feminist 'hen pecked' husband trapped in a loveless marriage, he is a ready victim to the alluring charms of Kitty March, the *femme fatale* he rescues from a beating at the hands of her boyfriend Johnnie. Although Chris has a somewhat limited knowledge about the history of modernism he recognises that if he had the strength of will of an artist like Paul Gauguin – another artist manqué trapped in a bourgeois existence – he could leave his wife, give up his day job, move to Tahiti and realize his ambitions, become a successful professional artist and live the good life! Ironically, Adele's first husband, a policeman whose photographic portrait glares down imperiously from the wall of their apartment, exercised more personal freedom by faking his death in order to extricate himself from personal debt and his marriage to Adele. Chris Cross is caught in the classic existential (Sartrean) dilemma of being for others or being for himself. When he exercises a measure of 'free choice' to pursue both Kitty and a studio (a room of his own), in which to paint without fear of criticism from Adele, his art succeeds by being legitimised in the art world, but he fails, by becoming a thief and a murderer. At the end of the film Chris is locked in the cell of his own personal hell. With less tragic results than *Scarlet Street*, the 'Gauguin option' for transcending creative frustration and *manquéhood* is played out in many popular films, for example *The Moon and Sixpence* (1942) based upon Somerset Maugham's Gauguin inspired story about a London based broker who gives everything up to live in Paris as a painter.

There are many other film and book narratives populated with frustrated and tortured artists *manqué*, misunderstood geniuses (*alter dei*) who struggle to realize their identity and mission as artists, which as Schopenhauer [8] and T.S. Eliot observed is to rise above mere talent, but who fail in their pursuit of success and the good life, turning their frustrations into self-hating, murderous or suicidal behavior that ultimately affects their family, those with whom they work and the community at large. *The Dark Side of Genius* (1994), a film directed by Phedon Papamichael recounts the story of an artist killer who murders his beautiful model and when paroled from prison he seeks out a new victim, a female reporter for an L.A. Arts weekly who is attempting to write a story about him. Ingmar Bergman's Gothic fantasy *Hour of the Wolf (Vargtimmen,* 1968), unfolds the story about the tormented inner life of a painter (Max von Sydow) who lives a solitary life with his wife on a northern island of the coast of Sweden. *Gothic* (1986), is director Ken Russell's stereotyped exploration of the laudanum-addled lives of tortured genius Byron, Percy and Mary Shelley at the Villa Diodati in June of 1816. One scene includes a powerful evocation in Mary's waking dream of spectres provided by Fuseli's painting *The Nightmare* (1781), suitably accompanied by theatrical flashes of lightning.

There are also films that represent the lives of artists who struggle with their patrons; for example *Close to the Wind* (1969), in which a sculptor comes into conflict with those who provide him with economic support to act out his neuroses, and Michelangelo's (Charlton Heston), epic struggle with the Pope over the painting of the Sistine Chapel represented in *The Agony and the Ecstasy* (1958), directed by Carol Reed. A different illustration of an artist manqué is provided in the cult film *Performance* (1970), an artful thriller directed by Nicholas Roeg and Donald Cammell. The film stars Mick Jagger who plays the role of a fading pop star – another manqué stereotype – who is contrasted with Chas (James Fox) a powerful gangland boss who is described "as an artist…. a real performer." The characters of Dr. Hannibal Lecter and Buffalo Bill in *Silence of the Lambs* are also presented as artists manqué, which makes their psychopathic behavior more diabolical than if they had been more transparent and 'conventional' serial killers.[9] Their 'life enhancing' [pro-] creative talents, Dr. Lecter's (Lector/Lecteur), classical drawing skill and Buffalo Bill's talent for fashion design, patterning and sewing, contrast markedly with their desire to kill. Arguably their art and design talents could have lead them to pursue different career objectives, but not, of course, if their artist sensibilities were somehow *ideologically inscribed* in their psychopathy. Other films about the art world represent an artist's mid life crisis as an opportunity to assume manquéhood. For example Martin Scorsese's abstract expressionist artist (Nick Nolte), in *Life Lessons* (*New York Stories*, 1989), struggles with his mid-life crisis and a troubled career by succumbing to the charms of a younger woman. Stourley Kracklite (Brian Dennehy), the unsuccessful architect in Peter Greenaway's film *The Belly of an Architect* (1988), also undergoes a mid-life crisis, losing his career, his wife and child, finally taking his own life to transcend his manquéhood. Dozens of films (see appendix I), contain accounts of the struggles of frustrated and tortured artists manqué who fail in their attempt to realize their visions. Even prototypical geniuses like Leonardo and Freud had their own moments of manquéhood – frustration, doubt and at times failure – in their inability to complete their masterpieces, or at least derive a modicum of satisfaction from their work. Freud was so concerned about these problems that he had to investigate Leonardo's childhood in order to understand his own predicament.[10]

The line between genius and madness, it must be reiterated, like the line between success and failure in the arts, is very fine. The history of the genius /madness conflation from which we derive the manqué theory of lack has been, and continues to be, a powerful ideological force in western culture, one which has been neglected in most of the literatures, except those that nominate Adolf Hitler as the exemplary artist manqué whose artistic rejections apparently precipitated a world war![11] Many books and films suggest that Hitler's assumption to power was somehow a result of his frustrated desire to become an artist, with historians noting the importance of his "oedipal struggle" with his father.[12] When he announced at the age of twelve that he wished to become an artist, his father's reported response was "not as long as I live," or words to that effect. And in 1907 at the age of eighteen, when Hitler failed in his drawing examination to obtain entrance into the Academy of Fine Arts in Vienna, he was unable to admit this failure to anyone. Seventeen years later in *Mein Kampf* he wrote "I was so convinced that I would be successful that when I received my rejection it struck me as a bolt from the blue." [13]

In his book *Hitler and the Power of Aesthetics* (2003), Frederic Spotts details several instances of Hitler's subordinates' opinion of him as an artist; for example Goebbels' boast that "His (Hitler's) creativity is that of the genuine artist no matter [in] what field he may be working." His diary entry after a meeting with Hitler in July 1926 notes that: "He talks about the future architectural image of the country and is thoroughly the architect. After, he paints a picture of a new German constitution and then is entirely the political artist." [14] He notes also that Hitler's view of statesmanship was not *Staatswissenschaft* but *Staatskunst* (Statecraft) that he elevated to "an intuitive art, like every art a product of genius."[15] Hitler's view of artists was also infused with ideology:

> Crime itself was forgivable in Hitler's eyes if it was committed by an artist. Informed on one occasion that a painter of his acquaintance had swindled a bank out of more than 1 million marks, he responded: 'the man is an artist – I am also an artist. Artists understand nothing about financial affairs. I forbid any action being taken against the man.'[16]

Oscar Wilde himself could not have manufactured a better defense of art and crime. Spotts recounts another important feature of Hitler's opinion of artists. Although Hitler was convinced that homosexuality was rampant in the Catholic Church and had no reluctance in sending priests to jail, he turned a blind eye ("don't ask don't tell") to homosexuality among artists.[17] Spotts and others concluded that Hitler transformed his thwarted creative energy – his manquéhood – into his political and architectural aspirations. "As an artist he was impotent, unable to do what he later did in politics and architecture - create a world instead of merely copying one." Although I believe it unwise to seek a reductive justification such as manquéhood for Hitler's despotism, the studies undertaken by Stern, Adams, Thewelweit, Eitner, Spotts and others[18] are useful in that they demonstrate that Hitler was not immune to the ideologies that sustained stereotypical notions of the artist and architect as *alter dei* although his subsequent behaviour as the führer demonstrated that he resisted the conflation of genius with madness and drew a line against the agonist, antagonist, and activist characteristics of the avant-garde.[19] The following section of this chapter explores the social construction and cultural representation of the artist manqué as outsider/other God figure, a phantasmatic construction that is part of the topological foundation and ideological fabric of western culture. I will conclude with a brief discussion of two exemplary figures, Vincent Van Gogh and Guy Debord who both committed suicide after demonstrably successful lives as artists, yet whose character and behaviour was nevertheless marked by manquéhood.

Genius and Madness

The late 18th and C19th century witnessed the hardening of various stereotypical images of the artist as priest, magician, physician, rebel, aristocratic hero, neurotic genius, sexual deviant etc.   These stereotypes had their infancy in antiquity and were firmly established by the Renaissance, but with the institution of the disciplines of art history, psychiatry, criminology and sociology these stereotypes began to take on the character of a law. With the proliferation of legitimating institutions such as art galleries, museums, art journals and art schools, by the mid-nineteenth century, artists were not only perceived as different from other members of their society, but also thought of themselves as different.[20] As Geraldine Pelles notes: "The place of the painter - artist in the pantheon of the great is relatively new."

> [So] a montage like picture of the artist has been built up in which he appears to be lazy, withdrawn, and anti-social, or exhibitionistic, explosive, and rebellious; sexually potent and promiscuous, or feminine and passive; a transcendental spiritual being or a social and political rebel. At any rate, the artist is regarded as deviating in some way from the general norms by which most people appear to conduct their lives.[21]

In the first chapter to their book *Born Under Saturn* (1963), art historians Rudolph and Margot Wittkower provide some important insights into the image and changing status of the western artist throughout history. The authors discuss documentary evidence for the position of artists in society from antiquity up to the French Revolution. Their investigation is diachronic and as such, is predicated upon understanding the place of artists in our own society as being other to, or simply *different* from their fellow human beings. They ask themselves if this had always been so, and if not, when and under what circumstances did change occur, and what manifestations in behaviour in particular did artists exhibit in order to merit this mantle of alterity. Their answer, which became the primary thesis for their book, is that the modern notion of difference, 'otherness' or separateness of artists from their society, occurred in the Renaissance, although they claim that documentary evidence reveals that the signs of change in status for the artist began somewhat before this time and the origins lie in antiquity. Perhaps the blame could be laid at the feet of Seneca whose dictum *'nullum magnum ingenium sine mixtura dementiae fuit'* – 'there never has been great talent without some touch of madness' – a comment that is often quoted in the context of discussions about Plato's *furores*.[22]

The Wittkowers advance a core distinction between the artisan and the artist to reveal the gradual emancipation of artists from a class of "cheerful, lively men of action," born under the patronage of Mercury, the fleet footed messenger of the Gods in Roman cosmology, to a class of solitary, brooding, contemplative and melancholic individuals under the patronage of Saturn, the large slow moving planet. Hermes, the Greek equivalent to Mercury was venerated as the deity of commerce and the inventor of music, science and art. In the astrological tradition being born under this sign would predispose one to become a painter, sculptor, watch maker or organ builder, perhaps also a thief and a cheat. Under Mercury's patronage the technical rather than creative achievements of artisans were valued. The Wittkowers attributed the early Renaissance neo-Platonist Marsilio Ficino with the task of shifting the patronage for the visual artist from Mercury to Saturn. They note that both Plato and Aristotle assigned the position for the visual arts below that of music, poetry and philosophy. Plato distinguished between clinical and creative insanity, reserving the latter solely for poets, and Aristotle placed visual arts below the registers for the language based arts, rhetoric and philosophy. Divine inspiration was reserved solely for philosophers, poets and musicians. Aristotle linked black bile, the fourth of Hippocrates' basic humors to creative talent and an artistic temperament. According to Giorgio Agamben this was "an ancient tradition [that] associated the exercise of poetry, philosophy, and the arts with this most wretched of humors. "'Why is it,' asks one of the most extravagant of the Aristotelian *problemata*, 'that all men who are outstanding in philosophy, poetry, or the arts, and some to the extent that they are infected by the disease arising from black bile?"[23]

According to Greek cosmology, from the disposition of the planets at birth we potentially derive an imbalance of humors that will determine our temperament. Being born under the sign of the planet Jupiter for example may predispose one to have an excess of blood in one's body and therefore to become more sanguine than others; if one has a preponderance of phlegm, one becomes phlegmatic, yellow bile, choleric and black bile, melancholic.[24] Plato's *mania* (divine enthusiasm), did not include visual artists because they were engaged with mimesis – image-makers – their images thus being mere imitations (aping) of the divine and intangible universe. The beginnings of a discursive shift began to take place in the fifteenth century. Marsilio Ficino's *Theologica Platonica*, an important foundational text of Renaissance neo-Platonist philosophy introduced some of the new metaphysical requirements for change: "In paintings and building the wisdom and skill of the artist shines forth. Moreover, we can see in them the attitude and the image, as it were, of his mind; for in these works the mind expresses and reflects itself not otherwise than a mirror reflects the faces of a man who looks into it." [25]

With this text and *De Vita Triplici* (1482-89), Ficino, as a key early Renaissance ideologue, tempered the Platonic antagonism towards the visual arts and endorsed Aristotle's position, thus reconciling both Aristotle and Plato's views on the sources of creativity and genius. Agamben suggests that Ficino himself was melancholic and points out that as his horoscope showed Saturn ascendant in Aquarius it therefore seemed natural for him, as an exemplary Florentine intellectual, to privilege a melancholic Saturnine disposition for himself and his cohort. He therefore contributed to a paradigm shift that had powerful ideological consequences throughout the following centuries. "The rehabilitation of melancholy went hand in hand with an ennobling influence of Saturn which the astrological tradition associated with melancholic temperament as the most malignant of planets, in the intuition of polarised extremes where the ruinous experience of opacity and the ecstatic ascent to divine contemplation co-existed alongside each other."[26] Aristotle's *pazzia* (melancholy) became the companion of Plato's *mania* (madness), and "the melancholy of great men became simply a metonymy for Plato's divine *mania*."[27]

Agamben implicates Ficino's intervention with the reproduction of Aristotelian phantasma that had evolved during the Middle Ages into the elevation of melancholic *acedia* (the noon day demon), as a dialectical "leavening capable of reversing privation as possession." And further, "since its desire remains fixed in that which has rendered itself inaccessible, *acedia* is not only a flight from, but also a flight toward, which communicates with its object in the form of negation and lack."[28] In another passage Agamben discusses the centrality of the phantasm for Aristotelian thought, describing it as a psychic constellation that he summarizes graphically with a diagram showing sensation as a force directed towards the phantasm, and language, sensation, memory (paramnesia *déjà vue*, ecstasy), dream divination as forces moving outward. Agamben suggests that the semantic character of language itself is "indissolubly associated to the presence of the phantasm," and explores the importance of this with respect to Medieval and Renaissance thought.[29] And although in this context, Agamben does not implicate the phantasmatic in the construction of ideology, this "indissoluble" focus upon the semantic character of language itself, says as much, and the results in subsequent cultural discursive formations (or regimes) may be manifold particularly if we (after Bourdieu), take ideology to be a legitimating discourse that operates through complicitous silence. "The most successful ideological effects are the ones that have no need of words, but only of *laissez faire* and complicitous silence.[30]

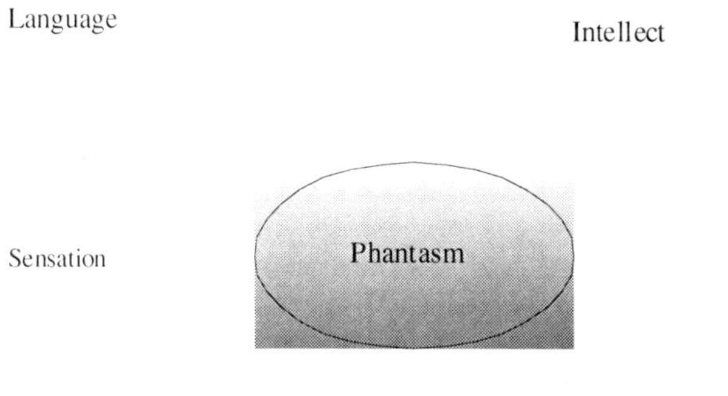

6. Phantasm as Ideology

Ficino did not fully acknowledge that the visual artist's enterprise was equal to the poets, rhetoricians and philosophers, members of the elite *literati,* of which he was a member. For him they remained artisans and it was left to the artists themselves (painters, sculptors and architects), to attempt to raise their own status in the eyes of their literate contemporaries through building upon the publication of treatises such as Leon Battista Alberti's *On Painting* (1436), Cenino Cennini's *Book on Art* (c. 1437), and Lorenzo Ghiberti's (d. 1455), important book on art and artists that includes the first known biography of an artist.[31] Alberti, probably with the medieval notion of the *deus artifex* (God the architect) in mind, suggested that as the artist, like God creates something out of nothing, then *he* (gender specific), "might well consider himself as another God, an *alter deus,*" a notion that certainly elevated the artist's position above other members – certainly women – within their community. And where Michelangelo speaks of his madness and melancholy, melodramatically represented for popular consumption by Charlton Heston in the film *The Agony and the Ecstasy,* his rants to the Pope while completing the Sistine Chapel frescos cannot be divorced from the Platonic and Aristotelian concepts that were given wide currency during the Renaissance. "It is true that Michelangelo by using the word *pazzia* to characterise his state of mind refers to his non-conformist obsessions rather than to Platonic madness. Yet such almost narcissistic emphasis on *pazzia* would be unthinkable without a familiarity with Plato's concept of *mania* by which poets and seers are possessed. It is well known that Renaissance artists appropriated inspired frenzy for themselves for it gave their art the *aura* Plato conceded to poetry."[32]   A wave of melancholy – as an evident behavioral product of ideology –swept the art world, such as it was then constituted, of the 1500s. The Wittkowers cite from the painter Giovon Battista Amenini's text: "An awful habit has developed among common folk and even among the educated to whom it seems natural that a painter of highest distinction should show signs of some ugly and nefarious vice allied with a capricious and eccentric temperament springing from his abstruse mind. And the worst is that many ignorant artists believe to be exceptional by *affecting melancholy and eccentricity*."[33] (Emphasis added) After quoting various examples of such affectation, Amenini adds that "artists must keep away from the vices of madness, uncouthness and extravagance, nor should they aim at originality by acting disorderly and using nauseating language."[34]

Through their topological overview the Wittkowers postulated a pattern of conformity and non-conformity in the conduct of artists throughout the centuries. Until the C17[th] philosophers and other members of the *literati* made little distinction between art, craft and fine art. They suggest that the emancipation of the artisan to artist was very gradual and that even as late as 1719 Abbé du Bos could refer to Michelangelo as "an artisan." They stress that there are always exceptions to their generalized overview of the emancipation process and that individualism was not specifically a Renaissance phenomenon; that indeed, many instances may be found up until the later Middle Ages when the maintenance of the *status quo* and rigid models of artistic behaviour were achieved through the guild system. The emancipation of artists from the guilds, which culminated in extreme individualism and alterity, was re-enacted in the eighteenth century when the romantic artists struggled for liberation from the academies. It should be noted that when they were first formed the academies encouraged individualism but as competition between artists increased and hierarchies developed, a new trend toward conformity arose, one that is best exemplified in the gentlemanly conduct of the of 17th artists such as Bernini and Rubens whom younger artists strove to emulate.[35] However by this time the proverbial 'die was cast' and the conflation of madness and genius began to become part of the ideological superstructure of the institution art. This was enabled through a variety of means such as artists behaviour, books and essays, for example in the occasionally contradictory writings of the Abbé Du Bos whose *Reflexions critiques sur la poésie et sur la peinture* (1719) contains the following paragraph about the character of genius:

> Vivacity and delicacy of feeling are inseparable from genius. Genius is not to be found in a man of cold temperament and indolent humour. It is the artists of genius who have much more exquisite sensibility than normal people. [36]

The Italian criminologist Cesare Lombroso (1836-1909) wrote the influential treatise *Man of Genius* (*Genio e Follia*, 1864), subsequently translated and published in a series of books on Contemporary Science. Lombroso was also one of the first to equate criminality with creativity. In literature and science, a tendency to puns and plays upon words, an excessive fondness for systems, a tendency to speak of oneself, and substitute epigram for logic, an extreme predilection for the rhythm and assonance of verse in prose writing, even an exaggerated degree of originality may be considered as morbid phenomena. [37]

Schopenhauer viewed genius, as a result of "surplus brain activity," a more powerful development than is required by "the service of the will" for which it originally came into being. As he wrote: "Therefore strictly speaking, physiology could to a certain extent class such a surplus of brain activity, and with this of the brain itself, among the *monstra per excessum*, which as we know, are coordinated by it with the *monstra per defectum* and the *monstra per situm mutatum*"[38] which translates as deformities through excess, through defect, and through wrong position. He makes some remarks on the individuality of genius quoting Aristotle's *Problemata* 30:1 "all men of genius are melancholic" (*omnes ingeniosos melancholicos esse*), and a poem by Goethe, the last two lines of which read: "Hence the poet's genius relishes the element of melancholy." For Schopenhauer genius serviced the whole human race as the intellect serves the individual and was divorced from capital and the profit motive. "The work of genius may be music, philosophy, painting or poetry; it is nothing for use or profit. To be useless and unprofitable is one of the characteristics of genius; it is their patent of nobility."[39]

In the 19th and early 20th centuries clinical (empirical) diagnosis attempted to confirm the long held assumption that there was indeed an alliance between genius and madness. It was assumed that artists are subject to Oedipal complexes, guilt complex and homosexuality or heightened bisexuality; were victims of their super ego or their neurotic frustrations and psychic traumas. For many years psychiatric opinion reinforced these opinions through clinical study, lectures, professional associations, publishing and various communications through the media to the lay public. Even a sentient writer such as Proust could maintain that individuals who are in some way deemed neurotic have produced everything significant in the world – "They alone have founded the great religions and composed the masterpieces."[40] The 'research' of Moreau, Lombroso and Möebius had considerable influence upon 20th century psychiatrists, as did Freud's study of Leonardo's childhood, which as later commentators have remarked, was as much a study of Freud himself.[41] Over the course of the next three decades several publications examining the character of genius appeared: Hermann Trück's study on genius in 1896, followed by a study undertaken by Albert Reibmayer (1908) in two volumes. In Leipzig Wilhelm Ostwald studied the biology of genius, 1910 and Ernst Kretschmer's 1919 university lectures on genius were published in 1929, shortly after the appearance of W. Lange-Eichbaum's famous volume on genius and madness, that concluded that most geniuses in all fields were psychopathically abnormal and neurotic. In the United States the field was lead by Lewis M. Terman from Stanford University whose *Genetic Studies of Genius*, Volume I appeared in 1924, Volume II (by Catherine Cox), in 1925, and Volume III (by Burks, Jensen, and Terman), in 1930.[42] These studies influenced or coincided with research in Germany and both American and German research on intelligence was based largely on the French Binet-Simon intelligence test (1904), which although it was designed for an altogether specific purpose, was adapted by researchers in several countries for other types of testing.[43] Scientific legitimacy for the genius/madness conflation was proclaimed often on the slimmest of evidence provided by the historical record of paradigmatic geniuses, 'corroborated' by dubious intelligence testing of large groups of subjects, often from within the military.

The tests themselves have since been shown to be inflected/ infected with hard to interpret (gendered and racist), ideological markers that render their broad applicability suspect.[44] The folly of attempting to construct meaningful correlations between results from intelligence quotient testing – when the meaning of intelligence itself still remains a question – and transposing these results onto a matrix of historical examples that are themselves constituted through ideology has not yet fully registered in the minds of proponents of IQ tests and the legions of individuals who flock to genius clubs such as Mensa when their 'test scores' register into the stratosphere.[45]

Lionel Trilling wrote that the connection between mental illness and artistic genius is one of the most characteristic notions of our time.[46] The romantic discourse around notions of genius remain familiar to those who teach in art schools still today – vision, enthusiasm, naïveté, spontaneity, the unique, individual approaches to style –even the term genius, now frequently used ironically, peppers studio conversations and critiques. This is the legacy of Romantic artists such as Blake who passionately asserted that "taste and genius are not teachable or acquirable but are born within us;" Goya, that an artist "may remove himself entirely from nature and depict forms or movements which have only existed in his imagination," and Courbet the exemplary 'realist', who could say "I cannot teach my art nor the art of any school, since I deny that art can be taught, or in other words, I maintain that art is completely original." These are but three examples of statements made by literally hundreds of artists whose discourse about teaching, the role and behaviour of artists, the value of art and creativity is peppered with ideological markers incepted in the Renaissance and before. Attendant to conflations of genius and madness, alterity and alienation is inevitably the problem of suicide.

Suicide

The Wittkowers note that although melancholy and a suicidal disposition are closely connected, few Renaissance and post-Renaissance artists "succumbed to the death wish." They conclude that the "excitement and rapture of creation ...may have compensated for the lack of pleasure which are dear to others." They discuss fourteen cases of artist suicides that occurred between c.1350 and 1800, five in Italy and nine in Northern Europe, tempering their discussion with the understanding that these are extremely small numbers for the tens of thousands of artists working in Europe during this time. The first names to appear in art historical literature were the artists: Giovan Battista Fiorentino (1494-1540), Francesco Bassano (1549-92) Francesco Borromini, and Pietro Testa (1607 [11?] -1650, the seducer of Artemsia Gentillischi; followed by the French artists Francis Le Moyne (1688-1737), Jean-Louis Sauce who first killed his lover before throwing himself out of a window at the age of 28. The documentary record also lists Eric Paulsen (1749-90) and the sculptor Johannes Wiedewelt (1731-1802), two Danish artists who committed suicide. The Wittkowers reveal that four of the fourteen suicides were committed at the end of the eighteenth century and the turn of the nineteenth at a time when suicide had lost some of its stigmas and had become, partly through the impact of the publication of Johann Wolfgang von Goethe's *The Sorrows of Young Werther* (1774),[47] "much more common among professionals and intellectuals than ever before."[48]

With the exception of a few celebrated examples (Caravaggio and Cellini), discussed in the literature, there is little evidence to suggest that murders committed by artists were as prevalent as suicides but as I noted previously, in film and literature there are dozens of examples of both, mad genius artists who kill themselves at the drop of a hat and artist killers, craftily elevating murder to a form of high art. Data collection undertaken in various countries around the world now link occupational groups to instances of suicide. In the US where 30.000 people take their own lives annually, statistics remain inconclusive and "assertions about which occupational group (police officers, dentists, artists) have the most suicides float around like urban myths." In 1997 a U.S. based study reviewing death certificates from

1980 to 1984 by all occupations and causes of death found "statistically significant elevated rates of suicide for white male physicians, black male guards (including supervisors, crossing guards, police, protective service occupations, but not correctional institution occupations), and white female painters, sculptors, craft-artists and artist printmakers." A more recent study examined records for half a million people over a period of nine years of who 545 committed suicide. After controlling for variables (age, sex, health, class) the researcher found that only labourers and the unemployed had significantly higher risks. This study affirmed, that the "top predictors for suicide are diagnosable mental disorder, co-morbid substance use [drugs and alcohol], loss of social support and availability and access to a firearm."[49]

7. Vincent van Gogh

Is an artist's suicide or anyone's for that matter, to be considered the *sine qua non* of failure? To whom is the suicide of Vincent Willem van Gogh (30 March 1853 – 29 July 1890) addressed? Like Derrida, I have returned late and had to leave you on the way. "Who was it, I don't remember now, who said, 'there are no ghosts in Van Gogh's pictures, no visions, no hallucinations.' It is the torrid truth?"

> "– that was Artaud protesting another way of suiciding Van Gogh (*Van Gogh, le suicidé de la societé*). This delegation of ghosts and hallucinations is, according to Artaud, a manoeuvre by society, delegating its psychiatric police.
>
> But 'to suicide' someone isn't that to make him come back as a ghost or to make him stay as a ghost, where he is, in short pretty well buried having only his 'nots' left. Not a revenant. Not a name."[50]

In the translator's note this last statement of Derrida's refers to the phrase *ne disposant plus que de ses pas. Pas de revenant. Pas de nom* meaning "having only his steps left at his disposal. Step of a ghost. Step of a name." Did van Gogh's suicide at the age of thirty-seven signal his personal sense of frustration, lack of fulfillment – failure – or was it his recognition of death as the penultimate moment to leap into the abyss/bliss to escape the purgatory of existence? Did he recognize his creative life as a failure when he decided to commit suicide or were the physiological symptoms of Ménière's disease (vertigo, loss of balance, nausea and vomiting), so debilitating that he felt he should end it all? Art historian Bogomila Welsh-Ovcharov writes: "Van Gogh's decision to commit suicide remains a complex conundrum and many attempts have been made – by artists as well as writers and psychiatrists – to unravel the causes of that final tragic act. We shall never know exactly why he decided to shoot himself that Sunday, July 27, in the wheat fields behind the Château of Auvers. Tellingly, in his last letter to his mother and Will he reported 'a mood of almost too much serenity '– a chilling note before the calamity."[51] If the evidence available in the letters to his brother Theo are used as a measure, Van Gogh's suicide was unexpected, and a momentary lapse of judgment, but even this is in dispute, especially given the time he spent in the mental institution under the care of Dr Gachet and also the other available evidence such as Emile Bernard's detailed account of the event, which he sent in a letter to Aurier:

> I imagine that you have already guessed that he killed himself
> .'. . On Sunday evening he went into the Auvers countryside,
> left his easel against a haystack and went behind the Château
> and shot himself with a revolver. From the violence of the
> impact (the bullet passed under the heart) he fell, but he got up
> and fell again three times and then returned to the inn where
> he lived (Ravoux, place de la Mairie) without saying anything
> to anyone about his injury. Finally, Monday evening he
> expired, smoking [the] pipe he had not wanted to put down,
> and explaining that his suicide was absolutely calculated and
> lucid. Characteristically enough, I was told that he frankly
> stated his desire to die –'Then it has to be done over again'–
> when Dr. Gachet told him that he still hoped to save him; but,
> alas, it was no longer possible.[52]

Then it has to be done over again? If we follow Hume, or
Schopenhauer who sagely offered the questions: "who has not
acquaintances, friends, and relations who have voluntarily departed
from this world? And should we all regard these as criminals? *Nego
ac pernego* (I say no, certainly not)."[53] Certainly not, but to what
extent was van Gogh as much a victim of ideology as his own
personal psychology? Could we now read his struggles as socially
and culturally instigated as much as response to his psychological
traumas? Is Vincent van Gogh's suicide another product of black bile
phantasma? Unlike Emile Durkheim, Arthur Schopenhauer takes a
very practical response to the problem of suicide. "As soon as the
terrors of life outweigh those of death," he offers in a matter-of- fact
way, "man puts an end to his life."

> If in horrible dreams anxiety reaches its highest
> degree, it causes us to wake up, whereby all those
> monstrous horrors of the night vanish. The same
> thing happens in the dream of life when the highest
> degree of anxiety forces us to break it off. [54]

Suicide, Schopenhauer suggests, may be the most autonomous free
act that any individual can commit. And yet how free are one's acts
if they are complicit with, or a product of ideology?
Phenomenologically, life - *being* - is always on the threshold; that is,
being with (*mitsein*) death. If Heidegger's *dasein* is ontically

construed as "a being for death" then perhaps van Gogh's death choice was governed by what Jean Luc Nancy refers to as "the phantasm of metaphysics," already, as he says, "proposed in Christian theology," in which the ego, the subject/ I, pronounces his/her own death (the Cartesian *ego sum mortuus*), and secures an afterlife — transfiguration (*nachleben*). Nancy writes: "I cannot say that it is dead, if the I disappears in effect in it's death, in the death that is precisely what is proper to it and most inalienable it's own, it is because the I is something other than a subject."[55] This is the crux of the phenomenological das/(s)ein, where subject hood meets the hermeneutic challenge(s) of life before an ego (I) can be (ir)rationally constituted. [56] And what if the hermeneutic challenge precipitates questions about the value of (a) life that has been marked by frustration lack – failure – manquéhood? Notwithstanding Artaud's prohibition as indicated by Derrida, Vincent van Gogh's death may also be an opportunity to recognize the phantasmatic character of ideology for *magisters ludi*, with suicide as the compensating mechanism to ameliorate failure and transform the end into a redemptive prelude to transfiguration and apotheosis. I would like to now (re-) consider the suicide of Guy Debord a contemporary 'artist ghost'.

The Case of Guy Debord

Guy Debord (1931 - 1994) filmmaker, author of *The Society of the Spectacle* and a founding member of the International Situationists committed suicide on 30 November 1994 at the age of 63. Debord's successes as an exemplary political theorist and avant-garde artist in the context of the International Situationists will be discussed in the final chapter. Here I would like to consider his cultural apotheosis through his manquéhood. I will argue the possibility of reading his last major film *in girim imus nocte et consumer igni (we turn in the night consumed by fire*, 1978) as a prelude to his final exemplary political/creative act which was his suicide.[57]

8. Guy Debord

Debord withdrew his six films from circulation in 1985. This protest action was taken as a result of the murder of his friend and patron Gerard Lebovici, the film producer and editor of *Editions Champ Libre*, the publishing house for both the I.S. and all of Debord's books. In their reportage of the event, the Parisian press attempted to link Lebovici's death to the associations he and Debord purportedly had with the French urban terrorist group Action Directe. Debord refuted these allegations in a long essay "Considerations sur l'assassination de Gerard Lebovici" published in 1983, but thereafter his taste for life seemed to become unhinged. Debord's many published statements revealing his antipathy toward the institution of cinema; "I have scarcely begun to make you understand that I don't intend to play the game" ("Je commence à peine a vous faire comprehendre que je ne veux pas jouer ce jeu la") *Critique of Separation* (1961) were carried beyond mere rhetoric.

The obituaries and personal testimonies attending Debord's death all spoke of his importance as a political theorist but also recognized his struggles to achieve his political and cultural aspirations. On the occasion of the publication of Anselm Jappe's biography *Guy Debord*, for example, T.J. Clark wrote in his Foreword for the book that we should be "driven and haunted" about the nature of "Debord's achievement," (i.e. 'success'); but he poses the question: "how we are to understand the obvious (but scandalous) fact that in Debord's case politics was largely writing" and how is it that this writing in its "inimitable polemical and expository style - the only political writing of our time, can survive its circumstances." Clark and Jappe speak of Debord's embattledness, isolation, paranoia, that led Debord in the 1970's and 80's to believe that "everything and everybody stood in his way." And although Clark did not dwell on the word "alienation", one of the key manifestations of capitalist life that the Situationists through their example attempted to dispel, this is also apparent between the lines of his Foreword.[58] Keith Sanborn is another commentator who wrote about Debord's struggle in compelling terms in his *Artforum* Review of Debord's final publication *Panegyric* (Verso 2005).

> The violence of passions raised by Debord, and the hatred of the empty writings that attacked him, has always stunned me. As for me, in all the controversies I witnessed, and in all those whose echo reached me, I can't think of an instance in which Debord wasn't totally right! I then tend to believe him in all those cases in which I personally don't have adequate information, before, of course, further verification has been made."

Sanborn discusses the contents of the first two volumes of Debord's publication that contain a wide variety of images, maps, drawings, paintings, collages, détourned images that he compares (rather extravagantly), to Benjamin's *Arcades Project* and Brecht's *War Primer*. He quotes Debord from this text: "People will at last be able to see what I looked like at various ages of my life, the kinds of faces that have always surrounded me, and what kind of places I have lived in." In another quote, Debord reiterates his desire to "strike a blow against the reigning deceptions of the time," which are "on the point of making us forget that the truth may also be found in images." Debord emphasizes the 'aesthetic' considerations that went into the manufacture of the book: "Of all the truths which go to make up this [second] volume of *Panegyric*, it will be acknowledged that the most profound resides in the very manner of assembling and presenting them together." Sanborn states that Volume Three of *Panegyric* that was in progress at the time of Debord's suicide was destroyed after his death at his instructions. In this volume Debord "was to have cleared up several details concerning his life and work that still remained obscure." Sanborn completed his review with the observation that Debord's suicide ended the physical suffering of what Debord himself diagnosed as "alcoholic polyneuritis."[59]

A contrasting view of Debord's suicide is offered by Pierre Guillaume who quotes from testimony provided in an article published in Le Figaro by Ricardo Paseyro. "Three days later, I learned that he (Debord) committed suicide. I didn't read anything of what the media reported, except an article cut from *Le Figaro* sent to me by a friend: the testimony of his friend Ricardo Paseyro, which looked true and well-disposed. It confirmed what I had been thinking" Guillaume quotes from this article:

> Arranged since long, his suicide doesn't hide any secret: Debord refused to sickness the right to ravish his independence. He wasn't a 'mysterious' man: he was a rare person, impossible to tame, constrain or manoeuvre. He wouldn't alienate his freedom to anything – neither to life, which he loved, nor to death, which he mastered.

"I never thought it could be a desperate suicide," Guillaume continues, "but a stoical suicide, since his health was getting ruined, seemed to me in the logic of the life he wanted to live." After this estimation of Debord's act, Guillaume offers a personal recollection of some of their meetings with members of the *Socialisme ou Barbarie* group. "I remembered our meetings at the Contrescarpe place. And the matchless and, maybe, typical way he had to leave the table, when the conversation" interest declined, or, rather, threatened to decline. He suddenly greeted everyone. He usually paid for all the drinks, and abruptly disappeared. And all the guests felt dismissed. Unlucky guests at life's banquet!" Guillaume concluded his testimony with an aphorism worthy of a Situationist tract.

> "Marxism knows neither 'immortals' nor corpses. With those that are called so by the common oratorical art, life converses."[60]

It is possible to interpret the script that Debord wrote for his last film *In girim imus nocte et consumer igni* as a final statement on the state of the world, both as he saw it and his place in it. At this stage in his life (at the age of 47), nearly two decades before his suicide, Debord was playing out his struggle with life, politics and art. He felt he had been the victim of general obloquy some twenty years before his suicide and it is possible to recognize in his ironic *dedoublement* the obsequies (funeral rites) for his life's work. *In Girim* begins with two familiar disavowals also trumpeted in 1952 in *Hurlements en faveur de Sade*, his first film: that he was "offering no concessions to the public in this film" and making no concessions to "the dominant ideas or ruling powers of his era."[61] This is followed by a litany of familiar complaints and criticisms about contemporary society, many of them previously published in *The Society of the Spectacle*, letters to other members of the SI and essays in the Situationist Journal. For example:

> This life and this cinema are equally paltry, which is why it hardly matters if one is substituted for the other.
> Our era has not yet managed to supersede the family, or money, or the division of labour; yet one could say that these people have already been almost totally deprived of their practical reality through sheer dispossession. Those who never had any substance have lost it for the shadow.

> *For a long time I have been perhaps the only person to offend it [the public] in this domain [cinema]* (my emphasis).

> The cinema I am talking about is a *deranged imitation of a deranged life*, a production skillfully designed *to communicate nothing*. It serves no purpose but to while away an hour of boredom with a reflect on of that same boredom"[62]

Compared to his earlier film scripts, essays and letters, the intrusion of the 'I' is more apparent in these statements. For example he acknowledges that his cinema has possibly been *the only film* to offend the public and describes the means by which this offence has been obtained.

> In the present film (*Im noctus*), for example I am simply stating a few truths over a background of images that are

> all trivial or false. This film disdains the image scraps of
> which it is composed. I do not wish to preserve any of the
> language of this outdated art, except perhaps the reverse
> shot of the only world it has observed and a tracking shot
> across the fleeting ideas of an era. *I pride myself on
> having made a film out of what ever rubbish was at hand;*
> and I find it amusing that people will complain about it
> who have allowed their entire lives to be dominated by
> every kind of rubbish. (emphasis added)

Debord's subsequent statements become even more pointed and
personal, if distanced through irony and his third person mode of
address. At one point he states, "It has to be recognized that there has
been neither success nor failure for Guy Debord and his extravagant
pretensions." This and other statements in the film are powerful
indicators, I believe, of his feelings of alienation at the time, which he
was simultaneously avowing and disavowing through his work. His
statements typically spiral through antinomies.

> *I have merited the universal hatred of the society of my
> time,* and I would have been annoyed to have any other
> merits in the eyes of such a society. But I noticed that it is
> the cinema that I have aroused the most extreme and
> continuous outrage. This distaste has been so intense that
> I have even been plagiarized much less in this domain
> than elsewhere, up until now at least. *My very existence as
> a filmmaker remains a generally refuted hypothesis.* I thus
> see myself placed outside all the laws of the genre. But as
> Swift remarked 'it is no small satisfaction to present a
> work that is beyond all criticism.'

His comment about plagiarism is revealing in that for many years essays
in the IS journal complained about the appropriation of Situationist
cinema by Jean-Luc Godard and other commercially successful French
filmmakers. Like the Surrealists before him, Debord reflects on writers
Swift and T.S. Elliot who were important models, and inserts a comment
about his first highly charged film *Hurlements en Faveur de Sade*, which
became a *success de scandal;* a film that consisted of nothing but voice
over a blank screen interspersed with black leader and long passages of
silence which he produced at the age of twenty-one.

> Some no doubt, would like to believe that subsequent experience led to a more mature development of my talents and intentions. Experience of what - of some improvement in what I had already rejected? Don't make me laugh. Why should anyone who strove to be so intolerable in the cinema when he was young turn out to be more acceptable once he's older? What has been so bad can never really improve. People may say, "As he has aged, he has changed"; but he has also remained the same."[63]

Debord understood that he was not about to "play the game" as early as 1952 and for the next four decades of his life he argued that all of the identities: 'artist' 'film maker' 'politician' or even 'revolutionary' were not only redundant but contrary to any revitalized political project. His manquéhood – intentional failure – was a necessary model for those following to consider new models of political praxis. Guy Debord's suicide may therefore be appreciated as the ultimate act of *détournement* and this *Magister Ludi* could be laughing from the grave.

---

[1] "Maxims and Interludes" # 137 in Nietzsche, Friedrich *Beyond Good and Evil: Prelude to a Philosophy of the Future* Translated by R.J Hollingdale with an introduction by Michael Tanner London, Penguin Books, 1973, 1990

[2] CBC News Report July 25th 2005 and The Globe and Mail Michael Kesterton Miscellany July 25th 2005

[3] Ronell, Avital. *Stupidity* Urbana and Chicago, University of Illinois Press 2003:44

[4] I have adopted the neologism *manquéhood* (cw sisterhood, manhood, childhood, statehood), to signify the condition or state of *manqué*.

[5] I am indebted to my EGS colleague Klaus Ottmann whose PhD thesis *The Genius Decision: The Extraordinary and the Postmodern Condition* introduced the challenging notion that the genius decision is "defined as an active-passive activity of the postmodern artist who is engaged in an activity of failure."

[6] Derrida, J. *The Truth in Painting* trans. Geoff Bennington and Ian McLeod Chicago, New York, Chicago University Press 1987: 42-3

[7] Ibid p45

[8] "The person endowed with talent thinks more rapidly and accurately than do the rest; on the other hand, the genius perceives a world different from them all, though only by looking more deeply into the world that lies before them also, since it presents itself in his mind more objectively, consequently more purely and distinctly." Schopenhauer, A. "On Genius" in *Schopenhauer: Philosophical Writings* (ed) Schirmacher, W. New York, Continuum, New German Library, 2002:83

---

[9] See Leyton, E. *Hunting Humans: The Rise of the Modern Multiple Murderer* London Blake Publishing 2001 Leyton argues that Hannibal ('the cannibal') Lecter, the aristocratic serial killer of fiction and film bears no resemblance to his real-life counterparts Bundy, Berkwowitz, Dahmer *et al*, who are mostly from the working classes. Leyton's contention is that serial killers are not diabolical geniuses or insane, but a product of their environment particularly influenced by American mass culture.

[10] Freud, S, *Leonardo da Vinci and a Memory of His Childhood*, New York: Norton, 1964

[11] Here the signal example is provided by Adolf Hitler who author J.P. Stern describes as "an artist manqué" see Stern, J.P. *Hitler: The Fuhrer and the People* Berkeley and Los Angeles: University of California Press. 1975 p.45 fn and Spotts, Frederic, *Hitler and the Power of Aesthetics* Overlook Press (2003)

[12] Adams, P *Art of the Third Reich* (1992), Barron, Stephanie *Degenerate Art; The Fate of the Avant-Garde in Nazi Germany* (1991) *Architecture of Doom*,

[13] Spotts, F. *Hitler and the Power of Aesthetics* Woodstock, NY Overlook Press 2003:124) and Hitler, A., *Mein Kampf* (1925)

[14] Ibid p.73

[15] Ibid p.43

[16] Ibid. p. 85

[17] Ibid.

[18] See Stern (1975), Spotts (2003) and Thewelweit, K. *Male Fantasies* Vols I&2 Translation Carter, E and Turner, C. Forward Rabinowich, A and Benjamin, J., Minneapolis, University of Minnesota Press 1989

[19] The three A's- Agonism, Antagonism and Activism are Renato Poggioli's definition of the avant-garde. See Poggioli, R. *The Theory of the Avant-Garde* Cambridge University Press 1968. See also Adams and Barron op cit 12

[20] See Holt, E. G. (ed) *The Triumph of Art for the Public: The Emerging Role of Exhibitions and Critics* Documents from the Period 1785 to 1848 Anchor Books 1979 and *The Art of All Nations 1850-73 The Emerging Role of Exhibitions and Critics* New York, Anchor Press Doubleday 1981

[21] .Pelles, G. "The Image of the Artist" Journal of the Warburg and Courtauld Institutes p119 and Pelles, G. *Art Artists and Society: Origins of a Modern Dilemma: Painting in France and England 1750-1850* New Jersey, Englewood Cliffs, Prentice Hall 1963

[22] Wittkower, R. & M. *Born Under Saturn, The Character and Conduct of Artists. A Documented History from Antiquity to the French Revolution* New York, Norton Random House 1963: 98

[23] Agamben, Giorgio, Ronald L. Martinez (Translation). *Stanzas: Word and Phantasm in Western Culture*. Theory and History of Literature, Vol. 69. Minneapolis, University of Minnesota Press. 1993:12

[24] The four humors corresponded with the four seasons spring, summer, autumn and winter and the elements earth, air, fire and water. Thus blood (air, spring, sanguine), phlegm (water, winter, phlegmatic), yellow bile (fire summer, choleric) black bile (earth, autumn, melancholic).

[25] : Wittkowers, p103

[26] Ibid

[27] Ibid

[28] "In so far as his or her tortuous intentions open a space for the epiphany of the unobtainable, the slothful testifies to the obscure wisdom according to which hope has

been given only for the hopeless, goals only for those who will always be unable to reach them. The nature of the "noonday demon" is just that, dialectical. As of mortal illness containing in itself the possibility of its own cure, it can be said of *acedia* that "the greatest disgrace is never to have had it." Agamben, *Stanzas* p 7.

[29] Agamben p76, 77.

[30] Bourdieu, P. *The Logic of Practice* Stanford, Stanford University Press 1990:133, original Paris, Les Editions de Miniut 1980.

[31] Wittkowers, p15

[32] Wittkower, R. "Individualism in Art and Artists: A Renaissance Problem" *Journal of the History of Ideas* Vol 22: 296, 1961

[33] ibid p. 92

[34] ibid

[35] Wittkower, R. & M. *Born Under Saturn, The Character and Conduct of Artists. A Documented History from Antiquity to the French Revolution* New York, Norton Random House 1963 Wittkower, 94 (from Ficino, M *Opera Omnia* Bale 229; quoted after Gombrich, E. 1945,59).

[36] ibid Du Bos *Reflexions critiques sur la poésie et sur la peinture* (1719) 1747 ii 19f., 54, 96, 366

[37] Lombroso *Man of Genius* quoted in Regenia Gagnier "Sexuality, the Public, and the Art World" in Gagnier R. (ed) *Critical Essays on Oscar Wilde* Toronto, Macmillan 1991

[38] Schopenhauer 2: 84

[39] Ibid p..96

[40] O'Brien, J. (ed and trans) *The Maxims of Marcel Proust* New York 1961 requoted in Wittkowers, p99

[41] Freud, S, *Leonardo da Vinci and a Memory of His Childhood*, New York: Norton, 1964 Freud, S, *Moses and Monotheism,* New York: Knopf, 1939, Kris, E. *Psychoanalytic Explorations into Art New York: International University Press,* 1952

[42] Autobiography of Lewis M. Terman Murchison, Carl. (Ed.) (1930). *History of Psychology in Autobiography* (Vol. 2, pp. 297-331). Clark University Press, Worcester, MA.1930   Clark   University   Press.   Republished   in psychclassics.yorku.ca/Terman/murchison accessed July 2005

[43] Binet worked with physician Theodore Simon on the problem of retardation in French school children. Their test consisted of a series of questions with graduated levels of difficulty to measure attention, memory and verbal skills. "Binet cautioned people that these scores should not be taken too literally because of the plasticity of intelligence   and   the   inherent   margin   of   error   in   the   test" psychcentral.com/psypsych/Stanford-Binet accessed July, 2005

[44] See Claude S. Fischer, Michael Hout, Martin Sanchez Jankowski, Samuel R. Lucas, Ann Swidler, and Kim Voss *Inequality by Design-Cracking the Bell Curve Myth* Princeton University Press, 1996

[45] Mensa boasts "100,000 Mensans in 100 countries throughout the world. There are active Mensa organizations in over 40 countries on every continent except Antarctica." www.mensa.org

[46] Trilling, L "Art and Neurosis in *Art and Psychoanalysis* 1957: 503 requoted in Wittkowers p.99

[47] Goethe, J W The *Sorrows of Young Werther* translation and introduction Michael Hulse London, Penguin Books 1989

[48]Wittkower, R.and M. 1963: 148

[49] Augustine Kposowa, PhD www.apa.org/monitor/jan01/*suicide*.html accessed July 2005

[50] Derrida, J. *The Truth in Painting* Bennington, G. and McLeod, I.,Trans. Chicago, University of Chicago Press, 1987:379-80

[51] Welsh-Ovcharov, B. *Van Gogh in Provence and Auvers* Hugh Levin Publishers 1999 pp273

[52] Ibid

[53]Schopenhauer, A. "On Suicide" in *Schopenhauer Philosophical Writings* Ed Schirmacher, W. New York, Continuum New German Library 2002 p 43

[54] Both essays translated are contained in *Arthur Schopenhauer Philosophical Writings* (Wolfgang Schirmacher ed.) NYC The German Library Continuum (1994, 2002)

[55] Nancy, J-L 1991:18

[56] Schopenhauer p. 47

[57] This title is a well-known Latin palindrome.

[58] Clark, TJ Foreword to Jappe, A. *Guy Debord* available at http://www.notbored.org/jappe-foreword..html accessed July 2005

[59] Keith Sanborn is a lecturer in the Visual Arts program at Princeton University. He has translated several of the films of Guy Debord, Rene Vienet, and Gil Wolman into English.

[60] Guillaume, P. *Debord* (1995) op sit 56

[61] I am indebted here to Kenn Knabb's English translations of the film scripts for Debord's six films from Debord, G. *Oeuvres Cinematographiques Completes 1952_1978* posted on the website for the Bureau of public secrets http://www.bopsecrets.org/SI/debord.films/ingium.htm The English version of the book was published in 2005.

[62] Ibid pp. 3-5

[63] Ibid p.8

Chapter 4

Murder as one of the Fine Arts.

Art has two constant, unending concerns: It always meditates on death and thus always creates life (Boris Pasternak, 1890-1960) [1]

Violent acts [such as murder] compel an aesthetic response in the beholder in the form of awe, admiration or bafflement. If an action evokes an aesthetic response then it is logical to assume that this action- even if it is murder- must has been the work of an artist.(Thomas De Quincey 1785 –1859) [2]

This chapter discusses the critical neo-Kantian philosophical position on the aesthetic sublime adopted by Thomas De Quincey in his famous satire "On Consideration of Murder as One of the Fine Arts"(1822), and Oscar Wilde's novel *The Picture of Dorian Gray* (1890), that represent murder as a fine art, arguing that these extraordinary texts, ironic 'riffs' respectively on Emmanuel Kant's *Critique of Judgment* and Johann Wolfgang von Goethe's *Faust*, became important models for subsequent art/crime conflations in film and literature. Employing the critical strategies of irony, parody and satire these famous texts assisted in encouraging the reproduction of phantasmatic constructions 'hardened' into an ideological form that were subsequently absorbed into the cultural dominant. In previous chapters I discussed ideology, class, hegemony, and the status of the other upon which political agency and/or its lack often rests. I suggested that rather than using class and ideology as structures within which to seek an understanding of class dynamics from the 'outside in' that it is more efficacious to seek this from the 'inside out' recognizing, after Bourdieu, that not only does "the field of ideological positions reproduce(s) in transfigured form the field of social positions" but that ideology is necessarily inscribed in specific cultural artifacts.[3] But before engaging in a discussion of these two texts it is appropriate at this point to consider the use of the keywords irony, parody and satire. The intention of this chapter is to affirm the point at which aesthetic positions become eclipsed by ideology and moreover, where humour is used as a vehicle for cultural criticism, this may be understood as a key component of the struggle to both resist and achieve hegemony.

Parody, Irony and Satire

Most definitions of irony, parody and satire relate to texts rather than images. This privileging of the text has lead to a problematical use of these categories with respect to visual parodies and satires in film, television and other media. Thus far it may have seemed that I have been somewhat indiscriminate in my use of these terms; that I have either blurred the distinctions between the three, or rendered them interchangeable. This is not my intention. But what does distinguish them? What are the differences between textual and visual irony, parody and satire and how do they intersect with ideology and class?

With its expressly critical and political dimensions, satire has remained a somewhat problematic genre for historians of literary and visual humour. In his study of satire Feinberg (1967), suggested, "dissimulation is the richest source of satire," a human response to hypocrisy and pretence, ample evidence he writes, of a "double standard in the structure of our society."[4] He attributes this further to a sociological mismatch between what we desire and the actuality to which we address our desires. The satirist, he argues, is stimulated to attack by his/her perception of a "violation of social norms."[5] He suggests that parody may serve the purposes of critique through dissimilation such as "emphasizing the affectations and excesses of style, and the superficiality and absurdity of content."[6]

Johnson's introduction to his early anthology of great works of satire from Aesop and Juvenal to Thurber and Thomas Wolfe provide some indication of why satire is such a problematic genre for literary historians and lay people alike. "Everybody recognises satire," he writes but "nobody knows what it is."[7] Accordingly, he settles for a wide range of satirical types ranging from high-spirited mockery to torment, colourfully castigating those who have argued that there must always be an element of humour in satire. "No description of satire can hold water unless it takes all the aspects of satire into account. Sometimes the satirist tumbles in giggling, thumbing his nose, wielding slapsticks and bladders, smacking people on their fannies, and administering electric shocks. Sometimes he bawls abuse or hisses denunciations, flays his victim and then pours oil or acid in the wounds. Sometimes austere as Dante stalking through the murk of hell, he grimly describes evil fallen into its proper torments, plunged in flame or locked in thick ribbed ice." [8]

Johnson distinguishes two types of satire, direct and indirect. The direct is a form of invective that he relates to melodrama, which he further characterises as "violent emotional satire."[9] His model – here the altering or magnifying of parts of a subject to startling proportions is similar to types of visual or performative humour such as caricatures and burlesque. Melodrama, he links to burlesque, but unlike melodrama, "burlesque knows what it is up to." "When burlesque inflates things to grotesqueness just for fun, it is one of the forms of humour: when it inflates them in order to deflate them, it is satire." [10] In this sense, Johnson likens literary satire to pictorial caricature. He also distinguishes between a satirical and a grotesque form of burlesque. Thus he is somewhat of a proto-postmodernist in advance of his time, focusing upon description and interpretation rather than definition and analysis, privileging one word common to all of those cognitive processes – *criticism* – to satisfy his desire for categorisation. It is the urge to criticise, he suggests, that stimulates the producer of satire (and parody) to attack. Criticism precipitates a "kind of unmasking" and in this sense may be compared to forms of disavowal, dissimulation and/or dissembling.[11] These forms of humour can also be read concurrently as signs of resistance and in/subordination to a controlling figure or powerful institution.

Responding to studies from the 1960s by Macdonald (1960), Blackmur (1964), Feinberg (1967), and Paulson (1967), more contemporary discussions articulating the similarities and differences between irony, parody and satire, have continued to argue their cases by employing various theoretical models derived from literary criticism. The appropriateness of reading the semiotic interrelationships between the genres will, I hope, encourage an understanding of the polyvalent conditions for both analyzing and interpreting visual humour, thus providing further entry into the debates concerning the political economy of humour and the symbolic representation of class conflict. Lehmann (1963), offered a useful open definition of parody, but again confined it to literature:

> I understand here under parody only such literary products that formally imitate in toto or in part a known text, or secondary appearances, manners and customs, events and persons. This imitation is seemingly accurate, but in fact distorted, with conscious and recognisable humour.[12]

By way of contrast, Joseph Dane (1988) argues that like beauty, parody is in the mind of the beholder. The reader, he writes, "has the power to read any text as a parody."[13] He stresses also "there should be constraints on such power" to ensure that authors, critics and other literary specialists, have more control over their work and it's meaning. Of course this is comforting for postmodern readers, who assume that they have license to negotiate and articulate meaning irrespective of the author's intention. It should be acknowledged however that, as many differences exist between irony, parody, satire, as there are between beauty, ugliness and the grotesque. I will acknowledge here also, that these concepts are too contingent upon a multiplicity of situations to assume either conditionality or commonality as a virtue. Parody, Dane argues, has been "conflated with the plastic arts, its parasitical nature and its history too strongly constituted with its sister genres, the grotesque, caricature and pastiche." [14]

An examination of the literature however, confirms that the discussion of parody, if not satire, has been focused very much upon the literary and not the visual or performing arts. Although many writers have taken great pains to show the differences between the two genres, it is often the similarities that are privileged when specific examples are discussed. As Linda Hutcheon (1985) suggests, many theorists have explicitly and implicitly conflated parody with satire and yet, she writes: "calling parody satire seems a little too simple as an instant way to give parody a social function."[15] Some writers have bypassed the identity problem altogether and used the terms interchangeably. Hutcheon concludes that the major reason for the confusion of satire and parody is they are often used together. This is particularly true of caricatures and, as I argue throughout this book, films that take the institution art as their subject of critical negotiation. Hutcheon also questions those who attempt to differentiate between the two on the basis of binary oppositions, arguing instead that parody and satire may operate both positively and negatively – simultaneously. The French have the term *une belle laid* for the virtually untranslatable conflation in English of the beautiful/ugly, so too we must admit the possibility of androglossic concepts such as parodic/satire and satirical/parody without denying that the two regularly assume separate identities when the context or the occasion demands.

From Socrates to Schlegel, Mann, Richards, Frye, and Paul De Man, the literary critics and theorists of irony have each, in their various ways, raised the impossibility of defining irony, since the practice of ironising – disassembling – from its generic Greek root *eironeia*, meaning simulated ignorance (*eiron, dissembler*), invariably engages the notion of saying one thing, and meaning another. Many theorists consider irony to be the vehicle within which parody, satire and their various interrelated forms are able to function. Defining irony however, presents many problems. Muecke (1969) suggests that the art of irony is the art of saying something without really saying it. It is an art that gets its effects from below the surface, and this gives it a quality that resembles the depth and resonance of great art triumphantly saying much more than it seems to be saying.[16]

Irony theorists such as Muecke (1969, 1970), Enright, (1986), Dane (1991), and Hutcheon (1994), acknowledge the heteroglossic character of irony and warn of the limitations of reductive and formalist definitions. Dane for example, distinguishes between rhetorical irony, romantic irony and critical irony, arguing "the history of irony and the novel involves the disparity between the language of the novel and that of the critic."[17] Linda Hutcheon provides a useful definition of parody that encompasses both the literary and visual 'text.' She argues that parody is a form of imitation, "but imitation characterized by ironic inversion, not always at the expense of the parodied text."[18] She suggests that we must examine parody, satire and irony, in both their literary and visual forms, specifically as processes of reading and interpretation. We must negotiate "the enunciation of the contextualised production and reception of texts, if we are to understand what constitutes [them]."[19] Accordingly, she developed an overlapping Venn diagram consisting of three circles: Satiric Ethos, Ironic Ethos and Parodic Ethos, in order to better explain the interrelationships between each form. Hutcheon argued that while each ethos can harbour or invoke criticism, the satiric ethos has a slightly stronger proprietary interest in social critique and is therefore (potentially), more politically efficacious. Irony, she insists, is inscribed in most forms of parody and satire thus serving the interests of both humour and criticism.

Other humour researchers have used semiotic theory to reveal the coded relationships between the forms and functions of various humour genres. Ziva Ben-Porat's study of MAD T.V. satires, for example, examines the close semiotic relationship between parody and satire without making them synonymous. In her essay parody becomes the coded vehicle within which satirical intentions are mediated. She describes parody as an alleged representation, usually comic, of a literary text or other artistic object i.e. a representation of a "modeled reality," that is itself already a particular representation of an original reality. The parodic representations expose the model's conventions and lay bare its devices through the coexistence of the two codes in the same message. She offers a compatible description of satire as:

> A critical representation, always comic and often caricatural, of 'non-modeled reality,' i.e. of the real objects (their reality may be mythical or hypothetical) that the receiver reconstructs as the referents of the message. The satirized original 'reality' may include mores, attitudes, types, social structures, prejudices and the like.[20]

Ben-Porat's reductive and binary construction of a "modeled and unmodeled reality" presents some problems with respect to the constitution of the 'real' especially for any Lacanian, but her privileging of the reader and the utility of the genres, challenges many earlier models and legitimises the non-conventionality of her approach. A few other theorists have tended to differentiate between ironies; parody and satire on the basis of instrumentality or utility, demonstrating, in so doing, that the social and political use value for humour may be one defining attribute, even when the forms are coded together. For the purposes of this study I have taken satire to be more strategic than parody in its relation to its `target' and more predisposed towards the negative. Its intention(s) are often to subvert the power and authority of its object, without necessarily introducing, implicitly or explicitly, a replacement. For the purposes in this book, a comparison between examples of cinematic humour, reveal a strong disposition towards negative and pejorative criticism in satire, while irony and parody are more affirming, seeking often to induce in the spectator/reader an ironic and complicit distancing, without this becoming overtly rejective. For Hutcheon "irony's double voicing both allows the distance and makes inevitable the implication. It therefore allows a questioning from within."[21] If there are close formal relationships between irony, parody, satire and related genre ascriptions such as travesty, grotesque and burlesque, we may often distinguish the form(s) through their effect(s), in the same manner that we could judge the performance of a stand-up comic in the social arena. When the three forms work together, as Bahktin and others have suggested, the burden of interpretability is ultimately the readers. Like all readers' interpretations however, these may be reinterpreted when subjected to the machinations of various new contexts and discursive communities.[22] The distinguishing attributes of irony, parody and satire are often contested on the grounds of the intentionality of the author versus those of the viewer/reader. An intended parody may be read as a satire and vice versa, one as complementary, and the other perhaps as derisive or antagonistic. The spectator or reader's interpretative efforts may not after all, coincide with the producers, and the commonsensical position is that this is what happens all the time in social transactions – the phrase "I don't get it!" says as much.

It is possible to understand visual and textual humour transactions in social terms, as the articulation of ideologically accented signs whose meaning is dependent upon the complex interaction of an interpretive or discursive community. As Voloshinov has argued:

> Every sign, as we know, is a construct between socially
> organised persons in the process of their interaction.

> Therefore, *the forms of the signs are conditioned above all by the social organization of the participants involved* and also by the immediate conditions of their interaction. *When these forms change so does the sign.* And it should be the tasks of the study of ideologies to trace the social life of this sign. [23] (Emphasis in the original)

This theoretical model allows us to infer that every ideological sign and ensemble of signs – for instance a work of art, a film, television episode or a graphic image such as a cartoon – is shaped by social interaction, that come about through "the process of social intercourse" and is therefore interpreted by the "social purview of the given time period and a given social group."[24] In several chapters, I attempt to demonstrate this process occurring through my reading of films that employ irony, parody and satire, demonstrating how it is possible to assign a political dimension to this communication.

Thomas De Quincey's Murderous Aesthetics

In the opening preface of Thomas De Quincey's famous disquisition on murder as one of the fine arts he draws the reader's attention to several fictional societies: "The Society for the Promotion of Vice," the "Hell Fire Club" and in Brighton, "A Society for the Suppression of Virtue" (itself suppressed), the "Society for the Encouragement of Murder," and "The Society of Connoisseurs of Murder," whose members, he writes, "profess to be curious in homicides... in short murder fanciers." For this group of homicide 'dilettante' with each "fresh atrocity brought to their attention they meet to discuss and criticize as they would a picture, stage play or any other work of art." De Quincey offers his membership in the Murder Connoisseurs as an authoritative reason why he was invited to present the "William's 'Lecture on Murder' considered as one of the Fine Arts," named for a master murderer whose sublime homicidal deeds – the callous murder of two households – are described in great detail in "The Postscript." "John Williams, in one hour, smote two houses with emptiness, exterminated all but two entire households, and asserted his own supremacy above all the children of Cain."[25]

9. Thomas De Quincey

Having established his double voiced ironic/satiric *modus operandi*, in the sense described above, De Quincey provides an historical overview of murder as a fine art, providing examples from the birth of humanity (as represented in the Bible), to his own era. He begins his 'lecture' with the observation that it may have been easier to deliver it three or four centuries ago "when few great models (of murder), had been exhibited," asserting that there are more masterpieces in the (his) contemporary period and this therefore, represents and anticipates a different set of aesthetico-critical standards to be applied.[26] De Quincey introduces his notion of the murderous sublime in the exemplary figure of fine art killer, Mr. Williams. "Like Milton in poetry, (sic) Michael Angelo in painting, Mr. Williams has carried his art to a point of colossal sublimity," and furthermore, as Mr. Wordsworth observes, he (Williams), has in a manner "created the taste by which he is to be enjoyed." The judging of such work, he insists, demands an altogether other critical faculty than that observed by judges of law. It must be judged "aesthetically, as the Germans call it – that is in relation to good taste."[27]

The first example of the aesthetic sublime employed by De Quincey in his essay concerns not a murder as such, or even a waterfall, or pyramid, but a fire, which Kant's *Critique* relegates to a comparison with a babbling brook; not sufficient to engage a workable intuitive model of the sublime in nature or culture. As Kant wrote: "It is just as when we watch the changing shapes of fire or of a rippling brook; neither of which are things of beauty, but they convey a charm to the imagination, because they sustain its free play."[28] Throughout the murder essays De Quincey employs irony for his critical subversion (dissimulation) of Kant's *Critique of Judgement*. He recognizes that from his point of view, the philosopher is short on examples for a true appreciation of the aesthetic sublime and too rigid in his applications of judgement and taste, albeit, with a sublime (universal) 'out clause' called "common sense," to whit: "The condition of the necessity advanced by a judgement of taste is the idea of common sense."[29] De Quincey applies his subversive examples of Kantian aesthetics through three essays: "On Consideration of Murder as one of the Fine Arts," "The "Supplementary Paper on Murder," and "The Postscript," each of which reinforces his basic thesis; that crime, specifically homicide, is as worthy of being experienced within the terms of the aesthetic sublime, as any feature of nature or culture, including the solar system (the Milky Way), waterfalls, pyramids, Hellenic statues or beautiful flowers, promulgated by Kant. Essentially, De Quincey appropriates Kant's models: The Dynamically Sublime in Nature; "Nature, considered in an aesthetic judgment as might that has no dominion over us, is dynamically sublime," and the Mathematically Sublime, "Sublime is the name given to what is absolutely great. But to be great and to be a magnitude are entirely different concepts (*magnitudo* and *quantitas*)." De Quincey turns these propositions inside out by applying alternative historical and empirical examples that he assumes Kant would have had grave difficulty judging as worthy of "disinterested aesthetic contemplation." He offers as his example two contrasting murders – those of "mere necessity (for which) Williams was obliged to hurry," and "a murder of pure voluptuousness, *entirely disinterested*, where no hostile witness was to be removed, no extra booty to be gained, and no revenge to be gratified, it is clear that to hurry would be altogether to ruin. If this child, therefore is to be saved, it will be on *pure aesthetical considerations*"[30] (emphasis added) .In his first essay, De Quincey relates that he was having tea (with Samuel Taylor Coleridge), when their attention was drawn to a fire in a pianoforte makers in Oxford Street...that he states excited the aesthetic impulse in him but nevertheless was damned unanimously by Mr. Coleridge and his colleagues. In short order De Quincey indicts his group as neo-Platonists who could not see the aesthetic appeal in a conflagration and therefore felt compelled to condemn those who submitted to its enjoyment. He then goes on to illustrate how imperfections are able to be subjected to aesthetical judgement as much as perfections, which is a similar logic to the Renaissance subversion of the Platonic ideal from *bella perfetta* to *bella deformita* that gave birth to caricature - the loaded portrait (*portrait chargé*) in the Caracci and French academies. The thief and the ulcer provide two more examples for De Quincey to submit to the standards of Kantian and Neo-Platonic aesthetic theory. Quoting Aristotle's "Fifth book of Metaphysics" in which he described a "perfect thief," and one Mr. Howship, a fictional surgeon and author of the text *Indigestion* who was enamored with "a beautiful ulcer," he assigns the "truth (is) that, however objectionable *per se*, yet, relative to others of their class, both a thief and an ulcer may have infinite degrees of merit. They are both imperfections it is true: but to be imperfect being their essence, the very greatness of their imperfection becomes their perfection," and later in this section he writes, "even imperfection itself may have its ideal or perfect state."[31] With this counter Platonic point established, De Quincey then applies it carefully to various types of murders throughout history; from Cain, "the inventor of murder and therefore father of the art," to Mr. Thurtell, a contemporary, "who exhibited a rare talent but not genius."[32] He also approaches the celebrated murders in Shakespeare's plays of Duncan, Banquo and Gloucester (Act 3 Henry VI) but dismisses them as far too theatrical to be elevated to the sublime in the Kantian sense.[33]

De Quincey moves on quickly to the aesthetic potential of assassinations and provides several examples of statesmen and members of royalty who were assassinated. "In these assassinations of princes and statesmen, there is nothing to excite our wonder; important changes often depend on their deaths; and from the eminence on which they stand, they are particularly exposed to the aim of every artist who happens to be possessed by the craving of scenical effect..."[34] In this passage it almost seems as if De Quincey is comparing these forms of assassinations to varieties of genre painting

- still life or landscape. He argues that exemplary murders (meaning prototypical or patterned) are not worthy of being valorized as masterpieces because although they may exhibit obvious talent, they obviously lack the necessary prerequisites for genius. But he does single out several assassinations, those of philosophers themselves that are worthy for aesthetic delectation. "But there is another class of assassinations," he writes, "from an early period of the seventeenth century that really does surprise me; I mean the assassinations of philosophers." He offers the humorous proposition that every philosopher of last two centuries has been murdered, or very near it . . . all but murdered. De Quincey begins with Locke and (sic) Des Cartes who he recalls was "all but murdered by some thugs when he was traveling by sea from Emden (sic) to West Friesland)," but "no sooner had he got out to sea, than he made a pleasing discovery, viz., that he had shut himself up in a den of murderers his crew *des scelerats*...- not amateurs, gentlemen, as we are, but professional men - the height of whose ambition at that moment was to cut his individual throat."[35] De Quincey then quickly moves through the philosophical pantheon. "The next great philosopher of Europe, counter to popular opinion was murdered. This was (sic) "Spinosa died 21st February 1677, at age of 44 years." As for the case of Hobbes, De Quincey opines, "Why or on what principle, I could never understand, was [he] not murdered." [36] The next philosopher to be dispatched by De Quincey is Malebranche who "it will give you pleasure to hear was murdered and the man who murdered him is well known. It was Bishop Berkeley."[37]

When he arrives at Leibniz and Kant, De Quincey takes the proverbial 'high road,' suggesting that although Leibniz was not murdered, he died "partly for fear that he should not be murdered and partly of vexation that he was not." Kant, on the other hand, "who manifested no ambition in that way," – a function de Quincey infers humorously of 'aesthetic disinterest' – "had a narrower escape from a murderer that any man we read of except Des Cartes. So absurdly does fortune throw her favours."[38] He discusses the circumstance by which Kant escaped murder, noting that he used to take a constitutional walk everyday along a high road around Königsberg and but for the murderer's peevish morality," and thinking that an "old man must be laden with sins that he should concentrate on killing a younger subject and at a critical moment found a child of five years old upon which to perpetrate the deed." Black suggests that "by treating murder as an art form De Quincey demonstrated the aesthetic subversion of the beautiful by the sublime and more generally the philosophical subversion of ethics by aesthetics." He argues also that this, what he terms, 'lampooning' of Kant's moral philosophy may also have anticipated Nietzsche's critique of morality later in the century.[39] De Quincey's essay provides a quasi-philosophical rationale for homicide, suggesting in a parodic/ironic form that murder may evoke a feeling of sublimity so long as it is [a] disinterested (anaesthetic), malevolent act. Murder loses its claim on the aesthetic judgement if the assailant acts out of petty self-interest, as in the case of robbery, or if the victim turns out to be a thief or a killer himself instead of a helpless innocent.[40] "I could mention some people (I name no names) who have been murdered by people in a dark lane; and so far all seemed correct enough; but on looking further into the matter, the public have become aware that the murdered party was himself, at the moment planning to rob his murderer, at the least and possibly to murder him if he had been strong enough. Whenever this is the case, or may be thought to be the case, farewell to all genuine effects of the art"[41] De Quincey's *Postscript* and *Avenger* essays present the killer as an artist in his own right and murder as an aesthetic act worthy of contemplation and veneration as much as any painting or piece of sculpture. As Denis Porter writes: "De Quincey legitimates the idea that discriminating pleasure may be obtained not from the sight of inflicted pain – he is no de Sade – but from the spectacle of the artist at work in a medium that includes the human body. The shock of the murder is no longer in the act [itself] but in its aesthetic treatment."

> Kant who carried his demands of unconditional veracity to so extravagant a length as to affirm, that, if a man were to see an innocent person escape from a murder, it would be his duty, on being questioned by the murderer, to tell the truth, and to point out the retreat of the innocent person, under any certainty of causing murder. Lest this doctrine should be supposed to have escaped him in any heat of dispute, on being taxed with it by a celebrated French writer, he solemnly re-affirmed it, with his reasons.[42]

Oscar Wilde's *Picture of Dorian Gray*[43]

Since it first appeared in 1890, serialized in *Lippincott's Monthly Magazine*, Oscar Wilde's single novel *The Picture of Dorian Gray* has been the subject of much discussion, a few scholars teasing out the repressed homo-eroticism, others exploring the story as a quintessential Victorian morality tale, and still others reading it as a parody of Goethe's *Faust: A Tragedy* (1808-32).[44] As Black suggests, *The Picture of Dorian Gray* is a good example of a transitional work that bridges the traditions of the romantic criminal artist and the modernist artist as criminal.[45] The figures of Lord Henry Wotten (the alter ego of Wilde as the Paterian aesthetician), and Basil Hallward the academic artist are also variants of Pygmalion, the artist from Greek mythology who falls in love with his *objet de manqué* (object of desire) and through the beneficence of Aphrodite, his sculpted likeness of her named Galatea comes to life. Wilde's novel also presents a prototypical example of the spectral *tableau vivant* – the portrait that comes to life – that is such a powerful phantasmatic trope in subsequent literature, visual art and film, particularly in the work of Alfred Hitchcock and Peter Greenaway, whose work I will discuss in following chapters.

Wilde's preface to the novel contains many key motifs in aphoristic form that appear both in *Dorian* and his other works. A few of these aphorisms also enjoy the reputation of being among the most often quoted Wildean *bon mots* in speeches, reviews, critical essays and art school studio critiques. The first of these: "The artist is the creator of beautiful things. To reveal art and conceal the artist is arts aim," confirms the origins of his aestheticism not only in Pater's *l'art pour l'art* but also the Renaissance dictum, 'the painter paints himself' which reappeared during the Romantic period and was subsequently absorbed into Victorian (Pre-Raphaelite) and symbolist aesthetic theory.

Wilde plays with this notion by subverting it in his aphorism and then reproducing it in an early exchange between Harry (Lord Henry Wotton) and Basil Hallward, the artist.

> 'Harry,' said Basil Hallward, looking him straight in the
> face, 'every portrait that is painted with feeling is a
> portrait of the artist, not of the sitter. The sitter is merely
> the accident, the occasion. It is not he who is revealed by
> the painter; it is rather the painter who, on the coloured
> canvas, reveals himself. The reason I will not exhibit this
> picture is that I am afraid that I have shown with it the
> secret of my own soul.'[46]

In the first few pages, Wilde also introduces the important theme of fatality in life informing Lord Henry that "there is a fatality about all physical and intellectual distinction," that death is attracted to difference (rank and wealth - class), intellect and identity - "we shall all suffer for what the Gods have given us."[47] This statement is also linked to the appearance reality dialectic and the visible/invisible, the spectral forces that haunt the aesthetic discussions between Basil and Henry who is the dandy spectator, arguably a stand in for Wilde himself as the knowledgeable 'Professor of Aesthetics.' "It is only shallow people who do not judge by appearances. The true mystery of the world is the visible, not the invisible."[48] The novel negotiates the torturous paths of art, desire and death through an exploration of youthful vanity and inexperience. James Winchell describes this as "Henry's specular 'contagious' doctrine of surface aestheticism (which) works fantastically to suspend the visible results of crime and suffering on the body of his disciple Dorian, only to find them revealed in the play of images on the profoundly superficial surface of an invisible painting."[49] The opening chapters present opinions through the mouthpiece of Sir Henry 'the aesthetician' about the alterity of artists in exchanges such as the following, tempered as always with a typical Wildean *bon mot* that collapses antinomies into a humorous apothegm.

> What odd chaps you painters are! You do anything in
> the world to gain a reputation. As soon as you have one,
> you seem to want to throw it away. It is silly of you,
> for there is only one thing in the world worse than
> being talked about, and that is not being talked about.[50]

Hallward affirms his own alterity by saying, "You know we poor artists have to show ourselves in society from time to time, just to remind the public that we are not savages." This first chapter establishes Hallward's infatuation with Dorian who becomes first his, then Lord Henry's *objet de manqué*. He describes their first meeting and the double question of morality/mortality becomes centre stage in his transgressive desiring of this beautiful man. "I turned halfway round, and saw Dorian Gray for the first time. When our eyes met, I felt that I was growing pale. A curious instinct of terror came over me. I knew that I had come face to face with some one whose mere personality was so fascinating that, if I allowed it to do so, it would absorb my whole nature, my whole soul, my very art itself."[51]

This disquisition on a quasi-religious holy trinity - soul/nature/art - is followed by an observation made by the narcissistic Dorian about the demerits of growing old and the problem of mortality. "Lord Henry is perfectly right," says Dorian, "youth is the only thing worth having. When I find that I am growing old, I will kill myself." "How sad it is!" murmured Dorian Gray, with his eyes fixed upon his own portrait.

> "I shall grow old, and horrid, and dreadful. But this picture will remain always young. It will never be older than this particular day of June ... If it was only the other way!
>
> If it was I who were to be always young, and the picture that were to grow old! For this –for this –I would give everything!
>
> Yes, there is nothing in the whole world I would not give!"[52]

And with this extravagant wish, Dorian's Faustian bargain with his Mephistopheles – in the guise of Lord Henry Wotten and Paterian aesthetic theory – is established. Hallward's portrait of Dorian becomes the instrument through which Dorian's immortality is to be obtained but in the bargain he must sacrifice his morality, become a dissolute and dishonorable man, a cheat and a murderer. He destroys Sybil Vane his fiancée, kills his friend Basil Hallward and finally commits suicide, becoming in the process another exemplary victim of phantasmatic ideology. At one point in the narrative Basil wants to destroy his painting of Dorian realizing that it is beginning to control his life but Dorian resists this strenuously, which finally sets the seal for his fate.

> With a stifled sob he leaped from the couch, and,
> rushing over to Hallward, tore the knife out of his hand,
> and flung it to the end of the studio. 'Don't, Basil,
> don't!' he cried. 'It would be murder!'[53]

Lord Henry establishes the philosophical coordinates around the vitality of aesthetic representation through the dialogues between the three principle figures as well as through his interior monologues. When he steps out in the direction of Berkeley Square on his way to his Aunt Agatha's for high tea, Henry reflects upon Dorian's parentage that he recounts, as was crudely told to him:

> A beautiful woman risking everything for a mad
> passion. A few wild weeks of happiness cut short by a
> hideous, treacherous crime. Months of voiceless agony,
> and then a child born in pain. The mother snatched
> away by death, the boy left to solitude and the tyranny
> of an old and loveless man.[54]

This narrative enables Henry to countenance the tragic sublime: "Behind every exquisite thing that existed, there was something tragic," and the Mephistophelean control he was beginning to exercise over Dorian through his teachings and the poisonous French book that he gave to him.[55]

"He could be made a titan or a toy. What a pity it was that such beauty was destined to fade." Lord Henry then turns his mind to Basil, reflecting upon how interesting he was - "from a psychological point of view and this new manner of art, the fresh mode of looking at life" which he describes in neo-Platonic terms as an interior idealist vision: "The new manner of art, the fresh mode of looking at life, suggested so strangely by the mere visible presence of one who was unconscious of it all; the silent spirit that dwelt in dim woodland, and walked unseen in open field, suddenly showing herself, Dryad-like and not afraid, because in his soul who sought for her there had been awakened that wonderful vision to which alone are wonderful things revealed: the mere shapes and patterns of things becoming as it were refined, and gaining a symbolical value, as though they were themselves patterns of some other and more perfect form whose shadow they made real: how strange it all was! He remembered something like it in history. Was it not Plato, the artist in thought who had at first analysed it?[56] This reference to shadows and Plato, expressly presented as "the artist in thought," in Lord Henry's monologue concerns the "Allegory of the Cave" (Book VII of *The Republic*) in which Socrates introduces Glaucon to the metaphysical mysteries of representation. The dialogue between the master and student about the prisoners and the shadows in the *Allegory* presents several of Plato's major philosophical propositions including his belief that the world revealed by our senses is not the real world but only a poor (mimetic) copy of it, and that the real world can only be apprehended intellectually in metaphysical terms as a transcendental idea. "To them, I said, the truth would be literally nothing but the shadows of the images."[57]

The notion of the truth embedded in the artificial representation is articulated in many sections of the novel, even in Lord Henry's apothegm about people knowing the price of everything and the value of nothing, a phrase that now circulates in daily conversation. "So sorry I am late, Dorian," he says, "I went to look after a piece of old brocade in Wardour Street, and had to bargain for hours for it. Nowadays people know the price of everything, and the value of nothing." Questions about value, taste and distinction also appear in conversations between Lord Henry and Dorian, as for example in Lord Henry's opinions about artists in general and Basil Hallward in particular: "The only artists I have ever known who are personally delightful are bad artists. Good artists give everything to their art, and consequently are perfectly uninteresting in themselves." "A great poet, a really great poet," he continues "is the most unpoetical of all creatures. But inferior poets are absolutely fascinating. The worse their rhymes are, the more picturesque they look. The mere fact of having published a book of second-rate sonnets makes a man quite irresistible. He lives the poetry that he cannot write. The others write the poetry that they are unable to realize."[58]

Lord Henry and Hallward's opinion of the importance of artistic and poetic manquéhood are similar to Nietzsche's distinction between great men and mediocre men in the quotation with which I began the previous chapter: "Behind a remarkable scholar one not infrequently finds a mediocre man, and behind a mediocre artist, often a very remarkable man." Like Nietzsche, Oscar Wilde's apothegms function contrarily; he poses one judgment only to (sur) render (to) its opposite in the next phrase, which often lends his statements philosophical heft.

After Dorian takes possession of his portrait the pattern of dissolution begins to become established and Chapter VI of the book compromises his love for his fiancée Sybil Vane by her revelations about the artificiality of the theatre. She informs Dorian that acting is no longer a reality to her because it is the world of mere reflection and shadows (smoke and mirrors), which is another Wildean play on neo-platonic specular veracity in Paterian aesthetics. After her disastrous performance Sybil says to Dorian: "All art is but a reflection. You have made me understand what love really is. My love! My love! I am sick of shadows. You are more to me than all art can ever be." Dorian replies callously to Sybil at this demonstrative lack of commitment to the theatre. "You have killed my love. You used to stir my imagination. Now you don't even stir my curiosity. You simply produce no effect. I loved you because you were wonderful, because you had genius and intellect, because you realized the dreams of great poets and gave shape and substance to the shadows of art. You have thrown it all away. You are shallow and stupid. My God! How mad I was to love you! [59]

With his pact with Mephistopheles cemented and intact, Dorian proceeds to focus narcissistically upon his predicament and like Pygmalion's sculpture of Galatea, Basil's portrait of Dorian begins to become alive, a phantasmatic theme that will haunt hundreds of subsequent cultural productions throughout the next century.

> As he was passing through the library towards the door of his bedroom, his eye fell upon the portrait Basil Hallward had painted of him. He started back in surprise, and then went over to it and examined it. In the dim arrested light that struggled through the cream coloured silk blinds, the face seemed to him to be a little changed. The expression looked different. One would have said that there was a touch of cruelty in the mouth. It was certainly curious.[60]

Dorian reflects on the uncanny nature of his predicament and his (castration) anxieties increase as he gazes at the portrait and recalls his narcissistic desire to remain forever young. He had uttered a mad wish that he himself might remain young:

> And the portrait grow old; that his own beauty might be untarnished, and the face on the canvas bear the burden of his passions and his sins; that the painted image might be seared with the lines of suffering and thought, and that he might keep all the delicate bloom and loveliness of his then just conscious boyhood. Surely his prayer had not been answered? Such things were impossible. It seemed monstrous even to think of them. And, yet, there was the picture before him, with the touch of cruelty in the mouth.[61]

He painfully recognises that his own soul is looking out at him from the canvas and calling him to judgment, becoming older hour by hour; day-by-day as he remains young yet becomes increasingly immoral. "A look of pain came across him, and he flung the rich pall over the picture. No, that was impossible. The thing upon the canvas was growing old, hour-by-hour, and week-by-week. Even if it escaped the hideousness of sin, the hideousness of age was in store for it." For Dorian, the sharpness of the contrast heightens his fetishistic pleasure. "He grew more and more enamoured of his own beauty, more and more interested in the corruption of his own soul."[62]   Later, however he recognises the image as "some foul parody, some infamous, ignoble satire," and his feelings of rage towards Basil Hallward the artist lead him to exact his revenge, which is described in horrible detail: "He rushed at him, and dug the knife into the great vein that is behind the ear, crushing the man's head down on the table, and stabbing again and again."[63]The novel ends with Dorian becoming more and more psychotic and when he revisits the scene of his crime he does what he restrained Basil from doing earlier, stabbing the painting itself.

"As it had killed the painter, so it would kill the painter's work, and all that that meant. It would kill the past, and when that was dead he would be free. He seized it, and stabbed the canvas with it, ripping the thing right up from top to bottom."[64] The novel ends tragically with Dorian killing himself and the painting returning to its original inanimate form showing him as he had been as a beautiful youth and presumably morally intact. When they entered, they found hanging upon the wall a splendid portrait of their master as they had last seen him "In all the wonder of his exquisite youth and beauty." But in abject contrast to this.

> Lying on the floor was a dead man, in evening dress, with a knife in his heart. He was withered, wrinkled, and loathsome of visage. It was not till they had examined the rings that they recognized who it was.[65]

Since the 1890's the aesthetic and narrative motifs in Oscar Wilde's novel have had a remarkable vitality, appearing in literally scores of books, plays and films of all genres. The Pygmalion figure has also appeared in dozens of paintings – the myth was a favourite subject of the Pre-Raphaelite brotherhood – theatrical productions and films. The following chapter will explore the Pygmalion effect in films directed by Roger Corman, Michael Powell, Martin Scorsese and Graeme Campbell.

---

[1] "More vividly than ever before he realized that art has two constant, two unending concerns: it always meditates on death and thus always creates life. All great, genuine art resembles and continues the revelation of St. John." (Pasternak, Boris *Doctor Zhivago*. Trans. Max Hayward and Manya Harari New York Signet Books, The New American Library 1958: 78).

[2] De Quincey, T *On Murder Considered as one of the Fine Arts* Edinburgh Adam and Charles Black 1827

[3] Bourdieu, P. *Outline of a Theory of Practice* Cambridge, Trans R. Nice, London, New York, Cambridge University Press 1977: 112

[4] Feinberg, L. *Introduction to Satire* Ames, Iowa, The Iowa State University Press 1967:23

[5] Ibid p..33

[6] Ibid p.185

[7] Johnson, E. *A Treasury of Satire* New York, Simon and Schuster, 1945:3

[8] Ibid pp. 5-7

[9] Ibid p. 67

[10] Ibid

[11] Ibid p. 9

[12] Lehmann, P. *Die Parodie im Mittalter*. 2nd edition Stuttgart, Hiersemann 1963:3

[13] Dane, J. *Parody: Critical Concepts Versus Literary Practices, Aristophenes* to Sterne Norman and London, University of   Oklahoma Press 1988:11-12

[14] ibid.

[15] Hutcheon, L. *A Theory of Parody: The Teachings of Twentieth Century Art Forms* London and New York Methuen 1985:43

[16] Muecke, D. C. *The Compass of Irony* London Methuen 1969:7; see also Muecke, D. *Irony and the Ironic* London and New York Methuen 1970

[17] Dane, J. *The Critical Mythology of Irony* Athens Georgia and London The University of Georgia Press 1991:187

[18] Hutcheon, 1985:55

[19] Ibid

[20] Ben_Porat, Z. "Method in Madness: Notes on the Structure of Parody, Based on MAD TV Satires," Poetics Today 1 245-72, quoted in Hutcheon 1985; 49

[21] Hutcheon, 1991:142

[22] The discussion of discursive communities by Michel Foucault (1972, 1977) is the obvious reference point here. A number of studies Radway J., (1984), and Lutz C.A and Collins, J. L., (1993) have illustrated the relative importance of this approach.

[23] Volosinov, V.N. *Marxism and The Philosophy of Language* t. L. Matejka and I.R. Titunic, Cambridge Harvard U P 1973:21

[24] Ibid

[25] De Quincey "Postscript" p.61

[26] De Quincey pp. 1-5

[27] Ibid p..5

[28] Kant, E. SS 22 "The necessity of the universal assent that is thought in a judgement of taste, is a subjective necessity which under the presupposition of a common sense, is represented as objective" in *The Critique of Judgement* translation James Meredith p.47 http://eserver.org/philosophy/kant/critique-of-judgement.txt Accessed July 2005

[29] SS 220 p 43

[30] Ibid p. 97

[31] De Quincey "On Consideration" p.7

[32] Ibid p. 8

[33] Ibid p. 8

[34] Ibid p.14

[35] Ibid p. 20

[36] Ibid p. 23-4

[37] Ibid p. 25

[38] Ibid p. 4

[39] Black, J., *The Aesthetics of Murder: A Study in Romantic Literature and Contemporary Culture* Baltimore, The John Hopkins University Press 1991p 15

[40] Black pp 15-16

[41] Porter D., *The Pursuit of Crime: Art and Ideology in Detective Fiction* New Haven Yale University Press 1981:22, quoted in Black p.56.

[42] De Quincey p 39

[43] Wilde, O., *The Picture of Dorian Gray* Oxford, Oxford University Press 1974:5 A theatrical version of the novel subtitled "A Moral Entertainment" was adapted by John Osborne, London, Faber and Faber 1973. *The Picture of Dorian Gray* (1945) directed by Albert Lewin, with Hurd Hatfield as Dorian, George Sanders, Donna

Reed and Angela Lansbury, Peter Lawford, Lowell Gilmore, and Miles Mander. Another version of *Dorian* Gray, directed by Glenn Jordan was produced in 1974.

[44] Black, p. 39 see Cohen, E "Behind the Closet Door: The Representation of Homoerotic Desire in the Picture of Dorian Gray;" Gagnier, R "Sexuality, The Public and the Art," and Paglia, C. "Oscar Wilde and the English Epicene" in Gagnier R., (ed) *Critical Essays on Oscar Wilde* New York G.K Hall & Co Maxwell Macmillan 1991

[45] Ibid p.6

[46] Wilde, p 27

[47] Winchell, J "Wilde and Huysmans: Autonomy, Reference, and the Myth of Expiation" in Gagnier, 1991:225

[48] Wilde, p 37

[49] "Dorian having embellished Lord Henry's pagan views with his own ideas of investing sensuality with an intellectual quality, found in "The Yellow Book" a practical design of action through which to carry out his new vision. His plan was to make dandyism into a metaphysics, to make his own life into a work of art" Lawler, D. An Inquiry into Oscar Wilde's Revisions of *The Picture of Dorian Gray* New York, London Garland Publishing 1988: pp 27-28

[50] Wilde, O *The Picture of Dorian Gray* p. 36

[51] Ibid. p.56

[52] p. 27

[53] p. 89

[54] p. 90

[55] p.128

[56] ibid

[57] p.158

[58] Ibid

[59] p.173

[60] Ibid

[61] p.224

[62] p 223

[63] p.156

[64] ibid

[65] ibid

Chapter 5

The Pygmalion Effect [1]

"Some artists will bait a hook and let you die."
Maxwell Brock, *Bucket of Blood* (1959) [2]

"I've just got one thing to say....
You've got to kill yourself to make it in the art world."
Teddy, *Still Life* (1992) [3]

George Bernard Shaw's version of *Pygmalion* (1916), that became internationally popular on stage and screen is based upon the story in Ovid's *Metamorphoses* of Pygmalion the melancholic sculptor of Greek mythology who resided in the town of Amathus on the island of Cyprus. Although passionately devoted to his art, Pygmalion found pleasure and happiness only in the silent company of the statues of the deities that he sculpted from ivory and marble.[4]The artist's melancholy was attributed to his disgust at the wanton sexuality of the Propoetides, girls from his city-state who had denied the divinity of Aphrodite (Venus). To punish them the Goddess inspired in them such immodesty that losing all shame, they would prostitute themselves to all comers and as a result of their lasciviousness; they were punished yet again by being transformed into rocks. Pygmalion shunned women but fervently venerated Aphrodite and finding a perfect piece of ivory he decides to create a sculptured likeness of her that he named Galatea (Sleeping Love). In a short time he became enamoured with his sculpture and although he caressed and kissed her, the cold artifact did not respond to his passionate advances. Recognizing Pygmalion's devotion to her through this fetishistic attention to her likeness, Aphrodite took pity on him and while embracing the cold statue one day, the sculptor felt the inert figure move and his kisses were soon returned by his object of desire (*objet de manqué*). It takes some time for Pygmalion (like Narcissus) to recognize that the object of desire that he has lost, is actually he.[5]

The films discussed in this chapter represent a reversal of the original Pygmalion myth.[6] The artist takes a live subject, kills it and then turns it into a fetish object worthy of aesthetic contemplation. This reversal is the perfect incarnation of the fetish character of the art object (as discussed by Binet, Freud, Brosses, Fourier et al), and Agamben's phantasmatic revision to the Freudian "object of lack," providing another major axis for interpretation that subtend this continuing discussion of art, film and death.[7] Each of the films discussed in this chapter: Roger Corman's *Bucket of Blood* (1959), Michael Powell's *Peeping Tom* (1960), Martin Scorsese's *After Hours* (1985), Graeme Campbell's *Still Life* (1992), and a notorious videotape (2001) produced by young Canadian artists Jesse Powers and Anthony Ryan Wennekers[8] that documents the torture, killing and skinning of a cat in the name of art, reinforce what I previously discussed in the introductory chapters as the othering of the artist, thus stimulating the reproduction of several stereotypes of artists as dangerous individuals whose neurotic, psycho-pathological, sexually avaricious, perverse, and/or criminal behaviour threaten the social order – such as it is.[9]

In this continuing discussion of alterity I will revisit some of the theoretical paradigms of post-colonial discourse introduced earlier where one's otherness is articulated simultaneously "as an object of desire and derision," and a "fantasy of origin and identity."[10] In each film avant-garde artists working within the 'institution art' are subjected to the critical machinations of social stereotypy becoming in this process, sites for the symbolic contestation of meaning and nodal points in the continuing struggle for cultural power. The film examples discussed in this chapter also provide the opportunity for continuing the exploration of the means by which the humour strategies of irony, parody, satire and burlesque, provide various classes and class fractions with critical vehicles for the negotiation of the dominant culture's sub-cultural avant-garde. The chapter concludes with some observations on how ethical concerns may possibly transcend different modes of representation.

Bucket of Blood

The film *Bucket of Blood* (1959), scripted by Charles B. Griffith and directed by Roger Corman is among the first of a large group of films from the legendary master of the Hollywood 'B' film to successfully combine the two genres of horror and comedy.[11] A promotional line for the film: "He killed so his art could live" provides the primary insight into this narrative that once again links aesthetics with murder, thereby conflating art and crime.[12] One would only have to add the seemingly paradoxical comment "he killed so that both he and his art could live," for in a crucial sense, this Pygmalion, like the others I will discuss in this chapter, is alive and creative – that is procreative – only when he kills. The artists represented in these films are also *being there* at the reality point/*pointure* (puncture or prick), of death rather than simply existing (being) in space and time.[13] Killing others and ultimately themselves enables these artists to exist in the Heideggerian essent/sense of the *dasein / das ein* that is of being there, rather than simply here. In other words, their thrust (thrownness) into life is also an ascent/descent to death, beyond which lies the immortal acquiescent condition of a metaphysical life (perhaps) uncontaminated by the alienating features of unconsummated longing and lack. These artists murder in order to consummate their desire for immortality and in order to achieve this, like the murderer immortalized in Oscar Wilde's *Ballad of Reading Gaol*, they have to "kill the things they love."[14]

Bucket of Blood opens with the credits scrolling over a medium frontal shot of Maxwell Brock, a bearded beatnik poet/philosopher; an Allen Ginsberg type, sonorously reading an enigmatic poem to bohemian inhabitants of the club called The Yellow Door Café. Brock's poetry is accompanied by the mournful atonality of a jazz riff, tapping feet and clicking fingers in rhythmic appreciation. Black coffee, berets, beards and black stockings are the order of the day and the atmosphere is thick with the smoke of Gauloise, Gitanes and the mirrors of faux melancholic conversation. Rock's poetry sets the stage for the development of the pivotal *Ur* themes – art, desire, death, and transcendence – contained in this film. His poem contains some lines that at once parody modernist essentialism and ironise the received role and identity of the avant-garde artist of beatnik culture, circa 1955.

> "A preacher is a preacher, or an artist;
> A rock is a rock, or a statue;
> A canvas is a canvas or a painting;
> Some artists will bait a hook and let you die;
> Repetition is death!
> The artist is, all others are not!"

And the wryly humorous:

"Life is an obscure hobo bumming a ride on the omnibus of art."

Dick Miller plays the role of Walter Paisley a shy bachelor working as a busboy in this beatnik café who seeks acceptance and respect from the artists he serves but suffers only the indignities of rejection.[15] Recognizing that continuing his menial position, as busboy will only reinforce his subordination; Walter decides that his only opportunity to win the respect of these café cognoscenti is to become an artist himself. In an early sequence we follow Walter home to a first floor studio apartment owned by Mrs. Zwickert, his somewhat nosey landlady. After a short conversation with her about the fresh piece of halibut she has bought for his cat, Walter enters his kitchen and opens a can of soup to prepare his dinner. Waiting for the pot of soup to heat on the stove, he retrieves a large cloth-covered object from a corner of the apartment. Unwrapped, this object reveals a lump of modeling clay that Walter begins to manipulate vigorously, pausing occasionally to examine a framed photograph he is using for his model. As he works, we hear a product of Walter's conscience, an authoritative voice-over from beat poet 'laureate' Maxwell Brock who intones in his *basso profundo* voice: "a sound is a sound, or music; a canvas is a canvas, or a painting; a rock is rock, or a statue." After a short time has elapsed Walter begins to exhibit some frustration with his inability to model the clay to his satisfaction. The harsh sound of a cat meowing from somewhere in the apartment interrupts his thoughts. Investigating the source of this meow, he discovers that his cat Frankie is trapped in the wall.

"Frankie" he asks, "Why did you have to get yourself stuck in the wall?" Taking a knife with a long blade from the kitchen counter, he approaches the wall to cut the plaster away from the area where the cat is trapped. With his first knife thrust however, we hear the cat squeal in pain. Realizing what he may have done, he frantically spoons away at the wall, finally retrieving the cat's body, with the knife planted firmly in its left side, already displaying an advanced degree of rigor mortis. "Oh Frankie, I'm sorry" says a dismayed Walter reflecting on the previous exchange with his landlady. "Oh…and Mrs. Zwickert had a nice piece of fresh halibut for you." The remainder of this sequence shows Walter in a melancholy mood, but in his misery he dredges up yet another powerful line from Brock's poem: "Let them die and by their miserable deaths, let them become an ash tray or an art work!"[16] With this poetic stimulation from his powerful mentor, Walter has a flash of inspiration and decides to turn the hapless Frankie into a work of art. From a classically trained sculptor's point of view his modus operandi, simply covering the dead animal with clay and plaster, is somewhat deficient but he nevertheless succeeds in producing a very fine looking sculpture of the cat, retaining for shock value the kitchen knife in its side. Satisfied with his efforts, he decides to show his artwork to Mr. de Santis the café owner and his girlfriend Carla, with whom Walter is secretly infatuated. Appropriately titled *Dead Cat*, the sculpture is an instant hit and Brock pronounces Walter a genius before the assembled throng. "Mark well this lad. His is the dark voice of creation!" Naolia, a beautiful young Eurasian woman, and one of the café regulars is attracted to Walter's instant success and gives him a good luck charm to aid him in his creative work. Unfortunately (or fortunately, depending on one's perspective), the charm contains dope that provides Walter with his next subject. Suspecting that Naolia's gift to Walter is a drug deal, an undercover narcotics agent who had been posing as a beatnik patron of the café, tracks him to his apartment. Brandishing a gun he attempts to arrest the confused Walter for drug trafficking. Fearing that he is about to be shot Walter smashes the detective over the head with a heavy frying pans, killing him. When Mrs. Zwickert knocks to investigate the loud sounds emanating from Walter's apartment, he quickly hides the officer's body on a high shelf above the sink counter and as she casts her eyes furtively about the apartment, a shadow of the agent's arm drops down menacingly behind her. Before she can see it however, Walter forcefully propels her out of his apartment just as blood flowing from the arm of the narcotic agent's body begins to drip loudly into a bucket on the floor to thus reinforce the film's provocative title.

Meanwhile the *Dead Cat* sculpture, temporarily exhibited at the café, has attracted the attention of Leonard the gallery director and critic who accidentally knocks the cat onto the floor and discovers that it contains real cat fur, and that - surprise - there's a body attached! Initially repelled by this discovery he subsequently recognizes it as an avant-garde project worthy of conventional art world attention and from which he may profit. When an art collector shows interest in purchasing the sculpture, he acts on Walter's behalf as his dealer and sells it for $500.00. Later, suffering somewhat from guilt, Leonard half-heartedly attempts to convince Walter to switch to making "free form" sculpture. He cynically offers the artist $50.00 of the $500.00 he obtained from selling *Dead Cat* and Walter uses this money to hire Alice, a very Aryan looking blonde to use as his model. Alice quickly becomes victim number three and she too is exhibited before the admiring members of the arts community at The Yellow Door Café. Brock waxes eloquently over this new creation from the 'genius' with: "The soul has become flesh and Walter Paisley is born!"

10. Dick Miller as Walter Paisley

At the party to celebrate his arrival to the art world Walter sits on a makeshift throne, dressed in striped jacket and trousers, perhaps an ironic reference to clothing worn by prisoners, with a hastily constructed cardboard crown bearing a sculptor's hammer and chisel (not sickle) jauntily placed on his head, a 'royal' bathroom plunger as a sceptre held in his right hand and in his left, a large chalice of wine. Walter also wears a signature paisley cravat and a large five pointed silver star, similar to a sheriff's badge pinned to his lapel which given his stripped suit (read as concentration camp clothing) may be a strangely inappropriate allusion to a Jewish star of David. Least this reading of the Walter's clothing seem somewhat far fetched, this semiotic mélange must also be placed in the context of Walter's killing framed as an aesthetic act and the prescription provided by Brock's rather scary poem - "*let them become an ashtray, or an art work*" (emphasis added). The artist's *Murdered Woman* piece is quickly followed by *Severed Head*, a portrait bust of a carpenter that Walter has modeled using the worker's own circular saw. Impressed by the opportunity these works present to him as Walter's dealer, Leonard arranges a solo exhibition for him that is a great success. At the gallery opening for his first one man show, Walter basks in his art world canonization but still lusting after Carla to become his muse, he decides to trade the material fruits of his success for love. "I don't want to make statues any more," he pleads, "I want to marry you." But when Carla refuses his overture, he decides that in order to possess his object of desire he must kill again. "Will you let me make a statue of you?" he asks. Carla naively accedes to his wish but before she allows him to take her to his studio apartment and potential death, she accidentally discovers that *Strangled Woman* and all the other works of sculpture in Walter's exhibition contain real dead bodies. Confronting Walter with this appalling knowledge she is told the truth: "Don't you see, I have made them immortal and I can do the same for you!" A chase ensues, during which Walter begins to hear the voices of his victims in his conscience. "Walter! Walter! Walter!" Finally he is driven mad, punished effectively by a higher power (a legacy, perhaps of the Hays Code regulations instituted several years before), and is found hidden, as he says in the closing minutes of the film, "where they'll never find me" in a plaster suit of immortality as *The Hanged Man*, his final masterpiece.[17]

Compared to the original Pygmalion myth, there are three reversals operating in this diabolically humorous narrative. The first reversal is the summary rejection of Walter by those around him; for unlike Pygmalion, he doesn't reject society ...society rejects him. He must therefore secure admission by becoming an artist like those whom he admires. The second reversal is that Walter kills live subjects and turns them into works of art whereas Pygmalion, with Aphrodite's assistance, brings his inanimate statue to life. Thirdly, when Walter realizes that he cannot possess his object of desire, Carla his muse, he decides to kill her and when this fails, he commits suicide. Walter murders in order to live an exemplary creative life as a successful and respected artist but when this objective is not realizable, he kills himself, thus transcending life to become immortal like those he has murdered. Walter's expression of romantic desire – love – for his muse is clearly fated -- *fatum* -- as Nietzsche wrote in *The Case of*

Wagner, an expression of love as "fatality, cynical, innocent and precisely in this a piece of nature...that love which is war in its means, and at bottom the deadly hatred of the sexes. Don Jose's last cry, "Yes, I have killed her.... I...my adored Carmen!"[18] Nietzsche continues that "such a conception of love, (the only one worthy of a philosopher)," added parenthetically – as if philosophers were the only men worthy of misogyny – "is rare: it raises a work above thousands. For on average, artists do what all the world does, even worse – they misunderstand love. Wagner too misunderstood it."[19]   In an accompanying footnote Nietzsche acknowledges the fatal love of Shakespeare's Brutus in *Julius Caesar* and the refrain from Oscar Wilde's *Ballad of Reading Gaol* poem "for all men kill the thing they love...." as well as the deadly sense of the verb "lure" in the ending to Goethe's *Faust* "The eternal feminine lures us to perfection."[20] From a feminist critical perspective the misogynistic subtext of the Pygmalion myth remains essentially the same. With a gender reversal of Medusa's power, fallen women must be turned into inanimate objects.

Peeping Tom

Michael Powell's *Peeping Tom* (1960), made in London a year later than Corman's film, and a few months before Alfred Hitchcock's *Psycho*, is an unusually chilling example of the Pygmalion effect. The narrative concerns the figure of Mark Lewis (Karl Boehm), a handsome yet psychopathic cinematographer, who as a young boy had been psychologically brutalized by his father, a researcher in child psychology. As a young child Mark's father had sadistically engaged him in his research into dreaming and fear response in the young. He had wired the house with microphones and when he heard his son's nightmares in the middle of the night he used to awaken the youngster in order to film his response. The father also deprived his son of sleep, placed objects and animals such as a live lizard in his bed in order to document Mark's anguished cries upon waking. The viewer is provided with a film within a film montage of chilling sequences of these experiments from the father's documentary, shots of Mark in grief over the body of his dead mother and his father's courtship of a new woman. And when the father left the house to be with his new partner, he gave Mark his 16mm camera and dozens of reels of film.

As an adult Mark lives a solitary existence in the upstairs apartment of the large three-story town house that was his family home. The second floor contains an apartment he has rented to Mrs. Stephens, a blind alcoholic and Helen her daughter. Lewis works for a film production company as a camera focus puller but carries with him everywhere the 16mm camera and tripod, a special "amenable object" (after Winnicott), from which he is unable to be separated. He is like a somewhat obsessive artist, using his camera as a crucial apparatus of mediation between him and the social world from which he remains estranged. As an instrumental result of his father's abuse Mark engages in his own pathological research into the terror response in the women he murders, filming the facial expression of his victims at the exact moment of their death. Luring his victims to his camera by appealing to their narcissism and desire for him, the murder is accomplished with a long stiletto blade hidden in the leg of a tripod to which the camera is attached. A concave mirror affixed to the camera assists the recording of the absolute moment of terror registered in the distorted faces of his female victims as the knife blade penetrates their throats. As the narrative progresses we learn that the recorded look of terror on the faces of his first victims does not measure up to the perfect document that he hoped would satiate his desire; both for ocular and psychological verisimilitude – the truth of terror (the Lacanian réal) – and the resolution of his Oedipal struggle with his emotionally absent and abusive father.

Not surprisingly in the early 1960's when it was first exhibited in English cinemas *Peeping Tom* was picketed and subjected to some very vigorous criticism. Part of the anger was directed at Powell for placing himself in the role of the father and Columba his son as the young Mark Lewis. The film was rehabilitated in 1979 by Martin Scorsese, an admirer of Powell's films and within the past two decades *Peeping Tom* has been accorded attention, not simply as a period piece but also for its implicit critique of psychological behaviorism; as a demonstration of the political and psychic economies of the gaze, and also for its somewhat eccentric representation of gender relations. It is now a popular film for visual culture researchers armed with the post-Freudian theoretical paradigms of Lacan, Klein and Winnicott. Several important essays discussing this film in psychoanalytic terms have been published, among them: Reynold Humphries' "*Peeping Tom*: Voyeurism, the camera and the spectator"[21] and Linda Williams' "When the Woman Looks" that persuasively argues that *Peeping Tom* is one of the few films that enable the woman to exercise and take power of the look, a strategic revision of Laura Mulvey's famous essay (1975), that argued that all Hollywood cinema subordinated women to the power of the male gaze thus reproducing the patriarchal order.

Parveen Adams' essay on this film "Father, can't you see I'm filming?" draws upon Lacan's psychoanalytic framework to locate Mark Lewis' neuroses as a struggle between analyst and patient, the symbolic and the real. [22] Adams argues that the pursuit of the perfect look of terror in the faces of his victims provides Lewis with an opportunity to "free him from the torment of his own life," and further that "the promise of looking and its impossibility...rests upon the idea of the completion of terror in which the subject and the other, killing and being killed, seeing and being seen, are incarnated in a single object, in a single impossible moment."[23] After murdering two women in the first section of the film, Mark's continuation of his homicidal research is interrupted when Helen invites him to go to a film screening with her. When he meets Helen's blind mother before their date, she intuits something amiss with this young man and displays some anxiety (trust a mother's intuition) for the safety of her daughter. As Mark and Helen's friendship develops Mrs. Stephens' anxiety increases and like a blind philosopher she intuits that there is something not quite right about Mark's constant filming, saying in one scene "all this filming isn't healthy." The mother's blindness contrasts not only with the scopophilia manifested in the title and Mark's filming but also the viewers' complicity in his capturing of the look of terror. When he finally reveals his psychopathic tendencies to Helen, significantly on her birthday, he realizes that the final attempt to capture the look of absolute terror must be undertaken on him.

From a Freudian perspective, Mark's behaviour is an example of unresolved Oedipal conflict and the power of the death drive. As a victim of his father's abuse he is compelled to obsessively rehearse and repeat his childhood trauma even when the repetitive act fails to deliver the fulfillment of his desire, both for a happy resolution to his desire for the absent father and the quiescence that preceded his birth. In *Beyond the Pleasure Principle* Freud argued (contentiously) that the human psyche is locked in a struggle between two instinctive drives, Eros and Thanatos, that the power of the death instinct or death drive explains why the psyche of the human subject compels him/her to obsessively repeat painful and traumatic events, which is exactly how Mark responds to his childhood neuroses. When it appears that some transference may be happening with

Helen and possibly her mother, he is placed in the position of recognizing his murderous psychotic behaviour, giving himself up to the police or committing suicide that becomes his final act of being there *au point du réalité* without possibility for redemption. In Adam's essay *jouissance*, the réal, redemption and transcendence are at stake in Mark Lewis' perverse engagement with the world. Employing Lacan's category of *jouissance* and his model of the *petit objet à* that functions "as a hole and a cover for a hole," Adam's argues that Mark Lewis' perverse pursuit of the absolute look of terror in the death of his subject enables the symbolic order to be eclipsed by a confrontation with the real. Forty years later the film's violence appears very choreographed and theatrical in comparison to the average horror or slasher film but the script remains a chilling model of psychological trauma and it's conflation of sex and violence a troubling example of misogyny.

How is this film a Pygmalion reversal? Functioning as *l'artiste maudit* Mark Lewis is seeking both scientific and aesthetic perfection in the fear response in his subjects, and yet to do so, he must turn them into objects of terror destined for both aesthetic contemplation and empirical testing. The documentary that his father was making with him as his psychological research subject was interrupted when he took another woman as his wife, and as the victim of separation, Mark is convinced that to recover the absent love of his father – that was probably never there in the first place – and to measure up to his projection of father's expectations, he must kill his research subjects at the precise moment of their recognition of their death, when fear is registered at its apex, and in Lacanian terms, at the point when the symbolic is eclipsed by the real. In the final moments of the film when the screen fades to black his small boy's voice recorded for posterity on audiotape delivers the painful line "goodnight Daddy, hold my hand."

After Hours

A third example of the Pygmalion effect is illustrated in the cult comedy film *After Hours* (1985), scripted by Joseph Minion and directed by Martin Scorsese. The narrative of this film has a Baron von Munchausen like incredibility that centres around the art world, identifiably New York City, Soho, the East Village, Tribeca and their artist inhabitants. The film opens with the story of a computer analyst, Paul Hackette (an ironical inflection of hacker), played convincingly by Griffen Dunne, who is in search of a romantic interlude from his boring life as an uptown office worker. Marcy (Rosanna Arquette) a beautiful young blonde, one of many we meet in this film (like Hitchcock, Scorsese has a fondness for Aryan blondes), is attracted to Paul when she encounters him reading a Henry Miller novel in a diner near his apartment. They trade opinions about Miller's novels and Marcy reveals that she is also knowledgeable about avant-garde art, something about which Paul knows very little. Clearly attracted to him, as he is to her, she asks him innocently whether he is interested in purchasing a plaster of Paris cream cheese bagel paperweight made by her artist friend.[24] This somewhat *gauche* pick-up line is one of many ironic references to contemporary art and high/ low antagonisms sprinkled throughout the film. As an ironic homage to Roger Corman's earlier art world satire, Scorsese provides a cameo for Dick Miller who played Walter Paisley the serial art killer in *Bucket of Blood*. After providing Paul with her Soho telephone number, Marcy departs from the diner. [25]   Later that evening, 11.25 p.m. - the proverbial 'witching hour'- Paul casually calls Marcy to inquire about the plaster of Paris paper weights, with the object of "getting together sometime for coffee." She suggests he take a cab and come to her place that evening, and after a wild cab ride during which he loses his only $20 note out the window – this act at midnight signaling the beginning of his living nightmare – he arrives at her loft. He rings the buzzer and artist Kiki Bridges (Linda Fiorentino), Marcy's loft mate, throws him down the keys to the front door.[26]

Kiki makes life size paper maché sculptures of contorted figures, classy examples of mid eighties 'victim art,' which she is working on when Paul arrives.[27] He quickly reveals his lack of cultural capital by suggesting, "it looks like a work done by the guy who did *The Shriek*." Kiki corrects him curtly with "it's Edward Munch, and it's *The Scream*." Sizing him up somewhat attractive but incredibly naive, she asks him to help her with the sculpture on which she is working while Marcy is at the drug store. She offers to wash his shirt when it gets paper maché paste on it and complains about her sore shoulders. Paul offers to give her a massage and after being massaged for a short time, which presents one of the most erotically seductive scenes in the film, she falls asleep in his arms. Marcy returns and quickly reveals to Paul her somewhat manic depressive personality, relating to him a few odd details about her life, including a rape, problems with a former boyfriend and her previous husband. "He was obsessed with *The Wizard of Oz*. Do you know the film? And every time he... you know...came... he yelled, "surrender Dorothy!" Marcy decides to shower and this provides Paul with a little time to snoop around her bedroom in an attempt to find out more about her. They go out for a coffee; returning a short time later to talk but the increasing evidence of Marcy's neuroses encourages Paul to slip out and head for home. He decides to take the subway. Bad timing. At midnight the fare was increased to $1.50 and having previously lost his $20 in the taxi ride Paul now has only 97 cents to his name. He attempts to jump the ticket wicket but one of New York's finest is cruising the subway at that moment and chases Paul that prevents him from catching his subway train. From here on the narrative exhibits a von Munchausen complexity. A 'noirish' rain begins to fall. Some theatrical sounding thunder is later added and does not abate until the closing minutes of the film. Paul enters a bar where sixties 'bubble gum' music (The Monkees' theme song), is playing and meets his next neurotic artist, Julie (Teri Garr), described as "Miss Beehive 1965" a waitress who tells him that she hates her job. The male bartender offers to give Paul the money to get uptown on the subway but he finds that his till will not open. The till key is in his apartment at 158 Spring Street and he exchanges keys with Paul so that he can go and fetch it. Paul picks up the key, but is mistaken for a burglar by a couple of gay guys (brilliantly acted by Cheech and Chong) who live below the bartender's apartment.[28]

After turning down Julie's offer to stay the night, Paul returns to Marcy's apartment. Outside he encounters two burglars, ironically played again by Cheech and Chong, engaged in loading Kiki's *Scream* sculpture and a television set into the back of their beat up van. Upstairs he finds a scantily clad Kiki bound head to toe in the company of Horst her formidable looking leather bound companion. It is apparent that she is a sado-masochist who is into bondage games. Horst informs Paul that he has treated Marcy badly and guilt stricken, Paul decides to go and apologize. Entering her room he discovers that she has taken an overdose. Kiki and Horst leave him a note about meeting them at an art performance at the Club Berlin on the corner of W. Broadway and Grand Street. Paul returns to the sixties bar. The bartender receives a call, looks shocked and announces that his "girlfriend Marcy just killed herself," revealing to Paul that the bartender is the estranged boyfriend. Julie takes him up to her apartment. Declaring that she hates both of her jobs as waitress and assistant in a Xerox shop, she executes a portrait sketch of Paul, providing another explicit example of a high/low struggle over the aesthetics of (re) production. Both are tired and despondent. She wants him to stay but slowly becoming aware of her quirky personality Paul decides to exit to the Club Berlin to meet Kiki and Horst. This proves to be another bad decision. Here he encounters a mosh pit of punks and barely escapes receiving a Mohawk haircut free of charge, Scorsese's ironic reference to Travis Bickle's hairstyle in *Taxi Driver* his earlier film. He leaves, only to run into another neurotic, this time a male insomniac, who thinks that Paul wants to sleep with him. Meanwhile the jilted Julie – "hell" so the saying goes, "hath no fury like a woman spurned"— has made hundreds of xeroxed copies of her portrait of Paul with an attached text reading "This man is a burglar." Paul realizes with alarm that the loud groups of people roaming Soho are after him!

Fleeing members of the neighborhood vigilante mob Paul enters a conceptual art show, where there is nothing in the gallery, and meets June (Verne Bloom) another gorgeous blonde artist suffering from creative melancholy. June takes pity on Paul's plight and derives obvious pleasure from concealing him in a plaster and paper maché statue, essentially performing a gender reversal of the Pygmalion myth.[29] After completing her work of concealment she leaves him stranded in the sculpture, potentially to become an inanimate art object. Later that morning Neil and Pepe, the two burglars still on their mission, break into the basement studio and steal the seemingly lifeless statue containing Paul. One of the criminals declares his lack of cultural competency by confessing, "Art sure is ugly", to which his partner retorts knowingly, "That's how much you know, the uglier the art, the more it's worth!" They place the sculpture into their van and roar off into the night. As dawn arrives, they make a fast turn on a street and the back door flings open, depositing the statue on the road where it breaks into a dozen pieces. A very disheveled Paul gets out to discover that he has arrived back at his work place where the film began. Covered in plaster, paper and glue; confused from lack of sleep, he takes the elevator to his office floor and stands to stunned attention beside his desk and computer.

After Hours contains somewhat muted Pygmalion reversals. No one is murdered and Marcy is the only character who dies from a self-administered overdose. Paul is incarcerated in a piece of sculpture and his life is endangered several times throughout the movie but he manages to survive. Scorsese's satire of the art world, however, and the othering of art and artists in this film is similar to that demonstrated in Roger Corman's *Bucket of Blood*: In Scorsese's film, Pygmalion exists as the creative force in each of the female characters and like the original Pygmalion all of the women are socially and psychically alienated and therefore perhaps suitable cases for treatment. In Paul they sense a rare naïveté, an essential goodness, a purity that they themselves do not possess. He intuits their desire to consume him, hence his resistance to their various femme fatale/ spider woman strategies of entrapment. June the final artist Paul meets, is the closest approximation to Pygmalion in that her plaster sculpture for concealing Paul from his pursuers turns into a literal trap. The sculpture becomes his prison and she his guard, an omnipotent creator/ magus figure with total power over her immobile subject. Without the burglars who steal the sculpture, the indication is that Paul would have remained incarcerated in this sculpture forever.

Still Life

A somewhat more sadistic example of the Pygmalion effect is provided by *Still Life* (1992) a slasher film directed by Graeme Campbell from a screenplay by Michael Tan and Dan Parisot. The film stars Jason Gedrich as Peter Sherwood, an avant-garde musician, Jessica Steen, as Nelly Ambrose, an NYTV news reporter and Teddy (Stephen Shellen) as Peter's sycophantic and somewhat scary friend, a performance artist and clarinetist. *Still Life* ratchets up the trans/actions between murder and aesthetics, art and crime, by showing a serial killer who presents his victims as works of creative assemblage and signs them with his tag 'AK' for 'Art Killer.' Like the other films discussed in this chapter, *Still Life* conflates horror with comedy, although in somewhat less comedic (ironic/satiric) manner than either of the previous films. The film opens with Nelly the television reporter covering one of the Art Killer's latest works, a very dead vagrant hanging in a gilt frame. "The Art Killer has struck again with his version of Fatal Art" scream the media headlines. Predictably, the Art Killer has developed a following and groupies have been lauding each of his exhibits as examples of "very cool" art.

Nelly meets Peter when a terrorist bomb threat clears the bar in which he is about to perform. A relationship quickly develops between them and she moves into his loft. Teddy, who lives next door to Peter, rapidly becomes jealous of their relationship. Meanwhile Peter receives a suspicious looking videotape through the mail from a new music producer bearing the sinister name of Luther Wax, requesting a new composition to accompany his compilation of horrific images. Luther has been a suspect in an unrelated murder case, and when the next Art Killer victim is found, Wax is again arrested as a murder suspect. After Peter's successful gig at the bar, Billy and Frank simulate an Art Killer performance by ambushing Peter attaching him to a frame and then hanging him high from a building. But instead of killing him they simply sign the piece "A.K" and document it with a Polaroid camera.

From this production the film narrative develops to witness a scary performance by Teddy in which he threatens both Nelly his co-performer and a woman in the audience with his pistol. Nelly is upset by this unscripted gun performance and tells him loudly "you can fuck with people but you don't need to kill them!" and "if you even shoot at me again, I'll kill you!" Peter is found and becomes Nelly's next media assignment under the headline "Totally Screwed." And in what proves to be a somewhat suspicious act, Teddy reveals that he wants to use the media coverage of Peter's arduous experience to promote his music. As an interlude Peter is shown igniting a cockroach in a somewhat lame attempt by the scriptwriter to enlarge the cast of suspects. The next Art Killer victim is Maggie Stepanova an Eastern European immigrant, and a regular at the bar frequented by Peter, Teddy and their friends. The work produced as a result of her murder is sinisterly titled *Whistler's Mother Revisited.* Detectives interrogate both Luther Wax and Peter about their whereabouts at the time of the Stepanova murder. Suspicious of the fact that Peter is somehow in the vicinity of each of the killings "Other victims he kills, but you he sets up," the two detectives decide to place him under surveillance. Meanwhile, Peter has received another menacing video from Luther showing that Nelly has been taken hostage. "I've got a fish to fry for you" relates the voice on the tape; "Finish it Peter, or it's all over but for the frying." Peter stays up all night to finish the piece while the detective keeps his vigil. The serial Art Killer's sixth victim becomes Stan (the Man), a popular local liquor store vendor.

In the final sequences, Teddy dressed as a clown drags Nelly into Peter's loft revealing that he Teddy is the Art Killer. "Put the handcuffs on lover boy," he says to Peter. "Why are you doing this to us?" Demands Peter in return, "you're our friend!" "I'm tired of being ignored," replies Teddy, as the camera pans up to a poster on the wall showing them all under a text that reads "Real Performance Art." "I planned all this, the bomb scare, the art killings, and ah...Miss Nelly, I was your only story!" Outside the loft clown suited fans of the Art Killer chant in unison "A.K! A.K! A.K! AK!" Dave, Nelly's cameraman enters the loft and she appeals to Teddy's narcissism by suggesting that they do an interview for NYTV news. She questions, "Is this your final piece Teddy?" And "why are you doing this?" You're not going to kill us, man?" Asks Peter, to which Teddy manically replies, "I want the show to be over." With a final "I want to be with my people," he leaps through the window into the assembled crowd several stories below and lands heavily on the roof of a car parked below. Peter comforts him before he dies and says, "I love you man" to which Teddy replies, "I love you too." His last words are prophetic and a strict Pygmalion reversal if ever there was one. "I've just got one thing to say.... you've got to kill yourself to make it in the art world!"

In all four films, irony and parody provide the vehicles for the satirical intentions of the screenwriter and the subsequent interpretation of the script by the film director and his partners in crime. Corman's *Bucket of Blood* parodies the performance, behaviour and idiomatic language of fifties beat culture. *Peeping Tom* parodies psychoanalysis and documentary verisimilitude. Scorsese's *After Hours* satirizes the New York art nexus of the profligate 1970's and early 1980's, and the art genres of pop, minimal, conceptual art, performance and body art. *Still Life* is a cynical attack on the putative narrowing of the gap between art and life, announcing that "its all a performance!"

Cats, Art and Buckets of Blood

In the summer of 2001, many of these art crimes and misdemeanors were replayed in the realm of the social with a shocking artwork produced by Toronto art students Jesse Powers and Anthony Ryan Wennekers who were subsequently charged with cruelty to animals and public mischief after a downtown apartment was raided by police. Their arrest directly fomented another art controversy for a public stupefied by summer heat and not yet immured in fear by the September 11th terrorist attacks on The World Trade Centre in New York, the Pentagon in Washington, D.C. and the continuing shocking aftermath. The July 01 art controversy in Canada now seems trivial in comparison to the terrorist attack, a veritable storm in a teacup. But perhaps there are some lessons to be learned here with respect to ethics and aesthetics, not to mention the political economy and psychosocial dynamics of art practices that conflate art and crime.

In Powers and Wenneker's apartment police investigators found a headless skinned cat in the fridge, a rodent skeleton, several animal skulls and videotape documenting the prolonged torture of a cat. The artists' videotapes were confiscated and held as evidence for their trial on charges of cruelty to animals and public mischief. It would be fortuitous but probably unrealistic to think that one, perhaps all of the films described here provided an impetus for their thinking. But like the films themselves there is ample evidence to demonstrate that the historical contexts - the location - for art production, the scripts, performance film or video, provide material for aesthetic reproduction and perhaps even, "the marking of the limit."[30]   What if we compare the performance of these young artists to the actual killing and sometimes torture of animals in dozens of films and videos within the canon, for example: an obscene snaring and shooting of rabbits in Jean Renoir's *Le Regle Jeu* (1939); the ritualistic (and physically disgusting) execution of the pig in Jean Luc Godard's apocalyptic film *Weekend*, which in a remarkable montage is transposed with and compared to multiple highway crashes. Then there is the slaughter of dozens of ducks (for sport and pleasure), by the English nobility populating *The Shooting Party* (1985), directed by Alan Bridges. How different are these from the torture and killing of the cat in the video by Powers and Wennekers? There are of course many more cinematic examples in which animals, birds, rodents and insects have been killed to provide veracity to a narrative schema. And there are now legal restraints placed on film producers and film credits claim the ethical treatment of animals throughout a production. Even within the art world groups such as JAAG (Justice for Animals Art Guild), have begun to question the ethical treatment of animals in art. For art historical provenance the art students' cat performance/video should also be placed in the context of the use of cats in art from early Egyptian statuary to Manet's *Olympia* and artist Carolee Schneemann's *Up To And Including Her Limits* a performance memorial to Kitsch her beloved dead cat, who appears in an advanced state of rigor mortis in the performance and is the subject of a film titled *Kitsch's Last Meal*. Steve Baker's *The Postmodern Animal* explores the ethical boundaries of the use of live and dead animals in art in the work of artists such as Damien Hurst, Marco Everisti (Goldfish in Blender), Mark Dionne (*Library for the Birds of Antwerp* 1993) and Eduardo Kac whose transgenic (glow in the dark) rabbit became a cause célèbre for both the

animal rights groups and the apostles of gene splicing and techno culture.
[31] Baker writes: ".... the distinction between living and dead animal counts
for little in terms of the meanings generated in much contemporary art"
and "regardless of ethical stances, it is still materials that count here,
creating knowledge and encouraging open and imaginative thought."[32] He
goes on to add the rather chilling phrase that invokes the Pygmalion effect:
"The use of the living animal in art is most telling when it's caught
somewhere between life and death, between reality and representation."[33]
Baker's sentiment or better, political position, finds confirmation in an
OCAD Professor, Johanna Householder's defense of Jesse Powers who
took two classes in performance art under her instruction. In one interview
she offered that he is "a sensitive young man who thinks deeply about
questions of life and death." "My understanding is", she continued, "that
he is extremely concerned with the wholesale slaughter of animals for food
and other purposes."

If we suspend the issue, that is the means of representation for the moment,
it may be argued that each cultural product discussed in this chapter
provides the ground for the strange amalgam of fascination, desire and
repulsion for contemporary art and artists of the kind that Homi Bhabha
describes as stereotyped othering in a crucial chapter of his book *The
Location of Culture* (1994). Each film others artists in the stereotypical
ways that I alluded to previously, as obsessive compulsive, sado-
masochistic, narcissistic neurotic, melancholic, suicidal, alcoholic and
criminal. The artists in *Still Life* and *Bucket of Blood* commit suicide to
achieve immortality. "They kill, and die, so their art can live." Mark Lewis
in *Peeping Tom* continues his father's documentary on fear, completing it
as only he could with his own final spectacular fear response at the point of
his own suicide, recorded with a custom designed apparatus that is
simultaneously the instrument and recorder of death. And Wennekers and
Powers, students of this process, merely kill in order for their art to live,
but ironically they were the only artists who were actually prosecuted in a
court of by the law for their crimes, receiving for their pains, at the
Crown's pleasure, fines, suspended sentences, and hours of community
service.

Homi Bhabha argues that one's otherness is articulated stereotypically "at
once (as) an object of desire and derision, an articulation of fantasy of
origin and identity."[34]The other stereotype is a combination of both fear
and fetish to which he provides a Freudian twist. "There is both," he

writes, "a structural and functional suggestion for reading the racial stereotype of colonial discourse in terms of fetishism."

> Fetishism, as the disavowal of difference, is that repetitious scene around the problem of castration. The functional link between the fixation of the fetish and the stereotype (or the stereotype as fetish) is even more relevant.[35]

Bhabha's psychoanalytic gloss on fetishism is a perfect description of the dynamics of the Pygmalion effect, which is also a repetitious (phantasmatic) scene around the problem of castration. The chain of absence and presence and the disavowal of Pygmalion's estrangement by his fetishistic fixation on the statue he has created, a fixation that masks the difference/ lack and restores the original presence of his love for an-Other besides himself. In Freudian terms a fetish dominates "the object -choice" for these individuals. Freud explained this as a disavowal (*verleugnung*) process whereby a male child refuses to recognize the absent penis of the mother and substitutes a fetish to accommodate and resist the threat of castration.[36] In his reading of Freud, Bhahba argues that fetishism is always a 'play' or vacillation between the archaic affirmation of wholeness/similarity – in Freud's terms "all men have penises"; "All men have the same skin/race/culture" – and for our purpose here – all artists exhibit neuroses – and the anxiety associated with lack and difference. Again, for Freud "some do not have penises." "Some do not have the same skin/race/culture" and in this context, some artists are *not* neurotic. We should revisit Bhahba's explanation of othering and stereotypy that has relevance in this context:

> The scene of fetishism is also the scene of reactivation and repetition of the primal fantasy - the subject's desire for a pure origin that is always threatened by its division, for the subject must be gendered to be engendered, to be spoken. For both coloniser and colonised the "stereotype is the "primary point of subjectification.[37]

Giorgio Agamben's interpretation of Freud 's *Fetischismus* corresponds in this instance with Homi Bhabha's, in that the force of the fetish is one of both absence and presence, an essential ambiguity over a perception of reality that has a phantasmatic character both "symbol of something and it's negation."[38] Agamben argues that the fetish can only be maintained through a fracture of the ego (*Ichspaltung*) and further acknowledges how mental processes of the fetishistic type have a linguistic correlative "in poetic language: synecdoche and its close relative metonymy)."[39]

As if trapped in postmodern discourse, Pygmalion breathes love/life into his inert object, seeking the activation of his primal fantasy and simultaneous release from a repetitive cycle of saturnine melancholy and misanthropy. Recognizing his lack he metonymically substitutes the inert statue for his fantasy which thus breaks the chain of misidentification and provides him with his reason to be: a subject identity as a whole social being capable of being and needing to be loved. His art becomes life. In the films and performances discussed in this chapter, the obverse happens. The artists kill in order to create the art that will potentially ensure them immortality. In a powerful Nietzschean sense Thanatos overrules Eros, confirming the eschatological coordinates of culture, and also emphasizing *ars longa, vita brevis*.[40]

---

[1] This chapter was developed from a paper first presented at the Universities Art Association Conference, Université du Quebec, Montreal October 18-21 2001, in the session" "Rethinking Controversy in the Arts I: Transgressions, Art Crimes and the new politics of Aesthetics" Chaired by Dr Jan Marontante.

[2] From the script by Charles B. Griffith for Roger Corman's *Bucket of Blood* (1959)

[3] *Still Life* (1992), directed by Graeme Campbell from a screenplay by Michael Tan and Dan Parisot.

[4] *Pygmalion* (1938) directed by Anthony Asquith, and Leslie Howard with cast Leslie Howard as Professor Henry Higgins and Wendy Hiller as Eliza Doolittle. *My Fair Lady* (1964) directed by George Cukor with Rex Harrison and Audrey Hepburn in the leading roles. There are numerous other versions of the myth on stage and screen including *She's All That* (1999) starring Rachel Leigh Cook and Freddie Prinze, Jr., which is probably the weakest adaptation of the myth. And other films employ subtle references to the Pygmalion story such as Krzysztof Kieslowki's *White* (from *The Three Colours* Trilogy) in which Tomas (Zbigniew Zamachowski) the love sick Polish protagonist is shipped back to Warsaw from Paris in a suitcase carrying with him a life size plaster facsimile bust of his divorced wife (Julie Delpy). In one scene he kisses it and carefully patches it up when it is damaged in transit. Tomas is an award winning hairdresser a role that could also be characterized somewhat as a Pygmalion effect. Within the history of visual art there are numerous representations of Pygmalion including perhaps the most famous series produced by Edward Byrne-Jones under the themes: "The Heart Desires", "The Hand Refrains", "The Godhead Fires" and the "Soul Attains" (1875-78). In Schiller's poem *The Ideals*, the Pygmalion myth becomes an allegory for the love of nature in a youthful heart. In his version, as in William Morris, the statue is made from marble a more likely material with respect to scale of the figure for the original Galatea. "As once with prayers in passion flowing, Pygmalion embraced the stone, till from the frozen marble glowing, the light of

feeling o'er him shone, so did I clasp with young devotion Bright Nature to a poet's heart; till breath and warmth and vital motion Seemed through the statue form to dart. And then in all my ardor sharing, the silent form expression found; returned my kiss of youthful daring, and understood my heart's quick sound. Then lived for me the bright creation. The silver rill with song was rife; the trees, the roses shared sensation, an echo of my boundless life." Rev. A. G. Bulfinch William Morris tells the story of Pygmalion and the image in some of the most beautiful verses of *The Earthly Paradise*. This is Galatea's description of her metamorphosis: "'My sweet', she said, 'as yet I am not wise, Or stored with words aright the tale to tell, But listen: when I opened first mine eyes I stood within the niche thou knowest well, And from my hand a heavy thing there fell Carved like these flowers, nor could I see things clear, But with a strange confused noise could hear.'ʻ

[5]Agamben, Giorgio, Ronald L. Martinez (Translation). *Stanzas: Word and Phantasm in Western Culture*. Theory and History of Literature, Vol. 69. Minneapolis, University of Minnesota Press. 1993 Agamben includes a number of Pygmalion images from manuscripts in the Bodleian library and Bibliotheque Nationale

[6] I am indebted to Max Kozloff for the first part of the title to this chapter. This author's critique of performance and body art "Pygmalion Reversed" appeared in <u>Art Forum</u> November 1975. Ernst Gombrich also explored "Pygmalion's Power" albeit it in the traditional sense of bringing life to an inanimate object. See *Art and Illusion A Study in the Psychology of Pictorial Representation* New York, Bollingen Series Princeton 1969 pp 93-115. See also Barber, B., "Towards a Taxonomy of Performance and Body Art" in Bronson AA and Gale, P (ed) *Performance by Artists* Toronto, Art Metropole 1979.

[7]Giorgio Agamben *Stanzas: Word and Phantasm in Western Culture* (1993) has outlined epistemological and phantomatic origins of the fetish object *viz* "suggestively characterized as *objet de perspective (perspective object)* or *object de manqué* (object of lack), or to perceive the closeness of the fetish object to the domain of cultural creation" 33-35 and *passim*.

[8]At the time Powers and Wenneker were two fine art students studying at the Ontario College of Art and Design (OCAD).

Bürger, P. *The Theory of the Avant-Garde* Peter Bürger makes the distinction between the organic and the inorganic work, arguing that artists who produce   organic work treat their material as living whereas avant-gardist artists "kill the 'life' out of the material, that is "tearing it out of its original context that gives it meaning" (Bürger, P., 1984: 70).

[9] Kim Honey "But is it Art?" Globe and Mail Saturday July 21st, 2001

[10] Homi Bhabha *The Location of Culture* London New York Routledge 1994:67

[11] I am indebted to colleague Scott Mackenzie for bringing this film to my attention at an FSAC conference in St Johns, Newfoundland. Roger Corman produced two versions of *Bucket of Blood* one in 1959 and the other in 1990.

[12] Joel Black's *The Aesthetics of Murder: A Study in Romantic Literature and Contemporary Culture* (1996)

[13]The phenomenological problem *par excellence* discussed extensively by Martin Heidegger in his famous 1935   University of Freiburg lectures. See Heidegger, M. *An Introduction to Metaphysics* trans. Ralph Manheim New Haven London. Yale University Press 1987 (first published 1959, p9). Being there implies awareness of Being p.29.

[14]Wilde, O. *The Ballad of Reading Jail*

[15] Paisley as it is defined in the Shorter Oxford Dictionary has feminine connotations. "A distinctive detailed pattern of curved feather shaped figures. A soft woolen garment having this pattern (Scotland).

[16] This reference to mass killing resulting in the production of an ash tray is somewhat odd and may be an unconscious   reference to the fate of Jews at Auschwitz which in the 1950's was still sinking into the minds of North Americans.

[17] This is also how Christopher Cross the artist in Fritz Lang's film *Scarlet Street* is punished.

[18] Nietzsche, Friedrich *Beyond Good and Evil: Prelude to a Philosophy of the Future* Translated by R.J. Hollingdale with an introduction by Michael Tanner London, Penguin Books, 1973:158

[19] Nietzsche p.159

[20] Ibid p.161

[21]Reynold Humphries "Peeping Tom: Voyeurism, the camera and the spectator n Film Reader 193-200 (1980)

[22] Adams P. "Father, can't you see I'm filming?" in Brennan, T and Jay, M., *Vision in Context: Historical and Contemporary Perspectives on Sight* New York Routledge 1996 pp 205-214

[23] Ibid

[24] The plaster cream cheese bagel paperweights are a reference to the work of the New York based Pop artist Claes Oldenburg.

[25]The telephone number "two-four-three- three-four-six, Oh" is an expression of surprise or 9/13 making an unlucky combination.

[26] Kiki is also the name of a famous black American dancer and stripper working in Paris in the 1920's who was favoured by the Surrealists.

[27] Constructed by artist Nora Chavoosian.

[28] These two figures parody a couple of beatniks who appear in Roger Corman's *Bucket of Blood* although production codes would not permit the positive identification of a character's sexual orientation in films made at this time

[29] Some of the paper glued to Kiki's sculpture is money, including a $20.00 dollar bill that at one point Paul thinking that it's his, attempts to rip from the sculpture. With this detail Scorsese reinforces "the umbilical cord of gold" (Clement Greenberg) that connects art to capital is actually closer than the nearest gallery.

[30] Derrida J. *The Truth in Painting* Trans Bennington, G. and McLeod, I. Chicago, University of Chicago Press, 1987:6

[31] Baker, S. *The Postmodern Animal* London Reaktion Books 2000 See also Baker's essay "Animal Rights and Wrongs" in <u>Tate </u>Issue #26 Autumn 2001

[32] Baker, *The Postmodern Animal* p.43

[33] Ibid. p.44

[34] Bhabha, H. *The Location of Culture* 1994 .,75

[35] Ibid p. 67

[36] I am indebted to Giorgio Agamben's discussion of Freud's 1927 article on the Fetish (*Festischismus*) which originally appeared in the *Internationale Zeitschrift für Psychoanalyse* (Vol 13) also in the *Standard Edition of the Complete Psychological Works of Sigmund Freud* Vol 21 Translation and Edited by James Strachey London Hogarth Press 1961, p 152. Agamben, *Stanzas* Chapter 6 "Freud or the Absent Object" pp31-35

[37]Bhabha 1994 p.75

[38] Agamben 1993:32

[39] Ibid

[40] Seneca's rendering in De Brevitate Vitae sect. 1. Hippocrates (c. 460-357 BC)

Chapter 6

Hitchcock's Art Crimes

"Let's say I'm a painter who paints flowers. What interests me is the way in which things are treated. But on the other hand, if I were a painter, I would say: 'I can only paint something that contains a message.' " (Alfred Hitchcock)[1]

"I'm not self-indulgent where content is concerned. I'm only self- indulgent about treatment. I'd compare myself to an abstract painter. My favourite painter is Klee."(Alfred Hitchcock)[2]

As a member of the audience for a post-screening panel discussion of a newly revised print of *Psycho* (1960) at the Hitchcock Centenary Conference held in New York city in October 1999,[3] I had the opportunity to ask a couple of questions of screenwriter Joseph Stefano and actors Patricia Hitchcock, Janet Leigh and Teresa Wright.[4] I was curious about a few details in the film that had puzzled me for some time and asked Joseph Stefano, *Psycho*'s screenwriter about the significance of the date Friday, December Eleventh, 2.43 p.m. matted into the establishing shots of Phoenix, Arizona. I declared that my ulterior motive for asking this question was that I had the fortune, or misfortune, to share a birthday with this date, albeit a decade before the film was made. Stefano's answer was straightforward enough. It went something like this: "Christmas decorations were up in the city and we wanted to establish a time for the narrative that coincided with the actual date of the filming but that was nevertheless not the week of Christmas, so we settled on December eleventh…no significance really," he added nonchalantly, as a provocative or dismissive afterthought. My second question was addressed to all of the panelists. I opened with something I had gleaned from reading the Truffaut interviews with Hitchcock, the John Russell Taylor and Donald Spoto biographies:[5] "Mr. Hitchcock was fond of saying that 'it's all in the details' and you are aware that much has been made of some of the details in this and other

Hitchcock films.[6] My question is this: who chose the art works, paintings, sculptures, and other artifacts on the set, Hitchcock himself, the art director, the set dresser, or some combination of these three individuals?"[7] Their answer was unexpectedly swift. Stefano and Pat Hitchcock replied almost simultaneously, as if they had rehearsed and delivered the answer a hundred times, which perhaps they had: "The choice of how the set looked and what was used to decorate it was done collaboratively at meetings of all concerned. Decisions were arrived at through consensus." Now, steeped in the powerful array of authorial codes in Hitchcock's films that have become the stock-in-trade of Hitchcock scholarship and a substantive argument for auteurship itself, I had some difficulty with this response but I was not about to quibble over it in this context. I suspected that their answer was perhaps calculated to both protect Hitchcock from any imputed impropriety over his aesthetic choices in *Psycho* (for example, the type of shower curtain, or toilet he chose), and to obtain the greatest amount of cultural capital for some of his collaborators, many of whom are still alive and deeply in the shadow of the Master. I framed the panelists' answer in these terms and recognized that neither their response to my question, or indeed my conjectures about it, were the last words on the subject. I knew for instance that Hitchcock liberally applied his signature to many details throughout his films and the reader is probably familiar with these through the plethora of books, critical essays and reviews in the still rapidly expanding Hitchcock bibliography.[8] One has to think only of his cameo appearances, his fetishistic attachment to Aryan blondes for his female leads, the explicit references to food, sex and alcohol, the parergonal significance of mirrors and windows as frames within frames, strangling as his preferred *modus operandi* for murder, whistling and the endless parade of apothegms ("it never rains but it pours," "it's an ill wind that blows nobody any good," "a bird in the hand is worth two in the bush," *etc.*), that are sprinkled liberally throughout his films. These signature flourishes appear irrespective of whether they are part of the screenplay, play script or novel upon which the films are based. Donald Spoto, for example, acknowledges that there are references to brandy, Hitchcock's favorite drink, in at least 51 of his 53 films.[9] From his first British sound film *Blackmail* (1929) onward, whistling also appears in different guises in nearly every film, and although I set out to initially challenge the idea, references to art, artists and art history are almost as common.[10] It could be argued that this type of authoring or branding strategy was employed almost unconsciously by Hitchcock as a compensatory reflex action (a hidden injury of class perhaps), least the creative authority he had invested in the production process was not visible in the finished work.[11] I conjectured that given Hitchcock's early experience as an art director[12] and his penchant for total control of his *oeuvre*, it was probably safe to assume that many of the choices, if not all, were his, or at the very least influenced by his tastes and desires for the film. I was, however, attracted to alternate points of view, particularly those that could present a challenge to, or problematises the received wisdom on the matter.

11. Alfred Hitchcock 1960

It's all in the details

Since the 1960's identified by some scholars as the beginning of the institution of film studies as a separate field of academic endeavor, there have been several, what could be termed theoretical blind spots in the film studies project, particularly where auteurship and genre typing is concerned.[13] As an artist and a cultural historian, I am very familiar with these *punctum caecae* in art history but there is ample evidence of a similar scotomisation in cinema discourse, particularly within the overlapping discursive fields of director, genre and national cinema studies. What follows are some notes and reflections on a couple of these theoretical blind spots before I engage in a reading of Alfred Hitchcock's representations of art, artists and art history in his films.

It is perhaps a truism that no artist works alone, particularly in the production of film, and yet there exists a whole institutional edifice built upon the reductive principles of authorship that nominate the director as the primary creative source (author) of the work, irrespective of how many dozens or even hundreds of individuals have contributed to its existence. How often do we read a confirmation of authorship in those works that are associated with a putative author? Is "the personal factor as the criterion of reference," the classic auteurship pre-condition outlined by Andre Bazin in 1957, appropriate anymore for determining authorship? Or should we submit to Roland Barthes' "death of the author" and the consequent birth of the omnipotent reader who is *ipso facto* also an author? Perhaps we should endorse Michel Foucault's "pervasive anonymity of discourse," or Derrida's deconstructive strategies for our critical reading of the cinematic work of film directors? I suggested earlier that a parergonal reading of the artist's production is necessary for the signal operations of the *ecrivain* (author) to be distinguished from the *ecrivant* (writer). This is Jacques Derrida's third prescription for reading – understanding/comprehending – a work; any work. How then does a Derridian approach permit a critical reading of Hitchcock whose work has become a staple argument for the existence of auteurship itself? This chapter will attempt to provide a response to this question.

We should reflect once again upon the supremely ironic statement that Hitchcock made earlier in his career to Claude Chabrol and Eric Rohmer. "Let's say I'm a painter who paints flowers. What interests me is the way in which things are treated. But on the other hand, if I were a painter, I would say: "I can only paint something that contains a message."[14] At the time Hitchcock made this comment, as indeed now, flower painters were often dismissed as rank amateurs or painters of 'chocolate box' art.[15] But in this comment Hitchcock was probably displaying his characteristic British self-mocking humility; at once disavowing his directorial power but also (re-) investing his role with the symbolic capital of the high culture fine artist. Perhaps with his comment he had a Dutch genre painter in mind such as Jan Davidsz Heem, whose detail fetish is apparent in the aesthetic treatment of petals and leaves with light reflected through water and on glass vases and mirrors, an artist definitely worthy of emulation but one whose work, as far as Hitchcock is concerned, must carry a message! Hitchcock's reference to "the way things are treated" is also echoed in many other statements that reduce the complexities of performance and representation into trite processes and treatments. The final sentence of the statement "I can only paint something that contains a message" implies a social/moral dimension to his project and an implicit rejection of Paterian aestheticism – l'art *pour l'art* – and certainly any forms of modernist non-objective abstraction, although several decades later Hitchcock could happily compare himself to the abstract artist Paul Klee. "I'm not self-indulgent where content is concerned. I'm only self-indulgent about treatment. I'd compare myself to an abstract painter. My favourite painter is Klee."[16] Hitchcock also compared his role as film director to that of a music composer. Discussing the role of improvisation when he was beginning to work on *Topaz* (1969), he said: You can improvise and you should improvise but I think it should be done in an office, where there are no electricians waiting and no actors waiting, and you can improvise all you want -- ahead of time. Sometimes, I compare it to a composer who is trying to write a piece of music with a full orchestra in front of him. Can you imagine him saying "Flute, give me that note again will you? Thank you flute," and he writes it down. A painter has his canvas and he uses his charcoal sketch and he goes to work on that canvas with a pre-conceived idea. I'm sure he doesn't guess it as he goes along. So I'm not in approval of improvisation on the studio stage, while the actor is on the phone about his next picture, and that kind of stuff.... I shoot a pre-cut picture. In other words, every piece of film is designed to perform a function.[17]

To my knowledge Hitchcock never compared himself to a surgeon, an architect or a lawyer, and his attachment to the relative freedom – creative autonomy – of the artist (painter and composer), was not always as ambivalent as these statements would imply. Throughout his life he remained somewhat of an aesthetic conservative, resisting the creative extremes of modernism, particularly abstraction and avant-garde experimentation, while maintaining for his film productions a strong attachment to naturalism and careful preliminary planning to ensure that his films would meet with reception from as wide an audience as possible. In this sense he acted contrarily, paying tribute to the autonomy of the fine artist while simultaneously reinforcing the pecuniary interests of the artisan who endorses the notion that viable creative productivity could only continue with commercial success.

In Hitchcock's artisanal vocabulary "treatments" are closely associated with his use of the favoured word "details." In his Encyclopedia Britannica entry on "Film Production" Hitchcock divided the screenplay, which he considered the architectural 'blueprint' for the film, into three stages, first "the outline" providing the essence of the narrative or original idea, often derived from a book or play script, followed by the "treatment" which sets out rough dialogue, blocks movement for the actors and provides technical directions "to the art department for the sets, to the costume department, to makeup, to the music department and so-on." The third element is the "detailed screenplay [that] enables the director to hold securely to the unity of form and to the cinematic structure of the action, while leaving him free to work intimately and concentratedly with the actors."[18] Hitchcock stressed, "it's all in the details" but what did he actually mean by this rather casual statement? Taken literally "it's all in the details" could mean that the details: items, elements and artifacts both within and outside the main field of action provide the key to what is happening throughout the work. This is certainly the case, when one thinks of fetish items, and narrative drivers that appear in many of his films such as the glove (*Blackmail*), a ring (*Shadow of a Doubt*), keys and purses (*Notorious, Under Capricorn, Dial M for Murder, Marnie*) or tiepin (*Frenzy*),[19] about which much has been written by Hitchcock scholars: Robin Wood, Sydney Gottlieb, Tania Modleski, Raymond Bellour, Slavoj Žižek, Mladen Dolar among others.[20] Zizek discusses these details somewhat differently as *sinthoms* "characteristic details which persist without implying common meaning"[21] But perhaps Hitchcock is being somewhat more devious – opaque – with this statement about details. He may have used the phrase as an ironic dismissive - or perhaps even as a MacGuffin itself - to disarm any critics who thought they knew exactly what he and his films were about. Saying "it's all in the details" could also distance the director from affirming the extreme division of labor and collaborative processes that are so much a part of the business of film production.[22] Details that only he, Hitchcock as director had mastery of, signaled to others that he was an exemplary author, or better, a fine artist, who could boast, or others could boast of him, that he had the whole film registered in his mind before it was even shot; that he had, in the words of a celebrated phrase from another context, "signed the whole operation!" Ingmar Bergman, Jean-Luc Godard, Claude Chabrol, Roman Polanski, David Lynch and Peter Greenaway are other film directors who have asserted this (Wagnerian) omnipotent control - as the universal *regisseur* - assigning a privileged place for details to ensure that their imprimatur is engraved on each production.

Hitchcock's attachment to art was not always so confident - though ambivalent - as his statements comparing himself to both a representational genre painter and an abstract painter would imply. As I will attempt to elucidate, he remained throughout his life somewhat of an aesthetic conservative, resisting the creative extremes of modernist avant-gardes, particularly abstraction. While much has been made of Hitchcock's borrowing from German expressionist film, the primary attachment he craved through his association with art was to assume the symbolic capital of the high culture artist, but he resisted the temptation of adopting avant-garde strategies to achieve it. And although he maintained a strong interest in art and artists throughout his life and even built a credible art collection, his quixotic relationship to the work of the modernist avant-gardes is played out convincingly in many of his films and statements.[23] In an important sense Hitchcock was both of, and not of his time, a modernist with respect to his choice of the most contemporary medium of his time - film - but in his life and beliefs, as Paula Cohen

notes, very much the "stereotype of bourgeois caution and conventionality that Lyton Strachey and fellow modernists satirized and relegated to the dust heap of culture."[24]
As a teenager Hitchcock had demonstrated a fair aptitude for art and design, but he was encouraged by his family to pursue more useful skills. As a result his training as an artist was somewhat peripatetic and limited to a few night classes as London University during 1915 while he was working at Henley's Telegraph and Cable Company. As Spoto describes it:

> The work (at Henley's) did not engage his interest, and it was about the same time that he returned to classes in other subjects one or two evenings a week in London; art history, economics and political science lectures engaged him for a few months and then some additional classes in drawing. The job of estimator was to have been his stable form of endeavour, but his interest began to shift toward the arts. Eventually he took a course in painting. [25]

Hitchcock's art training provided him with a visual vocabulary and limited understanding of art theory --"the uses of colour, shadow and light"[26] -- and he had occasion to remark on some aspects of his training with Francois Truffaut. In a discussion about the problems involved in lighting colour films he said:

> We must bear in mind that, fundamentally there's no such thing as colour; in fact there's no such thing as a face, because until the light hits it is nonexistent. After all one of the first things I learned in the school of art was that there is no such thing as a line; there's only the light and the shade. On my first day in school I did a drawing; it was quite a good drawing, but because I was drawing lines, it was totally incorrect and the error was immediately pointed out to me.[27]

At this time art education in British art schools was fairly standardized, based on copy books developed in the mid 19th century, drawing from casts and the copying of paintings, life drawing, as well as the learning of perspective and some basic elements of design. It is interesting to compare the type of conservative art training that Hitchcock would have received at Goldsmiths College, London University during the early years of the twentieth century to the exhibitions then making the news in the London daily newspapers. When Roger Fry's exhibition *Manet and the Post-Impressionists* opened to the public on November 8th 1910 the paintings by Gauguin, Van Gogh and Matisse stimulated much negative commentary in the press about the maltreatment of the human body.[28] Fry's groundbreaking Futurism show at the Sackville Gallery in 1912 also incited much negative commentary and the appearance of many satirical cartoons in the popular press. Bold headlines appeared declaring: FREAK PICTURES, ART THAT ALARMS; FUTURIST PUZZLES, REBEL ART, SHOCKING ART and THE LATEST OUTBREAK. And much to the chagrin of many members of the public, representative works and artists from the European avant-garde began to trickle into several London dealer galleries. F.T. Marinetti the anarchist founder of Futurism lectured in London during 1913-14,[29] providing a rich ground for the introduction of early continental modernist aesthetics and avant-garde politics onto English soil, and directly stimulating the production of another whole crop of graphic satires and parodies.[30] In these satirical cartoon images (1914-18), modern art is often likened to the destructive forces of the war that was at this time consuming a generation of Europe's young men. Hitchcock must have been aware of the contestation over the terms and conditions for the reception of contemporary art but his sympathies in his early years probably lay with the satirists working for *Punch* and other popular journals of the time. In the United States the Armory show (1913) was scandalizing the public of the three cities, New York, Chicago and Boston that it visited and the Vorticists under Wyndham Lewis were firmly entrenched as the leading avant-garde movement in England. Hitchcock's training at Goldsmiths included illustration and composition, sketching from antique models and some drawing from life. With respect to this aspect of his art education, McGilligan mentions that one of Hitchcock's teachers sent the class out to draw people at railway stations. Hitchcock was a train spotter from a very early age and friends remember his extraordinary memory for the train timetable. Although he spoke little about his specific memories of art education at this time he did note a lecture by E.J. Sullivan an artist renowned for his fine illustrations for magazines, newspapers and books.[31]

The published accounts of Hitchcock's taste in art are few and far between but still tantalizing windows into the views of a man living in an age of great challenges to the dominant aesthetic tastes, the overturning of Victorian attitudes and the birth of modernism. He was familiar with the work of the English modernist sculptor Jacob Epstein but as a joke he had an Epstein bust made of his colleague, producer Michael Balcon and gave it to him as a salve for making a 100% profit from him over the sale of a script. "While we were shooting *Waltzes from Vienna*, at this low ebb of my career, Michael Balcon came to see me working at the studio. He had given me my first chance to become a director. He said 'What are you doing after this picture?' I said, 'I have a playscript that was written some time ago; it's in a drawer, somewhere.' I brought in the scenario; he liked it and offered to buy it. So I went to my former producer, John Maxwell, and brought it from him for two hundred and fifty pounds. I sold it to Gaumont-British, which was headed by Balcon for five hundred pounds. But I was so ashamed of the hundred percent profit that I had the sculptor Jacob Epstein do a bust of Balcon with the money. And I presented Balcon with Epstein's bust of him."[32]

Reading between the lines, this anecdote reveals much about Hitchcock at this time in his life; his class anxieties about money and profit – capitalism – his catholic appreciation of reciprocity, guilt and atonement for sin for profiting over someone whose generosity had benefited him, and perhaps his ambivalence over the type of modernist portraiture produced by Jacob Epstein. In discussing with Truffaut the difference between making a documentary and a dramatic film, Hitchcock was quite clear on issues of objectivity and verisimilitude in the cinematic representation of narrative as well as the difference between painting and colour photography. "To insist that a storyteller stick to the facts is just as ridiculous as to demand of a representative painter that he show objects accurately. 'What's the ultimate in representative (representational) painting? Colour photography. Don't you agree?' and later, 'We should have total freedom to do as we like, just so long as its not dull."[33]

When Hitchcock was directing *Spellbound* as a psychological thriller, he expressed a wish to "break with the traditional way of handling dream sequences through a blurred and hazy screen." He discussed his reasons for contracting the Surrealist painter Salvador Dali with Truffaut. "I asked Selznick if he could get Dali to work with us and he agreed, though I think he didn't really understand my reasons for wanting Dali. He probably thought I wanted his collaboration for publicity purposes." But the real reason Hitchcock disclosed was that he "wanted to convey the dreams with great visual sharpness and clarity, sharper than the film itself. I wanted Dali because of the sharpness of his work. (De) Chirico has the same quality, you know, the long shadows, the infinity of distance, and the converging lines of perspective." But he later admitted, "He didn't care for the scenario."[34] Hitchcock's art training and his early introduction to film as a scenographer certainly provided him with an excellent visual memory, reinforcing the meticulous control of set details that he used to provide key signifiers both to the action within the *mise en scène* and also to propel the narrative. For example in a key dramatic scene in *The Paradine Case* (1948), a 'fat' woman (large and overweight in today's politically correct language), is shown munching an apple to the side of a mid shot of the central protagonists in the film. Discussing this shot with Truffaut he said, "what I am trying to bring out is that these *elaborate details* are generally overlooked by the public because all the attention is focused on the major characters in the scene. Therefore you put them in for *your own satisfaction* and of course, for the sake of enriching the film"[35] (emphasis added). The apple scene in the *Paradine Case* provides an interruption in the film's diegesis. It is something that sticks out; in Lacanian terms.... *un petit à*, which also has been variously described as a "*punctum*" (Roland Barthes), "stain" (Pascal Bonitzer) or "blot" (Slavoj Žižek); in every case altering the libidinal and political economy of the scene, reinforcing the social verisimilitude of the event, yet providing another layer to the symbolic registers of meaning.

Unlike Freud's 'cigar' or Gertrude Stein's 'rose' in Hitchcock's world, a fat woman eating an apple is not simply a fat woman eating an apple. She paradoxically signifies pleasurable yet obsessive excess – gluttony – and paradoxically, health, "eating an apple a day keeps the doctor away" to provide the unspoken apothegm which would probably have registered in the mind of Hitchcock, who with his own weight problems, would have had no difficulty identifying with this woman or the Judge, the other overweight person in the film. And like the story of Adam and Eve in the Garden of Eden this apple eating is also a symbol of the Devil's temptation in utopia (the film's overall theme), a danger signal to gluttony and sexual obsession, the subversion of religious piety and the breakdown of morality.

In Hitchcock's textual world "it's all in the details," is often literally that. There are many implicit and explicit references to art, artists and art history in Hitchcock's films (see appendix 2), some appearing as 'details' and others in more prominent roles in the narrative. In six films: *Easy Virtue* (1927), *Blackmail* (1929), *Rebecca* (1940), *Rear Window* (1954), *The Trouble with Harry* (1955), and *Vertigo* (1957), artists figure prominently in the narrative. In *Easy Virtue* (1927) and *Blackmail* (1929), two artists are key protagonists, one a philanderer who kills his lover's husband; the other, an attempted rapist who is killed by his intended victim, thus providing at this early juncture in Hitchcock's work one bilateral axis – art and crime – upon which his work was to unfold for the next fifty years. Throughout his films Hitchcock also makes references to art and art history, even when he is closely following a script where art is of little or no consequence to the direction of the narrative, for example in the opening memorial sequence of *Secret Agent* (1936), a large painted portrait of a young soldier hanging on the wall becomes the object of the gaze of the one-armed attendant. Paintings also engage the attention of characters for periods of time in *The Lodger, Blackmail, Bon Voyage, Suspicion, The Paradine Case, The Trouble with Harry, Rope, Under Capricorn, Strangers on a Train, Rebecca, Vertigo, North by Northwest, Psycho* and *Frenzy*. In *Rebecca*, both X (Joan Fontaine) and her dead father are identified as artists and a painted portrait of Rebecca is instrumental in a key scene between X and Miss Danvers over the choice of dress she will wear to the costume ball that she pleaded her husband Maxim De Winter (Laurence Olivier) to arrange. In *Rear Window*, 'Jeff' L.B Jeffries (James Stewart) the press photographer laid up in his apartment is surrounded by neighbours who are artists: a sculptor, a composer, a dancer, an opera singer, and with Thomas de Quincey in mind, a murderer functioning as an artist (Raymond Burr). In *Vertigo*, Midge Wood (Barbara Bel Geddes) is a lingerie designer and painter, and a portrait of Carlotta Valdez in the

Palace of the Legion of Honour also holds the attention of Madeleine Elster who pretends to be the reincarnation of her great great grandmother. There are explicit and implicit references to art, artists and art history - the institution art - in over forty of Alfred Hitchcock's films - all of them, if *tableaux vivants* framed by windows, mirrors and doors are included in the tally.

The Exhibitions *Spellbound: Art and Film* (1996); *Notorious: Alfred Hitchcock and Contemporary Art* 1999 and *Hitchcock and Art* (Montreal Museum of Fine Arts) did less to provide insights into Hitchcock's own use of art and art history than to demonstrate the use other artists have made of his work. All three exhibitions profiled the work of dozens of artists and filmmakers who have profitably mined Hitchcock's films for their own creative endeavours, among them, Cindy Sherman, Tony Oursler, Chris Marker, Douglas Gordon, and Stan Douglas. The curators of *Hitchcock and Art* Guy Cogeval Director of the Montreal Museum of Fine Arts and Dominique Paini Director of the Cinémathèque Française produced a wonderful list of artists whose work they suggested was associated with Hitchcock: Beardsley, Munch, Vuillard, di Chirico, Klee, Ernst, Magritte, Hopper, Martini and others less well known such as Fernand Khnopff, Meredith Frampton, Carol Willink Leon Spilliaert, Ralston Crawford. But as one critic wrote for the *New York Times Review*, with this eclectic mix "Hitchcock's visual art would by this reckoning have been a kind of indigestible potpourri of the pre-Raphaelites, the Symbolists, the Blaue Reiter group, the Surrealists and every variety of Pop Culture from London music hall posters to the cover art of *Harpers Bazaar*."[36] The exhibition was so loaded with imagery that it became somewhat surreal, which judging from Hitchcock's comment about Dali's extravagant creative work on *Spellbound*, had he seen the exhibition, he may not have "cared for the scenario." In the introductory catalogue essay Paini warns his viewers not to expect a literal connection between the exhibited items and Hitchcock's film, but more of the associations that one would make in a waking dream. "We have placed our trust in intuitive constellations of images that stood out upon seeing the films again."[37] Although the voluminous 498-page catalogue contains eighteen essays, over half of the publication consists of illustrations of works in the exhibition arranged thematically under headings. For example, Oscar Wilde's "For Each Man Kills the Thing He Loves"(*The Ballad of Reading*

Gaol), places stills of Ingrid Bergman in *Under Capricorn* arranged with photographs by Julia Margaret Cameron and paintings by the Pre-Raphaelites, Dante Gabrielle Rosetti and Edward Burne-Jones, a comparison apparently aimed at revealing Hitchcock's attachment to representations of Victorian womanhood. Similarly Madeleine's dip into San Francisco Bay in *Vertigo* is placed in a comparative context with Millais' *Ophelia* and Schlobach's painting *The Dead Woman* (1890). Odilon Redon's famous drawings and paintings of eyes *Cyclops* (1880, 1898), *Eyes in the Forest* (1875), are compared to the peeping eye of Norman Bates, his Mother's empty eye sockets, and Janet Leigh's 'lifeless eye' in *Psycho*. With the exception of the two essays on Hitchcock's collaboration with Salvador Dali on *Spellbound*, Julia Tanski's "The Symbolist Woman in Alfred Hitchcock's Films" and Stephane Aquin's "Hitchcock and Contemporary Art" few of the contributors actually discuss art in Hitchcock's films but rather engage in impressionistic projections onto Hitchcock of his 'indebtedness' to popular culture and high art. This is not to suggest that there are not very specific relationships between Hitchcock's film and painting, that is tableaux *vivant* configured analogically in many scenes in his films, as well as the inclusion of specific art objects, and architecture in his work, but rather that these have to be more closely identified as indexical as opposed to merely referential, to give one famous example, the close similarity between the view of the Diner beyond Jeff's apartment block in *Rear Window* to *Nighthawks* (1942) the famous Edward Hopper painting of a city Diner and its late night inhabitants.

The Lodger

The Lodger A Story of the London Fog (1926),[38] Hitchcock's most successful early silent film, employs explicit references in the narrative to theatre and music, chorus girls, models, and five painted portraits of fair haired women are prominently displayed in the Lodger's rented room, one of which, an allegorical (eroticised) image of a naked woman in bondage tied to a rock, 'sticks out' – "a phallic anamorphosis" – as Slavoj Žižek would say. [39] In the context of the other more benign head and shoulder portraits of women, the woman in bondage image that appears for a mere one or two second period, seems totally out of place and raises the question why Hitchcock, and /or his art directors (C. Wilfred (Wilf) Arnold and Bertram (Bert)

Evans, would have placed this painting in the context of the Lodger's rented room of the Bunting's middle class household. I believe that the insertion of this image of the naked woman in bondage is an early example of an ironic detail put into the path of the camera for Hitchcock's personal satisfaction, and in this instance because it offers a contrast to the rather effete hand movements and languid mannerisms of the Lodger (Ivor Novello), who was openly homosexual. With this insertion, Hitchcock provides another set of signifiers – sado-masochism and castration – to the melodramatic look of anxiety and fear that Novello portrays when we see his image reflected in the mirror that also contains a reflection of one of the paintings of fair haired young women, one of Hitchcock's first triadic assays of an image within an image within an image. The Lodger is both attracted to and repulsed by these images and he attempts to turn the faces of these portraits to the wall exclaiming to his landlady Mrs. Bunting and her daughter Daisy: "I'm afraid I don't like these pictures." At his request Daisy and her mother remove the pictures from the room and it is only later when the Lodger, suspected of being the Avenger, is being interrogated by the police that his antipathy to these images is provided with another rationale when he produces a photographic portrait of his sister, another beautiful young fair haired girl who was the Avenger's first victim. This concern with the revealing concealing aspects of representation is reiterated in a scene where the Buntings are listening to the Lodger pacing in the room above and with an ingenious shot through a glass plate floor Hitchcock enables us to see what is in the 'mind's eye' of the listeners below by showing us a dynamic *sub rosa* view of the Lodger pacing his room.

In his camera direction, Hitchcock frequently employs mirrors, windows and doorways to frame a *tableau vivant*, this also becoming a common strategy to heighten tension, signal surveillance, and direct point-of-view dynamism and structure lighting design. For example the flashing neon light "Tonight Golden Curls" in the opening sequence to *The Lodger* is accompanied by a montage of medium and close-up shots of chorus girls in their dressing room laughing and preening themselves in front of mirrors, oblivious to the menacing Avenger who has claimed his sixth blond haired victim in the city precincts.[40] When the Lodger arrives at the Bunting's house we see his ominous looking silhouette image at the door which changes to a look of anxiety when he is reflected in the mirror of his room containing the portraits of the fair haired women. The Lodger is one of the first "wrong man" and double figures in Hitchcock's films. Spoto points out that Hitchcock would have been introduced to the double in school, noting that it would have been "reinforced in his moral education and his leisure reading. It is central, for example to Robert Louis Stevenson's *The Strange Case of Dr Jekyll and Mr Hyde* (1886), and to Oscar Wilde's *The Picture of Dorian Gray* (1891), popular works during Hitchcock's adolescent years, and works he read several times before beginning his film career."[41]

Downhill (1927), Hitchcock's fourth film again provides early sequences of a stage musical and chorus girls.[42] A mirror also features as an important framing device for some of the scenes and the actress Julia squirts perfume at a portrait of her leading man thus anthropomorphizing this image in a manner alluding to Oscar Wilde's *Portrait of Dorian Gray. Easy Virtue* (1927),[43] based on a Noel Coward play opens with an Art Deco silhouette of a camera with text reading "Virtue is its own reward they say but easy virtue is society's reward for a slandered reputation." The film contains a lengthy courtroom scene of a three-way scandal between Filton versus Filton and Claude Robson, the co-respondent a philandering artist who fell in love with his employer and murdered alcoholic husband. There are multiple references in this film to painting, art models, seduction and betrayal reproducing standard stereotypes about the role of the artist in society.

Blackmail

Claude Chabrol and Eric Rohmer argued that *Blackmail* (1929)[44] was the most important film in Hitchcock's oeuvre to establish his directorial strategies. With *The Lodger* and *Easy Virtue, Blackmail* also provided the template for Hitchcock's uses of art and artists. Crewe the artist (Cyril Ritchard, a dancer and comedian in real life) is killed accidentally by Alice White (Anny Ondra) the young woman he attempts to seduce and rape. Music and two portraits, "The Joker" and the other, a collaborative portrait caricature by Alice and Crewe, figure prominently in the narrative. The film also includes shots of the British Museum, antique sculpture and other artifacts prominent in the film's penultimate chase scene that was undertaken with the

Shüfftan rear projection process.[45] The primary narrative in *Blackmail* begins and ends with a whispered joke between a policeman and Alice that the viewers witness but do not hear. The play between appearance and reality, seeing and knowing, hearing and not seeing, and seeing and not hearing, figure in various ways throughout the narrative in this film, two versions of which were produced, one with sound and the other silent. The film opens with a parody of a documentary showing detectives from 'the flying squad' of New Scotland Yard racing in a van to an apartment building location in a working class district where they apprehend a criminal suspect, take him in for questioning and an identification line-up. The additive montage of this opening sequence beginning with a close-up of a spinning hubcap is similar to the dynamic editing of many British and European documentary films of the period with obvious references to Pudovkin's montage theory and the work of Eisenstein or Vertov. Although Hitchcock had profited from both German and Soviet film of the 1920's, the theoretical writings associated with both additive and dialectical montage had not yet appeared in English. Eisenstein published "The Cinematic Principle and the Ideogram" (originally as a postscript to N. Kaufmann's pamphlet "Japanese Cinema" in 1929, the same year that *Blackmail* was produced. This important essay and Eisenstein's "A Dialectic Approach to Film Form" from that same year were included in *Film Form* edited by Eisenstein, V.I. Pudovkin and G. V Alexandrov, one of the first film theory books to appear which Jay Leyda subsequently translated into English in 1949. Eisenstein's approach to film making was widely known and appreciated through the circulation of his films *Potemkin* (1925), *Strike* (1925), and *October* (1928). Hitchcock also learned his cinematic vocabulary through the work of F.W. Murnau *Tartuffe* (1922), *The Last Laugh* (1924), Fritz Lang, whose masterpiece *Metropolis* appeared to critical acclaim in 1926, and G.W. Pabst *Pandora's Box* (1928) and *Diary of a Lost Girl* (1929), which appeared the same year as *Blackmail*, and of course the signal work of D.W. Griffith whose films influenced them all.

Blackmail contains many Hitchcock motifs including a point-of-view shot of a mirror during the capture that shows the suspect that he is being surveyed by two policemen, and humorous shots of one of the detectives offering the apprehended suspect's trousers before they take him into custody and then back at the yard to offer him 'a nice cuppa tea,' while he chain smokes through the interrogation. Without the credits this section of *Blackmail* may have been mistaken for a documentary short before the main film and when it was first viewed it attracted the positive attention of many of Hitchcock's more political film colleagues for example John Grierson and Lindsay Anderson.[46] This documentary sequence showing the professionalism of Scotland Yard is followed by the meeting between the Detective Frank Webber (John Longden) and his awaiting fiancée, blond haired Alice White, one of the first of many Aryan blondes that populate Hitchcock's films. Alice has been waiting for some time to meet Frank from his shift and as he arrives the mustachioed sergeant at arms whispers a joke in her ear to which she responds by laughing uproariously, Frank joining in without knowing whether or not he is the butt of the joke. They cross crowded streets, take the tube where Hitchcock inserts his cameo, one of several scenes in *Blackmail* to show the impetuosity of youth in contrast to the staid behaviour of adults. In the tube train cameo Hitchcock is sitting behind a young boy who reaches over and pulls his trilby hat down over his eyes. And in another scene, that takes place outside Lyons Corner House in Coventry Street, Frank disobeys the order to go upstairs presented to them by the young boy door attendant wearing an oversized uniform, and steers Alice into the crowded ground floor of the restaurant. Here Hitchcock choreographs a humorous doubles scene by showing Frank and Alice and another older couple sitting uncomfortably across from one another. Both couples decide to get up simultaneously and move to smaller table; Frank leads Alice, and opposite them, the woman leads the man. The insertion of this short scene provides Hitchcock with the opportunity to visually comment upon what, at that time, was considered to be an emasculating characteristic of marriage, a woman leading a man. Alice soon picks a quarrel with Frank in order to spend some time with Crewe (Cyril Richard) a suave artist with whom she had previously made a casual agreement to meet at 6.30pm. Frank disgruntled disappears outside and Alice takes up with Crewe. The next scene reveals that Crewe has invited Alice to his studio and when they arrive at the building in which his studio flat is located they see a man outside surveying their entry. He calls out but Crewe doesn't acknowledge him and propels Alice into the foyer where he casually stops to pick up and check his mail then knocks on his landlady's door to question her about a note he has found. They finally begin to ascend the staircase to his studio apartment that is tracked by an impressive interior crane shot, one of many such 'bravura' shots, for example the towers sequences in *Vertigo*, which Hitchcock will employ over the next three decades. As they climb the stairs Alice and Crewe pass a framed painting of what resembles a devotional scene that is partially visible for a second or two through the upright 'bars' of the banister.

12. Crewe and Alice White painting in Alfred Hitchcock's *Blackmail* (1929)

When they arrive in the studio flat Alice looks around the studio and is clearly delighted by the tidy decor, the piano and the signs of an artist's studio, including a palette, brushes and a painting on one easel and a blank canvas on another. She goes to the window and looks down, a point-of-view shot to see a policeman walking his beat which momentarily allays any anxieties she or the viewer, may feel about her being in the lodgings of this dandyish artist. This apparent sense of safety dissipates in the next shot when she (and the spectator) gaze at the painting, a large three quarter length portrait of an opulent nearly toothless and somewhat angry looking jester in a classic Harlequin costume who is pointing and laughing - mocking the viewer(s). The shot of the jester figure contrasts with the previous shot of the policeman suggesting protection and Frank her cuckolded boyfriend, thus constructing a classic dialectical montage which signals warning! "I thay.... that's rather good isn't it? Alice says laughing hesitantly to allay her own fears. Joan Barry delivers this with a lispy RP (Received Pronunciation) accent of the upper classes, not the lower middle class accent of the daughter of a London shopkeeper. She then artlessly plunks a few notes out on the piano while Crewe is busying himself off camera whistling the vaudeville theme that he will later play. In another sign of her low cultural competency Alice makes an inept attempt to hold a large palette... Crewe helps her hold both palette and brush inviting her to "draw something Alice." "Shall I?" she asks, beginning to crudely scumble a childlike face on to the canvas. " Ooh look what I've done..."she exclaims. "Never mind" replies Crewe, "we'll finish this masterpiece together, taking her brush hand and following up with a flourish of deftly drawn lines with a "there... there and there" as he draws the breasts on this naked body... "Ooh.... you are awful..."she says in a coquettish fashion but then signs the painting with a flourish. He brings out the drinks and when she admires a shapely ballerina's dress with" I say how would I do for one of your models?" he urges her to put it on. "That's an idea..." Crewe replies " let's see it on you.." "Do you mean put it on?" Alice replies again naively, proceeding to cough as she takes a sip of the strong (probably brandy) alcohol, this response registering the fifth sign of her lack of experience and hence vulnerability. At first she hesitates to put the dress on and says she should really be getting along home. He feigns cool disinterest saying that he would have liked to sketch her in that dress and turns back to the piano to play the popular Noel Coward tune. She gives a small sign of resignation and goes behind the screen to change into the dress and as she does she says to Crewe "go on play something" as if to take his mind off her undressing behind the screen. "Just a minute.... how does that thing go?" he says, trying to recall a tune. In this tableau Hitchcock constructs a split screen effect to show Crewe playing the piano and singing while Alice is changing into the dress. "They say you're wild, an awful child... you are absolutely great...." "And that's a song about you dear" he says, after playing and singing a few bars. After slipping on the dress she pirouettes in front of him and announces "I can't do it up...." Crewe leans around to survey her body and replies "never mind" followed by, "wait a minute. That's not quite right," he says moving toward her and slipping the dress straps off her shoulders and then running his hands through her hair, he draws her mouth towards his and gives her a forced kiss. With a shocked expression on her face, Alice retreats and says quickly "I better go now..." In a somewhat unusual response Crewe turns away (in a half pirouette) hanging his head, and thrusting his hands deep into his pockets muttering almost resignedly, "I say...." The next shot of Crewe shows his face 'in a different light' with horizontal shadow bars introducing a switch of character from a Dr. Jekyll to Mr Hyde. Alice moves toward the screen partition and he quickly snatches away her dress from the top of this and flaunts it her as she says "please.... please" whereupon he throws it across the room saying "there it is..." and continues playing the piano. But before she can retrieve it he slams the lid on the piano then grabs her by the hands and pulls her towards his curtained bed. Alice screams and the film cuts to the policeman walking his beat outside oblivious to what is taking place inside. They struggle behind the curtain that moves violently back and forth with troubling sounds of escalating protestation from Alice. "No.... no..... no." Her right hand is seen groping around to connect with a bread knife resting on the bedside table, which she then draws back through the gap in the curtain, raises and presumably (because this is behind the curtain) stabs down with it or he falls onto the knife which enters some region of his body, critical enough that he expires within minutes. The struggle between the two subsides and Crewe's arm drops through the gap in the curtain, signaling his demise. Alice emerges looking wild eyed, shocked and disheveled but otherwise unscathed and bearing no signs of the blood that must have issued from Crewe's body on her ivory white foundation undergarments. She retrieves her dress that was draped over the Joker painting and with her right hand in a claw like clench, thrusts it down like a cat paw through the painting. Then on automatic pilot and looking somewhat like Cesare in *Dr Caligari* she wanders in a daze around the room, stopping momentarily before exiting - with some presence of mind - to erase the signature that could identify her from the caricatural 'masterpiece' that she and Crewe had painted together. Of course she left her gloves, one of which is obtained by Tracy the black mailer and the other by her suitor Frank, who recognizes it as belonging to Alice.

This murder scene and the so-called dream sequence that follows have been discussed many times from differing perspectives, some writers questioning the authenticity of the rape scene and thereby also the legitimacy of Alice's defendable position, should she be indicted; others describing it purely in formalist cinematic terms or concentrating upon the symbolism offered by the 'clown' or 'jester' painting. Maurice Yacowar for example, identifies the clown as "in the spirit of corrective comedy, recalling the shrew, manic wisdom of the jester in *King Lear*... The painting like its dapper, elegant artist, works as a test of the people it meets. It is the very spirit of irony, seeming innocent but a tricky test of its viewer's moral alertness."[47] Modleski suggests that the 'jester corrective' is the patriarchal response to the evident (temporary) control of the woman, arguing that if Yacowar "is right to see a self-reflexive element in the panting, to see that the artist in the film as a representative of Hitchcock the artist, then by extension, the film maker's work of art." She adds that it if this is so, "then *Blackmail* would be like the painting (of the jester) in the final shot, a cruel but not unusual joke on woman, a joke which the critic retells in his own style."[48] Modleski also employs a quote from Cixous to argue that if castration (after Mulvey) is always at stake for the male in Hollywood narrative, then decapitation is at stake for the female as elsewhere."

I will offer here a slightly different reading of the key signifiers in this scene. Crewe the artist is definitely a dandy in the Wildean sense, cultured, witty and urbane. He is dressed in a fashionable three piece bespoke suit with accessories (a matching overcoat, trilby and cane); he is obviously a talented portrait painter, musician (pianist and singer), well educated, judging by his upper-class accent, with a high quotient (in the Bourdieuian sense) of symbolic capital and all round cultural competency. He is older and single, and his performing of masculinity is more ambiguous than Modleski and other feminist film critics have been willing to admit. One has only to look at the languid manner he flips through his mail when they arrive at his apartment building and also the strange ambivalent movement he makes after his stolen kiss leads to Alice's request to leave, a half pirouette – matching Alice's in theatricality – followed by an effete resignation of power when he places his hands in his pockets with a politely resigned "I say...." Hitchcock uses Cyril Ritchard in the Crewe role precisely because his masculinity contrasts with that represented by other males in the film, particularly the rather stolid and predictable middle class male figures of Mr White, Alice's father, her fiancé detective Frank Webber, and the stereotypical working class criminals, one in the beginning documentary sequence and Tracy the blackmailer. This is the same contrast in masculinity that Hitchcock offers in *The Lodger* and many of his other films especially *Murder, Secret Agent, Strangers on a Train, Rope, I Confess*, and *Frenzy*. As a dandy Crewe conforms Baudelaire's perception that "they don't have erections," an opinion that would be hard to justify to Alice during her struggle behind the curtain but Hitchcock, I believe, wants the viewers to have ambiguous feelings about Crewe, to identify with him at the outset and then to recognize that he may not have deserved his fate and that perhaps Alice should not have gotten away 'Scot free' without a charge of manslaughter.[49]   Crewe is an altogether different male to the lascivious stereotype of an artist who is constitutionally (ideologically) predisposed to rape women at any given opportunity.

The Trouble with Harry

Hitchcock paid $11,000 to acquire the rights to British author John Trevor Story's novel *The Trouble with Harry* (1950), and in 1954 asked John Michael Hayes to produce the screenplay for this dark comedy released in 1955.[50] According to Hayes after completing *To Catch a Thief* Hitchcock wanted to do this film" just for fun and relief from what he was doing regularly."[51] His long association with composer Bernard Hermann also began with this film and this is only one of two Hitchcock films where a murder does not occur yet a corpse is present, the other film being *Number Seventeen* (1932).

Hitchcock always said he was attracted by the subversive sense of humour that pervades *The Trouble with Harry*. But the story also has the undertow of romance that balanced his best films. In fact, it boasts a double love story: a sweet courtship between an older couple, a shy spinster and a retired gentleman, which is paralleled by the spicier attraction between a perky, husbandless mother and a tortured artist.[52]

Some commentators have described this film as a comedy of errors, a dark comedy or a romance (Brill). Spoto terms it "a filmed parable on the death and resurrection of Christ, presented ironically." Hitchcock himself called it a "nice little pastorale."[53] It features Sam Marlow (John Forsyth) an artist struggling with his 'aesthetic identity,' Harry Worp a dead man who cannot remain buried, a retired seaman (Edmund Gwenn), Miss Gravely, a middle aged spinster, Mrs. Wiggs, a shopkeeper and seller of art, a young widow Mrs. Rogers (Shirley MacLaine) and her son Arnie. Hitchcock described this film... as "a quickie" but it contains more information about Hitchcock's attitudes towards art and artists than many of his other films. The establishing shot locates the narrative in a bucolic autumn setting in Vermont (where the premiere was shown in Barre, Friday September 30, 1955 (the novel was originally set in England) and a hunter, a retired seaman (Edmund Gwenn) taking three shots at a rabbit hears a cry and investigates to find the body of a dead man. Captain Wiles thinks he has inadvertently shot Harry Worp; "Harmless potshot at a rabbit and I'm a murderer." Later we learn that Jennifer Rogers, his 'wife,' and Miss Gravely also think they may have killed him. Over the course of several hours from early morning to late evening the four characters bury Harry and then disinter him four times. On one level this film is about the abstractions we live in daily life, time and space the question of being, and an example literally for Harry of being for death. A core theme for Hitchcock in this film, as for de Quincey and Wilde, is the mutability of life and immutability of art (*ars longa, vita brevis*). "When Truffaut insisted that *The Trouble with Harry* was shot in the fall, the season of decay, for symbolic reasons, Hitchcock had to agree. "I couldn't very well disillusion him, could I?"[54] The narrative is an allegory about the value of art, life and death or more specifically a dialogue between the art in death and the death in art (the images of Harry are foreshortened like Mantegna's painting *Dead Christ* and once again we see his feet sticking out of the bath, a Hitchcock insider joke about David's painting *Death of Marat* (1793). Harry functions as a still life (nature *mort,*), treated as an art object for disinterested contemplation and Sam's abstract paintings take on a life through their association with the various characters' desires. At one point Sam says "Don't you think about Harry. He's part of the earth. He's with eternity, the ages. Take my word for it, Harry's ancient history." Robert, Mrs. Rogers's first husband, and the father of Arnie, died before he was born and Harry, Robert's brother ("the Saint ... Harry the good), offered to marry her, but on their second wedding night she found out that his life was dictated by astrology and this made him totally unacceptable as a life partner. She moved away and changed her name and when he arrived on her doorstep demanding she accept the legitimacy of his offer of betrothal, she knocked him out with a milk bottle." Slavoj Žižek's Lacanian analysis of this film argues that there are two deaths, the real and the symbolic; Harry's death - the death of the father - is "a blot" isolated as an understatement but also a settling of accounts.[55] Ken Mogg has suggested that the body of Harry functions as a type of Winnicottian 'amenable object' which has no intrinsic value other than providing an opportunity to experience and learn from one's experiences, somewhat akin to the MacGuffin itself which simply exist in Hitchcock films as symbolic drivers of narrative.[56]

There are many art references throughout this film. Mrs. Wiggs' open-air store near the emporium sells cider and Sam Marlow's paintings. He approaches her with a new painting and expresses concern that she has not sold one of his works in some time.[57] She asks him to show her his new painting and he says "What good does it do to get you to see it when you can't sell any paintings... You don't deserve to see it." Not a picture sold... Do you think we would do any better on 5th Avenue?" Wiggs says "If there's more people there...." he says "Oh lots of people hundreds and thousands, billions of people... They're all little people..." He asks her for a cigarette, cuts it in half saying "I'll buy the other half tomorrow." When he does relent to show the new painting he has brought to Mrs. Wiggs for sale, she expresses admiration - "Oh Mr. Marlow its wonderful" she says, looking at it upside down and Marlow turning it back upright says. "I've been in a *tortured* mood lately" Wiggs "What is it? I don't understand your work but I think it's beautiful. So does Mrs. Rogers." Marlow pays attention to this statement and asks "Is that the pretty woman with the little boy? Does she talk about me?" he asks hopefully. To which Wiggs replies, "I only brought your name up when we were talking about *strange* people." Two stereotypical comments "tortured' mood and "strange" and one action, in which Sam corrects the orientation of his upside down abstract (the most common popular critique of abstraction) - accompany this exchange between the artist and Mrs. Wiggs. When Miss Gravely enters the emporium she looks at the paintings. "What gorgeous pictures she enthuses. Why don't you sell them and make a lot of money" to which Howard replies sardonically "I never thought of that" They are very professional, she continues" following with " Do you think so Miss Wiggs?" Her aesthetic approach to life is emphasized in the next scene when she picks up a large coffee mug and cradles it in her hand, contemplating it as an aesthetic object for several minutes before asking "whether this would fit a man's finger," in preparation for her afternoon coffee and blueberry muffins with Captain Wiles.

When Howard goes sketching in the country he finds when he sits down to sketch a copse of trees and sees the corpse - this pun would not have escaped Hitchcock - and says to the dead man in another Wildean moment: "Hey... do you mind getting out of my picture?" In another exchange responding to implicit criticism from Wiles about his abstract paintings he says, "Sam, I'll have you know that picture is symbolic of the beginning of the world." To which Captain Wiles wryly replies: "That's where I first heard of 'the world,' kindergarten."

A millionaire arrives in a chauffeur driven limousine and declares Sam's work to be that of a genius and offers to buy all his work. When asked what he wants, Sam says he is not willing to part with his paintings for "all the money in the world," – like Schopenhauer, his genius is not for sale, only service to humankind – but upon reflection he decides to part with his work by requesting all of those present at the Wiggs Emporium to reveal their desires. Jennifer replies by requesting fresh strawberries every month (summer and winter), for Arnie it's a "smelly chemical set"; for Mrs. Wiggs a chrome plated cash register; and for Miss Gravely, a hope chest full of hope, for Captain Wiles, fresh shirts and hunting outfit and a brown cap; while Sam requests the hand of Jennifer in marriage. For Lesley Brill and others this film is a quintessential Hitchcock romance but it also represents his views on art that coincide with those of Thomas de Quincey and Oscar Wilde. "We can forgive a man for making a useful thing as long as he does not admire it. The only excuse for making a useless thing is that one admires it intensely. All art is quite useless."[58]

Frenzy

Frenzy (1972)[59] is a Hitchcockian auteur film *à la lettre* with Hitchcock riffing on Hitchcock throughout.[60] There are references in this film to many of Hitchcock's signature motifs, obsessions and biographemes: a wrong man theme, doubles, classed difference revealed through accents and the contrasting of low and high taste in food, French gourmet (*cordon bleu*) cooking versus standard English fare, especially breakfast of sausages, (bangers) bacon, fried bread and tomatoes), tea; alcohol (brandy), strangling his preferred mode of dispatch, which occurs in sixteen of his films, several of the television series and a couple of notable photographs, (one showing off Hitchcock's chubby hands around his daughter Patricia's neck), jails, blondes, mother, shot through with favorite little Hitch apothegms, proverbs, stock phrases hackneyed sayings, ironic slogans, catchwords. "Bob's yer uncle;" "I'm alright Jack and pull up the ladder;" "you know what they say 'virtue is its own reward,'" and "everybody expects a bad penny to turn up sooner of later." *Frenzy* includes two whistling scenes, since *Blackmail* (1927), almost as common a feature in Hitchcock's films as his cameo, and each significant space for the interior scenes: apartments, pub bars, hotel room have specially chosen art works on the wall, providing some additional signifiers to the character of the protagonists, or to the film's diegesis. For example, Bob Rusk's walk-up apartment near Covent Garden has two famously reproduced and popular (factory produced) prints on the wall of black velvet paintings, beautiful Polynesian women inspired by the work of Albert Leetag, and a cheap reproduction of a group of flamenco dancers to emphasize his bachelorhood and low brow working class (low competency) attitude to culture. Hitchcock also uses these paintings of exotic women to contrast Rusk's statement "you know.... you're my kind of woman" that he offered to both of his blonde English victims. On the walls of the upscale market apartment of Johnny and Hetty who provide refuge for "Dicko" Blaney are several popular generic landscape prints, modernist yet blandly decorative and one mass produced genre painting of a game bird (a pheasant) symbolically acknowledging the game status of Blaney who is being hotly pursued by the police and indirectly affirming Hitchcock's continuing interest in avian tropes. The dinner scene in Brenda Blaney's Women's Club sports two art works that figure prominently in several key shots; an imperious looking marble sculpture of an C18th coiffed male bust and an oval landscape painting, a romantic image reminiscent of the sublime landscapes of Salvator Rosa which is located in the rear of restaurant framing respectively Brenda and Dick as they discuss Blaney's hard luck. The dining room and kitchen of the Inspector's house contain black and white documentary photographs on the wall and an unidentified approximately two foot high standing figure in the kitchen. The Coburg Hotel where Babs and Blaney spend a night in the Cupid Room has a long rectangular reproduction over the queen-sized bed of a generic reclining nude. The film contains a myriad of details that are not only the result of the production process but also the result of Hitchcock's own frenzied authorial investment in the film. These biographemes permitted him to both access and assess his career back on home ground in London where he was raised and also to convince those who needed convincing that Hitchcock's mastery was assured.

Donald Spoto's interviews with those associated with the production provide another interesting purview on Hitchcock's signature motifs. Everyone "connected with the project agreed that for a time Hitchcock was "in great humor and concerned himself with every detail." Among the details Hitchcock insisted upon in his early meetings with screen writer Anthony Shaffer were the use of the River Thames and Convent Gardens food markets for location shooting, The Old Bailey Court, with narrow alleyways between Bow Street, Oxford Street, County hall, the Coburg Hotel, pubs near Covent garden and for Bob Rusk the killer's residence a flat above Duckworth and Company where Clemence Dane another murderer had previously lived. According to Spoto and McGilligan, Shaffer also offered Hitchcock a few of his own suggestions for the locations; that as this was to be a contemporary film they should use the London Hilton and New Scotland Yard. Hitchcock was apparently as intractable about the dialogue with his screenwriters as he had been on many earlier films and took the opportunity to introduce many of his own favorite stock phrases and cockneyisms. "Hitch affirmed that he had "had a happy time with the writer of *Frenzy*" "It's a crime story but I wanted to avoid the inevitable scene among the detectives at Scotland Yard. So we had the plot points discussed by the inspector and his wife at home over meals. And I made the wife a gourmet cook."[61] Anna Massey who played the part of Babs, Blaney's mistress, stated that "[Hitch] had immense creative energy and a real mental zest and early on he was concerned about every detail, clothes and colors and set dressings. But then he got slow physically. Off the set the only conversation that seemed to interest him was about food - he taught me how to make a good batter - and later I realized that this was apt at a time when we were making a film so crowded with food."[62]

In the making of this film Hitchcock was clearly revisiting his early life history. According to his biographers he spoke to anyone who would listen about his childhood in London and of the Moroccan tomatoes available at Convent Garden in both 1901 and 1971 the year in which the film was made. He marveled at the citrus fruits from Israel, Spanish grapes, vegetables from California a constant reminder of his father's life as a green grocer in Leytonstone. Details about food in *Frenzy* became somewhat of an obsession for Hitchcock. In his conversations with Truffaut he spoke about doing "an anthology on food, showing its arrival in the city, its distribution, the selling, buying by people, the cooking, the various ways in which it is consumed. What happens to it in various hotels; how it's fixed up and absorbed. And, gradually, the end of the film would show the sewers and the garbage being dumped out into the ocean. So there's a cycle, beginning with the gleaming fresh vegetables and ending with the mess that's poured into the sewers. Thematically, the cycle would show what people do to good things. Your theme might almost be the rottenness of humanity"[63] As far as some details were concerned Hitchcock's closest associates including his partner Alma felt that he had gone too far. "Even after all of the business of the impotent frenzy of the killer and the hideous close ups of the strangling with the necktie; Hitchcock wanted to insert a close up of the dead woman's tongue dripping saliva. But at last he yielded to pressure and the shot was cut."[64]

But Hitchcock's focus upon details in *Frenzy* was curtailed somewhat by a minor stroke that Alma had during the shooting. "Suddenly according to actor Barry Foster (Rusk), he became tired and lazy "whereas earlier he had come onto the set and said the position of certain key lights would necessitate the repainting of a backcloth because of some small shadows, he soon changed. Some of our scenes were shot by the assist director (Colin Brewer) while Hitch went off to dinner with a visiting friend or a former actress from his films. And he looked forward to him having us all join him promptly at tea time - but not for tea, for vodka gimlets."[65] Spoto suggests that after Alma's stroke Hitchcock rose to the occasion for only three key scenes: the rape murder of Brenda Blaney, the justly famous reverse zoom tracking shot from the murderer's apartment door after he enters with his next victim and Rusk's frenzied search for the incriminating tie pin that was clutched by the hand of the corpse in the large sack of potatoes on the back of a truck.

The famous scene containing the single reverse zoom tracking shot is provided by the camera tracking away and down from door of Rusk's second story flat and it descends seemingly without a cut, to the ground floor level out of the front door of the building and then to the opposite side of Henrietta street. Always interested in the technically innovative Hitchcock in his discussions with Truffaut, spoke about the overhead tracking rail he used for the camera and the edit point made during the passage of a worker carrying potatoes across the camera's path.

The scene on the truck revealing the killer's attempt to retrieve his incriminating tiepin is pure De Quincey and would not have looked out of place in the description of one of the Williams murders in his "Postscript." Hitchcock's ironic conflation of the macabre and amusing is highly detailed. According to Hitchcock's description: "The scene on the truck is composed of one hundred and eighteen separate shots. When we finished filming it, I sat down with my secretary and dictated a complete list of the shots. It took about an hour. Each shot was listed on a numbered yellow file card. All the cutter had to do was refer to the number of each cut and splice it together." A few other details in *Frenzy* are worth acknowledging in passing. For example, the number of figures with a name beginning with B: Babs, Blaney, Brenda, Barling. Miss Barling (the secretary) impresses the inspector with her precision and eye for detail as she gives a picture perfect description of Blaney who becomes the wrong man identified as his wife's murderer. Dick calls Babs to pick up his clothes and he takes a cab to meet her taking her then to the Coburg hotel where he signs them in as Mr. and Mrs. Oscar Wilde which provides Hitchcock with another amusing reversal for comic effect.

In his Hitchcock biography Donald Soto exclaims that *Frenzy* (1972) is "among the most repellent examples of murder in the history of film."[66] Moreover, *Frenzy,* he argues "was at once a concession to modern audience's expectations and a more personal self-disclosure of the director's angriest and most violent desires. The Covent garden grocer simultaneously attracted to women and repelled by them, full of desire and full of loathing for that desire, commits in this film the ultimate Hitchcock murder - an attempted rape and the strangling toward which the director's life work had tended ever since *The Lodger*"[67]. Now, this is a strong accusation, highly psychologised, from one of Hitchcock's most influential and unapologetic supporters. Although one could argue that the principal rape murder scene is not as shocking to many viewers today, especially those weaned on slasher films in which the gratuitous display of sex and violence is the stock and trade of commercial success, part of what Spoto has to offer in this statement conveys some truth about the circumstances of both the making of the film and the condition of Hitchcock's career at this time.

By the late 1960's the director had been honored with many awards including a full scale retrospective at the Museum of Modern Art in (1965). But by this time Hitchcock was also beginning to recognize that he was somewhat trapped in his own success. How could he improve upon or transcend *North by Northwest, Psycho, The Birds* and *Marnie*? These films had secured him a privileged place within the pantheon of film, even without the coveted best director Oscar award from the Academy, which had consigned him, in his own words, to the status of "always a bridesmaid never a bride." During the filming of *Frenzy,* two more awards were bestowed upon the director, one from France and one from England, the first in March from Princess Anne on behalf of the Society of Film and Television Arts which presented him with its first honorary membership and three months later, in June, Henri Langlois of Cinematheque Francaise awarded him with the rank of Chevalier in the Legion of Honor and a commendation from Georges Pompidou himself.

[1] Chabrol, C. & Rohmer, Eric. *Hitchcock: the First Forty-Four Films*, Translated by Stanley Hochman, New York, Frederick Ungar, 1957/1979: xi

[2] McGilligan, P *Alfred Hitchcock: A Life in Darkness and Light*. New York, Regan Books Harper Collins 2003:476

[3] Both Teresa Wright and Janet Leigh died recently. Eva Marie Saint was also invited to be a participant on the panel but was unfortunately unavailable.

[4] Organized by Richard Allen, Sydney Gottleib et al The proceedings are available in Allen R. and Gonzales S. Ishi. *Alfred Hitchcock: Centenary Essays* London British Film Institute 1999

[5] McGilligan, P *Alfred Hitchcock: A Life in Darkness and Light*. New York, Regan Books Harper Collins 2003 was not available at this time

[6] Truffaut, F., with Scott, H.G. *Hitchcock* New York: Simon and Schuster, 1967:54

[7] Art Directors for *Psycho* were Joseph Hurley and Robert Clatworthy; special effects Clarence Champagne and titles, Saul Bass.

[8] See Sloan, J.E *Alfred Hitchcock The Definitive Bibliography* Berkeley, Los Angeles University of California Press 1993, 1995

[9] Spoto, D. *The Dark Side of Genius: the Life of Alfred Hitchcock* New York: Ballantine Books, 1983:280

[10] Although I strongly suspected that Hitchcock used art as a signature device in many, if not all of his films, I consciously set out to challenge this belief. After purchasing fifty of Hitchcock's films, viewing them all several times as well as teaching several courses on his work ('Reading Theory Through Hitchcock,' and a director's course titled 'Hitchcock's Films') my students and I recognized that Hitchcock was almost as consistent in his use of art, artists and art history as he was his other signature strategies, including brandy, blondes and his cameo appearances.

[11] See Sennett, R. and Cobb, J. *The Hidden Injuries of Class* New York, Vintage Books 1973

[12] After working briefly for Players Lasky where he produced titles and lettering for approximately eight films Hitchcock worked for the independent producers Michael Balcon and Victor Saville later of Gainsborough Pictures who contracted him to be set designer and art director for two successful films *Woman To Woman* (1923) and *The Passionate Adventure* (1924). (McGilligan pp.50-4)

[13] Sklar, R., and Musser, C., *Resisting Images: Essays on Cinema and history* Philadelphia Temple University Press 1990

[14] Chabrol, Rohmer, 1957: xi

[15] See Barber, B *Popular Modernisms: Art, Cartoons, Comics and Cultural In/Subordination* (Chapters 3&4, forthcoming)

[16] McGilligan p.476

[17] Spoto, p. 540

[18] Hitchcock, A. "Building the Screen play " in Auiler, D. *Hitchcock's Notebooks* Klond Avon Books 1999 pp.21-2

[19] See Demonsablon, P., "Lexique mythologique pour l'oeuvre de Hitchcock Cahiers du Cinéma 11: no 62 18-29, 54-55 1956 An alphabetical listing of recurring objects and motifs in Hitchcock's films, rings, keys, cats etc. also in Manz, H P *Alfred Hitchcock: Eine Bildchronik* Zurich, Sancoussi 1962

[20] Raymond Bellour "Symbolic Blockage" (on *North by Northwest*); Gottlieb, S

(Ed) *Hitchcock on Hitchcock Selected Writings and Interviews*: L.A. University of California Press; Peucker, B. *Incorporating Images: Film and the Rival Arts* Princeton, Princeton University Press 1996

[21] Žižek, S. "Hitchcockian Sinthoms" in Žižek S. (ed) *Everything You Always Wanted to Know About Lacan (But Were Afraid to Ask Hitchcock)* London, Verso, 1992

[22] A MacGuffin is the mysterious element that drives the plot in several Hitchcock films. The term was introduced by Angus McPhail, a friend and colleague of Hitchcock and derived from an anecdote he told about two men traveling from London on a train to Scotland. On man looks at a oddly wrapped parcel in the luggage rack and says "What do you have there?" "Oh that's a MacGuffin, replies the other man. "What's a MacGuffin?" he says curiously. In reply the other man says "it's a device for trapping lions in the Scottish highlands" "But there aren't any lions in the Scottish highlands" replies the first man. "Well then, I guess that's no MacGuffin" McGilligan, p.159-60 Classic MacGuffins: The plans in *The 39 Steps*. The microfilms in *North by Northwest*, the encoded melody in *The Lady Vanishes* and the secret clause in the Defence treaty in *Foreign Correspondent*.

[23] Hitchcock's art collection: "One of Hollywood's noted art collectors, McGowen would go on to help Hitchcock build his growing art collection, including abstracts by (Paul) Klee" McGilligan, pp.324. "Hitchcock hated wallpaper, preferring walls of simple vanilla, with maybe a dash of colour - a Utrillo here, a Picasso there. Art was probably his most expensive indulgence, and Hitchcock's small but noteworthy collection divided its loyalties between the English and the French. Especially at Bellargio Road, the walls were hung with post-impressionist favorites - Maurice Utrillo, Chaim Soutine, Raoul Dufy, Maurice, de Vlaminck, Amadeo Modigliani. (McGilligan 476-77, 495)

[24] Cohen, P M *Alfred Hitchcock: The Legacy of Victorianism* Lexington, Kentucky: University Press of Kentucky, 1995::199.

[25] Spoto, p..38

[26] McGilligan p. 27

[27] Truffaut: p.133

[28] Wees, W. *Vorticism and the English Avant-Garde* Toronto University of Toronto Press 1972 p.20

[29] Several newspaper articles on Futurist music appeared as a result of a performance at the Coliseum "Noisy Tuners at a Rehearsal" appeared in Pall Mall Gazette 12 June 1914:1(quoted in Wees, 1972:255

[30] See Barber, B *Popular Modernisms, Art, Cartoons, Comics and Cultural In/Subordination* (forthcoming)

[31] McGilligan McGilligan, P *Alfred Hitchcock: A Life in Darkness and Light.* New York, Regan Books Harper Collins 2003: 27

[32] Truffaut:59

[33] Ibid p.70

[34] Ibid p.118

[35] Truffaut, 1967:54.

[36] O'Brien, G. *Hitchcock: The Hidden Power* New York Time Review November 15 2001 p.23

[37] Paini, D and Cogeval, G. (Eds) *Hitchcock and Art: Fatal Coincidences* catalogue of the exhibition Montreal Museum of Fine Arts/ Milan: Mazzotta 2001 p19

[38] Screenplay Eliot Stannard from a novel by Marie Adelaide Belloc-Lowndes.

[39] I have not yet identified the exact origin of this image but it is one from a genre of bound women that appeared in the late nineteenth century *The Victorian Nude Morality and Art in 19th Century Britain*

[40] The name Avenger may have been borrowed from Thomas de Quincey's "Avenger " story in which the killer is described as an artist. See De Quincey, T. *The English Mail Coach and other Writings* Edinburgh A & C Black and Collected Works

[41] Spoto p. 276

[42]Screenplay by Eliot Stannard based on a play by Ivor Novello and Constance Collier.

[43]Screenplay Eliot Stannard

[44] *Blackmail*'s screenplay written by Benn [W] Levy (dialogue); Alfred Hitchcock (adaptation) based on a play by Charles Bennett.

[45] For a fuller account of this process and the production of B*lackmail* generally see Ryall, T. *Blackmail* London, BFI Classics 1993:25

[46]Ibid p33

[47] Yacowar, M. *Hitchcock's British films* Hampden Connecticut, Archon 1977, p135 cited in Modleski p.20

[48]Ibid

[49] Gagnier, R. *Critical Essays on Oscar Wilde* New York, G.K. Hall & Co 1991:4

[50] According to Donald Spoto Hitchcock instructed Herman Citron an MCA agent to act on his behalf (without using his name) to negotiate a good price for the screening rights to the novel. "Story and his publisher were somewhat disenchanted to learn the identity of the buyer after they had agreed to the price of $11,000. They went through with the deal, however, since they has long give up any thought of Hollywood interest" Spoto, p379

[51]McGilligan p.502

[52] Ibid p503

[53] Reviewers typically treated *Harry* as a black comedy with a light theatrical romance. Philips, L "The Burden the living bear" Armchair detective 19: 3: 293-98 1986. None of the characters feel guilty but try to shift the blame for Harry's demise on someone else.. *The Trouble with Harry* Filmcritica 32:311 January: 48.

[54] McGilligan p513

[55] Žižek, S. Hitchcock October No 38 Fall 1986:99-111

[56] Mogg, K. http://www.labyrinth.net.au/-muffin/univesral_c.html page 2 accessed May 2005

[57] The artist who produced the paintings and sketches produced by John Forsythe's character is John Ferren

[58] Wilde, O. *The Artist as Critic*; Critical Writings of Oscar Wilde "Preface to the Picture of Dorian Gray" Edited by Richard Ellmann, New York, Vintage Books Random House, 1969:236

[59]*Frenzy* Screenplay Anthony Shaffer based on Novel *Goodbye Piccadilly, Hello Leicester Square* by Arthur La Bern

[60] Gabriel Miller "Hitchcock's wasteland vision: An examination of frenzy." Film Heritage 11:3 (spring 1976) pp1-10. Miller describes the film as a portrait of "total decay". One critic even composed a poem about the murder of Babs "Hitchcock's Violence: A Fans Notes Journal of Popular Film and television 6, No 3:239 (1978). Dennis Turner "Hitchcock: Moral Frenzy in the declining years" Film/Psychology Review 4:1 (Winter/Spring 1980) pp 56-69 seeks to rescue Frenzy from the evolutionist perspectives on Hitchcock's work that describes it as self-consciously repetitive and therefore false. Turner's analysis describes ways in which the viewer is challenged to participate in its production via the films self-reflexiveness"

[61] Spoto, p. 542

[62] Ibid p.543

[63] Truffaut in Spoto, p. 544

[64] Ibid p546

[65] Ibid

[66] Spoto, 1983:545

[67] Ibid.

Chapter 7

A Perfect Murder

MARGOT
(*To MAX*)
Do you really believe in the perfect murder? (*pause*)
MAX
Absolutely - on paper. And I think I could plan one better than most
people ----
but I doubt if I could carry it out.
TONY
Why not? (TONY *rises and moves to fireplace.*)
MAX
Because in stories things turn out as the author plans them to ...
in real life they don't ---- always.

Frederick Knott *Dial "M" for Murder* playscript (1952).

1999 marked the centenary of Alfred Hitchcock's birth on August 13th 1899 and this date stimulated more than the usual number of retakes, remakes and riffs on his work, among them:[1] the late Christopher Reeve's remake of *Rear Window* (1998), directed by Jeff Bleckner; *A Perfect Murder* (1998) directed by Andrew Davis and Gus van Sant's *Psycho* (1998), a shot by shot reconstruction of the Hitchcock original.[2] In each of these films, art, artists and art history figure prominently, arguably as much, if not more, than in their Hitchcock models. In Bleckner's *Rear Window* for example, the killer who the paraplegic architect Jason Kemp (Reeves) surveys with his video equipment through the rear window of his apartment, is Julian Thorpe (Ritchie Foster), an English sculptor, replacing Lars Thorwald (Raymond Burr), the travelling salesman of Hitchcock's original. In Davis' *A Perfect Murder*, based on Hitchcock's *Dial M for Murder*, (1954), and the successful play of the same title by Frederick Knott, the avant-garde artist (Viggo Mortensen) with whom Gwyneth Paltrow is having an affair, is blackmailed into murdering her by Stephen Taylor (Michael Douglas), her financier husband, who replaces

Tony Wendice (Ray Milland), the ex-Wimbledon tennis star in the original. The artist in this case replaces both Mark Halliday (Robert Cummings) the American crime writer having the affair with Margot Wendice (Grace Kelly), and Captain Lesgate/Swann (Anthony Dawson) who is blackmailed by Wendice to kill his wife. In keeping with Hitchcock's strategies, Gus van Sant's version of *Psycho* (1989)[3] affirms the parergonal truth in painting with the signal importance of pictures, windows and mirrors as frames for controlling audience subordination to the film's suspenseful diegesis.[4] Both versions of *Psycho* also employ specific references to art and artists through paintings, prints, sculpture, stuffed birds, as well as Norman's preserved mother who, with his assistance, becomes both animate and inanimate. Gus van Sant's version places somewhat more emphasis upon art and sex than the original. Norman for example, proceeds to masturbate while peeping through a hole in the wall at Marion Crane undressing in the washroom next door to his motel office, something that Hitchcock in 1960 would not have been able to get away with – even if the thought had probably crossed his mind -- because of Production Code restrictions. In both films, the peephole through which Norman surveys Marion is hidden behind a reproduction of the painting *Susannah spied on by her elders,* an allegory about modesty and purity based on the Old Testament story in Apocrypha (*Susannah* 15-24).[5] In this story the beautiful and virtuous Susannah bathes in her garden and is spied on by two elders who threaten to accuse her of adultery if she does not sleep with them. Refusing to submit to this patriarchal blackmail, Susannah's innocence is subsequently proven and she is thus saved from being stoned to death.

Tania Modleski insisted, "The issue of sexual violence must be central to any feminist analysis of the films of Alfred Hitchcock."[6] I have no difficulty endorsing Modleski's claim but it should also be recognised that the representation of violence in the films of Alfred Hitchcock remains contested ground for those who recognize the complexities of desire, pleasure, pain and death and who do not necessarily endorse the reductions offered by some feminists that "pornography is the theory, and rape is the practice."[7] Hitchcock himself argued in a famous statement that the shocking characteristics of the representation of violence in film could actually be beneficial to society, providing a moral panacea to what he discerned was a certain psychological numbing of the masses. At a

Hollywood press conference in 1947 he stated his views in these terms:

> I aim to provide the public with beneficial shocks. Civilisation (humanity) has become so protective that we're no longer able to get our goose bumps instinctively. The only way to remove the numbness and revive our moral equilibrium is to use artificial means to bring about the shock. The best way to achieve that, it seems to me, is through a movie.[8]

This statement implies a kind of social Darwinism, possibly a Hitchcockian gloss on the repressive sexuality hypotheses of Freud, Reich, Lacan and others; even a Bataillian surrealist dialectic of prohibition and transgression through the cathartic use of violence. But beyond these grandiose claims about the ameliorative affects of shock tactics, violence in Hitchcock's films has always been made palatable for popular consumption through its imbrication with the erotic pleasures of food, sex, and art. This chapter explores the famous murder scene in Hitchcock's *Dial M for Murder* (1954) and compares this with the original Frederick Knott playscript and Andrew Davis' recent interpretation of that script in *A Perfect Murder* (1989).[9] The films are explored generally with respect to their use of art to reinforce the discussion of Hitchcock's own attitudes to art, artists and art history reviewed in the previous chapter. But before discussing these two films I would like to digress somewhat to review briefly another aspect of Hitchcock's own attitudes toward art in an attempt to understand how these may have influenced the direction of his films.

Sociological studies of the artist and the art world influenced by Pierre Bourdieu have focussed upon the accumulation of symbolic capital as a basis for understanding cultural and class distinctiveness. In his review of the critical reception of Hitchcock's work the sociologist and film historian Robert Kapsis suggested that Hitchcock's transformation from "popular entertainer to distinguished auteur" was assisted by the American (British and French) publicity machines of the 1950's, the rise of auteur theory in the late sixties and early seventies, and subsequently the development of feminist discourse, beginning with Laura Mulvey's famous essay (1975), that convincingly established the importance of his oeuvre, both in academic (gender politics) and aesthetic terms.[10] The 1965 retrospective of Hitchcock's work curated by Peter Bogdanovich for the Museum of Modern Art, certainly reinforced the public perception and probably his own, that he was indeed a master whose work and life had achieved historical, that is museological importance, and that he could be placed in the pantheon of the great masters of western culture. Notwithstanding this view and his present iconic position within the history of film, Hitchcock's life reveals the hidden injuries of class that registered with a number of his personal acquaintances, who made note of his attraction/repulsion to bourgeois life, and his antagonism towards classed society in general. Screenwriter John Houseman provides one important instance of Hitchcock's class-consciousness from the late 1930s that is documented in Spoto's biography:

> I was instructed to use my British background, as well as my cultivation and charm, to establish good personal relationships with Hitch and to cajole and encourage him into conceiving and preparing an "original" screenplay.... I had heard of him as a fat man given to scabrous jokes - a gourmet and an ostentatious connoisseur of fine wines. What I was unprepared for was a man of exaggeratedly delicate sensibilities, marked by a harsh Catholic education and the scars of a social system against which he was in perpetual revolt and which left him suspicious and vulnerable, ultimately docile and defiant.[11]

It is no accident that Alfred Hitchcock's films are riddled with references to art (see Appendix 2). As I suggested previously, Hitchcock used art, artists and art history in several ways: to enrich the visual *mise en scene* and enhance the hermeneutic complexity of the narrative; to invest his films with symbolic capital derived from their association with high culture and as a critique of the role of the artist and his (usually) ties to a privileged culture from which Hitchcock – as a classed subject and popular culture producer – was somewhat alienated. As his principal biographers, Spoto, Taylor and McGilligan, and legions of Hitchcock scholars have asserted, apart from Hitchcock's cameo performances that reinforce his authorial stamp on nearly every work, he also inserted details about his personal life into scripts, making references to his Irish Catholic and East End Cockney origins, his relationships with his family, friends, colleagues and his likes and dislikes with respect to literature, art, theatre, food, sport, animals (pets), the law, crime, architecture, theatre, ethnicity, gender, sex…literally and liberally applying his biographemes to every production, at least since *The Lodger. A Story of the London Fog* (1926), which was his first internationally successful film that he directed at the age of 27. Notwithstanding his use of the above biographemes and signature forms, which have provided stimulus to a large number of writers within the Hitchcock Studies community,[12] including Tom Cohen's "user guide"[13] that provides an alphabetized lexicon of such effects.

13. Anthony Perkins as Norman Bates in Alfred Hitchcock's *Psycho* (1960)

Hitchcock makes specific references to art, artists and art history throughout his films, even when he is closely following a script where art is of little or no consequence. *Dial M for Murder* is one such film.

About this film Hitchcock reportedly said:" There isn't very much we can say about that one is there?"[14] And although Truffaut professed an increased enjoyment of the film each time he saw it, *Dial M for Murder* remains one of the films least discussed in the Hitchcock bibliography. Despite the diffidence that he expressed to Truffaut, Hitchcock's meticulous attention to detail is very evident throughout this classical thriller. As the camera movements were limited for much of the film to the set construction of the apartment, Hitchcock paid close attention to specific details within the *mise en scene*. With the assistance of Edward Carrere his art director, Hitchcock chose two prints by Rosa Bonheur, Wedgwood and Staffordshire figurines, oriental Buddhas, Victorian teacups and tennis trophies for the mantelpiece of the Wendice apartment in Maida Vale, a tony district of London. He also inserted one of his most inventive cameos, a photographic image of himself with others at a school reunion dinner. After the first take of the famous scissors scene, in which Grace Kelly stabs her assailant in the back, Hitchcock reportedly said: "This is nicely done but there wasn't enough gleam to the scissors, and murder without gleaming scissors is like asparagus without a hollandaise sauce." Hitchcock frequently links murder with food. Spoto observed that food sequences containing the preparation and consumption or celebration of food are important to many of Hitchcock's films, linking hunger with sexuality, through the representation of insatiable appetites. This is an important feature of the libidinal economy of Hitchcock's films, where the desire for food is often configured as a compensation for sex – sublimated desire – in the classic Freudian sense. Dinner, luncheon or breakfast sequences are also crucial for character revelation and development, for example in *Blackmail* where Alice White's problem cutting bread with the knife after she had used a similar instrument the previous night to kill Crewe the artist. The first dinner scene in *Shadow of a Doubt* provides Uncle Charlie (Joseph Cotton) with an opportunity to display his ego, delivering presents to the family, including a mink stole for his sister Emma, but niece Charlie jealous of the attention displayed to her mother removes herself from the table, claiming sulkily that she doesn't want any gifts; that just having him with the family is enough. Uncle Charlie follows her to the kitchen, later giving her a ring which she immediately notices has the wrong person's initials engraved inside, thus providing a major shadow of doubt in her mind about his past.

In *Psycho* Norman offers sandwiches to Marion commenting as he carefully surveys her "you eat like a bird" which in the context of his motel office full of stuffed birds and a house with a preserved mother, lends this scene a sinister air. The kitchen scene in *Marnie* when her mother pours syrup for a pecan pie is accompanied by the discussion of the beautiful young girl that she looks after that provokes a jealous Marnie (Tippi Hedren) to complain "why don't you love me mama?" Food is also linked with images of nausea in *Rich and Strange, Lifeboat* and *The Birds* and different types of culinary tastes are contrasted in *Frenzy* to signify different classes in English society. The aftermath of Bob Rusk's rape murder scene in *Frenzy* is accompanied by apple eating and tooth picking which links this apple to the one eaten by the 'fat woman' in *The Paradine Case.* In *Sabotage* three narrative movements escalating in tension are marked by meals before the terrorist bomb blast destroys the bus carrying young Stevie. A formal dinner party occurs in *The Paradine Case* at the London home of Sir Simon, the fat and surly judge who is one of the principal protagonists in the narrative. An elaborate dinner party is held in Squire Pengallan's home in *Jamaica Inn* that also provides the site for the introduction of a life-like figurine that is pronounced "not alive" thus providing an implicit reference to the Pygmalion story. And in *Under Capricorn,* a gala dinner scene takes place in Minyago Yugilla a Spanish style mansion, during which a fight breaks out between cooks in the kitchen who attempt to strangle each other. In *Rope* food is placed as if for a sacrament on the *cassone* (marriage chest) that doubles as a coffin containing the strangled body of David Kentley. The dialogue exchanges between Brandon and Phillip in *Rope* also conflates Nietzschean *ubermann* (overman) philosophy with De Quincey's model of murder as one of the fine arts. At one point soon after the murder of Kentley, who they disparaged as "the Harvard undergraduate," Brandon states: "The Davids of this world merely occupy space, which was why he was the *perfect victim for the perfect murder*" (emphasis added), and a little later, further justifying their murderous act, he says "The power to kill can be just as satisfying as the power to create....do you realise that we have actually done it?" The dining room table is set with flowers and candles and Philip initially expresses his anxiety about the dinner party informing Brandon "don't you think the party's a mistake..?" to which he confidently replies, "of course not, it's the signature of the artist." Nothing could be closer to an affirmation of what Derrida terms the *ductus* (idiom of the *trait t* / trace as the draftsman's signature)[15] but Brandon's take on the contiguous relationship between murder/art, and the sacraments of celebration/communion – with food (the breaking of bread and wine) as its centre piece, is also linked allegorically -- perversely – to such events within Christian theology, including the major one, the last supper where Christ is offering communion with his disciples, one of whom betrays him. Analogically this last supper for David (a Jew), ties Hitchcock's *Rope* to Leonardo da Vinci's painting of *The Last Supper*. If food is an important feature of the symbolic economy of his films, Hitchcock also enjoyed linking murder with sex and art, the latter providing a neat squaring of the circle/circling the square – art/sex/food/murder – that could be expressed graphically thus:

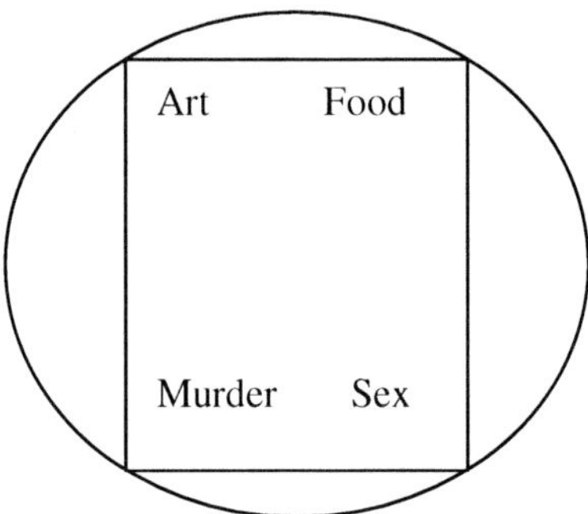

14. Squaring the circle, circling the square

Rather than being a source of cheap entertainment, the art of murder for Hitchcock, following the exemplary models provided by de Quincey and Wilde, should and could be compared to the transcendent perfection idealised in the work of the great artists - masters (Leonardo da Vinci, Michelangelo, Raphael et. al.) – within the art historical canon. And if a few artists had to be murdered in the quest to achieve immortality, so be it. In this respect it is interesting to reflect of Hitchcock's public reference to Thomas De Quincey's murderous aesthetics in a recorded speech delivered to the Film Society of the Lincoln Centre (Monday April 29 1974). His remarks were documented on film.

> "Finally I think I can best describe the insidious effect of murder
> on one's character by reading a paragraph from Thomas de
> Quincey's delightful essay "Murder as one of the Fine Arts." He
> said: "If once a man indulges himself in murder, very soon
> becomes to think little of robbing, and from robbing he comes
> next to drinking and Sabbath breaking, and from that to incivility
> and procrastination. Once begun on this downward path, you
> never know where you are to stop. Many a man dates his ruin
> from some murder or other that perhaps he thought little of at the
> time" They tell me that murder is committed every minute, so I
> don't want to waste any more of your time. I know you want to
> get to work. Thank you."[16]

The art of murder almost achieves aesthetic perfection in *Dial M for
Murder*. Tony Wendice (Ray Milland), an ex-Wimbledon tennis champion
decides to do away with Margot (Grace Kelly) his beautiful, wealthy but
adulterous wife, and blackmails Captain Lesgate (Anthony Dawson), an
old school chum to do the job. The plan devised by Wendice calls for
Lesgate to obtain access to the apartment with a key that he has left hidden
under the staircase carpet outside and to strangle Margot at home while he
is establishing an alibi at the stag dinner he is attending with Mark
Halliday (Robert Cummings), his wife's lover. Hitchcock reportedly spent
a full week filming the murder scene (out of thirty-six days spent on the
entire film), and it's clear references to sexual struggle with shot inserts of
the actress' shapely legs pushing against her attacker, the diaphanous night
dress that plays the light evocatively off her body and the use of scissors
as a vulgar Freudian castration symbol, make this a clear example of
Hitchcock's aesthetic interests.

The murder scene takes place 100 minutes into the film (82 pages in the
playscript), and from the moment the phone rings, through to the struggle
and the stabbing of the assailant, takes less than five minutes, with the
sequence containing 31 shots with two cutaways to the stag party where
Tony Wendice is anxiously looking at his watch to give the signal to his
accomplice. Lesgate meanwhile, has been waiting anxiously by the
apartment window for the telephone call to summon Margot to the phone
so that he can undertake the murder. When Wendice finally telephones,
after realising that his watch had stopped, Margot answers with "hello"
(hullo), a full seven times (a typical Hitchcock suspense evoking strategy),

three times punctuating her response with the "tap, tap, tap," of the telephone receiver. In the Knott play in contrast, Margot says "Hullo" and jiggles the receiver a mere two times before her attacker assaults her. The description and directions for of the murder scene in the play are quite detailed and were obviously closely followed by Hitchcock, with Knott's assistance, in his interpretation for the screenplay and its subsequent translation into film. Grace Kelly's icy beauty and diaphanous dress in *Dial M for Murder* connotes to be looked-at-ness and the strangling scene itself is a tightly choreographed aestheticisation of violence in the De Quinceyian manner providing, like so many of Hitchcock's other film murders, an example of his crime as high art.

Hullo...(*She listens for several seconds then louder*) Hullo!
MARGOT *does not notice* LESGATE *as he comes from behind the curtains. His gloved hands hold each end of the silk scarf in which two knots have been tied.* MARGOT *has had the phone in her left hand. She puts the phone down and jiggles the receiver with her right. Just as she is jiggling the receiver* LESGATE *attacks her throwing the scarf over her head and drawing it back sharply against her throat. With a strangled gargle she drops the phone.* LESGATE *holds her back against his body but* MARGOT'S *hands catch hold of the scarf and try to tear it away. They struggle for a moment, then* LESGATE *winds the scarf, with his left hand, right around her neck and at the same time she turns around so that she faces him with the scarf crossed at the back of her neck. He pushes her against the end of the desk and forces her down until she is bent right back along the top of the desk with her head downstage. In his efforts to tighten the scarf he leans right over her so that his body almost touches hers.* MARGOT's *right hand leaves the scarf and waves over the end of the desk, groping for the scissors. She grabs them and strikes with one of the points into* LESGATE's *back.* LESGATE *slumps over her and then very slowly rolls over the left side of the desk landing on his back with a strangled grunt.* MARGOT *continues to lie back over the desk, completely exhausted. Then she manages to get to her feet, all the time fighting for her breath. She tears the scarf away from her throat but it remains looped around her shoulders. She grabs the telephone. At first she has difficulty in speaking. A sharp "Hello" from* TONY *can be heard from the receiver.*[17]

15. *Dial M for Murder* Strangling scene

16. *Dial M for Murder* The Scissors

A number of critics and reviewers noticed the 'baroque quality' of the strangling sequence. It was filmed originally for 3D viewing, but shown flat. In 1980 a 3D showing of the film occurred in New York at the 8th

Street Cinema.[18]   During the murder sequence, the axis points are located in the bedroom through to the location of the phone in the living room. Rohmer and Chabrol noticed the pivot and bending of the bodies as instrumental in constructing a deep space appropriate for the 3D production.[19] They argue that two explicit goals can be distinguished. The first involves the elaborate choreography of the scene to make the crime more suspenseful. While the killer tries to strangle Grace Kelly from behind with the scarf, she pivots, bends almost at an impossible angle, and with her shoulders touching the table top she stretches her right arm out behind her to grasp the scissors placed on the table at the end of the visual field. Almost with her last gasp, her body snaps back up in a sharp reflex action, and she plunges the instrument into the back of her assailant, who pivots in turn and falls backward toward the lens of the camera and heavily on to the scissors which are thereby plunged further into his back. Tracing this superbly choreographed movement demonstrates how it heightens tension and dynamism but retains balance to the whole sequence. A subsequent shot when Tony Wendice returns, frames the foreshortened body of the murder victim in a manner which may be compared to the representation of dead bodies in a number of paintings from the historical canon, including deposition images of Christ by Mantegna, Caravaggio and possibly Manet's *Dead Matador*, some of which Hitchcock may have seen reproductions of, or in museums during his many trips to Europe. The first two paintings may have also been discussed in art history lectures that he attended at London University in 1915.

The cinematographic camera tricks in the strangling sequence hark back to the German Expressionist film makers, particularly to Murnau and Fritz Lang, but Hitchcock is less interested in disrupting the proscenium frame, which he does just once in the sequence, than in reinforcing its hegemony. Hitchcock claimed to not be interested in watching other directors direct, but for many years he kept up with the newest releases and took a keen interest in the critical responses in the media. His aesthetic interests in this film are not limited to the graphics in the tiles and credits, the choice of objects on the mantle, the murder itself or even the disposition of the body.[20] In this film Hitchcock also provides two detailed shots to reinforce the links between death and high art. As the camera pans over the body of Lesgate it pulls back to take in a pile of three large folio size art history books, monographs of Renaissance masters: Giovanni Bellini, Leonardo

Da Vinci and the third title on the spine, although difficult to read, is possibly that of Michelangelo or Raphael. The pile of art history books is on screen for a split second, an insert during the sequence in which Tony is consoling Margot while he is pocketing the key that he retrieved from Lesgate's body. These books were obviously placed here by Hitchcock, another detail "for his own satisfaction" to signal the close affinity between the fine arts of painting and murder. The split second images of these art monographs provide a contrast to the popular arts of knitting signified by ball of wool and knitting needles in the knitting basket on the table from which Grace Kelly grasped the pair of scissors that she used to defend herself from the murderer. The scissors were also previously alluded to by Wendice in the scene where the three are having martinis and Margot shows Mark the clippings from Tony's tennis career that she is pasting into his scrap book. At this point they also embark on a discussion about "the perfect murder" for Mark's detective story.

Although he is credited with saying "the best way to do it is with scissors" the quintessential and aesthetically transcendent murder endorsed by Hitchcock seems to be strangling which provides an opportunity for viewing a protracted struggle -- *a life* and *death spectacle* – between two or more protagonists.[21] Instances of murder by strangling appear in fifteen of his films: *The Lodger, Shadow of a Doubt, Notorious, Stage Fright*, the late version of *The Man Who Knew Too Much, Vertigo* and *North by North West*; strangling is graphically detailed in *The Lady Vanishes, Jamaica Inn, Rope, Strangers on a Train, Dial M for Murder, Rear Window, Torn Curtain* and *Frenzy*.[22] The strangling sequences in *Rope* and *Dial M for Murder* are the most sexualised in their connotations. In *Rope*, the strangling is unseen but the audio image provided by Hitchcock intimates that this is a pleasurable act similar to a sexual climax (*un petit mort*). After the act Brandon and Philip even light up cigarette and one asks the other "how do you feel?" as if they had just engaged in vigorous sex.

17. Ray Milland and Grace Kelly in *Dial M for Murder*

I would like to shift register at this point to briefly discuss Andrew Davis'
A Perfect Murder to illustrate the resilience of De Quincey's model of the
fine art of murder in contemporary film and to underline the use of food
art and sex to further this goal. Art, food, sex and film references abound
in *A Perfect Murder* that could be described as Hitchcock thriller to the
letter. Not only does this film represent a riff on *Hitchcock's Dial M for
Murder* but Davis has also quoted the work of many other filmmakers,
providing a panoply of cinematographic and directing styles of directors

such as Orson Welles, Brian de Palma, Martin Scorsese and Peter Bogdanovich. The film opens for example, with a Wellesian travelling aerial shot through the skylight windows into an artist's studio loft to survey the lovemaking of Emily (Gwyneth Paltrow) and painter David Shaw (Viggo Mortensen).[23] David Shaw whom we learn later was educated at Berkeley and Cal Arts (California Institute for the Arts) dresses fashionably in black. Emily Taylor works as a translator to a UN Ambassador, and is from a wealthy background with a 100 million inheritance. Stephen Taylor (Michael Douglas) her husband, is a multi millionaire financier who is about to undergo a financial meltdown, described by one of his consultants as "the equivalent of the Chernobyl disaster."[24] Recognizing that his options are limited he decides to blackmail Shaw into killing his wife. Taylor has done his homework on his wife's lover and on a pretence of interest in seeing and perhaps collecting some of his artwork, he discloses his knowledge of the affair as well as the extensive research he has undertaken on the artist, contemptuously reciting details of David's (aka Winston's) miserable life "made up of depressing little scams" for which he has spent three years in Soledad prison, which is where he learned how to paint. Asked by Shaw what's in it for him, Taylor says "my agenda doesn't concern you."

The set up for the murder is similar to Hitchcock's in *Dial M*, although both depart somewhat from some of the details in the Frederick Knott play. The husband is to take his wife's latchkey and place it in a spot for the murderer to retrieve and Shaw is then cued to attack the wife at a predetermined time as she answers the telephone. The husband's alibi is a high stakes card game and a phone call at the expected time of death to his stockbroker. In *Dial M for Murder* the alibi for Tony Wendice is provided by a Stag party that both he and his wife's lover attend. In the Davis version, the husband is expecting David the lover to be the murderer, not as it turns out, one of his prison acquaintances. Before he leaves the loft where he makes the arrangement Stephen tells David that the murder should appear to be "spur of the moment...the word bludgeon comes to mind." Janine, the Taylor's African American housekeeper has made one of her legendary roasts and the meat thermometer that subsequently becomes the domestic murder instrument, is thrust into the neck of the roast with a resounding "thwack!"

The murder scene employs typical Hitchcockian suspense evoking edits, cross cuts and inserts between Gwyneth relaxing seductively in her bath, this invoking the vulnerability of Janet Leigh in *Psycho*, and the murderer stealing his way into the apartment. At his card game Stephen makes two calls on his cell phone, one to his broker and the next to Emily. Knowing she is in the bath he lets it ring until she answers it... "Hello," she says, "hello," (three times). "Who is this?" and at this signal the masked intruder springs to strangle her. Like the Hitchcock original this is also a highly choreographed but much more violent sequence. Emily is literally thrown across the kitchen counter. The assailant gropes after her and with his hand in a strangle hold around her throat; he attempts to reach up with his other to grasp an appropriate bludgeoning instrument, an overhanging fry pan. In a reverse shot to the Hitchcock, Emily reaches back into the sink to pick up a sabbatier knife which is knocked out of her hand and then, with what seems to be her last breath, she grabs the needle sharp stick thermometer that Janine had previously set down into the drying tray, picks it up and thrusts it into the jugular vein of her assailant's neck, spurting blood - in a 'gross out' imitation of a slasher movie - in all directions. As the thermometer enters the neck it makes the same repulsive 'thwack' sound it had previously, being thrust into the roast by Janice -- enough to turn a hardened carnivore into a vegetarian. *A Perfect Murder* also employs many postmodern ironies. For example inspector Hubbard (John Williams) in the original *Dial M* is replaced by the inimitable David Suchet, who plays Hercule Poirot the famous detective in the Agatha Christie stories, profiled to great acclaim on the PBS Mystery Series. In this film Poirot's Daliesque waxed moustache is gone, a contrast to the full brush moustache worn by Inspector Hubbard in *Dial M for Murder*. Like its model in Hitchcock, this perfect murder turns out to be not so perfect, not quite reaching the perfection of high art removed from the banality of domestic life - that is cooking in the Davis film and knitting in *Dial M for Murder*.

---

[1]Expanded interest in Hitchcock is also the result of the release of some of his work from excessive copyright controls.

[2] Jeff Bleckner also directed *Brotherly Love*; *Target: Favourite Son*; *When Your Lover Leaves* and *White Water Summer*

[3] Gus Van Sant also directed *Drugstore Cowboy* and *My Own Private Idaho*

[4]Wittkower, R. & M. *Born Under Saturn. The Character and Conduct of Artists. A Documented History from Antiquity to the French Revolution* New York: Random House, 1963.

[5]Dozens of painted versions of this story exist, the most famous by Ludovicio Caracci (1916) Guido Reni (c1620), and Johann Carl Loth c. 1675)

[6] Modleski., T. *The Women Who Knew Too Much: Hitchcock and Feminist Theory* New York, London Methuen 1988:117

[7] Dworkin, A and McKinnon, A. (eds) *In Harms Way: The Pornography Civil Rights Hearings* Cambridge, Mass. Harvard University Press, 1998

[8]Truffaut, 1967:149

[9] Bordonaro, Peter "Dial M. A Play by Frederick Knott/a film by Alfred Hitchcock" Sight and Sound 45:3 summer 1976:179 1976; Michael Kerbel "3D, or not 3D" Film Comment 16, No 6 Nov-Dec 1980 11-20; Fulvio Contenti *Dial M* Filmcritica 32:11 (January, 1981), 45.

[10] Kapsis, R. *Hitchcock: the Making of a Reputation* Chicago: University of Chicago Press, 1992:2

[11]Spoto, D. *The Dark Side of Genius: the Life of Alfred Hitchcock* New York: Ballantine Books, 1983:262

[12] See the *Hitchcock Annual* (Vol: 1-15) Gottlieb, Sydney and Allen, Richard (eds), Sacred Heart University Fairfield CT

[13]Cohen, T. *Hitchcock's Cryptonomies* Volume I. *Secret Agents* and Volume 11 *War Machines* Minneapolis, London, University of Minnesota Press 2005

[14]Truffaut, F., with Scott, H.G. *Hitchcock* New York: Simon and Schuster, 1967:156

[15]Derrida, J. *The Truth in Painting* Trans., Bennington, G. and McLeod, I., Chicago, University of Chicago Press, 1987:10

[16] Spoto, D., pp563-4

[17] Knott, F. *Dial M for Murder* New York, Random House, 1953:82-3

[18] Hollywood's 3D phase was very brief starting and ending in 1952. The craze was over before Hitchcock's *Dial M for Murder* hit the screen and it was therefore shown flat.

[19]Rohmer, E and Chabrol, C. Hitchcock: *The First Forty-Four Films* translated by Stanley Hochman, New York, Unger 1979

[20] The opening title for the film shows a black telephone with the camera then focussing upon a red letter 'M" on the dial with the rest of the title script forming above and below it, accompanied by romantic theme music composed by Dimitri Tiomkin.

[21] *Paraphilia* is a term used in psycho pathology to categorize a clinically defined deviancy that causes those afflicted to seek sexual gratification by raping, stabbing and throttling women and children.

[22] Spoto, 1983:353

[23]This shot is a quotation from Orson Welles travelling aerial shot into *Citizen Kane*'s Xanadu.

[24]This is a reference to the meltdown of the Chernobyl nuclear reactor in the Ukraine

Chapter 8

Art and Death in the Films of Peter Greenaway

> The five thousand year history of western painting is more important for my aesthetic interests than one hundred years of cinema critique. (Peter Greenaway)[1]

> In the last analysis, the artist may shout from all the rooftops that he is a genius: he will have to wait for the verdict of the spectator in order that his declarations take a social value and that, posterity includes him in the primers of Artist History. (Marcel Duchamp)[2]

Peter Greenaway is arguably one of Britain's most articulate contemporary film makers, a polymath, seigniorial in his bearing and disposition, yet in many ways also a somewhat private individual who alternately savours and disavows his position as that country's most successful avant-garde film maker;[3] one who has regularly disparaged, before Lars von Trier's *Dogme* Manifesto made an international movement out of it, commercial (Hollywood) cinema for its manipulatory cinematic conventions and classical narrative schemas.[4] This chapter and the next explore *representations* of art, artists and art history in the films of Peter Greenaway with a specific focus upon the conflations of art and death in several films: *The Falls* (1980), *The Draughtsman's Contract* (1982), *A Zed and Two Noughts* (1985), *The Belly of an Architect* (1987), and *The Cook, The Thief, His Wife and Her Lover* (1990).[5] Like Alfred Hitchcock, Peter Greenaway's film directing sensibilities are marked by his relationships with his family, his class background and education, particularly his early training as a visual artist, and a less discernable, yet none-the-less important quality, his 'Britishness'; that is a certain predisposition to recognize the complexities of class, history, colonial power, language, behavioral traits, and last but not least, humour. Peter Greenaway was born on 5th April, 1942 (an Aries) into what he has described as a "a *petit bourgeois*" family in Newport a town in southern Wales.[6] In several interviews he has spoken of spending his early years living in a working class house in the industrial area of Newport, and with his father away during most of WWII, being raised by his mother, grandmother and aunts. His early education took place at Forest School, a public school in Newport and when the war ended the family moved to the east end of London to be somewhat nearer his father's family in Essex.[7]

 In 1960 Greenaway turned down an undergraduate placement at Cambridge University to enroll in Walthamstow College of Art to pursue an NDD (National Diploma of Design), where one of his fellow students was Ian Dury (1942-1999),[8] subsequently the popular lead singer of the post-punk band Ian Dury and the Blockheads.[9] Peter Blake (now Sir Peter Blake), the famous British painter taught at Walthamstow for three years from 1961 to 1964 and Greenaway probably experienced some close first hand contact with Blake who at that time had a developing reputation as a Pop artist with a strong interest in Elvis, Marilyn Monroe and The Beatles. A recent graduate from the Royal College of Art, Blake taught at four of the London based art schools and in these positions he had the opportunity to traffic many art ideas back and forth between them, some of which, for example the post surrealist collaging together of a diverse selection of images and text excised from popular media, are identifiable in Greenaway's early aesthetic approaches to drawing and painting. In 1963, Greenaway saw his first solo exhibition of works of R.B. Kitaj, an expatriate American artist, at the Marlborough Art Gallery.[10] This exhibition strongly impressed him and reinforced his interest in mining both art historical and contemporary media images as well as using text in his art. In an interview in 1990 Greenaway affirmed that Kitaj's work provided valuable legitimation for his own artistic directions.

> Kitaj legitimized text, he legitimised arcane and elitist information, he drew and painted as many as ten different ways on the same canvas, he threw ideas around like confetti, ideas that were both pure painterliness and direct Warburg quotation; there was unashamed political passion and extravagantly bold sexual imagery. His ideas were international, far from English timidity and English jokiness, and the English timid and jokey pop art.[11]

In interviews undertaken throughout the 1980s and 90s, Greenaway provided many other illuminating insights into the various artistic influences to which he was subjected during the late 1960s and early

1970s. He identifies three major ones: "Land Art, Minimalism and Conceptualism. My fascinations within this local contemporary public baggage journeyed through the work of Richard Long, Ian Hamilton Finlay, Walter De Maria, Robert Morris, Frank Stella, R.B. Kitaj, and as with everyone else, Marcel Duchamp, and their visual overspill into a cinema language somewhere between and including Hollis Frampton and Alain Renais." Declarations by artists about their creative beginnings should be treated with some caution as for many reasons some experiences may be privileged and others repressed. Absences in an artist's creative origin narratives are therefore occasionally more revealing than articulated presences. Greenaway is quite candid about his artistic origins and his sardonic display of critical self-consciousness for his own rites of passage are a welcome change to the auto-hagiography that subtend the musings of many artists. In his origin narratives Greenaway does not directly acknowledge the various aesthetic struggles that were going on at the time in London as a reflection of international pressures wrought by the displacement of Paris as the international centre of contemporary art and New York's increasing hegemony in the art world. Indirectly however, he does acknowledge this differential in cultural power. Just two of the artists identified in his list, Richard Long and Ian Hamilton Finlay, are British; five are American who, with the exception of Kitaj, forged their careers in the United States. Duchamp and Renais are the only European (French) artists Greenaway mentions, both of whom were acknowledged as internationally important figures in both French and Anglo-American contexts. Early on it seems Greenaway identified his art with an international rather than a local, regional, or national context. At Walthamstow College of Art Greenaway was provided with a foundation to European art history and specifically the work of historically important English artists such as Reynolds, Hogarth, Gainsborough, the pre-Raphaelites, Wyndham Lewis and the Vorticists, and probably English modernists such as Henry Moore, Ben Nicholson and Barbara Hepworth, who had by this time developed international careers and were lionized by the British art establishment. Outside Walthamstow, Greenaway was exposed to the work of more contemporary British artists. In the late 1960s and early 1970s a larger group of English artists, in addition to the American expatriate Kitaj, were becoming more prominent on the international stage, and it is revealing that Greenaway does not acknowledge at least some of these individuals in his origin narratives: for example Francis Bacon whose work he quotes in several films and also: David Hockney, Allen Jones, Richard Hamilton, Brigit Riley, Eduardo

Paolozzi, Peter Philips, Derrick Boshier, Pauline Boty, William Tucker, William Pye, to name a few. Like other young English artists with a close eye on their contemporaries, Greenaway would have been exposed to the work of British artists represented in the book *Private View* (1964), and probably read it. This book enjoyed wide circulation in England and elsewhere including Britain's former colonies, Canada, Australia, and New Zealand.[12] Edited by John Russell and Brian Robertson of the Whitechapel Gallery, *Private View* contained large black and white and colour photographs taken by Anthony Armstrong-Jones, then husband of Princess Margaret. A large and glossy book, *Private View* was a comprehensive celebration of the artists of this time, many of whom were recent graduates from the RCA, and included information about the major art institutions, galleries and collectors, mostly in and around London. With its intimate photographs of artists posing or at work in their studios, this book has been described as a type of *zeitgeist* text, and its presence in the mid 1960s was as much a sign of London's 'swinging sixties' as The Beatles, Cilla Black, Carnaby Street fashions and Antonioni's film *Blowup* (1966). The influence of *Private View* on the subsequent development of the English art scene is hard to measure but judging by the meteoric rise in the reputations of some artists represented in the book, as well as the subsequent dominance of certain art styles during these two decades, it was probably considerable.[13] It is also intriguing that Greenaway does not mention Pop art in this interview except to disparage it as "jokey English Pop art." Pop was probably the most important contemporary style to which Greenaway would have been exposed, at least informally, through his education at Walthamstow College of Art. The staples of art education at this time in most British art schools continued to be representational drawing, perspective study, anatomy, life drawing, copying from the masters and technical training in conventional techniques associated with the fine arts (painting, drawing, printmaking, sculpture and photography), design, and less frequently, some exposure to craft. Paul Melia co-editor of *Peter Greenaway Artworks 63-98* indicates that most of the NDD diploma paintings at that time were domestic interiors, portraits and landscapes, "Impressionism mixed with social realism - as interpreted by the Camden Town Group and the Euston Road School. With few exceptions art schools were immune to Continental or North American modernism."[14] But if the milieu was somewhat conservative in many British art schools, ambitious students like Greenaway tended to absorb everything cultural within their domain and given the evidence of his art work from this time, for example the three panel *Nativity Star* (1963), and other works from his final year at art school, it is obvious that his fine art education had a certain breadth and depth, both practically and academically. His paintings and drawings from this period suggest that Walthamstow fine art graduates were not totally immunized against contemporary developments in art.

Greenaway graduated in 1964, the same year as The Beatles appeared in the film *A Hard Days Night* and the Tate Gallery mounted its important survey exhibition *Art of A Decade*. The dominant international art movements at this time were Abstract Expressionism, Pop and Op art that were about to be superceded in the next few years by Fluxus, Minimalism, Conceptual art and *arte povera*. The influence of the International Situationists (1959-1972), in visual art, film and politics, was also considerable in England during the sixties (T.J. Clark and Christopher Gray were members) but the IS influence on British art and film remained unacknowledged by most art and film historians well into the 1980s.[15] The English art critic Lawrence Alloway introduced 'Pop' art --the neologism a contraction of 'popular' into cultural discourse in 1952. The Pop aesthetic itself was forged over the next few years in the crucible of the Institute of Contemporary Art by the so-called Independent Group (IG), consisting of Alloway, the architects Allison and Peter Smithson, art and architecture historian Reyner Banham, and the artist Richard Hamilton, whose collage *Just What Is It That Makes Today's Homes So Different, So Appealing* (1956), became an international icon of Pop sensibility, followed a few years later by the signal work of the American Pop artists: Johns, Rauschenberg, Warhol, Lichtenstein, Oldenburg, Dine and Rosenquist. Many of the discussions undertaken by the Independent Group centred on: popular culture, post-war mass consumerism, billboards, science fiction, comics, the new technologies, robotics and contemporary American cinema. Out of these discussions developed a so-called 'anti-aesthetic' as well as much of the foundational critical discourse, vocabulary and processes of Pop art, including a reconstituted collage/montage aesthetic adopted from the lessons of the historical avant-gardes: Cubism, Dada, Futurism, Russian Constructivism, Productivism and French Surrealism. The IG also introduced the term "New Brutalism" (1954) to describe the technologically expressive functionalism of the Smithson's modernist architecture. In many interviews Greenaway identifies Kitaj as a major formative influence on his work yet Peter Blake who actually taught at Walthamstow and produced the iconic design for the cover of the Beatles' album *Sgt Pepper's Lonely Hearts Club Band* during Greenaway's time as a student is passed over in silence. Perhaps the reason for this was because he was producing "jokey Pop art," or was a Marilyn Monroe and Elvis fan, contrasting with Greenaway's increasing involvement with more contemporary music, including a developing interest in the avant-garde, especially the work of the American composer John Cage, but not it seems, Cornelius Cardew, who was the English vanguard equivalent. Greenaway's developing interest in Cage's musical innovations reinforced his understanding of Marcel Duchamp's critical nominalism and *objet trouvé* aesthetic which by the late 1960s and early 1970s had been absorbed into many art world contexts, including university art programs and art colleges. It also led him to appreciate the work of Phillip Glass, Brian Eno and Michael Nyman who collaborated with Greenaway on many projects.

Kitaj, Blake and David Hockney were recent graduates from the RCA, the school that Greenaway also had applied to enter, but in the company of several hundred other applicants in his application year he was unsuccessful which must have been a major disappointment for both him and his family who expected much from their ambitious son.[16] Greenaway considered his subsequent employment for eight months as a doorkeeper and attendant ("a minion" as he describes it), in the film distribution department at British Film Institute as a temporary 'stop gap' measure toward fulfilling his ambition to become a film maker, which he had already signaled with the purchase of a Bolex 16mm camera. The BFI turned out to be an excellent context for a young film maker and Greenaway undertook "a crash course in film history" by screening every film that he "could lay his hands on" and later enrolled in a BA in Film Studies. His rapid introduction to film editing at the BFI subsequently enabled him to obtain continuing employment at the wonderfully named Central Office of Information, where he worked for the next ten years as a film editor and director of so-called 'information films' for the Government. This position provided him with further excellent opportunities to consolidate his training in film production and to obtain a better exposure to film history. The position at the COI also gave him some time to pursue his own painting and filmmaking.

Peter Greenaway, like Alfred Hitchcock before him, is a product of the British class system, and although his parents were upwardly mobile *petit bourgeois*[17] who, in the company of millions of other Britons, believed in the value of hard work, determination and a good education (effort, perseverance and success), they were also aware of the rigid social structures that inhibited class mobility and transcendence to people with

Welsh origins like themselves, who for generations had worked in the service of the titled and landed gentry "as gardeners, horticultural people, who looked after estates."[18] It is interesting to note that in this comment Greenaway inserts the somewhat scientific term "horticulture" and the phrase "who looked after estates," perhaps to provide these tasks with a little more symbolic capital and therefore distinguish his origins as being on a somewhat more elevated plane than tenant farmers, game keepers, farm labourers or peasants.[19] In common with other British working and middle class youths it was primarily education, not kinship, or family connections that provided young men like Greenaway with the necessary symbolic capital to transcend their social register. And like Hitchcock and many other artists and intellectuals with working and lower middle class backgrounds, for example, Raymond Williams, his Welsh countryman, the hidden injuries of class are never much below the surface in either his writing or his work as an artist.[20]

In interviews and conversations Greenaway has occasionally cited Francois Truffaut who "said that a film maker always gives himself away with his first film" cheerfully offering that his own early films established "all the leitmotifs, recipes, agendas, obsessions and fascinations of all the subsequent years of film making." Notwithstanding his endorsement of Truffaut's assumption, which was originally directed towards Alfred Hitchcock, Greenaway's first few films do reveal a few, although not all of his "leitmotifs, obsessions and fascinations," but the ones that are evident have remained with him for over three decades. His first film, *Death of Sentiment* (1959-62), prefigures a developing obsession with art, melancholy and death, which feature as major leitmotifs in most of his subsequent work.[21] In a 1997 interview he stated, with some irony, that *Death...* "is a work of juvenilia made with a friend, Brian Love. It was made in Super 8 in black and white, about churchyard furniture, crosses, flying angels, typography on grave stones....filmed in four large London cemeteries, the most famous being where Karl Marx is buried. It was also filmed in a graveyard close to where William Hogarth used to live, so his tomb is in it, there are references to painters as well - a romantic essay on melancholia."[22] It is interesting that Greenaway identifies two political names here, Karl Marx and William Hogarth whose drawings, prints and paintings representing the foibles of the upper classes as well as the injustices and absurdities of the English class system as a whole, must have impressed him, for he quotes Hogarth images from the *Rake's Progress*, *Harlot's Progress* and *Marriage à la mode* in several films, including *The*

Draughtsman's Contract. The spectres of Marx and Marxism haunt several works and are most present in Greenaway's trenchant critique of class politics and *laissez faire* capitalism in *The Cook, the Thief, His Wife and Her Lover* (1990).

Art, melancholy and death accompanied usually by Eros, figure frequently in Greenaway's paintings, films, installations and operas. For example, *The Death of Webern and Others* (1994) conflates art and death literally in what Greenaway termed "a musical theatre in ten parts;" the ten narratives exploring the deaths of several composers, two real historical figures, both assassinated, Anton Webern (Schonberg's most talented student), and John Lennon of the Beatles; the others, fictitious: Samuel Bucket (a play on the names Samuel Becket, the Irish writer and Charlie Bucket a character in Roald Dahl's *Charlie and The Chocolate Factory*), Geoffrey Fallthius (from *The Falls)*, Antonio Merseil and Manuel De Rosa. Many of Greenaway's early films reveal his other themes and obsessions: maps, art history, Greek and Roman mythology, the naked human body, water (in all states), body fluids, birds (in honour of his father who was an amateur ornithologist), language, (foreign languages, puns, anagrams and acrostics), alphabets and numbers. A few biographeme and signature symbols such as rams (sheep and lambs) - a personal homage to his astrological sign Aires - also appear occasionally, for example in two sequences in *The Draughtsman's Contract*.

Train (1966) Greenaway's short 'homage' to the first film in the history of cinema produced by the Lumiere brothers as well as J. M. W. Turner's painting *Rain, Steam and Speed: The Great Western Railroad* (1844), documents the powerful energy of a steam powered train arriving at Waterloo Station, subsequently accompanied with a *musique concrète* score. *Tree* (1966), a 16mm five part film (5 minutes) accompanied by Webern's *Five Pieces for Orchestra*, is a nature versus culture 'narrative' woven through several shots of a Wych Elm adjacent to the Royal Albert Festival Hall. *Tree* is also included in *The Falls* (1980), with appropriate death imagery as biography # 83, Geoffrey Fallthew. *Revolution* (1968) is a 3 minute film of a demonstration in central London edited to The Beatles' song *Revolution* also produced during that year. *5 Postcards from Capital Cities* (1968), a film 35 minutes in length, concentrates attention on the ports in five cities, and *Intervals* (1969), consists of a short compilation of Italian alphabet corrections accompanied by Vivaldi's *Winter* composition from *The Four Seasons* concerto. Greenaway's most ambitious film from this period, *H is for House* (1973), is a complex meditation on the letter H, the Human body, bird names beginning with H, and an encyclopaedic review of many other 'H' topics, including H for Hannah, Greenaway's daughter to whom the film is dedicated. *Windows* (1974), represents a landscape seen through windows with the addition of statistics about the 37 (reversal of the date, 73) people who jumped out of windows in the parish of "W' in 1973. *Goole by Numbers* (1976), consists of shots of numerals edited together in sequence acquired in the town of Goole on the Humber River, followed by *1-100* (1978), a collaboration with Michael Nyman, again a compilation of shots of sequential numbers 1-100, taken from five European city contexts, Berlin, Paris, Rome, Florence and Brussels.[23] In all these works, numbers and language provide the primary elements and *raison d'être* for the film, linking Greenaway to a large number of Fluxus, *arte povera*, Minimal, and Conceptual artists, among them: Andre, Brecht, Ono, Graham, Long, Tremlett, Morris, LeWitt, Merz, Ruscha, Kosuth, Art and Language, Kawara, Gilbert and George, Darboven and Smithson all of whom, during the late 1960s, and early 1970s, employed language and number in their work. There were also a few film makers for example Norman McLaren, the Scots Canadian animator who made animated films using numbers and letters during this period but the most important links are to Jean Luc Godard and Hollis Frampton, the American experimental filmmaker whose work shares similar structural, temporal-spatial and thematic concerns to Greenaway. Frampton's *Hapax Logomena* (1971-72), for example, appears as the name of an important VUE language in *The Falls*.[24]

Peter Greenaway has frequently affirmed that "the five thousand year history of western painting is more important for [his] aesthetic interests than one hundred years of cinema critique" and the fact that many of his films are constructed from still shots endorses Roland Barthes notion that "the still is the major artifact of the projected film."[25] To reinforce his belief in the importance (omnipotence) of painting and art history, Greenaway's films are frequently constructed as an ensemble of still lives (*tableaux vivants*) and at times resemble an episodic grouping of theatrical sketches or works of performance art. In a response to a question regarding painting and cinematography in *The Draughtsman's Contract* Greenaway offered "there are three reasons for this. First, the facetious reason: paintings don't move. Secondly, with a still camera you throw the emphasis on the dialogue and the soundtrack...thirdly, it is a sheer reaction to the St. Vitus dance of film making over the last few years. It seems to me that most camera work is done for no good structural reason, or even good emotional, or mood reason."[26] Arguing that Greenaway is a neo-baroque artist Christina Degli-Espositi Reinert has encapsulated in one paragraph many of the painters whom Greenaway has quoted in his films. We see Turner, Constable, Tiepolo, Veronese, George de la Tour in *the Draughtsman's Contract*; Jan Vermeer of Delft in *A Zed and Two Noughts* (1986); Piero Della Francesca and Velasquez in *The Belly of an Architect*; Rubens, Velasquez, Mantegna in *Drowning with Numbers*; Frans Hals in *The Cook, the Thief, his Wife and her Lover*; de la Tour, Antonio Da Messina, Bronzino, Veronese, Titian, Botticelli, Michelangelo, Rembrandt, Velasquez, Piranesi, and Breugel in *Prospero's Books*; and Bellini, Carpaccio, and Caravaggio in the baby of *The Baby of Mâcon*. [27]

There are actually many more, at least three times as many references to artists, and specific artworks in each of the films mentioned including more contemporary artists than most Greenaway critics are willing to countenance. Reinert is familiar with the Mannerist, Baroque and postmodern strategies of historical quotation and is concerned (with Umberto Eco and Paul de Man) that over interpretation can also present problems in reading the work of an artist such as Greenaway. Other Greenaway scholars, Dayana Stetco for example, have also voiced concern with the problems of interpretation that are presented to readers of Greenaway's work. "His texts humiliate hermeneutics and saturated with allusions, remove completely the allusion of finiteness."[28] In his writings, lectures and interviews[29] Greenaway has argued that all major works of art are "encyclopaedic in nature,"[30] and the evidence available in his own work, from the earliest paintings and films to his most recent meta cinematic magnum opus, *The Tulse Luper* project,[31] certainly reinforce his commitment to construct a dense matrix of meaning for his paintings, films, and operas, both individually, and as part of a coherent body of work. "The works of art that I admire, even contemporary ones *Like One Hundred Years of Solitude* [Marquez], or any three page story by Borges, have that ability to put all the world together. My movies are sections of this world encyclopaedia."[32] Keeping company with his favourite film makers: Ingmar Bergman (whose film *The Seventh Seal* (1956) he acknowledges as an important early influence),[33] Fellini, Pasolini, Antonioni, Godard, Bertolucci, Rohmer, Straub, and Renais,[34] Peter Greenaway is also an *auteur* in the best sense of this overused term, and as such, he is acutely aware of protecting his creative autonomy as an artist/author, even when on occasion, he registers his strong criticism of the auteur, genre concepts and other keywords in the film studies lexicon.[35] There is one other name, arguably more important to Greenaway than those above, Alfred Hitchcock, whom he rarely mentions in interviews or conversation, yet pays discrete homage to in several works and occasionally borrows from, for films such as *The Falls* (1980), *a Zed and Two Noughts; The Belly of an Architect, The Cook, the Thief, his Wife and her Lover* (1990), and others, a point which has not gone unnoticed by a few of his critics. Amy Lawrence for example, notes that there are many covert and overt references in *The Falls* to Hitchcock's *Psycho* (1960), *The Birds* (1963) and *Marnie* (1964). She also notes the omnipresence of the death theme in the work of both filmmakers.

> "As in Hitchcock's work, criminality covers or stands in for the frequently violent relationships between men and women. *Marnie* alone filters male- female relations through such crimes as embezzlement, blackmail, the use of aliases and disguises, prostitution, child molesting, rape, and more. In *The Falls*, the innumerable crimes, disappointments, and misunderstandings between men and women mirror the hostility of the universe. Death colours everything."[36]

With Hitchcock and his other favourite film makers - *auteurs* all - Greenaway's signature is always represented in the details of his films, providing continuity from work to work, assuming a richly woven totality that he recognises as a product of his aesthetic intentions and the overarching goal of his project, which like many artists is to construct an extraordinary artistic life worthy of ordination to the art historical canon, if not strictly canonization itself.[37] There is something Wagnerian in his multi-layered production of film, visual art (painting, drawing, installation), opera, installations, books, as if it he has taken very seriously the notion of the *gesamkunstwerk* (the complete or total art work), as a prescription to willfully construct not only the powerful *oeuvre*, but also the *exemplary* life in art. Greenaway cites Jorge Luis Borges, and occasionally Joyce, Tolkien and Marquez, as models for literary complexity, but his allegorical mining of art and literature is also similar to Walter Benjamin's quoting from the historical ruins of encyclopedic knowledge. As Benjamin wrote in one of his exquisite aphorisms, "quotations in my work are like robbers at a graveyard who relieve an idler of his convictions." Similarly, Greenaway's use of quotations issues distinct challenges to his spectators and readers - some of whom have registered their displeasure in surprisingly trenchant reviews - to engage in exemplary, even heroic acts of interpretation, in order that they too, may be relieved of their convictions. Every element within a given *mise en scene,* and even outside of the frame of a Greenaway film, opera or installation, is prefigured as semiotic *mélange,* or "postmodern pastiche," functioning simultaneously to enrich the meanings available in his films and to reveal the fecundity of the creative mind - both his, and the reader's.[38] Greenaway functions like an archaeologist, a taxonomer, philologist, numerologist, digging, mining "cannibalizing" the history of art, ideas and philosophy, quoting and appropriating imagery and texts at will from the works of 'the masters' to whom he is occasionally compared.[39] This eclecticism is arguably an identifiable mark of his British art education in the 1960s, and his intelligent apperception of the social and ideological dynamics of art history provide him with the recognition that quoting, borrowing from the canon, not only further valorizes the work of the artists thus used, but also ensures maximum potential for the quoter's own art practice to be recognized as worthy for insertion into the pantheon of art.[40] The history of modernist art demonstrates that this appropriative/ expropriative process is a symbolic overturning - a 'killing' of the masters - the *de jure* method to (re) constitute and affirm the signal importance (omnipotence) of the contemporary innovations of the avant-garde. Historical researchers of the historical avant-gardes (Hadjinicolaou, Bürger, Clark, Guilbaut, Krauss, Crow) have articulated the ideological structures operating within vanguard formations, reinforcing the notion that these often exhibit an oedipal trajectory, a symbolic killing of the father by artists who borrow, quote, appropriate/ expropriate *from* art history in order to insert themselves *into* art history. This is a profoundly ideological; a teleological movement towards an (in) finitude - as well as evidence of a tautological progress and/or egress - an eschatological "tarrying with the negative" (Žižek, 1998), in the sense that it becomes, ultimately and irrevocably, a dialogue/dance with [im] mortality.

To read a Greenaway film competently it is often necessary to employ all of the deconstructive tricks of Jacques Derrida, that is circumnavigating four times, and then some. The titles of Greenaway films, artworks, books and operas provide the literate reader with an opportunity to construct a multiplicity of meanings even before one has entered the time space of the *mise en scène.* Ockham's Razor (less is more), the apodictically reductive *modus operandi* of the Minimalists and Conceptualists he cites as major influences, may actually have less significance for an artist like

Greenaway, whose strategic methods for producing layered meanings, meta-textual puzzles, ironical juxtapositions, palimpsests, are more typical of baroque art and surrealism's "chance meeting on a dissecting table of a sewing machine and an umbrella."[41] This is to say that his film titles and the names of characters typically become an occasion for readers to recognize a puzzle, and if its not there in the artifact, to assume the task of creating one. Accordingly, his interpreters are stimulated to search for the anagram, acrostic, linguistic or visual pun, the numerical series or alphabetical reference that subtend and/or augment the work. Some of these puzzles are archly simple, like a newspaper crossword; others are highly problematic and contradictory; a Byzantine or baroque myriad of complexity; mythology, geometry, numerology, ornithology, taxonomic and language games, all of which become opportunities for Greenaway's creative manipulation. As he writes:

> "If a numerical, alphabetical or colour coding system is employed, it is done so deliberately as a device, to construct, counteract, dilute, augment, or complement the all pervasive cinema interest in plot, in narrative, in the 'I'm now going to tell you a story' school of film making, which nine times out of ten begins life as literature, an origin with very different concerns, ambitions and characteristics from those of cinema.[42]

Film titles and the names of characters are therefore very intriguing in this respect, for example *Gang Lion* contracts to 'Ganglion' (a knot of nerves cells, centre of interest) but retains the privileged meanings of both words, similarly *Gang Lion and the Visual Flush* and *The Water Papers* (a set of 50 drawings), register his interest in chance, fluidity, contingency and excess. *Tulse Luper and the Centre Walk* and the paintings and drawings in *A Walk Through H* (1978) signal his cognitive investment in mapping, autobiography, taxonomies, kinship, language, English rural and urban life, and the environmental artwork of Richard Long. *The Falls* represents simultaneously Greenaway's fascination with waterfalls, the 'regime of coincidence' (Duchamp), nomenclature in the telephone directory, fear of flying, failure and the Fall of Man, among other things. Like Borges and Foucault, the order of things, the identity, naming of things (nominalization) are of crucial importance for Greenaway, and several of his critics have reflected on the puzzles and multiple meanings contained in his work, some of which may not have been intended, but nevertheless are implicated in his aesthetic strategies for meaning making. For example there are twenty-seven possible variations for Kracklite, the extravagant surname of the American architect obsessed with Étienne-Louis Boullée in Greenaway's film *The Belly of an Architect*. The most conceptually intriguing in terms of the director's obsessions and the film's narrative are: "Ark Tickle", "Leak Trick", "Track Like", "Later Kick" and "Alter Kick." The anagrams for the draughtsman/artist Neville, his lovers Mrs. Herbert and her daughter Sarah Tahlmann in *The Draughtsman's Contract* are similarly revealing. For Neville there are seven, including the symbolically relevant, "Level In", "Even Ill" and "I've Nell"! The anagrams for Mrs. Herbert also reflect humorously upon her (and Neville's) sexual behaviour in the film: "Bert Her", "Beth Err" and "Bet Herr." The name Tahlmann for the Herbert's' daughter Sarah Tahlmann delivers the working class acronyms "Malt Nan" and "Malt Ann". [43] And for the name Tulse Luper which appears in many Greenaway films and projects including *The Falls*, and now provides the title of his most recent mega project, there are several hundred anagram variations, among them: "peters lulu," "pester lulu," "tree pull us," "leer lust up," "teler up us," "letup rules," "tuple lures,"" tuple rules," "rules let up" and "ruse et pull." Greenaway may not be an obsessive anagram user, but number and language games remain a constant in many of his films, paintings, operas and art installations, and they therefore routinely become a natural stimulant for reviewers, critics and historians to exercise their own analytic and hermeneutic talents.

The Falls

The Falls (1980) is an important Greenaway film, not only because it provided him with his first notable success as an award winning film maker, thus laying the foundation for his future feature length films, but also because it includes so many of his key themes and obsessions: art, birds, flight, mythology, numerology, doubles, language, chance, coincidence, irony, melancholy, and death. The film consists of 92 (the atomic number of Uranium),[44] short biographies of individuals whose name begins with FALL, all of whom have been affected by the catastrophic VUE (Violent Unknown Event), with 19 million Britons and millions of other individuals around the world, instilling in them the desire to speak in bizarre languages, to be attracted to water, and to attempt to fly like a bird. Members of this population have also been afflicted with unusual, occasionally bizarre, physical and psychological symptoms such as: heart palpitations, high blood pressure, digestive and skin problems, limb growth abnormalities, hair loss, bone calcination, psychoses, neuroses, gender reversals and hermaphroditism. For example biography #2 Constance Ortuist Fallaburr "is a Sackamayer-speaking middle aged woman and she would be the first to admit that her interest in flight has been a long one. Since the Violent Unknown Event Constance has gradually developed an earth-bound shape due to an engrossed coccyx." Biographical Information provided in the voice-overs relate that some VUE victims have engaged in murder or been murdered and others have committed suicide. Not surprisingly, the over arching trope in this film is provided by the Greek myth concerning the deity Icarus. According to legend, King Minos imprisoned Icarus and his father Daedalus, an artisan and inventor in the Minotaur's labyrinth that Daedalus had previously designed to be escape proof. Daedalus artfully fashioned some wax wings for Icarus to escape from the labyrinth. The wing design worked perfectly but when Icarus flew too close to the sun the wings melted, causing him to fall into the sea, which was subsequently named the Icarean Sea in his honour. Greenaway links Icarus to a multitude of human fall, flight and water fantasies, establishing connections to various philosophical, religious (The Books of Genesis and Daniel), literary, and occasionally obscure anthropological texts for example "Why is the Cassowary not a bird?" the title of an important essay by Ralph Bulmer, a New Zealand anthropologist who discusses the allegorical and political economic significance of the Cassowary bird to indigenous tribes in New Guinea. Greenaway also borrows and quotes artifacts from the canons of art and film history, including some major works of art by J. L. David and Piero Della Francesca, cinematic stills appropriated from Hitchcock films and flight related footage from early documentaries.[45] He also places himself in a cameo role (#81) as a documentary film interviewer of a pop star. At one point in the film the voice over asks, "Why are we not interested in Daedalus, the father of Icarus?" This question could stand as a mantra for the whole film, perhaps even Greenaway's life as an artist, with its intimation of an intelligent and creative, yet emotionally absent father, who apparently left a vacuum in Greenaway's life that he attempts to fill with surrogates like Tulse Luper and several other alter ego characters.[46] Greenaway may also be intending to make homage to the character Stephen Daedalus in James Joyce's *A Portrait of the Artist as a Young Man* (1916) who is attempting to escape his own labyrinth in Dublin.

In each FALL biography the description of the VUE effect differs and some of these texts are extremely truncated; for example, #80 Ascrib

Fallstaff "Pernicious inclusion of a fictional character. Criminal charge pending and #84: Morryen Falltrick "Deaf mute with cerebral palsy and wings." Several FALLS (Fallaby, Fallaspy, Fallbutus, Fallcaster) are related through kinship or marriage and their biographical snippets are connected to produce more complex narratives. The overall schema suggests that all of the FALLS are related to one another, if not by phylogenetically, or genealogically, then by chance or circumstance. Some other biographical descriptions from the VUE Directory will serve to illustrate the unusual symptoms of this event. For example, biographical anecdote #60 Edio Fallenby is classified as an elderly woman who "spoke Untowards with a Yorkshire accent and suffered from fluttering eyelashes, excess numeracy and a high blood pressure." Throughout the film there are scattered references to suicide, murder (patricide and fratricide), and immortality, this latter 'condition' the Commissioners underline, as the most extreme and desirable VUE effect because it ensures the mythic flight opportunity of elevated transcendence- an apotheosis. Biography #16 Ipson and Pulat Fallari are "brothers in fiction...inseparable. The fourteenth edition of the VUE Directory declared the brothers to be dead - shot in an airport hotel in Media-Sidonia by the only legitimate son of their father." For Brenda Fallbutus the individual of biography #40, " it was the excitement about immortality that kept her from cutting her wrists." The pulsing Nyman musical composition acts as a prelude to each voice over narration, primarily provided by Colin Cantlie, Greenaway's favourite narrator, who has the perfect broadcasting voice and accent, the (RP) received pronunciation of the educated middle and upper classes. With its episodic structure, sight gags and complex information delivered by Cantlie as the professional (voice of God) interlocutor, *The Falls* can be loosely categorized as an ironic parody of the type of documentary (soft propaganda) films that Greenaway used to edit and direct for the Office of Information. The film maintains throughout a very similar pacing to some of these documentaries, and with the conventional voice over, albeit tempered in *The Falls* with an ironic *faux* didacticism, the film evokes the authoritative tone of scores of films made by the OI on behalf of the British Government. There are also echoes of the hit television series *The Prisoner* (1967-68) starring Patrick McGoohan as number #6 , who is being held as a prisoner with dozens of others who also have numbers in the eccentrically designed village of Portmeirion on the northern coast of Wales. *The Prisoner* was a huge hit and now has a large international cult following. Its 60's counter culture themes, surveillance, mind control, dream manipulation and identity theft wrapped in surreal narrative appealed strongly to members of Greenaway's generation. The final episode *Fall Out* (#17) even has a similar title to *The Falls*. This episode generated much controversy when it was broadcast because there was little plot structure and no dialogue leaving it totally open to viewer's interpretation. The large number of irate calls from viewers apparently jammed the switchboard. When Number Six (McGoohan) finally meets Number one, the all-powerful controller of the village, he tears off his mask to find the mask of a chimpanzee underneath, and then tears this off to discover his own doppelganger! At times, with their humorous references to class and gender, *The Falls* anecdotes also resemble zany dialogues from *Dr Who* another hit television series. What they all share is a type of class inflected British humour, hovering between artful zaniness and intelligent irony.

There are several sequences of appropriated footage in the film, not enough to make it a pure Compilation film, but certainly comparable to the appropriative and subversive strategies of other experimental filmmakers such as Hollis Frampton.[47] A famous early film clip of a man wearing a pair of artfully engineered wings - an 'Icarus' figure attempting unsuccessfully to fly - is inserted into several of the biographies. The film also contains humorous sequences of human interactions with vehicles such as biography #71 Agostina Fallmutt who is seen in a wide angle crane shot, driving a Landrover around and around in circles on "a New Zealand beach," and #75 Afracious Fallows, another shot of a car driving around in a circle, which in the contemporary context resembles a more recent skit by the English comic actor, Mr. Bean (Rowan Atkinson). The humour is artfully zany, understated, cerebral and elegant, occasionally mildly prurient - a hallmark of British humour - with a few scatological references and gender bending absurdities inserted for good measure. There is also much word play and several parodic educational or media (radio and television) 'Quiz Show' inserts, for example: "Starting at the buzzer, name for me as many birds as you can starting with the letter 'P'." Hitchcock references are also inserted into several of the FALL biographies. For example biographies #9 and #17 contain a famous still shot of Janet Leigh from Hitchcock's *Psycho*; and #67 Bird Gaspara Fallicut contains a reference to Hitchcock's *Birds*. #68 Obsian Fallicut "has a theory that the VUE was an expensive and elaborate hoax to provide an ending to [Hitchcock's] *Birds*." The biography for # 56 Appiroquine Falcatti contains an ambiguous statement which sounds like "cinematic iguana" or "cinematic guano", a sly reference perhaps to Duchamp's famous punning equation *"arrhe* is to art as *merdre* is to *merde.*"[48] There are also several other references to art and art history, for example: the biography for #30 Coppice Fallbeter identifies her as an art historian obsessively undertaking research on the presence of birds in European paintings; and #70 Ashille Fallke, a man who died in his bath like Marat, is accompanied by images of Jacques Louis David's famous painting of *The Assassination of Marat* (1793). Biography #55 Raskao Fallcaster is of a retired farmer who quietly invented maps from the hides of his cows accompanied by images of cows painted with numbers, which may be an arcane reference to Warhol room installations (1966, 1970) that are decorated with screen printed cow wallpaper. If *The Fall's* contains some complicated associations for the modern era, *The Draughtsman's Contract* continues some of the same themes albeit in the context of 17th England.

18. Peter Greenaway's *The Draughtsman's Contract*

The Draughtsman's Contract

The long and beautifully calligraphed credits for *The Draughtsman's Contract* are accompanied by the voice of a counter tenor singing a Greenaway penned libretto. The credits take several minutes to scroll over several *tableaux vivants* revealing conversations between the principal figures in the narrative who establish the context and important features of the back story. An early close-up shows Mr. Noyes the estate manager, a

C18[th] gentleman with powdered wig and face, eating a large juicy plum, delivering the insider information that Mr. Herbert, his employer "has spent more time with his gardener than his wife." All of the principal characters in the film, estate owners, Mr. and Mrs. Herbert, their daughter and son-in law Mr. and Mrs. Tahlmann, friends, Fraser and Anne Louise Lambert, Mr. Noyes (Neil Cunningham), a former suitor to Mrs. Roberts, now estate manager, are introduced to the accompaniment of composer Michael Nyman's hypnotic neo-baroque music played upon a clavichord and later by a chamber orchestra. In common with Thomas Gainsborough's *Mr. and Mrs. Andrews* (1750) a famous painting of the landed gentry and other significant images - conversation pieces - of country life that *Greenaway* quotes in this film, *The Draughtsman's Contract* is about property, patronage, patrimony, art and crime. The plot is somewhat convoluted and not too dissimilar in structure to an Agatha Christie or Arthur Conan Doyle 'who-dun- it' murder mystery. The primary narrative consists of a contract between Mrs. Herbert and Mr Neville (Anthony Higgins) a landscape and architectural artist who makes his living drawing prospects of country houses for the titled upper classes and landed gentry. His contract is to produce twelve scenes from various vantage points of the Herbert's estate, Compton Anstey.[49] We are informed that the scenes are to be a gift ("a supplicant") from Mrs. Herbert to her husband to ameliorate their marital problems. "You Mr Neville" says Noyes, "are to be the instrument of a hopeful reconciliation." Neville is tall, dark and handsome, an arrogant Adonis figure, dressed fashionably (for both the 17th and late 20th) in black attire and upon his arrival to the estate he immediately attracts the attention of all of the women sequestered there, including the almost invisible maid servants.[50] The film was originally three and half hours long and included more material about the work undertaken by the servants on the estate (and class conflicts) but unfortunately this was excised before the film's release. The contract is formally negotiated, under the light of a centrally placed single large and very phallic candlelight, by Noyes seated between Mrs. Herbert on the left, and Mr Neville on the right. This scene is one of many secular *conversazione* lit by candlelight throughout the film, a self conscious effort by Greenaway to quote the paintings of Georges de la Tour and to heighten the light and dark contrasts - *chiaroscuro* - in a manner reminiscent of the paintings of Caravaggio and Rembrandt. The contract between the artist and his patron stipulates that Mr Neville will receive full board and eight pounds per drawing and that he is to "meet with Mrs. Herbert in private and reply to her requests concerning his pleasure." After six drawings (and several other sketches) have been completed the contract is amended to include sexual favours for Mrs. Sarah Tahlmann, the Herbert's' daughter whose husband, a somewhat fey German protestant, is unable to produce an heir to enable primogeniture to continue the family title to the property. In keeping with Greenaway's critique of classical film language and cinematographic convention, the camera movements are very minimal, geometric, employing static shots of four basic types: long establishing shots, wide angle shots of the landscape, architecture and dispositions of people in large open spaces; and frequent point of view shots through Mr Neville's drawing aid which is on an easel with an adjustable grid frame within the frame, an apparatus that several commentators have linked to ocular drawing aids of the Renaissance represented for example, in Albrecht Durer's Perpectival Apparatus from the *Unterweisung der Messung*, 1525.[51] Only once do we receive an oblique view through Neville's frame that is made to appear like an aberration - a dissimulation - given the structural limitations placed on the rest of the film. The other camera shots consist of medium wide angle shots of groups of people engaged in conversation, and a very sparing use of close-ups, usually of some individual engaged in eating (or disgorging), significant architectural details and artifacts (a swinging plumb bob in one shot), and the drawings themselves, executed by Greenaway himself.

There is an almost total absence of sutured 'shot reverse shots', which many film theorists have argued is the staple of the conventional realist cinema. Panning and tracking movements of the camera are severely limited, thus restricting spectator identification with the characters, which is a common cinematic strategy in many Greenaway films. There are only three clear tracking shots, movements frontally back and forth across an evening indoor dinner gathering and outdoor luncheon table, a camera movement that Greenaway himself has described as "inorganic and very mechanical."[52] Half way through the execution of the contract during which discussions between Neville and his employers and their guests increase in aggressive intensity, the dead body of Mr Herbert is found in the moat near the equestrian monument and Neville is set up to become the chief suspect. The film begins and ends in darkness with characters eating; Noyes eating a plum in the beginning and at the conclusion the animated sculpture from the equestrian statue eating a chunk of Neville's pineapple, finding it sour, spitting it out as if to register his distaste for the whole sordid narrative.

19 *A Formal Garden*   20. *Magdalene*

Ludolf de Jongh's painting *A Formal Garden: Three Ladies Surprised by a Gentleman* (1676) housed in the Royal Collection is a convincing model for the overall schema for *The Draughtsman's Contract*. The painting shows a similarly designed estate garden with a statue, and the intrigue represented between the three ladies and the gentleman, is very close to Greenaway's screenplay and at least two perspective shots in the film.[53] Several paintings by Georges de La Tour have also been employed as models for scenes including *The Card Sharp with the Ace of Clubs* c 1620-1640, during a dinner scene, *The Nativity c. 1630-40*, *St Joseph the Carpenter* 1640's, *Paid Money* also known as *The Money Lender* and *the Payment of Taxes* (1625-27) during the first meeting between Neville and Mrs. Herbert to negotiate the contract, and *St Sebastian Tended by St Irene* (1634) 1643) and the famous *Repenting Magdalen* also called the *Magdalene in a Flickering Light* (1635-37) which shows the pregnant woman holding a skull, a common symbol of mortality on her lap, in the scene where Mrs. Herbert is crying in penitence with her daughter at her side. David Pascoe has indicated that William Hogarth's *The Lady's Last Stake* (1758-59) is the source for the important tea-drinking scene between Neville and Mrs. Herbert. Most of these art associations have been noticed by other commentators but there are possibly also more contemporary art references in this film, including *trompe l'oeil* 'images within images,' for example surrealist René Magritte's famous painting *The Human Condition* (1934), and the metaphysical painting (*pittura metaphysica*) of de Chirico. Greenaway is not averse to quoting famous art work from several epochs in the same film to enrich the *mise en scene* and diegesis. For example, the garden scene where Neville and Mrs. Herbert engage in sexual intercourse behind the large black parasol is a common Freudian symbol of coitus and a possibly an allusion to several famous impressionist paintings of women with parasols by Seurat, Monet, and Renoir or late nineteenth photographs of men and women with umbrellas that became almost a sub genre of urban photography. The problem of distinguishing representation from reproduction (in art as in life), is at the core of this film and is played out frequently in Greenaway's animation of the inanimate, or the reverse situation. The Pygmalion effect is also evoked when the stone statue of a naked man on a plinth at the entrance to the estate becomes animated. Greenaway describes this figure as a "statue-figure-/genius/loci/priapic, Pan."[54]

The placement of such a figure in the grounds of an estate is also closely associated with the Roman God Hermes (Greek, Mercury), the fleet of foot herald/ messenger of the Olympians, originally a Greek phallic deity associated with fertility and good fortune but also paradoxically, tricksterism and thievery. It is common practice for statues of Hermes rather than Pan to stand guard over the entranceways of country estates. This figure in Greenaway's film even resembles a very life like, individualized bronze statue of Hermes seated on a stone in the national museum of Naples. If, as Greenaway suggests, the figure is specifically of Pan (the son of Hermes, from a liaison with Aphrodite), then this phallic divinity and protector of shepherd flocks, is also the equivalent of the universal god of Mysia in Asia minor, who was called Priapus. According to legend Hermes also fathered three daughters, Peitho (the personification of persuasion and seduction) Tycho and Eunomia. He and Aphrodite also had a son called Hermaphroditus, who became joined in one body with the nymph Salmacis) from whom we derive the term *hermaphrodite*.[55] Neville is allegorically linked both to Priapus and Aries the Ram, the first sign in the Zodiac and also Greenaway's birth sign, which binds him also to Neville as his creative alter ego in this Pan/Priapus/Hermes mythological constellation. At one point a feature of this allegorical connection is emphasized when Neville chases sheep with his black cane, waving it in the air as a surrogate shepherd's crook. The animated Pan statue appears four times in the film twice pissing, the first time holding a flaming torch (fire) and the second time pouring water from a jug, lending a playfully masculine and alchemical air to these sequences. The first time he appears as a statue in the garden standing almost chameleon like against a stone wall while Tahlmann is instructing his young nephew, (sent to England to escape his Catholic mother), the fine art of being a Protestant gentleman, "not chasing sheep like that fellow Neville." When the young boy notices his presence Pan 'pulls a face' in a puckish gesture that goes unnoticed by Tahlmann. The next occasion the animated figure appears it is evening and he is seen lifting an obelisk off its base (obelisks are priapic/phallic trophies of war), taking its place on the base and pissing while holding his right arm up and out from his body mid torso holding a flaming torch and his left hand high above his head. In Pan's next appearance we see him rearranging his genitals before pissing, and as he relieves himself he simultaneously pours from a jug of water held in his left hand. This startling image is a reference to neoclassical sculptures of naked standing or sitting figures, occasionally young boys pissing in a fountain. It is also a regendered ironic homage to J-D Ingres' *La Source* (1820-56) the famous allegorical painting of a nude woman pouring the 'life source' from a pitcher of water. The final appearance of this figure occurs in the last scene after the blinding and killing of Neville and the torching of his drawings. He dismounts the equestrian statue, crosses the moat to pick and take a bite from Neville's pineapple. But for two characters, Tahlmann's nephew and Mr. Clark who flicks Pan away with his hat before reporting the news of the finding of Mr. Herbert's body in the moat in front of the equestrian statue, the estate inhabitants are oblivious to the presence of the animated sculpture in their midst.

During the first coital act between Mrs. Herbert and Neville, he lectures her about horticulture and the growing of pears, and as he does so, he surveys her naked body for the first time. He takes her arms back and metonymically makes a tree out of her limbs saying "the angle between the branches and the main trunk is too steep. But the original work is good and what of the pears themselves?" (Feeling her breasts) adding "Are they presentable?" The next edit shows Mrs. Herbert, spewing, (not fully vomiting) what appears to be semen from her mouth, one of many allusions to body fluids, water and a general 'wetness' associated with sexuality, life and death in this film. Another coital scene takes place under a large black parasol, the opening and closing of the umbrella being a well-known Freudian symbol for sexual intercourse. On another occasion Mrs. Herbert and Neville are shown in a hayloft framed in an approximation of Oskar Kokoshka's painting *Bride in the Wind* (*The Tempest* 1914). The conflation of art and murder is most clearly evoked during the fourth tryst between Mr Neville and Mrs. Herbert when Neville brandishing a pair of fabric shears undertakes her deshabille. He discusses the painting identified as the *Allegory of Newton's Service to Optics* (1785) by the German painter Juanuarius Zick. "The reason I asked you to come here is because I have borrowed this painting from the house." He continues his dialogue with "your husband surprises me with his eccentric and eclectic taste. While most of his peers are content to collect portraits of family connections, Mr Herbert seems to collect anything." A close-up of the painting follows this declaration. "Perhaps he has an eye for optical theory.... or the plight of flowers, or the passing of time...."is accompanied by another close up of the sun dial in the painting. "Perhaps Madam he has.... I would stand by him on this ...an interest in the pictorial conceit.... can you see why your husband had reason to buy it...?" Neville continues snipping her dress back with shears as Mrs. Herbert replies..."it is of a garden which is probably reason enough." "True, true..." says Neville "but what of the events in it?" "Shall we peruse it together? Do you see madam, a narrative in these supposedly unrelated episodes...there is drama, is there not, in this over populated garden... What intrigues here.... do you think the characters have something to tell us? Would you know if your daughter had any particular interest in this painting?" (Another sundial close-up.) "Madam could you put a season to it?" and "Madam do you have an opinion...of infidelities? This exchange is accompanied by several close up shots of symbolic details in the painting. Do you think...that *murder is being prepared*?" Mrs. Herbert remains silent. With this exceptional preparatory framing of the murder that is being prepared is Neville's and the allegorical conflation of art and death laid bare. David Pascoe has engaged in a close reading of the Zick painting identifying the figures of Newton, Euclid (the Mathematician) and Diogenes (the Cynic), suggesting that Newton's genius and scientific discoveries were banishing the ignorance and prejudice of an earlier age, supplanting the knowledge of previous generations to inaugurate a new age of scientific enlightenment.[56] One would be hard pressed to recognize the drama in this painting as preparation for a murder unless one was engaging in over interpretation but the libidinal economy between Mrs. Herbert and Neville is another matter. The point that Greenaway is trying to make through Neville is that this painting has too many signifiers that make it open to wide interpretation.

As is common for Hitchcock, birds appear often in Greenaway's films, a self-conscious homage to his father, an amateur ornithologist who encouraged the younger Greenaway in his interest in biology and especially insects, and also his obsession with systems of classification, taxonomy and philology. Many of the bucolic daylight scenes feature Constable like cloud studies and the sound of birds permeate the audio tracks in the film, rarely competing, mostly complementing Nyman's score, but contrasting sharply with the incarcerated (love?) birds held in two cages in Mrs. Herbert's boudoir. The mythological counterpart for Mrs. Herbert is probably Demeter ("spelt mother" the Ceres of Roman mythology), the Greek goddess of grain and fertility, both agricultural and human. Homer recounts a number of stories about Demeter and Persephone her daughter, including one that may have been in Greenaway's mind when he wrote the screenplay for this film. The myth of Demeter and Persephone is recounted in the *Hymn to Demeter* in which Hades abducts Persephone and takes her to his domain in the underworld. Demeter becomes distressed by the taking of her daughter and searches the underworld for them both, neglecting her duties on earth that as a result becomes barren. Zeus, concerned for their plight, intervenes to return Persephone to her mother but before she leaves him, Hades gives her a pomegranate a powerful allegorical symbol of fertility to eat in order that she would be forever connected to his world.[57] With Mrs. Herbert as Demeter, her daughter Sarah Tahlmann is allegorized in this film as Persephone, the goddess of the underworld and wife of Hades. In Greek mythology Persephone is described as "a divinity of dazzling brilliance" but also "she who destroys light."[58] Greenaway is probably familiar with the famous painting of Persephone titled *Prosperina* (1874) by the pre-Raphaelite artist Dante Gabriel Rosetti that hangs in the Tate Gallery, and *The Return of Persephone* (1890-1) by Frederick Leighton, which is in the Leeds Museum. In her important pre-coital exchange with Neville, Sarah Tahlmann reinforces some of the major aesthetic positions regarding knowledge, representation and death, with a reference to scotomisation that prefigures Neville's final literal blindness (and revelation) at the hands of Messrs. Tahlmann, Noyes and company. Painting requires a certain blindness; a partial refusal to be aware of all the options, an intelligent man will know more about drawing than he will see. And in the space between knowing and seeing, he will become constrained, unable to prove an idea strongly, fearing that the discerning - though he is eager to please - will find him wanting if he does not put in only what he knows, but what they know as well. In her speech Sarah Tahlmann emphasizes the mismatch between perception and cognition, seeing and knowing, between *avoir* and *savoir*; implying that knowledge is contingent, and the seemingly apparent may be an illusion or disguise; that in order to represent the truth a certain play of blindness, presence of absence and concealing in revealing is necessary. This is a very Derridian soliloquy: "Non-presence is presence. Différance, the disappearance of any originary presence, is *at once* the condition of possibility and the condition of the impossibility of truth."59 The difference(s) between seeing and knowing also play a major role in Greenaway's next film, again richly scripted with a multitude of textual and visual cues for [herme] neutic exploration.

---

[1] Greenaway, EGS Seminar August 2002

[2] Duchamp, M. "The Creative Act," presented at the Convention of the American Federation of the Arts, Houston Texas, April 1957

[3] Greenaway now lives in Amsterdam.

[4] Greenaway describes *Tulse Luper* as "my alter ego as a super-polymath" Leon Steinmetz and Peter Greenaway *The World of Peter Greenaway* Boston, Tokyo: Journey Editions 1995 p.7. In another passage Luper is identified with Greenaway's heroes "parts of heroes and parts of lesser divinities": John Cage, Buckminster Fuller, Marcel Duchamp and "certainly my father and later Sacha Vierny, cinematographer"(for Alain Renais and later Greenaway), "Samuel Johnson, Edward Gibbon, Laurence Sterne, Thornton Wilder Linnaeus, Darwin, Newton, Boullée, d'Alembert, Audubon, Arbuckle." (p.18)

[5] There are several books and essays that discuss Peter Greenaway's practice as a visual artist and the use he makes of art history in his films. Melia, P., and Woods, A., *Peter Greenaway: Artworks 63-98* Manchester University Press 1998; Pascoe, D. *Peter Greenaway: Museums and Moving Images* London Reaktion Books 1997; Steinmetz., and Greenaway, P. "The World of Peter Greenaway Boston Journey Editions 1995; Hacker, J and Price, D., *Take Ten: Contemporary British Film Directors* New York, Oxford University Press, Elliot, B and Purdy, A. *Peter Greenaway, Architecture Allegory* London: Academy Editions 1997

[6] The full quote reads: "My *petit bourgeois* parents (who were embarrassed generally in public) were aghast that they had a child walking the street with only one shoe on. And ever after there seemed to be an association of cinemas and lost clothing which hung around my head." Quoted in Lawrence, Amy *The Films of Peter Greenaway* Cambridge University Press 1997 p.8

[7] Lawrence, A. 1997 *passim*

[8] Ian Dury and the Blockheads created the hit song "Hit me with your rhythm stick" which in the year it was released sold over a million copies. Dury appears as the character Fitch , one of Spica's henchmen in *The Draughtsman's Contract*. He died at the age of 57.

[9] Greenaway and Dury are among Walthamstow College's most celebrated graduates.

[10] Melia, Paul, "Frames of Reference "in Melia, P and Woods A, *Peter Greenaway Artworks 63-98* Manchester University Press 1998 p7

[11] Woods, Alan *Being Naked and Playing Dead* Manchester University Press 1996 p.106 requoted in Pascoe, D. *Peter Greenaway Museums and Moving Images* London Reaktion Books 1997 p.43

[12] This is where I came across it in the late 1960's.

[13] This generalization is based upon my own exposure in the late 1960's to RCA educated teachers at the Elam School of Fine Art, University of Auckland, New Zealand.

[14] Melia, P and Woods A, *Peter Greenaway Artworks 63-98* Manchester University Press 1998:3

[15] During its years of operation (1958-69) The IS had 70 members from 16 countries, six of who were British see Raspaud; J_J and Voyer, J_P *L'internationale Situationiste 1958_1969* Paris, Editions Champ Libre 1972.

[16]His parents had also previously been very disappointed in their son's decision to turn down a placement in Cambridge University to pursue an education in fine arts. (Lawrence p.9) Ian Dury his colleague from Walthamstow was accepted into the RCA.

[17] *Petit Bourgeois* is traditionally defined as a member of the lower middle classes.

[18] Lawrence, A. p.7

[19] On a personal note as someone with a similar class background to Greenaway, and also Hitchcock, I recognize the insertion of symbolic capital that elides the material socio-economic circumstances of one's origin. As E.P Thompson the English Historian "a class makes itself as much as it is made" but he and other writers on class for example Raymond Williams and Pierre Bourdieu have argued that education or marriage are powerful mechanisms for transcendence.

[20] In subsequent interviews he mentions that his father was "a businessman" but whose ambitions to become an ornithologist were frustrated by his lack of education.

[21]This film does not appear on all of Greenaway's filmographies which begin in 1966 at the age of 24 with *Train* 5 minutes and *Tree* (16 minutes)

[22] Willoquet-Maricondi, P., and Alemany-Galway, M. *Peter Greenaway's Postmodern/ Poststructuralist Cinema* Lanham, Maryland and London, The Scarecrow Press 2001:.301

[23] I was fortunate to be able to view several of these early films in Peter Greenaway's EGS Seminar on his work, Saas-Fee, August 2002

[24] For a discussion of Greenaway's work in the context of experimental film in the 1970's see Testa, B. "Tabula for a Catastrophe" in Willoquet-Maricondi, P., and Alemany-Galway, pp. 80-85

[25] Barthes, R. *Image Music Text* translation Stephen Heath New York, Hill and Wang 1985:61

[26] Jeahne, Karen "*The Draughtsman's Contract*: An Interview with Peter Greenaway" Cineaste 13:2 1984 p 14. This was a point reinforced in two presentations Greenaway gave to EGS Faculty and Graduate Students in Saas-Fee. Greenaway is a vociferous opponent of conventional film making, especially Hollywood films that "deodorize, glamorize, and sentimentalize" (EGS seminar notes August, 2002)

[27] Christina Degli-Espositi Reinert "Neo- Baroque Imaging in Peter Greenaway's Cinema" in Willoquet-Maricondi and Alemany-Galway M., *Peter Greenaway's Postmodern/Poststructuralist Cinema* Latham, Maryland and London, Scarecrow Press 2001, p. 63

[28] Dayan Stetco "The Crisis of Commentary: Tilting at Windmills in Peter Greenaway's *The Cook, The Thief, His Wife and her Lover*" in Willoquet-Maricondi, P., and Alemany-Galway, M.. Eds p 204

[29] Peter Greenaway lecture presentation at the European Graduate School, August 2002

[30] Pally, Marcia "Cinema as a Total Art Form: An Interview with Peter Greenaway <u>Cineaste</u> 18:3 1991 p.6

[31] The *Tulse Luper* series of works is planned to consist of several CD's dozens of DVD's, books, museum installations and websites.

[32] Pally, M.,"Order versus Chaos: The Films of Peter Greenaway" Cineaste 18:3 (1991) p 6 requoted in Lawrence, A. P 2 and fn p 193

[33]Greenaway cites his viewing of Bergman's *The Seventh Seal* as a revelatory experience

[34]The director of cinematography Alain Renais' film *Last Year at Marienbad* (1962) was Sacha Vierney who Greenaway subsequently contracted for several of his own films.

[35] Greenaway August 2002 EGS Seminar notes.

[36] Lawrence, A. p37

---

[37] These thoughts were gleaned from several conversations I was privileged to have with Peter Greenaway at the EGS summer seminars Saas-Fee in August 2002 and 2003

[38] Lawrence, 2; see also Willoquet-Maricondi and Alemany-Galway M., *Peter Greenaway's Postmodern/Poststructuralist Cinema*

[39] Woods, Alan *Being Naked, Playing Dead: The Art of Peter Greenaway*. Manchester, Manchester University Press 1996

[40] This may be a questionable assumption but my own training by English educated art historians and studio instructors corroborates this form of education.

[41] *The chance meeting on a dissecting table of a sewing machine and an umbrella* Lautréamont's poetic line from *Les Chants de Maldoror* adopted by Breton as a quintessential surrealist image.

[42] Greenaway, P. *The Early Films of Peter Greenaway* London British Film Institute 1991:3

[43] Anagrams generated by Brendan Connell's On Line Anagram generator http://mbh.edu/bconell/cgi-bin/anagram accessed 12.4. 2005

[44] Uranium named after the planet Uranus is the heaviest element, and its crystal shape is orthorhombic with seven energy levels.

[45] Bulmer, R. "Why is the Cassowary Not a Bird? A Problem of Zoological Taxonomy among the Karam of the New Guinea Highlands" *Man* 2 (I): pp.5-25.

[46] See Lawrence, Amy and Willoquet-Maricondi and Alemany-Galway op cit.

[47] For a discussion of Greenaway's work in the context of experimental and structuralist film see Testa, B. "Tabula For a Catastrophe: Peter Greenaway's *The Falls* and Foucault's Heterotopia" in Willoquet-Maricondi and Alemany-Galway M., *Peter Greenaways Postmodern/Poststructuralist Cinema* Latham, Maryland and London, Scarecrow Press 2001 pp. 79-112

[48] Duchamp, M. *Notes and Projects for the Large Glass* with an introduction by Arturo Schwarz London, Thames and Hudson 1969 p.88

[49] The real country house is Groombridge Place, Kent built in 1652 by John Packer

[50] Neville's mode of dress resembles a self-portrait of the Dutch painter Jan Vermeer.

[51] See Pascoe, p. 72.

[52] Jeahne, Karen "The Draughtsman's Contract: an Interview with Peter Greenaway" <u>Cineaste</u> 13:2 1984 p. 14 requoted a footnote in Lawrence, A *The Films of Peter Greenaway* p.199

[53] Alain Renais' *Last Year at Marienbad* (1961) has also been cited as a major source for *The Draughtsman's Contract* by Greenaway and other authors. See Alemany -Galway, M.. "Postmodernism and the French New Novel: The Influence of *Last year at Marienbad* on *The Draughtsman's Contract* in Willoquet-Maricondi, P., and Alemany-Galway, M. *Peter Greenaway's Postmodern/ Poststructuralist Cinema* pp.115-135

[54] Lawrence endnote p.201

[55] Mercury was one of the most popular deities adopted by the Celts in the North, who became the patron of all the arts, commerce and the safety of travelers. He was worshipped in preference to Jupiter, Mars, Apollo and Minerva. See The Larousse *Encyclopaedia of Mythology* trans Aldington, R., Ames, D. London New York Hamlyn 1968 p, 238, and Hermes pp's 115-19; 123-4 and passim.

[56] Pascoe, p. 67-69

[57] Before he undertakes his last drawing (the unlucky #13) Neville delivers to Mrs. Herbert a gift of three pomegranates as a symbolic peace offering.

[58] Larousse *Encyclopaedia of Mythology* p.165

[59] Derrida, J "Play from the Pharmakon to the letter and from blindness to the supplement" in *Disseminations* University of Chicago Press 1981:168

Chapter 9

The Belly of an Artist

The belly is the reason that man does not so easily take himself for a God. (Friedrich Nietzsche)[1]

Are animals like car crashes - acts of god or mere accidents - bizarre - tragic, farcical, plotted nowadays by an ingenious storyteller M.C. Darwin? (Peter Greenaway)[2]

A Zed and Two Noughts

In common with *The Draughtsman's Contract* discussed in the previous chapter, Peter Greenaway's *A Zed and Two Noughts* (1985).), opens with an additive montage of short film clips – *tableaux* – interspersed with credits and accompanied by the pulsing rhythm of Michael Nyman's score. The first scene of a few seconds in length is an evening shot of a noirish rain soaked road, with at centre stage, a teenage girl with a younger fair-haired boy of about twelve years of age both struggling with a Dalmatian dog that is straining on it's leash to go in the opposite direction (a Dalmatian also appears in the opening sequence of *The Cook, the Thief, his Wife and her Lover*). The three are in front of the entrance to the ZOO, signified by huge illuminated blue letters and under the watchful gaze of a security guard who checks the time on his watch, one of many different time signals operating throughout this film.[3] The next scene reveals a tiger pacing up and down in its cage, with on the floor, the half eaten head of a Zebra. This is followed by another montage of quick shots of a fair-haired man, whom we learn subsequently is the zoologist Oliver Deuce (Eric Deacon). He is counting the pacing tiger's steps with the aid of a chronometer upon which we see a close-up of the numerals 676, the square of 26, a number that becomes an important numerical motif in the film.[4] Over this image is montaged a sound image of a dog barking off camera, a squeal of tires and the crunching sound of a car crash, a debt to Hitchcock's famous extra diegetic sound images. This sound then cuts to an image of the car crash itself that has just taken place in front of an ESSO advertisement on a billboard adjacent to the Zoo bearing the familiar advertising image of the tiger and the now darkly ironic text "Quality at Work." The image of the crash reveals the wings and broken neck of a large white (mute) swan that has been hit by the car; these shots implicating the Dalmatian dog as in some way responsible for the crash. The next ensemble of images consist of close-ups from the top and side of a medium format camera taking still photographs of a pacing gorilla in a cage who is missing his right leg. The camera operated by Oliver's twin brother Oswald Deuce (Brian Deacon), a dark haired zoologist who is the other O (Nought) in the Z&OO title. We read the frame counter of this camera that is close to the previous number albeit this time incrementally as single digits 7, 8, 9...

Numbers, names, colours, and the letters of the alphabet are key signifiers in this film. For example, the swan, car and driver, are white. Alba Bewick (A/B; has a daughter called Beta), and is wearing a white dress with feathers. Her first name Alba in Italian translates as Dawn. *Alb* is a white vestment used by priests from *Albatus* (L) = white, as in Albatross and the surname Bewick corresponds with the name of a rare type of swan that migrates from Siberia to England..[5] Symbolically the scene now represents a bizarre coincidence - a white swan has crashed into another, yet different, white swan thus establishing time/space co-ordinates for the film concerning gratuitous events and nominal coincidence. Venus de Milo, named after the famous Greek sculpture of the armless woman, and Van Hoyten the Zoo's keeper of the owls (in the script) both wear black.[6] But Greenaway has *detourned* (diverted) the symbolic order and made the colour white equivalent to death, and black, life. The car is a Ford Mercury with a hood ornament figure of the Greco-Roman deity Mercury (Hermes), the messenger of the Gods. Mercury is named for the fastest planet in the cosmos and being the fleet footed patron of messengers, and within Greek cosmology, is also the patron planet of artisans, tricksters and thieves. Half-way through the smashed window screen lies the body of a screaming woman, Alba Bewick the driver of the car (phonically Bewick can also be read as Buick, another brand of American car), and in the rear seat lie two other women cosmetically enhanced (and erotically charged), wearing bright red lipstick, who appear seriously injured or dead.

Like Hitchcock, Greenaway often conflates art and death with Eros. One wag once said, "Hitchcock treated his murders like love scenes and his love scenes like murders." A similar comment could be made of Greenaway. The shot of the victims is followed by another of the scene of the crash now attended by ambulance medics, the police and members of the fire department who employ special equipment to cut the bodies out of the automobile. A voice crackling over a walkie-talkie radio in conversation with a policeman poses questions: "A swan? What sort of swan? Leda? Who's Leda? Is she the injured woman? Laid by whom? By Jupiter? What was the cause of death? A female swan! How do you know it was female? Eggs! Egg (s) bound? Was it wild? Perhaps it was a wild goose. Did it come from the zoo?" In this exchange Greenaway presents other mythological references. In the question "By Jupiter?" he turns the usual exclamation "by thunder!" into an interrogative thus permitting the generic Jupiter to stand alone without the performative as a signifier for the Roman God of celestial light, weather and war.[7] In Greek mythology Leda, a deity of the night was one of the married women with whom Zeus formed an adulterous relationship. According to legend, he disguised himself as a beautiful swan so that she might sleep with him and she subsequently became the bearer of his two children Pollux and Helen. Leda was also the mother of Castor and Clytemnestra of Tyndareus her legitimate husband.[8] "Egg(s) bound" is a homonym for "expound" and "perhaps it's a wild goose" is a contraction of the apothegm "a wild goose chase," meaning a waste of time. And "laid" is a near anagram and homophone of Leda. The travelling shot to the two women lying in the back of the car dissolves from colour into a black and white still photograph on the front page of a tabloid newspaper with the headlines

SWAN CRASH TWO DIE.
TWO WIVES
DEAD IN CAR.

Again like Hitchcock, Greenaway never misses an opportunity to insert meaningful details into a scene and this front page contains ironic insights into his themes, the Z&OO narrative and his next film *The Belly of an Architect* (1986), then in preliminary stages of production. In the upper left column of the newspaper is placed a cropped image of the head of a Greek statue without a nose (a reference to the enigmatic figure, perhaps a 'criminal artist' chipping noses off the faces of classical figures in that film, and below this, the punning text **A COLD**

SMELL. In the same column appears another headline reading **PANICKED ZEBRA** and centre page, superimposed over the image of the car wreck, is Greenaway's writer and director credit. The top section of the right column is the headline, **A HOT BATH HEART ATTACK** with below this **ARCHITECT DIES**, announcing the death of the American architect Stourley Kracklite, the key protagonist in *The Belly of an Architect*. In common with other Greenaway films the opening scenes of Z&OO establish the allegorical matrix for the entire film that can be described on at least one important register, as a complex meditation on art, life (desire) and death. In a short space of time and with an impressive array of means, Greenaway introduces some of his other core themes, motifs and formal concerns. For example, the stripes on the tiger and zebra also appear in other contexts throughout the film, including police tape, Venetian blinds and toys, introducing issues of representation, the nature of disguise, and figure/ground (positive/negative) ambiguity that is later replayed in a conversation between Venus and Van Hoyten. "Do you think a zebra is a white animal with black stripes or a black animal with white stripes?" This ambiguity is similar to classical 'multistable" images discussed at length by Ludwig Wittgenstein, Ernst Gombrich, and W.J.T. Mitchell such as the rabbit/duck image, or the image that flips between a figure of an old lady with a big nose, or a young lady with a long neck.[9] The stripes also allude to optical dynamism in the painting of Brigit Riley and other Op artists whose work Greenaway would have seen during his art school days and after, perhaps also the exemplary striped work of the contemporary French artist Daniel Buren. Dots, stripes, numbers, colour and language resonate powerfully in these few minutes of viewing time; for example the Dalmatian is also an aesthetic black and white, figure/ground 'problem,' simultaneously signifying popular images of Dalmatians accompanying fire engines and the Disney adventure film *101 Dalmatians*. And once again, there are references to classical mythology, doubles, twins, symmetry and asymmetry. Binaries figure prominently in other ways: nature/ culture, light/dark, purity/pollution and decay, and fire/ water. Oscar and Oswald Deuce are twin brothers, zoologists who lose their wives simultaneously in this impossibly gratuitous car crash and the resulting narrative enables Greenaway to construct a series of tableaux that explore eschatological themes, grief, gratuitous death, decomposition, coincidence and evolutionary biology. In Greek mythology Castor and Pollux – the Dioscuri – are the brothers Castor and Poly*deuces* from which Greenaway has also obtained the allegorically useful surname Deuce, conveying the multiple meanings: double or twin, a surprise or annoyance, and the two noughts on a dice, considered the worst possible throw. Deuce also conveys the meanings, bad luck and misfortune, and metaphorically, the Devil in the phrase "who the deuce are you?" [10] According to legend Castor and Pollux were very affectionate toward one another, never rivals and neither acted alone or without consulting his twin brother. The Greek sea deity Poseidon gave them the power to assist shipwrecked men. The zodiacal constellation and astrological sign representing the twin brothers is Gemini and like their mythological prototypes Oliver and Oswald are also close, sharing everything together as one, from their birth to their death. They share the same profession, appearance, albeit wearing different clothing, hairstyles and coloring in the first half of the film. They also share the same behaviour, an inability to properly express their emotions, and after their wives die, they share a relationship with Venus de Milo, seamstress and zoo 'prostitute,' and Alba Bewick the driver of the Mercury automobile that crashed. At first blaming Alba for the accident that killed their wives, they soon form a threesome, but when she subsequently gives birth to twins, they question the babies' paternity. The Deuce brothers probably have their origins in *The Falls* twins Ipson and Pulat Fallari Biography #16 who are "brothers in fiction, inseparable." When they are in a bed scene with Alba Bewick notices scars on their bodies that enable Oliver and Oswald to share the secret that they were previously joined at the hip as Siamese twins who had to be separated after birth. Greenaway has made some interesting observations about the themes in Z&OO.

> How do animal behaviourists think about their subject - how do they relate their anxieties with their studies? The greatest loss I could imagine would be the death of my wife. So kill the twin's wives in a car-crash - the most possible and yet gratuitous events. Grief stricken, the twins try to use what they know best - natural history - to comprehend the event. To complete the circle, the crash is caused by an animal - a swan. We now have the beginnings of a plot to explore many things: the absence of meaning in gratuitous death; is death predetermined? How do religion and science deal with the problem; is Genesis or Darwin the most likely myth; what other myth systems try to answer these questions [11]

Beyond the 'myth systems' provided by Greek mythology, religion and evolutionary biology, the other systems that Greenaway is registering in this film are provided by art history, medicine and mathematics. In the operating theatre the surgeon Dr. Van Meegeren (who has an unfulfilled desire to become an artist like Vermeer) ascertains Alba's injuries from the accident. He has to amputate one leg and is concerned about the viability of the other. The scene in the surgery begins after the operation to remove one of her legs has been accomplished and we witness him abusing the doctor patient relationship by kissing her between the breasts, a signal for the window blinds closed for the operation to slowly open and bathe the room in sunlight, thus highlighting the uncanny presence of a frame or mirror to the right and rear of the theatre containing a half-length image of Van Meegeren's wife, Caterina Bolnes, who shares the same name as the wife of the famous painter Vermeer of Delft. She wears a wide brimmed felt red hat matching that worn by the female subject in Vermeer's famous painting *Girl with a Red Hat* (c.1665). The image of Bolnes reflected in the mirror, appears behind vertical bars as if in a cage, analogically reproducing the cages we have been previously introduced to in the tiger and gorilla scenes as well as providing allusions to caged birds and the marriage bond itself, a trope that Greenaway employed previously in *The Draughtsman's Contract*. Bars are also a familiar metaphor in Hitchcock's films. The disposition of this uncanny image, that function simultaneously as a mirror and an animated portrait, is similar to the mirrored image depicted in *Las Meninas* (*Maids of Honour*), the famous painting by Velasquez discussed in the first chapter of Michel Foucault's *The Order of Things*. This painting provided Foucault with the opportunity to articulate some important theoretical arguments about representation, knowledge and being, which are also three principal concerns of Greenaway in *A Zed and Two Noughts*. The mirror in the rear of *Las Meninas* offers the beholder "the enchantment of the double" that Foucault argues is denied us as spectators. Of all the representations figured in the painting he insists, "This is the only one visible but no one is looking at it" and "that tiny glowing rectangle which is nothing other than visibility, yet without any gaze able to grasp it, to render it actual and to enjoy the suddenly ripe fruit of the spectacle it offers."[12] Foucault notes that the mirror reflects nothing in the space of the room itself or anything represented in the picture. It is not the visible it reflects like the mirrors in most Dutch and Flemish paintings of the period, excluding the extraordinary painting of the mirror in Jan van Eyck's painting *Giovanni Arnolfini and his Bride* (1434), a painting that Greenaway is also alluding to in this and other scenes that take place in Meegeren's surgery/clinic/gallery. The mirror in Velasquez's painting "cuts straight through the whole field of representation, ignoring all it might apprehend within that field, and restores visibility to that which resides outside all view." And yet, Foucault insists, this invisibility is not the invisibility of that which is hidden; rather, he argues, "it addresses itself to what is invisible both as a result of the painting's structure and its existence as a painting." He thus offers a philosophical revelation to this phenomenon. "The mirror provides a *metathesis* of visibility that affects both the space represented in the centre of the canvas, what in the painting is of necessity *doubly invisible*."[13] The inserted mirrored image in Van Meegeren's operating room figures exactly in this Foucauldian sense of revealing/rendering the presence of an absence and the visible invisible, a theme that Foucault takes up again in *The Birth of the Clinic*.[14] In its incompleteness the image functions metonymically as the phantom lost leg of Alba Bewick, Vermeer's ('legless') portrait of Bolnes and the unfulfilled creative desires of Dr. Van Meegeren, artist *manqué*. From the clinic the scene shifts to Oswald's laboratory where we see him despondent over the death of his wife. A slow tracking zoom shot to where he sits at his light table takes in several laboratory experiments and displays, a Bunsen burner, bones, plants and biological specimen jars under blinking lights. The sounds of invisible cheeping laboratory chickens are accompanied by Nyman's pulsing sound track, keeping time with the syncopated lights as the distraught Oswald attempts to review his large format photographic negatives of the Zoo's one legged Gorilla. Greenaway juxtaposes the legless human with the legless ape this providing an odd symmetry between these two hominids. Behind Oswald standing in a containment area with a glass window is a white cow with what appears to be a black heart or spade shaped marking on its body. The presence of this cow is an *aide de memoir* to the cows bearing numbers in *The Falls*. The scene in Oswald's laboratory cuts to a perspectival vista shot of Oliver and Oswald carrying flowers away from the church where the funeral service for their wives has taken place. Standing in the middle of a neo classical colonnade Oswald asks his brother "How long does it take for a woman's body to decompose?" As scientists they both have difficulty comprehending the absolutely gratuitous nature of the deaths of their wives and engage in what could be considered, an inappropriate scientific discussion about the rotting of the body which Greenaway suggests is the only way that they can make sense of this tragic event. Oswald's question about putrefaction leads Oliver to launch into a technical discussion about the numbers of pathogenic bacteria in the gut as compared to the mouth, followed by a comment about the transfer of bacteria occasioned by the first kiss between Adam and Eve and the cardinal sin introduced to humanity with the eating of the forbidden apple. This is followed by a scene change back to the accident site where the Deuces reverentially place their flowers in the spot where the crash had taken place, now cleared of broken windshield glass, some shards of which Oliver had previously taken as a memento or 'souvenir' of the tragic event. In the background four white coated figures are covering up the ESSO sign with white paper in preparation for a new sign (screen) and the audio track at this point carries the familiar voice of the famous British naturalist David Attenborough narrating a section of text on the origin and mutability of life from the television series *Life on Earth.* This scene cuts to a full size image of a large garden snail moving majestically across some flowers. Snails and the village Escargot, Alba Bewick's place of origin, figure prominently in the diegesis as symbols of decay and regeneration. Besides being a French culinary delicacy, the snail provides other allegorical meanings for Greenaway. Snails are members of the gastropod (stomach foot) family that evolved from the sea over 600 million years ago. They breathe through lungs, are deaf and have 'eyes' on sensing 'stalks.' In addition they are nocturnal hermaphrodites, have spiral shaped shells and feed on decaying plants and soil. Attenborough's voiceover intones "...to contemplate how life can be made apparently out of nothing...and in the beginning life's origins..." We next witness Oliver's despondency as he sits in the Zoo theatre watching the Attenborough film and drowning his sorrows with a bottle of Scotch. The following tableau is of Alba in hospital dressed totally in white resembling an angel, an allusion reinforced by a section of the bed frame making a crescent shaped halo above her head.

"How are you feeling?" asks Oswald, to which she replies "In the realm of the legless." The camera tracks backwards to reveal Oswald and Oliver on either side of her bed. On the side table and the bed lay bouquets of red and white roses all of which appear about to wilt thus illustrating the dialectical phenomenon of life within death. This tableau is followed by close-up shots of the pyramidal arrangement of green apples (Granny Smiths), on the right table and with other items, a small toy zebra (from A to Z) on the left. Alba laconically relates a crass anecdote about a legless whore during the war who lived in

Marseilles with "no limbs to inhibit entry...imagine that gentlemen..." an exclamation that stimulates Oliver to absent mindedly pick up the toy Zebra, followed by Oswald who takes an apple from the pile on the table next to him. With the reverse tracking shot, the bed is now revealed to have two circles O's (Zeroes/ Noughts) at either end. We learn from Alba's story that the woman from Marseilles had many lovers but died young and was buried with artificial legs made for a legless man named Philippe Arc-en-Ciel (Rainbow) saying that she will have to find her own Philippe Arc-en-Ciel in order to ensure her happiness. The film returns to Oswald's lab where we see him taking a bite out of the apple and beginning a time lapse film of its decomposition, the inaugural chronophotographic experiment that is repeated eight times in the film, following the numeric pattern of scenes that structure Attenborough's series *Life on Earth*. The time lapse animations documenting the process of decay begin with #1 the apple, followed by various representatives from the Linnaean classificatory system Fish #2 shrimps and #3 the angel fish, a Reptile, #4, the crocodile, a Bird #5, the swan, followed by Mammals #6 the dog (man's best friend), #7 the zebra and then finally #8 the Deuce twins themselves, who after Alba's death, decide to commit suicide together in the field at Escargot, injecting each other with a poison while lying naked on a Muybridge like raised grid platform under the watchful eye of the time lapse camera and to the cheerful orchestration of the "Teddy Bears Picnic." Although we witness hundreds of snails slowly tracing the brothers' anatomy this is the only decay that we are not privileged to witness in its entirety. Signs of life and death as a figure/ground problem are apparent in and between each tableau. For example in the scene where Oliver is obsessively watching the origin of life section we view a full frame close-up insert shot of a microscopic prawn swimming across the screen that jump cuts to an image of Alba's empty hospital bed where Oswald is opening a package of cooked prawns. Functioning like a grammatical construction within a sentence this tableau then shifts to a text sign excised from a magazine accompanied by a woman's clipped voiceover "called mute because unlike the Bewick it is rarely heard" and "Egg bound...there were no (sic) childeren" This is a reference to Alba's allegorical significance for viewers who didn't make the initial identification to the name Bewick with a white Swan in the opening shots. This scene is followed by a tableau in Oliver's apartment that has the appearance of being an extension of his laboratory decorated with lighted glass display cases, plants and classification charts displayed throughout the space. The camera frames Oliver and Venus (Frances Barber), both naked on the bed, Oliver playing with a group of slimy snails on a broken plate of glass resting on his stomach, (stomach foot to stomach), a belly trope that will reappear in Greenaway's *The Belly of an Architect.* Venus asks, "Why do you like snails? To which Oliver replies," because they are a nice primitive form of life, they help the world decay and they are hermaphrodites and can satisfy their own sexual needs." Venus retorts, "I don't believe it," to which Oliver unconvincingly replies: "Neither do I." Venus changes the subject to introduce an economic theme. "The server says by leasing out the jar of honey that the bear had two profitable sources of income" to which Oliver reading between the lines, replies, "This is just another whinging story about money and I disapprove of services" to which Venus responds indignantly, "...and I disapprove of zoos." Affronted by her impertinence Oliver pushes her out of his apartment, and as she exits, she begins to sing the "Teddy Bears Picnic" song framed cinematically as a "nude descending a staircase" in reference simultaneously to Duchamp's famous painting of 1912 and the chrono-photographic series of Edweard Muybridge, a source for Duchamp's (and the Futurists'), representation of movement in painting. "If you go down in the woods today you better go in disguise...if you go down to the woods today, be sure of a big surprise... What sort of stories would your brother Oswald like? At six o'clock their mummies and daddies will tuck them off to bed because they're tired little teddy bears...." And with a parting gesture as Oliver thrusts her clothes out the door, Venus adds, "and leave those little snails alone.... you dirty old man...!" The shot of the building's facade alludes to another Duchamp work, his *magnum opus*, by approximating the two halves of *The Large Glass,* with all of the iconographic baggage (the bride and the bachelors, the agricultural machine and the chocolate grinder etc.) implicit in this connection.

Venus de Milo as the Nude Descending a
Staircase

The dark silhouette of a security man in front of the building witnesses Milo's exit and a toy camel in the right foreground provides an uncanny presence. Venus de Milo, who bears the name of an antique sculpture from the art historical canon and also represents a conflation of Venus/Aphrodite/Eve/prostitute, has several exchanges concerning money with Oliver and later Van Hoyten (Joss Ackland) that provides other interesting libidinal and political economic vectors for this film. In scene #16 in the early morning outside the Zebra enclosure we view Venus the zoo prostitute (the oldest profession), walking sedately in high heels, wearing her trademark black clothing and smoking a cigarette. A cyclist passes cheerily saying, "good morning Venus, how are the zebras doing?" To which she answers cryptically "black and white" that besides being a humorous retort, is a literal description of the Zebra's appearance. Following this exchange Van Hoyten, the sinister looking keeper of the owls who, like his charges, seems to be nocturnal, approaches her. Van Hoyten also dressed in black, takes off his dark glasses (in the dark) and in a *basso profundo* theatrical sounding upper class voice ventures a "good morning Milo. How are you doing?" to which Venus replies, "just coming to see if you are looking after the animals properly." Van Hoyten slyly says, "You could come and look after me..." to which Venus replies, "Back there behind the cages.... is there a bed there?" "Since when did you need a bed?" questions Van Hoyten. "Since my back hurts which is now." Van Hoyten then states his terms. "I'll give you five pounds and two pounds of zebra steak," to which Venus replies cryptically "Do the owls go hungry for your pleasure?" Hoyten responds with "...owls aren't that fussy, they'll eat anything, even a lizard. Would you rather have a lizard or a zebra afterbirth?" She takes a drag on her cigarette and Van Hoyten then delivers a zebra puzzle question. "Tell me Milo. Do you think a zebra is a white animal with black stripes or a black animal with white stripes? She replies to this question by stubbing out her cigarette, and demanding "carry my shoes for me. There used to be a bed in the back of the vulture cages" "Ah," says Hoyten "but you were younger then...now you have less to bargain with." Continuing this witty repartee Venus retorts, "now I have experience...." With animals?" he asks. Van Hoyten then offers her "four pounds and some meat" and her rejoinder, "I'll take 10 pounds for half an hour and the tail feathers of an American bald eagle." The transactions in this scene are laced with bestial innuendo presenting differing rates and terms of exchange for 'sexual services' that are never fully disclosed. The absurd dialogue vacillating between the eschatological and scatological is framed by a surreal misogyny.

In a following hospital ward scene a hostile Oliver angrily confronts Alba with the accusation that she is responsible for the death of his wife "It's all your bloody fault...Because you were wearing white feathers... you were asking for trouble." Alba quips back in reply "Am I supposed to have a pilot's license?" Oliver continues "and because you said you took mercury to procure an abortion...." Alba, "how did you know I was pregnant...?" to which he replies, "because pregnant women are notoriously unreliable, especially when they are trying to procure an abortion!" While this odd exchange is taking place Caterina Bolnes, wearing a light pink dress and darker pink hat with furry trim, manicures Alba's toenails. Oliver continues with "it's all your fault you bitch!" accentuating this statement by throwing dead flowers in water

22. Oswald walking in his apartment

and the container of fruit into her lap. Outside the room is a sculpture of a figure on the roof, a Mercury or Icarus figurine that in a subsequent scene becomes a Sphinx. The insert following this contains the time lapse film of the decaying apple, followed by a powerful tableau of naked Oliver sitting drunk on the floor of his bathroom, surrounded by papers and magazines, an electric heater, and two empty red wine bottles. This tableau with its foreshortened figure of Oliver resembles several deposition images of Christ and the foreshortened figure of a murdered man on top of his child in *Rue Transnonain* (1834) a famous lithograph by Honoré Daumier. Oliver in desperation attempts to imbibe some of the glass from the smashed windscreen of the Mercury car. Venus arrives at his apartment door (#26) and when he doesn't answer she looks through the letterbox, which provides a tableau of Oliver on the floor, and recognizing the dangerous situation he is in she rushes him to the hospital. This is followed by a tableau vivant of the Zoo attendant/(Mercury) messenger quizzing Beta about the letters of the alphabet and the names of animals (a reprise of similar scenes in earlier Greenaway films *H is for House* and *The Falls*) "J is for?" And the answer, "Jaguar;" "K is for? Kangaroo" "L is for?" "Lion" "M is for?" - "Monkey." This scene shifts to images from the life cycle of the shrimp.

Successive tableaux build upon the themes established in the first section of the film with scenes taking place in the hospital the Deuces' apartments, the theatre, Van Meergeren's surgery with its reproductions of Vermeers and the reptile house and Zebra enclosure at the Zoo. Oswald Deuce's Apartment he restaurant scene continues the economic theme previously established where Oliver is challenged by Beta to ascertain what colour underwear Bolnes is wearing. When he is challenged by Bolnes to inspect under her dress, she slaps his face and tells him "that will be forty pounds."   Many scenes contain art references both contemporary and historical. The scene with Oswald walking in his apartment, tracking back and forth across the stage in front of the static camera resembles the tracking movements of Robert Wilson's opera in *Einstein on the Beach*. The blue screen of a television set, provides the lighting in the left foreground of the scene and two fluorescent tubes, another light source, causally leaning against the back wall resemble Dan Flavin artworks in a private collection. The three scenes in Meergeren's surgery looking more like a studio/gallery reinforce some the key themes about the ambiguity of representation and the value of art. On the walls are several paintings, from the major genres, a landscape, a still life, a nude and Vermeer's *Lute Player At The Window* (1664) In the first scene with the assistance of Catarina Bolnes, Van Meergeren attempts to fit an artificial leg to Alba and she asks if he has sold her other amputated leg. In a subsequent surgery scene, Van Meergeren is seen wearing a similar costume to the one worn by the artist in Vermeer's allegorical work *The Art of Painting*. The camera tracks back to reveal that the surgeon /artist manqué is producing photographs of Caterina Bolnes still wearing her signature red hat. The third scene in the Van Meergeren surgery opens with five paintings: Vermeer's *The Concert* (1666) and four others that contain women wearing the black and white /yellow striped dress, which become an analogue to the Zebra question. Alba is standing with her new black prosthetic leg. In the rear are Bolnes and Milo who is standing before a mirror. Van Meergeren commands Milo to dress Alba in the dress represented in Vermeer's *The Soldier and the Laughing Girl, Girl Reading a Letter at an Open Window* and *The Music Lesson*. Alba sits at the piano (similar to the woman in *The Music Lesson*) complaining that she is just "an excuse for medical experiments and art theory" and begins to play "The Teddy Bears Picnic" song. All 26 of Vermeer's works (the same number of letters in the alphabet) are referenced in Z&OO, even the three dubious authentications that Greenaway acknowledges through Alba's quip about her daughters name Beta, the second of twenty-three letters in the Greek alphabet. The scene in which Van Meergeren orders his wife to dress in special art historical clothing to provide him with aesthetic pleasure is similar to Scottie Ferguson's (James Stewart) demanding treatment of Judy Barton (Kim Novak) in the famous dressing scenes of Hitchcock's *Vertigo. A Zed and Two Noughts* may be read as something more than an essay on mortality, morbidity and money, or an allegory on the fate of Vermeer. Michel Foucault's discussion of the visible/invisible is again instructive here. "To see death in life, immobility in its change, skeletal, fixed space beneath its smile, and, at the end of its time, the beginning of a reversed time swarming with innumerable lives, is the structure of a Baroque experience"[15] With its allegorical systems Z&OO is a work of baroque complexity but also a phenomenological excursion with life itself as a zero-sum game as this was described in the game theory formulated in the 1940s by John von Neumann and Oskar Morgestern. In mathematics the term 'zero-sum' describes a situation in which a participant's gain (or loss) is exactly balanced by the losses (or gains) of the other participant(s). It was named 'zero-sum' because when the total gains of the participants are added and the total losses subtracted they will "sum to zero." Cutting a cake is zero- or constant-sum because one player taking a larger piece for him or herself reduces the amount of cake available for others. Situations where participants can all gain or suffer together such as a country with an excess of bananas trading with another country for their excess of apples where both benefit from the transaction are referred to as non-zero-sum.[16] J.Von Neumann and Oskar Morgestern proved that any zero-sum game involving n players is in fact a generalized form of a zero-sum game for two persons; and that any non-zero-sum game for n players can be reduced to a zero-sum game for $n + 1$ players, the ($n + 1$) the player representing the global profit or loss. The characters in a *Zed and Two Noughts* also suffer (and gain) together. When Oliver and Oswald realize their loss is incommensurate with their gains - a zero-sum - they decide to commit suicide to the accompaniment of the Teddy Bears Picnic song, "they're sure of a big surprise."[17] Finally a note about the scene in which Alba provides Oswald with the key to her cottage in Escargot that provides an insight into both the art of film making and deconstructive criticism. When Oswald slips his hand into Alba's slim white handbag -- another Hitchcockian operation with Freudian sexual connotations – to obtain the key to Escargot where she encourages Oswald and Oliver to stay, he finds dozens of keys to choose from. "Good Lord Alba which one?" he asks, tipping them all out on her bed in front of her for her to choose the right one. "Why do you keep all these (keys)?" to which she answers, "I've always had them..." she says, adding archly, "you should never throw a key away." If Alba had added that the key is often beveled, this would have an excellent invocation of Derrida's truth in painting. The *passé partout* in Derridian terms is not simply a master key but a matt and matrix for the cultural artifact but as he warns, the "internal edges of a *passé-partout* are often beveled."[18] With multiple keys one has to choose whichever best fits the text and if one doesn't work then one must pick the lock.

The Belly of an Architect

Thanatos, Eros, art and architecture, figure prominently in the first montage of travelling shots accompanying the credits of *Belly of an Architect* (1986), arguably Greenaway's most accessible film for general audiences and according to many commentators, his most personal. The American architect Stourley Kracklite (Brian Dennehy) and his wife Luisa are making love in the train carrying them into Italy, and shots from the train show a wooden cross, church and a graveyard, with medium close-ups of headstones with artificial and dead flower arrangements. The graveyard shots hark back to Greenaway's first film *Death of Sentiment* (1959-62), his first cinematic essay on art, melancholy and death. As they simultaneously cross the border and reach a climax in their love making Kracklite says "what a lovely way to enter Italy" and Louisa replies, "absolutely, the ideal way" one of several references to idealism, Platonic, and neo-Platonic in this film about unfulfilled ambition (the artist manqué), frustrated desires, adultery, and the power of art, architecture and history. This introductory railway sequence also quotes a familiar train scene in Hitchcock's *North by Northwest* (1959) that occurs in the final moments of the film when Roger Thornhill (Cary Grant) is holding on to Eve Kendall (Eva Marie Saint) who is about to fall from a ledge of the Mt. Rushmore monument. At the most suspenseful moment the film cuts to show them engaging in the same struggle to safety with Thornhill reaching for the hand of Eve and pulling her up into the top bunk bed of the sleeping car of the train as they speed into a dark Freudian tunnel.[19]

The next scene in *The Belly of an Architect* is a celebratory party in the open air with a dual purpose: to honour the arrival of Kracklite, the

American curator of a major retrospective of the work of the visionary C18th French architect Étienne Boullée, and to celebrate his forty-fourth birthday symbolized for the occasion with a huge iced cake surrounded by candles after Boullée's spherical design (1784) of the cenotaph for Sir Isaac Newton. Kracklite demonstrates his appreciation for his hosts friendly gesture by showing them an English pound note bearing a portrait of Isaac Newton and as he points out, the apple blossom, a reference to the falling apple with which the scientist hypothesized the existence of gravity. Like book ends the pound note and the force of gravity appear in the penultimate tragic scene of the film. We learn that in the seven years (another significant digit) he has been married to Luisa he has started but been unable to complete many projects, which has its analogue in Louisa's inability to carry a pregnancy to full term. Kracklite is a frustrated architect manqué who like his idol Boullée has had little success in constructing any of his buildings and must seek his symbolic capital in his extravagant curatorial project to reinforce the genius of his mentor, and hopefully in the process, obtain some much needed prestige for himself. This film once again contains many of Greenaway's core tropes, obsessions, art history and mythological references Icarus and Mercury, adding a few more such as Silenus and Dionysus with references to paintings such as Galeazzo Mondella's *The Cortege of Silenus* c 1500, and Piero Della Francesco's *The Flagellation of Christ* (1455-60). The magnificent architecture of Imperial Rome from which Greenaway has chosen eight major buildings also features prominently throughout this film[20] There are also more contemporary references to the modernist work of Warhol, Kitaj, late modernist and postmodern reprography, process and architectural photography.

When the Kracklites arrive in Rome they are at first treated royally by their hosts and co-curators of the Boullée project, the architects Io Speckler (Sergio Fontani) senior, Caspasian Speckler (Lambert Wilson) his tall dark handsome son, and daughter Flavia, a photographer of art and architecture. The other major character in the film is Frederico Boccini, a close friend of Caspasian and the model maker for the Boullée exhibition. During the course of the exhibition planning and installation of the scale model of the Newton cenotaph at the Victor Emmanuel building, Kracklite begins to experience debilitating attacks of stomach pain, at one point, at the suggestion of his Italian hosts, enduring a full rectal scopic examination that reveals stomach cancer. As a result of these attacks that he first attributes to dyspepsia his concentration on the curatorial task at hand begins to diminish and Louisa becomes irritated by his self-pitying obsession with his body. She begins to have an affair with Caspasian and Kracklite becomes more and more obsessed with his belly, making art projects with postcards he borrows (steals) of neo-classical statues of male figures with bulging stomach muscles that he obsessively enlarges on a copying machine, then covers the walls and floor of his lavish studio apartment. He also obtains 26 postcards (another alphabet reference) of famous architectural sites around Rome and throughout the film these appear as full screen inserts with the camera shifting from the frozen tableau to the site itself thereby producing a phenomenological investigation of time and space referenced to past and contemporary history, the work of Boullée and by extension Kracklite, the architect associated with Chicago and that city's austere neo-classical modernism introduced by Louis Sullivan the famous American architect. Kracklite also writes on the verso of the postcards but never sends them, a neat quotation of Derrida's concept of the *lettre en souffrance* - the lost letter or one held in abeyance - the lost letter or one that does not or can not reach its destination.[21] Like Derrida, Kracklite, (Greenaway's alter ego) recognises that "even by arriving.... the letter carries the sense of not arriving. It arrives elsewhere, always, several times. You simply cannot take hold of it. That is the structure of the letter."[22]

Kracklite's obsessive appropriative and reproductive task is similar to a Warhol or Kitaj art project and is contrasted with another project being undertaken by an artist who Kracklite meets during one of his outings around Rome. In a scene reminiscent of Bernard Malamud's *Pictures of Fidelman*, this art criminal is obsessively chiseling noses off the faces of classical sculpture for a collection that he exhibits privately at a later point in the film. His *arte povera* excisions give these statues an immediate historical gloss, a reminder of famous Greek statues from the Hellenistic period that are also noseless but usually as a result of other circumstances.

The underlying key numeral for this Greenaway film is nine, a reference to the last nine months of his Kracklite's life during which he loses control of career, his wife and his future, that also coincides with the gestational period of Louisa's pregnancy. The film narrative also concludes nine months after it started, the 12th February 1986, coinciding with the anniversary of Boullée's birthday, Louisa giving birth and Kracklite's death. Kracklite's cancerous belly, with the word itself serving as an ironic play on the name of the French architect Boullée, becomes another character in the film, at one point being compared to the lives of the Roman emperors but not as Nietzsche does with God - "The belly is the reason that man does not so easily take himself for a God." Where many of Greenaway's other films exhibit a baroque sensibility, *The Belly of an Architect* explores neo-classicism particularly with respect to the architecture and paintings that Greenaway quotes throughout. The major themes in this film are configured around problems of production, reproduction (human and mechanical) and representation, of art, architecture, history and memory.

Caspasian begins to flirt with Louisa and later Flavia with Kracklite who he discovers is also an obsessive artist, voyeuristically photographing every experience to which she has access, even her brother's affair with Kracklite's wife. Another major theme concerns historical legacy both personal, given Kracklite's manqué inspired mid life crisis, and public, concerning the separate agendas of museum and State. At one point in a conversation Flavia points out to Kracklite that Albert Speer, Hitler's favourite architect was also influenced by Boullée and the links between the architecture of Imperial Rome, Fascist Italy, Germany and American modernism are a thematic thread coursing through the rich fabric of images in the film. Caspasian's plan to obtain money to restore Mussolini's Foro Italico by milking the Boullée exhibition budget is a spectral reminder of Italy's Ghost and how rehabilitation is often linked to reproduction. But as one of Walter Benjamin's "Theses on the Philosophy of History" posit "There is no document of civilization which is not at the same time a document of barbarism. And just as such a document is not free of barbarism, barbarism taints also the manner in which it was transmitted from one owner to another." [23] Kracklite commits suicide by falling backwards, in a very non Icarus-like manoeuvre, from the Vittori Emmanuel II monument site of the exhibition of Boullée's work at the exact moment his wife is giving birth, probably registering as one of the fastest births on film.

The Cook, the Thief, His Wife and Her Lover

The Cook, the Thief, His Wife and Her Lover (1990) is a film that has frequently been discussed in Greenaway literature as a critique of consumer society during the Thatcher years, primarily as a result of several interviews that he gave to the press. "This film is about greed... a society's..." – he quotes a *bon mot* from Oscar Wilde – "and a man who knows the price of everything and the value of nothing."[24] Greenaway's signature themes and tropes: art, artists and art history, food, water (ice and steam), body fluids, the nude body, sex and sexuality, books, reading, knowledge, and of course, death (two murders) appear again in this film.[25] Class struggle, elided in many of his other films, here takes central stage. The contrasting themes in this film, like *A Zed and Two Noughts* and many other Greenaway productions, are configured in matching pairs, doubles, twins, *doppelgangers*, or as binary opposites: light/dark, male/ female, open/closed, soft/hard, wet/dry, left/right, front/back, up/down entrance/exit. Greenaway's binaries however are rarely fixed, they may become doubles, one may slip into – be imbricated or conflated with – the other at a moment's notice. Light slips into dark, liquid will become solid, water may be represented as ice, then entropically as steam, a top may become a bottom, left to right, a front becomes a rear, male/ female, and life will become death. An implicit ambiguity or sharp contrast between opposites (thesis and antithesis) may resolve dialectically into a third (synthesis) but most often become they are mutually canceling. This is evident in the architecture configured within many of his films, including the *Le Hollandaise* restaurant in *The Cook, the Thief...* where the 'entrance' to the restaurant that leads through the kitchen and pantry areas to the dining room is also the principal 'exit' through which Mr. Spica and his cronies pass. In some ways the architecture of the restaurant is configured like a body with the dining room as the head with the kitchen and its ancillary spaces, cheese room, bread pantry, configured as the internal organs, the stomach and intestines, the piano (that remains silent), the heart, corridors and the wash rooms become the digestive system and reproductive organs between the freezer and the stoves.[26] The sphincter and anal areas for the passage of effluent is at the rear of the building where the garbage and dogs are kept. In Greenaway's lexographic schema front could become back, arse could become face – arse about face – a Janus like contiguity that is strongly configured in the first two sequences of the film. This is a medieval hall rather than a restaurant and the *mise en scene* is bathed alternately in an erotic reddish brown chiaroscuro with gradual highlights in the foreground areas, or an eerily acidic yellow and clinical white light, the kitchen and dishwashing areas enveloped in entropic steam.[27] Even the sizes and colours of the dogs have been carefully chosen to provide allegorical (and classed) emphases to the diegesis. The spotted black and white Dalmatian (a 'fire dog' that also appears in the opening shot in *A Zed and two Noughts*), the black and grey of the Alsatians, and the black and tan Rottweilers, all working animals, guard dogs and hunting and retrieving (water) dogs.

The film opens with a shot of a cage with a central bar bisecting the screen behind which the large hungry dogs are seen noisily ravishing carrion and/or leftovers from the restaurant, which also serves analogically as a school, butchery, slaughterhouse, and prison. At the beginning of his films Greenaway typically leaves the options open. It is early evening and the scene is selectively bathed in lights that provide strong contrasts between dark and light (chiaroscuro) accentuating the saturated colours: red, white, black, blue, green and brown, employed in Greenaway's palette. Allegorically there is a Greek mythological reference here in the figure of Cerberus the vicious dog that guards the entrance to Hade's underworld, for under his influence Spica's favourite restaurant has become a type of underworld or hell. The credits scroll down slowly to the ascending accompaniment of a pulsing neo-baroque orchestral composition scored by Michael Nyman. The camera does a slow vertical pan up from the underworld bowel of carnage to the above ground reality of classed privilege, debauchery and subordinated drudgery. The vertical pan stops at a low shot introducing the backs of two (twin) 'footmen' dressed immaculately in red and black with long white gloves who walk away from the camera to draw the dark curtains back from the stage set, soon to become an amphitheatre for a degrading spectacle. An automobile arrives and moves off screen, stage left and then two white provision vans arrive into view for an establishing shot, a white car containing Albert Spica and his wife driving between the two vans to face the stationary camera. A neon sign in the background spells "Luna" (moon) which is a symbol of madness, love, and with its association with women's menses, sexual desire and fecundity. The camera shifts to a reverse shot

23 *The Cook, the Thief, His Wife and Her Lover*

24. Jan Davidsz Heem
Still life with Lobster

25. Jan Davidsz Heem
Flower Arrangement

to show the rear of the vans with open doors revealing that they are fish and meat suppliers, the first of a series of *tableaux vivant* presented by the open vans displaying their contents. The vans also have gender specific attendants, a meat boy and a fish girl.

Taking his cures from Greenaway's assertion that he accorded more importance to the history of painting than with film, William Van Wert an early reviewer, identified several paintings employed throughout this film. The open vans have the appearance of Dutch genre paintings by artists such as Gerrit Dou *The Grocer's Shop* (1647) *Woman Peeling a Carrot* (1630) and *The Poulterer's Shop* c.(1679); Jan Davidsz Heem, *Still life with Lobster* 1645-50 and *Flower Arrangement*; Jan Steen *The Bean Feast* 1668, Peter Claesz *Breakfast Piece* (1646). Many of the restaurant table shots also resemble Dutch genre paintings.

The first scene shows in graphic detail the physical degradation of an individual named Roy (Willie Ross) by Albert Spica (Michael Gambon), the film's *nouveau riche* thief/lout, identified (caricatured) by language and demeanor with obvious working class Cockney origins, who is the central protagonist of the film. Within the first three minutes we learn from Spica's unremitting diatribe that Roy is the owner of "a dirty little canteen" who owes him money. His shirt is stripped from his back and he is forced to bend backwards over the trunk of the car and suffer the abject degradation of having dog faeces smeared in his mouth and all over his half naked torso. "Open your mouth... you've got to learn that they don't appreciate the food you serve in that dirty little canteen of yours..." says the grotesque bearded and balding figure of Spica, dressed in a bespoke dinner suit with a large blue military sash. "You must learn the rules" Have you never heard of Chicken à la Rhone (sic) 'Pourine', Oyster Mornay or Frogs Legs Parisienne..." says Spica. "Of course you haven't!" Spica imperiously orders his henchmen to "take his pants down," an order that he also delivers at two other critical points in the film. The scene is marked by the baroque twisting of Roy's body as Spica desecrates his body until he falls to the ground in front of the car.... where he apparently defecates in fear. Spica responds with the first of many scatological comments in the film "Oh dear, oh dear, didn't your daddy teach you to wipe your bottom?" At this point Georgina who had previously been sitting in the car smoking a cigarette gets out and shouts "Albert ...leave him alone." The scene is medieval, out of Chaucer or Rabelais in its 'carnivalesque' mixture of scatological profanations, filth and degradation. Spica is a figure larger than life, no ordinary gourmand or restaurateur. He struts about and introduces himself and his wife "This is Georgina (Helen Mirren), "she's got a heart of gold and a body to match and I'm Albert Spica (Michael Gambon) with a heart of gold and money to match." Spica's cockney accent[28] identifies him as a working class lout, or rather a caricature of how the upper and middle classes view the working class, particularly the threatening nouveau riche gangsters such as the notorious Kray brothers, twin gangsters who operated in East London in the 1950s and 1960s who were immortalized in a TV series in the 1990s. After identifying himself in grandiose terms he then points to his victim "And you are Roy and you've got nothing except what you owe me" At this point in the diegesis we obtain a three quarter rear view of the hulking figure of Spica, who says to Georgina I'll be as quick as I can, recoils at the smell of excrement on his hands, slaps one of his attendants on the face saying "'ere you... go, get me some water, soap and a towel ...eh...?" and begins to poke Roy with his phallic walking stick, proceeding to berate him with "you 'ave 'umiliated yourself in front of a lady.... 'umiliated yourself in front of us" followed by, "Now I've given you a good dinner and now you can have a nice drink...." proceeding to open his fly and piss on the unfortunate prostrate figure at his feet, threatening the near comatose Roy as he does so, to "behave yourself in future and pay up... or next time I'll make you eat your own shit after forcing it out of your dick like toothpaste!" Spica then speaks abusively to one of his cohort. "Put that away Spangler, we don't want to see your shriveled contribution." At this point in the proceedings two young kitchen workers, one albino Caucasian, one Asian appear with the bowl of water, soap and towel that Spica had asked for. "I never liked that Chinese food.... but looking at you I like it even less...." and follows this with a hand flourish to upend the bowl of water on the unfortunate Asian. By this point we are approximately five minutes into the film and have been introduced to Spica as an absolutely grotesque, working class, racist, homophobic, misogynist, misanthropic pig, a gangster boss and successful racketeer involved in the protection business, extortion, probably money laundering and murder. Spica is making a 'friendly visit' to Le Hollandaise his favourite restaurant and in an attempt to encourage Richard Boarst the French chef to build a 'business' partnership, he delivers two vanloads of fresh fish and meat and the large letters for the sign that announces their impending union. Later he delivers boxes of cheap silverware all of it presumably stolen or in payment for 'protection.'

The opening scene with dogs barking, Spica barking and harsh lighting looks less like an up market restaurant for the chattering classes than an abusive prison or concentration camp. The two open vans filled with bodies of animals and fish have been compared to two Dutch still life paintings and the middle scene of the dogs mauling each other, growling, barking around the naked male torso is reminiscent of several powerful paintings by Francis Bacon featuring naked men and dogs, alluding to bestiality and fear which we have previously see represented in *A Zed and two Noughts*. Other Dutch genre painters provide models for the panoply of *tableaux vivants* in the restaurant kitchen, for example Gerrit Dou's painting *The Poultry Shop* (1670). Greenaway, like Hitchcock packs the *mise en scene* with a myriad of significant details to enrich the potential for meaning. For example the license plate on Spica's car reads HEX Q832. Greenaway does not simply reference the literal definition of "hex" as a spell placed on some individual by a malevolent witch or wizard, but also loads the other letter and numbers with other signifiers. "Q" as a homophone may be linked to the cue and the phallic stick that Spica carries and use as a weapon to intimidate his intimates and potential victims. Q may also signify a question. The numbers on the plate 832 added equals 13 a traditional unlucky number associated with the devil. Greenaway is not beyond teasing his viewers with H=8 E=5 X=23. The first numbers 8+5=13 and 23 is 32 reversed. The literate viewer of a Greenaway art project is also made aware of some other relevant signifiers 'made to measure' for the libidinal and political economy of this artfully constructed film. Spica reversed is Aspic; a sticky jelly like substance made from rendering cow bones that is used widely in cooking as a thickening agent. "Mr. Spica" which Richard the Cook calls him, is also phonically tied to Mr. Speaker, the key point man within the British Parliamentary system, and the House of Lords, through whom every member must speak. *Le Hollandaise* the name of Spica's restaurant also provides some other coordinates for the reader of symbols in Greenaway's films. Hollandaise is a French béchamel (white) sauce used as an accompaniment for game and vegetables, often asparagus which figures prominently in the first table scene. Hitchcock famously said about his *Dial M for murder*, "a murder untaken without a gleam on the scissors is like asparagus without Hollandaise sauce!" Hollandaise also provides a reference to the interior theatrical tableaux, the many allusions to Dutch still life and domestic genre scenes and the large wall sized reproduction of Franz

Hal's *Banquet of the Officers of the Saint George Civic Company* (1616) which is the centre piece of the restaurant and the heart of the allegorical matrix of meaning for the film.

26 Table scene with Franz Hal's painting *Banquet of the Officers of the Saint George Civic Company* (1616)

Again, in company with Hitchcock, Peter Greenaway has a vested interest in maintaining the power and autonomy of the visual artist and correlates his work to the singular role and genius characteristics of the artist rather than the more fragmented role of the film director that is typically characterized by an extreme division of labor. He therefore employs art for many reasons, political and aesthetic. Greenaway thinks visually as a director, and because he was trained as a painter he necessarily brings his archive of images to mind when he is working on a script. In company with many other film directors and visual artists he quotes, Greenaway may borrow and appropriate from art history in order to (consciously or unconsciously) insert himself into art history. The paintings that Greenaway uses in this film include Andrea Mantegna's *Dead Christ* (1500), also a favourite painting of Hitchcock's that with its deep foreshortening becomes the model for the foreshortened view of Michael the dead lover. There are multiple references throughout *The Cook*...to other famous artworks from the canon including: Rembrandt's *Anatomy Lesson of Dr Deyman* and *The Anatomy Lesson of Dr Tulp* (1656), Eakin's *The Gross* clinic, Andrea del Castagno's *The Last Supper* (1436), Rembrandt's *The Syndics of the Drapers Guild,* Jan Vermeer's *The Cook* (1657), and also the work of more contemporary painters such as Francis Bacon and perhaps even the performance artists Marc Chaimowicz and Stuart Brisley who were producing challenging abject performance works during the 1970's at a time when Greenaway was a avid participant in the London art world.

After the first scene the camera tracks horizontally to follow Spica and Georgina into the restaurant. This tracking is a favourite Greenaway cinematic strategy to phenomenologically mark time and space for his viewers. Their entrance is accompanied by the exquisite voice of Pol Pot a young albino male soprano (an ironic allusion to the Cambodian despot and castrati of classical Italian opera), replacing the counter tenor in *The Draughtsman's Contract,* who sings a Greenaway libretto about his role as a dishwasher thus representing a conflation of high culture and low social status. Spica stops briefly to listen to the boy, gaze lasciviously at his body then scornfully flicks a coin into one of his bowls as if to signal his status as a beggar.

The new electric sign for the restaurant "Spica and Boarst" is raised and in the next scene we are introduced to Richard the elegant French cook (chef and restaurateur) who is sitting facing the camera and plucking the feathers from a large duck.... that we learn is destined for the meal to celebrate Spica's anniversary. Spica proclaims loudly "[it's been]… three months since I invited you to become my favourite restaurateur..." to which the cook replies, "We can also leave the feathers on and cook it..." At this point a raw egg is thrown by a shadowy figure from a top gantry overlooking the kitchen that seems to signal for Spica to do an excited little dance, a hop and a skip...entreating his "favourite restaurateur" to "come, come" and see the new electric sign that he had installed. The neon sign is switched on with a flourish but this is followed by a splutter of lights and a flash behind the sign, a symbolic overload demonstrating that the power has died and a portent of what is to come. A waiter enters to see the cook and says "it's dark in the restaurant" to which Richard replies in an aside..."yes, Phillip thanks to Mr Spica... it's dark everywhere..."

The next scene resembles the performance of a Catholic religious rite as waiters move slowly in procession lighting the candles of all those present in the space. Spica follows the cook repeating after him in tortured French the names of the menu plan that he and members of his entourage are about to consume. At this point the camera cuts to a close-up of the French menu that Spica continues to read in very bad French... and that the *haute* and clearly exasperated Georgina corrects. Albert says "Poison...."which Georgina quickly corrects as "Poisson...." and in response he slaps her with the menu, and questions her arrogantly three times with, "what did you say?" To which she repeats softly, "Poisson, Poisson, Poisson." At this point there are several intercut tableau shots of the rear of the vans containing fish and meat, an Asian woman strangely licking a block of ice, and close ups of the products. The sequence ends with two shots of Roy slowly arising from his beating at the hands of Spica. There is an exchange between Spica and the cook about ' protection' that indicate the Spica and his gang are in the extortion racket, providing 'protection' against food poisoning that they would initiate if resisted by their 'clients.'

Another long tracking shot through the various rooms of the restaurant carries viewers to the table occupied by Spica and his guests dressed now in formal dress code with red military sashes replacing the blue. The backdrop for the table is a large reproduction of Franz Hal's painting *Banquet of the Officers of the Saint George Civic Company* (1616) who are also in the 'protection business' thus presenting a suitable allegory for the *haute bourgeois* pretensions of Spica and his gang. Ten figures are seated at a circular table and the first non-verbal communication occurs between Georgina, dressed alluringly in red with a black hat and pendulous black earrings delicately eating a phallic spear of asparagus with her fingers and Michael, her future lover. While her husband prattles on with his scatological remarks, she continues to gaze demurely Michael who is dressed conservatively in a brown suit.

Greenaway's palette references are blacks, reds and whites with green accents provided by the potted palms and other foliage. Spica makes specific references to art in his bellicose manner "I'm an artist the way I combine my business and my pleasure...money...my business and food is my pleasure." Michael and Georgina continue to exchange alluring glances toward one another while Spica continues his vulgar outbursts: "Shut yor ma'f Mitchell!" Every time you open it you show 'ow vulgar you can be." At this stage the viewer is approximately

27 Table Scene

sixteen minutes into the film and there is a cut to Georgina in the very
pristine white ladies room. The spectator witness two-tableau shots of
Georgina and Michael who appears meekly shrugging his shoulders to
reveal that he is in the wrong room. They circulate one another without
speaking, sexual tension clearly palpable. She offers him a cigarette, he
declines and they return to the restaurant. Georgina looks at the book
(with a green cover) that he is reading, one of three that are on the
table. Albert remains his usual bellicose and scatological self. "Did
you wipe the toilet seat before you parked your bum... caus' you never
know what you might catch off a toilet seat these days. Every toilet seat
is a minefield." This scandalous remark is followed by a contrasting
close up of the plate with its gleaming metal covering resting on the
table an ironic reference to sanitization. Georgina soon gets up to return
to the bathroom, excusing herself with the statement that she has left
her cigarette lighter behind in the toilet. At the adjacent table, Michael
notices and follows her to the ladies room. They meet in the red foyer
where she takes his hand and places it to her breast.

They have another erotic liaison in a toilet stall that is interrupted by a
woman who enters to check the mirror. After she leaves Georgina
continues to engage in a sexual act with Michael until curiosity gets the
better of Spica who enters the ladies room loudly demanding to know
what she is up to. Michael stands on the toilet seat to conceal the fact
that there are two people in the stall while Spica struts around the
gleaming white space demanding to know what his wife is doing. He

then makes some more endearing remarks about the danger of toilet seats before he exits announcing "I've ordered you some *gateau poivre* and (sic) profiteroles." He pretends to go out and then returns in a suspenseful moment saying when he sees her "...you're all sweaty wash yer hands... and I'll give you a kiss." After the initial liaison in the ladies room the love scenes that Georgina and Michael engage in progressively escalate in intensity, framed aesthetically in various sectors of the kitchen and pantry: the bread room, the cheese room the dead bird room, the book room. The scene of Michael and Georgina making love in the bakery is contrasted rhythmically with intercut close-up shots of the kitchen workers erotically cutting vegetables, a cabbage and red pepper and a cucumber. The camera tracks left on the longitudinal axis from the rear rectal entrance of the restaurant past the belly through to the head that is the dining room itself and Spica's table.

The Cook.... is openly scatological; sexist, racist, and xenophobic. Homophobic references in the dialogue and visual tableaux also saturate the film. Spica wears a very long phallic tie on a red shirt. When Georgina returns from another time in the ladies room he again asks her with paternalistic (and xenophobic) menace "Where have you been...wiping your bum...did you use your right hand like I told you to?" During one scene Spica aggressively passes Michael's table knocking his books to the floor then lectures him about high art versus graffiti. "More people read the graffiti in the bathroom than read books.... reading gives you indigestion...didn't you know that?" He invites Michael to join the Spica table and addresses him in front of the others with an implicitly racist comment: "what's your name...Michael?'.... Michael...is that a Jewish name?" The conversation turns to Georgina who announces that she is infertile. "Being infertile makes me a safe bet for a good screw." In another example of gross brutality a scene follows in which an attempt to move a table to enable a floorshow to begin allows Spica to confront another patron in another scandalous scene "Naughty Willie... naughty little Willie" he addresses the patron "How would you like to be spanked on the bottom?" He then force-feeds this hapless character before kicking him out of the restaurant.

The scene changes with a return tracking shot past Pol Pot washing dishes where Spica ingratiates himself saying, "I was choir boy once." One of the female members of Spica's entourage finally divulges the secret love affair between Georgina and Michael and Albert goes on the rampage, invading the Ladies Room kicking open the stall doors on all the frightened women, then careering through the kitchen to destroy anything in his path. The cook hides Michael and Georgina in the freezer and then whisks them out the back door to the van filled with rotting carcasses. They are taken to Michael's book depository as a refuge and hosed down by a black attendant in an exceptional tableau between four neoclassical columns, possibly a neo-classical painting reference to a work by the French painter Gerôme. They settle down to the comfort of the book depository and the boy soprano from Le Hollandaise delivers them a bottle of wine and some food. While they lounge together (we receive a rear view) on a couch for another Dionysian tableau, Pol Pot looks at the books and Michael suggests that he take one with him when he returns the dishes to the restaurant but returning he is soon discovered by Albert, his dogs and henchmen who are in hot pursuit of the couple. Their meeting appears like a confrontation between red riding hood and the wolf, with Spica proceeding to throw everything out of the boy's basket.... tasting the leftovers in the dish he is returning to the restaurant... "A fish.... profiteroles..." continuing with "Georgina likes profiteroles" but spying the napkins with Georgina's lipstick, he then aggressively rips a button from the boy's tunic and holding his nose, stuffs it into his mouth demanding as he did with the assault on Roy in the opening sequence.... "Take 'is pants down.... take 'is pants down!" This attracts the attention of a couple of passersby – figures in silhouette— who Spica quickly warns away with the homophobic comment "Go away we don't want no fairies here!" Spica then continues to torture Pol Pot who screams and begins to choke. Inspecting the books that the boy has borrowed, he discovers the stamp address for Books Unlimited The Book Depository Falconer Court, (a bird reference which is another Greenaway signature). The following scene, takes place in the dark, with the sound of dripping water and dirge like passages of music composed by Michael Nyman. Richard takes Michael and Georgina some more food and tells them that Spica has attacked the young boy. Georgina immediately dresses and returns leaving Michael alone.

The next sequence begins with a long tracking shot of Georgina following two nurses in Victorian nursing clothes to the boy who is lying in a hospital bed accompanied by a powerful men's chorus that with the boy soprano's voice heightens the Catholic/ Protestant binary. This cuts to a tableau of Spica and Mitchell force-feeding Michael pages ripped from his books. A foreshortened shot of the bookkeeper reveals that his chest is lacerated, bleeding but Spica is in high spirits. "God piss in your wound...God alive Mitchell you can always be guaranteed to say the wrong thing at the right time." "I didn't mean you literally had to chew his bollocks off... I meant it metaphorically..." "I can see the news now 'Jewish book keeper savaged by young sex maniac." To which Mitchell replies dumbly," What does that mean?" This exchange invokes some of the previous exchanges between Spica and Mitchell regarding the eating of sheep's testicles at the restaurant and especially Spica's early advice to Michael "Reading gives you indigestion." Spica subsequently invokes De Quincey's prescription for a murder worthy of aesthetic delectation.

> I don't want this to look like a sex murder... I want it to appear as a revenge murder...an affair of the heart...'a crime *passionelle*' poison/passion/poisson. They going to say that this was a dignified revenge killing.... they are going to admire the style.... ...he was stuffed and Albert liked good food and they might even smile...he was stuffed with the tools of his trade...he was stuffed with books.

Georgina begins her return to the restaurant as the camera tracks past a couple kissing.... alighting on Albert teaching three of his cronies how to eat crayfish by biting the head off snapping the shell and digging out the insides. Albert informs his cohort that he doesn't want to destroy the evidence of the murder. He wants Georgina to see it and we cut to her pulling a crumpled sheet of paper out of Michael's mouth opening up a bloody page that shows the book's title *The French Revolution*. A close-up of Albert Spica ruminating on the deed follows with his particular brand of humour. "What did he say that the French Revolution was easier to swallow than Napoleon".... a patsy... Napoleon was fond of food his favourite dish was oysters Florentine...Churchill liked seafood.... amazin' 'ow all the great generals were fond of seafood.... what did Hitler like.... clams? Mussolini liked squid..."

The next scene returns us to Georgina who has slept the night with her dead lover and she now delivers a soliloquy about Albert, an important disclosure to her dead lover and to channel her anger towards Albert. "He beat me...you know that but after we returned from the restaurant he made me get a wet towel and I would have to wipe his ... he had a suitcase with all kinds of objects in it a tooth wooden spoon, a plastic drain and wine bottle and he would insist on using them...or me using them..." Georgina approaches Richard the cook asking him if he could cook the body of her dead lover informing him "he has a reputation for a wide range of experimental dishes..." "He might taste good." She offers asking him what his favourite things to cook are to which he replies, "Black...the most expensive items are black" and "eating black food is like consuming death." She offers herself to Richard or 11.000 pounds if he will cook Michael but he tells her to put the money away.

In the final scene Albert arrives with his entourage, Grace, Mitchell, Harris, enters the restaurant and in the background there is an uncanny spectre of a woman holding a net moving in consort with them. Spica confronts Georgina with his usual diatribe, "where have you been bitch... slut..." continuing with "I'll bloody kill yer for what yer did t' me...I'll make yer pay yer slut.... I'll kill you...I'll make yer pay ...your bottom's going to be very sore for weeks." Georgina quietly addresses him with "Happy anniversary Albert...." to which he replies "What yer talk'n abart...it's not me birfday."

In a calm voice Georgina offers that "It's an anniversary I will always be able to celebrate...you vowed that you would kill him and you vowed to eat him.... What's the matter Albert? Have all those table manners gone to waste?" This tragically ironic exchange is interrupted by a funeral procession of the well-roasted Michael on a pyre under a white sheet. Georgina intones the sacramental rites "Mitchell can pour you a drink... Grace will pour for you .... the body of Christ." And then she levels a gun at him... The first of Albert's victims Roy pours Albert a final drink. A rarity in Greenaway's films, the camera circles the body that is laid horizontally between Georgina who is standing and Albert who remains seated. Georgina says "Try the cock Albert. *Bon appetit* ...it's a delicacy and you know where its been...."Albert vomits..."Go on Albert.... eat..! .It's French!" Georgina then shoots him.

About the political economy of this film Greenaway has said: "*The Cook, the Thief, His Wife and Her Lover* is a passionate angry dissertation on the rich vulgarian Philistine anti-intellectual stance of the present cultural situation in Great Britain...There's a lull in the film where Spica says to the lover (Michael) who is reading, "Does this book make money?" "That really sums up this theme. In England now there seems to be only one currency, as indeed one might say about the whole capitalist world."[29] And yet in terms of political economy this is arguably a deeply conservative film, a caricature of how the upper class views the vulgar *nouveau riche* (working class) contamination of the privileges of the natural order of rule in classed society. The film may be less the staging of the bourgeois imaginary than a staging of bourgeois anxiety about the take over by the working class armed with the injustices of their class.[30]

But we should provide the last word to Greenaway in this discourse on art, desire and death in his films that will secure a bridge to the final chapter. In answer to the question "Do you think you will be pursuing your cinema increasingly with Godard in mind after this?" Greenaway responded: "Well he's always been a great hero.... the three for me.... the triumvirate.... there's Eisenstein, who created cinema; Orson Welles, who consolidated it; and there's Godard who throws it away. And now, we haven't got any cinema. Cinema is now dead."[31]

---

[1]Maxims and Interludes # 141 Nietzsche, Friedrich *Beyond Good and Evil: Prelude to a Philosophy of the Future* Translated by R.J Hollingdale with an introduction by Michael Tanner. London, Penguin Books, 1973:101

[2]Greenaway *A Zed and two Noughts* p 15 requoted in Pascoe p.115

[3] Several of the Z&OO sequences were shot at the Rotterdam Zoo

[4] Close but one to 666 the numbers associated with the Devil. 676 is the square of 26 which is also the car plate number NID-26-B/W Oliver's apartment number and the number of letters in the alphabet.

[5]The Bewick Swan Cynus Columbianus is also referred to as the so-called Whistling Swan

[6]The Venus (Aphrodite) de Milo (130 BC) sculpture is thought to be of Venus Vitrix holding a golden apple presented to her by Paris of Troy. The sculpture was originally attributed to the Greek sculptor Praxiteles but is now recognized as the work of Alexandros of Antioch. (Encyclopaedia of World Art New York 1968)

[7]The Larousse *Encyclopaedia of Mythology* trans Aldington, R., Ames, D. London, New York, Hamlyn 1968:203

[8]Ibid. p.105

[9] See Gombrich, E. *Art and Illusion: A Study in the Psychology of Pictorial Representation* New York Bollingen 1969: 5; Wittgenstein, L., *Philosophical Investigations* tr. G. Anscombe Oxford University Press 1953:194 and Mitchell, W.J.T *Picture Theory* Chicago University Press 1994:45-52

[10] *The Shorter Oxford Dictionary*

[11] Interview Take 10 pp 218 requoted in Pascoe p..96

[12] Foucault, M, *The Order of Things: An Archeology of the Human Sciences* New York, Random House 1971:7-8

[13] Ibid. p. 8

[14] "The figure of the visible/ invisible organizes anatomo-pathological perception." Foucault, M. *The Birth of the Clinic: An Archeology of Medical Perception* New York Vintage, 1975:170

[15] Ibid.

[16] Neumann, J and Morgenstern *Theory of Games and Economic Behavior* Princeton University Press 1944

[17] Original author unknown

[18] Derrida, J. *The Truth in Painting* pp. 12-13

[19] Ernest Lehmann wrote the screenplay for North by Northwest.

[20] The Coliseum, the Pantheon, the Baths of Villa Adriana, the Piazza and Dome of St Peters, the Forum, the Piazza Navona, Augustus Mausoleum and the EUR building. Seven of these buildings influence Boullée. Greenaway stated that together these buildings represent 25,000 years of architectural history that puts Kracklite's nine-month predicament into perspective.

[21] -Derrida, J. *The Post-Card: from Socrates to Freud and Beyond* Trans. A. Bass Chicago, University of Chicago Press 1987

[22] Ibid p.135

[23] Walter Benjamin, "Theses on the Philosophy of History" in *Illuminations,* ed with an introduction by Hannah. Arendt, New York, 1969:256

[24] So sorry I am late, Dorian. I went to look after a piece of old brocade in Wardour Street, and had to bargain for hours for it. Nowadays people know the price of everything, and the value of nothing." Wilde, O. *The Picture of Dorian Gray*

[25] Toward the conclusion of the film Neville brings Mrs. Herbert a peace offering of Three Pomegranates in a box.

[26] See Elliot, B.., and Purdy, A. *Peter Greenaway. Architecture and Allegory* London Academy Editions 1997

[27] Steam also figures prominently in Greenaway's early film *Train* and in the Roman bath scene in *The Belly of an Architect.*

[28] There is some slippage in Spica's accent but his "shut yor maaf Mitchell" sets his accent somewhat apart as Cockney. The cockney accent is considered one of the broadest accents in Britain and is heavily stigmatized as the epitome of the working class accent of Londoners and in its somewhat more diluted form also of other areas. The area and its colorful characters and accents have often become the foundation for British comedies and soap operas such as the "East Enders" "The "mouth" vowel is a "touchstone for distinguishing between 'true Cockney' and popular London" and other more standard accents. Cockney usage would include *monophthongization* of the word mouth. Example: mouth = [ma:f] (maaf) rather than [mae:f] mouth. Wells, J. C *Accents of English An Introduction* Cambridge University Press 1982 www.ic.arizona.edu/~lsp/CockneyEnglish (Accessed June 2005)

[29] Joel E. Siegel "Greenaway by Numbers" City Paper (6 April 1990), p.22 requoted in Pascoe, D. p.173

[30] Johnston Ruth, D "The Staging of the Bourgeois Imaginary in *The Cook, The Thief, his Wife and her Lover* Cinema Journal 41, No.2 Winter 2002

[31] Paula Willoquet-Maricondi interview with Greenaway in Willoquet-Maricondi, P., and Alemany-Galway, M.. *Peter Greenaway's Postmodern/ Poststructuralist Cinema* Lanham, Maryland and London The Scarecrow Press p. 320

Chapter 10

The Death of Film
Cinematic Subversion and the Theory of the Avant-Garde[1]

> Among other possibilities the cinema lends itself particularly well to studying the present as an historical problem, to dismantling the processes of reification.   .
> (René Vienet 1959) [2]

> What is untimely will have its own times. That is true of philosophy.   (Martin Heidegger 1935) [3]

The reverse or shadow side of the art/crime conflation is naturally the crime of art itself, an obsession of the necrophiliacal historical avant garde movements of the modernist era, that initiated and engaged in the usurping of the symbolic authority of previous vanguards, an Oedipal ritualistic killing of the father in order to secure the identity and omnipotence of the son. Like other avant-garde artists reiterating the Oedipal narrative trajectory, Peter Greenaway isn't the first filmmaker artist to have pronounced the death of cinema, or Lars von Trier and a host of other contemporary filmmakers and video artists critical of cinematic convention and the so-called 'classical' Hollywood cinema. But these filmmakers arguably owe less of a debt to Jean-Luc Godard, the officially accepted and canonized film avant-gardist of the post WWII era than to Guy Debord and the International Situationists c.1957-1969 whose exemplary cultural interventions and critical strategies, after a long hiatus, have resonated so powerfully throughout the past two decades within vanguard Western culture. In some discussions the International Situationists represent the final death throes of the historical avant-garde before it became a simulacrum of itself, a neo-avant-garde with film as one of the victims. But arguably the IS strategies for superseding the death of cinema have since provided avant-garde film with a *dénouement* and revitalized life within bourgeois society, one that many media artists,[4] including Peter Greenaway, have either consciously or unconsciously absorbed into their practice. This chapter will review the historical roots of IS with a focus upon the concepts of cinematic subversion, *détournement* and the death of cinema, as this interpolates this continuing investigation into cultural in/subordination and the conflation of art/crime. Before outlining the parameters of the discussion of these important concepts, we should briefly review the Situationist problematic as it applies to social relations and the production of culture within capitalism.[5]   From this we will follow with an introductory examination of Situationist film theory,[6] in particular the related critical concepts of intervention, détournement and subversion, as these are represented in the writings of Vaneigem, Vienet, Wolman and especially Guy Debord, whose writings and films have provided much of the critical grounding for this chapter.[7]   We will conclude with a brief overview of the successes and failures of the Situationist critique as this pertains to the theory and practice of 'experimental' or a term I prefer, 'neo-avant-garde' film making (Bürger 1974,1984), and with this, attempt to recuperate, some aspects of the IS's revolutionary program that remain tenable today.[8]

The Spectacle

The Situationist problematic is based on a description/diagnosis of 'late' capitalism that Guy Debord dubbed the "society of the spectacle." From the early 1950's, the *spectacle* was used metaphorically to designate "a one way transmission of experience; a form of 'communication' to which one side, the audience (consumers) can never reply; a culture based on the reduction of almost everyone to a state of abject non creativity: of receptivity, passivity and isolation."[9] As expressed In Guy Debord's famous theses:

"The entire life of societies in which modern conditions of production reign appears as an immense accumulation of spectacles. Everything that was expressed directly has been distanced in a representation" (Thesis 1) "Spectacle in general, as the concrete immersion of life is the autonomous movement of the non-living. Spectacle is not a collection of images, but a social relation between people mediated through images." (Thesis 4). [10]

With Debord's theses, the IS applied the term *spectacle* with its various connotations (simulacrum, sight, play, theatrical presence), to all aspects of socio-cultural relations under monopoly capitalism. At its most incisive the term represented the hegemonic tendencies sustained/subsumed under, and reproduced by capitalist ideologies.[11] As many commentators have acknowledged the spectacle is even more integrated now - a "spectacular phantasmagoria" - than it was in 1967 that as Agamben notes, "makes the implacable lucidity of [Debord's] his diagnosis all the more remarkable."[12] As Debord theorized it, the society of the spectacle described a system of power relations, one in which alienation is naturally 'inscribed' (Derrida), 'institutionalized' (Bürger), (folded (Deleuze), "interwoven" (Agamben), and reproduced (for un-reconstituted Marxists). For the IS, the antidote, or, in terms less psycho/physiological, and more contemporary -- the counter - hegemonic agents -- and the loci of resistance, became the adventitious 'construction of situations', which from the beginning involved the notion of intervention.[13]

> The construction of situations can only begin to be effective as the concept of the spectacle begins to disintegrate.[14]

From the very first issue of the IS journal, the character of 'the situation' was described in terms that revealed the fundamental importance of intervention as a post - theoretical, post --experimental, practical and therefore grounded, aspect of their critique. During the next ten years the political efficacy and indeed, urgency, of this aspect of their project was debated constantly by members of the IS. In late 1961 and early 1962 the divisions of opinion actually lead to several rifts within and exclusions from the group. The theoretical problems attending this negotiation of practicality were finally subsumed under various and at times conflicting ideologies of cultural practice which relegated direct political action and the formation of praxis, to the backburner; that is until the weeks leading up to the events of May/June 1968 which once again, foregrounded several of the original foundational (political) premises of the IS association.

It is not too grand a claim to suggest that no aspect of cultural production: art, theatre, literature, poetry, architecture, advertising, urban planning, fashion, television and film, was left untouched by the Situationists. This can be demonstrated adequately enough through a quick examination of the semi-official chronology and bibliographical index compiled by Jean-Jacques Raspaud and Jean-Pierre Voyer that summarizes in brief the contents of the IS journal as well as their echoes in the popular and specialty press.[15] A closer examination of the primary and secondary texts, especially those contained in the IS Journal the group's central organ, reveal that like the Dadaists and Surrealists before them, theatre (performance) literature, visual art and criticism played vital roles in their political theorizing, particularly the so called 'construction of situations'. Cinema, with respect to its special role in 'consciousness forming' (interpellation in Althusser's sense), ideological reproduction, and the formation and reproduction of the spectacle itself, was also accorded special attention. Many of the IS's key concepts and critical techniques were elaborated, or better, "played out", to use a key IS phrase, in relation to film. From the pre-International Situationist, IL (International Lettrist) texts by Chtcheglov (1953), Debord (1955), Debord and Wolman (1956) and Asger Jorn (1957) and later within the IS proper, those essays and broadsides produced by Debord, Vienet and Vaneigem, cinema, if not mentioned directly, is implicitly recognized (often as a negative agent of reification) in the attempts to theorize a way out _ to repudiate (negate, in IS terms) _ the passive reproduction of alienation in daily life.

In the important early text "Methods of Detournement" (1956) co-authored by Guy Debord and Gil J Wolman, there are several references to film as a site for critical intervention.[16] This essay contains two key passages that deserve to be mentioned in this context. In their introduction the authors suggest that with respect to political efficacy, " only extremist innovation is historically justified."[17] The foundational arguments of this statement do not initially strike one with their radicalism; they are similar to other pronouncements made by the historical avant-gardes of the first decades of the twentieth century and reiterated in various forms ever since. However a closer reading of the entire text soon changes this observation and establishes its avant-gardist credentials, and moreover, distinguishes this text from the pronouncements of the earlier historical avant-gardes. "since the (avant-gardist) negation of the bourgeois conception of art and artistic genius has become pretty much old hat, [Duchamp's] drawing of a moustache on the Mona Lisa is no more interesting than the original version of that painting. We must now push this process to the negation of the negation. Bertolt Brecht, revealing in a recent interview in the magazine *France Observateur* that he made some cuts in the classics of the theatre in order to make the performances *more educative* is closer than Duchamp to the revolutionary orientation we are calling for"[18] (emphasis added).

Detournement and Deconstruction

In their essay Debord and Wolman proceeded to discuss the principal categories of *detournement*:[19] minor, deceptive and ultra detournements, the characteristics of which were later to inform IS theoretical discussions attending the construction of situations. These primary types of détournement are related conceptually to re-contextualizing and re-constructing methods as well as the more conventional collage and montage techniques of Cubism, Futurism, Dada, Productive, and Surrealism with however, a few important differences that from our contemporary perspective align them more specifically to the critical methods of *deconstruction* as these were formulated by Jacques Derrida, Paul de Man and their followers: the challenging of binaries with the recognition of a double movement, difference to différance (not "a/ not a", "a/b") and the dependence of the major on the minor term, to avoid (suspend) closure; to practice inclusion as opposed to exclusion, hybridity, inter-textuality, appropriation, scission/ excision, weaving, folding, erasure (*sous rature*) and parenthetical [suspension].[20] Derrida stated in a 1971 interview that the general strategy of deconstruction is designed "to avoid both simply *neutralizing* the binary oppositions of metaphysics and simply *residing* within the closed field of these oppositions, thereby confirming it"[21]

In the simple terms developed by the IS, collage, dialectical and additive montage techniques draw their meaning from the new contexts and juxtapositions of the auto-produced or appropriated 'ready-made' or 'assisted' cultural material -- semiotically -- the intended result becoming the establishment of new, often highly charged signifier/signified relationships. Debord and Wolman's strategies of *detournement* (diversion) differ significantly from these, now classic techniques of the historical avant-gardes, placing more emphasis upon the context in which the detourned image may be read.

For example, with minor *detournement*, which depending upon the circumstances, may be described as a somewhat conventional strategic mode of 'turning' (subversion), an element (image or text) that has little importance in itself, is placed in a new context from which it draws its meaning; to use Debord's examples here, "a press clipping, a neutral phrase, a commonplace photograph." For those familiar with the subversive strategies of the historical avant-gardes the potentially subversive and negative character of the strategy of detournement is relatively clear in this description. For, depending upon the circumstances - if we consider the Brecht example - the context, this could become a radical strategy for the critical apprehension, deformation (erasure and/or suspension) and critical reformation/reformulation of meaning -- *deconstruction* -- to be accomplished. The radical altering of the context, and moreover, the investiture of primary meanings in the new context is different in character to most of the conventional techniques of the post-cubist collage or montage artist. The intention in the conventional collage or montage work is the reconstitution of the base elements or fragments in some way as to creatively produce a whole; the result -- here I paraphrase Peter Bürger's *Theory of the Avant-Garde* (1984) -- is an "organic work" which in all senses of the term represents a "false sublation" of a quintessential avant-garde intention the sublation (erasure) of the separation between art and life, and the formation of praxis. In Bürger's terms the organic work serves only to reproduce the bourgeois category of the autonomous work (of art), thereby sustaining the institutionalism of artistic practice. One of the key phrases in this text is "the neo-avant-garde institutionalizes the avant-garde as art and thus negates genuinely avant gardist intentions."[22] In the conventional collage or montage work the substrate of the given material may be detourned, subverted, reconstituted yet there is usually some attempt by the author to retain some identity for the original elements and meaning of the work, including its context. Alternatively the new `aesthetic' or institutional (art) context is reinforced. The obvious historical examples here are Duchamp's ready-mades, although these retain an essential ambiguity within Bürger's theory of the avant-garde, as they did for the Situationists. Asger Jorn's detourned paintings of 1957-9 may be closer to the models of minor *detournement* discussed by Debord and Wolman. Jorn's interventionist mediation consisted of cheaply purchasing paintings by unknown artists at second hand stores and flea markets then repainting and later reinvesting them with his signature into art world contexts. Debord and Jorn's book *Memoires*, composed entirely from prefabricated (appropriated) elements that may be read in any direction, is also a useful example of the strategy of minor detournement which the

I.S. described in somewhat recondite yet clearly from today's perspective, deconstructive terms, as "negation and prelude."[23]

Deceptive detournement which Debord and Wolman also called "premonitory proposition detournement" is more politically efficacious than minor detournement. Here a significant element from the original work is detourned and because of the relative importance of the original i.e. again to use their examples: "A slogan of Saint Juste" or "a sequence from Eisenstein" the act of detourning or deconstruction grows in significance. A comparison is invited here between Burger's examples of the politically efficacious work of John Heartfield, specifically his AIZ montages. However, with respect to the overt agitational and propagandistic function of Heartfield's montages there are some important differences to be considered. For the I.S. detournement "as rational reply" or "reversal" - techniques of agitprop - was considered to be less effective, ostensibly (this was contradictorily argued within IS texts), because it precipitated extreme rejective and prohibitive responses from those at whom it was aimed, thus negating its didactic function and thereby allowing the power differential to be maintained or worse, reinforced. This is clearly not in the interests of the deconstructive methodology that as Derrida has insisted must be in the final analysis "affirmative."[24]

Wolman and Debord elaborated upon the so-called "laws"_ what can be called more usefully, the conditions of detournement, that sustain in a relatively comprehensive (and less pseudo_ scientific) fashion, the various meanings subsumed by their definitions: *Detournement*: short for: detournement of preexisting aesthetic elements; the integration of present or past artistic production into a superior construction of a milieu. In this sense there can be no Situationist painting or music, but only a Situationist *use* of these means. In a more primitive sense, detournement within the old cultural spheres is a method of propaganda, a method which testifies to the wearing out and loss of importance of these spheres.[25] The 'rules' of detournement were reduced to a group of quasi-formulae. The first rule articulated by Debord and Wolman insisted that: Law #1 "It is the most distant detourned element that contributes most sharply to the overall   impression, and not the elements that directly determine the nature of this impression."
 Law #2 "The distortions introduced in the detourned elements must be as simplified as possible, since the main force of a detournement is

directly related to the conscious or vague recollection of the original contexts of the element."
Law 3 "Detournement is less effective the more it approaches a rational reply. (i.e. forms of agitational propaganda)."
Law #4 "Detournement by simple reversal is always the most direct and the least effective. (Agitprop)

The authors suggested that their first 'law' was "universal and essential" while the other three were applicable solely to deceptive detournements.[26] The last two laws introduce the related problems of parody and propaganda that were discussed at length, if at times incoherently, in subsequent IS essays and theses. From the perspective of contemporary strategies of deconstruction the first two are interesting because they focus on memory and sets of relational meanings _ they invoke a *hermeneutic* _ one in which meanings politically mediated by context and time remain negotiable.

It is possible that the various forms of detournement may be also conceptually allied to Walter Benjamin's concept of allegory, closer perhaps than is montage, the process/technique and forms of which Peter Bürger uses in his arguments for sustaining the legitimate and authentic work of the avant-garde; critical procedures that he argued resolve the contradictory features of normative avant-gardist and therefore bourgeois intentions. The emphasis on meaning 'substitution' or 'sublimation' as a prelude to critical consciousness in Debord and Wolman's conception of premonitory detournement is also a form of redemption that is similar to the historical distantiation and quest for transcendence elaborated in Benjamin's theory of allegory. The Situationist notion of distantiation _ of decomposition (the destruction of conventional cultural forms) parallels the `surrealist inspired' tropes that Benjamin employed in his discussions of allegory.[27] Debord and Wolman's conception of cultural exhaustion and the oppositional use of the strategies of detournement to resist and overcome this symptom of monopoly capitalism finds its homiletic in Benjamin's "...profound fascination of the sick man with the isolated and insignificant [is] succeeded by that disappointed abandonment of the exhausted emblem." [28] For in both strategies, the symptoms, or better, syndrome of alienation, is seen as responsible and responsive - the *pharmakon* - "poison and drug" for both the sickness and the cure.[29] For Benjamin, Debord and Wolman critical consciousness only comes to those who have realized their own alienation as a part of the political (collective) present. For Benjamin redemptive criticism and for the IS the construction and deconstruction of situations represent a possible alternative to the passivity and isolation _ the political death of those who acknowledge the central paradoxes inherent in our time. In Wolman and Debord's terms, it becomes (therefore) necessary to conceive of a parodic serious stage where the accumulation of detourned elements, far from aiming at arousing indignation or laughter by alluding to some original work, will express our indifference toward a meaningless and forgotten original, and concern itself with rendering a certain sublimity.[30]

In the final sections of their important essay, Debord and Wolman outlined détournement strategies with respect to film, which in view of its importance deserve to be quoted in full. "It is obviously in the realm of cinema that détournement can attain its greatest (political) efficacy, and undoubtedly, for those concerned with this aspect, its greatest beauty." He follows with:

> The powers of film are so extensive, and the absence of coordination of those powers is so glaring, that almost any film that is above the miserable average can provide innumerable polemics among spectators or professional critics. Only the conformism of those people prevents them from discovering features just as appealing and faults just as glaring in the worst films. To cut through this absurd confusion of values, we can observe that Griffiths' *Birth of a Nation* is one of the most important films in the history of cinema because of its wealth of new contributions. On the other hand it is a racist film and therefore does not merit being shown in its present form. But its total prohibition could be seen as regrettable from the point of view of the secondary, but potentially worthier, domain of cinema.[31]

With this minor concession to the institution of cinema that was subsequently reiterated in other theses by Vienet and Debord the authors continued with a remarkably subversive strategy worthy of deconstruction strategies today: "It would be better to détourn it (*Birth of a Nation*) as a whole, without necessarily altering the montage, by adding a sound track that made a powerful denunciation of the horrors of imperialist war and of the activities of the Ku Klux Klan, which are continuing in the United States even now"(1956). The authors insisted, with some irony, that this critical work on Griffith's film would be a moderate détournement, "in the final analysis...the moral equivalent of the restoration of old paintings in museums." Those with an investment in the maintenance of a pantheon of masters would view their strategies differently.

The Cinema of Guy Debord

How is this radically subversive and proto-deconstructive activity sustained in Debord's other writings and particularly in his own films? This is an interesting question, one that we should now examine briefly and discuss with respect to the propositions of so-called 'experimental', 'new wave' (*nouvelle vague*) _ or neo-avant-garde cinema and the formation of an adequate postmodern critical strategy worthy of operative cultural producers for the new millennium.[32] Debord produced a total of six films, three near feature length (80'_ 90') and three shorter films of some 20 minutes duration. They are all 35mm, on b&w film stock; the full scripts and 'shot descriptions' (or appropriated image synopses), are available in his *Oeuvres Cinématographiques Complète 1952_1978*.[33] It can be argued that it is in Debord's films that we obtain the clearest explication and summation of his deconstructive strategies of cinematic détournement and subversion. It is significant in understanding the degree of importance he placed in cinema as a means of communication and political action, that Debord attempted to film "in its entirety" his book *The Society of the Spectacle*" (*La Société du Spectacle* 1973) and when this film met with critical resistance in 1975 he filmed a critical response to his detractors under the title *Refutation de toutes jugements, tant élogiuex qu'hostiles, qui ont éte jusqu'ici porte sur le film La Société du Spectacle.*

There are several important modal characteristics of Debord's films that establish their absolute political character and from the perspective of today, their inviolable condition as exemplary avant-garde projects. In each of the film's text/language is primary; image is secondary and frequently absent. The result of this revision (minor detournement) of conventional cinematic language is that the film resists becoming an ensemble of phantasmagoric representations and subsequently for Debord, a commodity. His withdrawal of the films from circulation in 1985 (reversed after his death by suicide on November 30th 1994), took this act of decommoditization to its ultimate and natural consummation as *un action exemplaire*. [34] It is fortunate, ironically that this withdrawal has not disturbed or violated the 'traffic' in his ideas, it actually enhanced their transmission and acceptance. Debord's films neither activate the spectator/viewer's scopic drive, nor do they initiate or facilitate the formation of the spectacular or to use, a useful term borrowed from contemporary film discourse _ "the phantasmagoric experience." However with its primary emphasis on text, the visual and especially the audio phonic transmission of language, the Debordian Situationist film may invoke what Lacan and Metz termed called *la pulsion invocante*, (the auditory drive) the desire to listen. In a fundamental sense, the film's presence as political agent is assisted by its absence of conventional cinematic cues for looking or, more precisely (here I paraphrase the early work of Roland Barthes, Christian Metz, Julia Kristeva and that of the *Screen* critics, Wollen, Mulvey et. al.), the viewers are restricted from obtaining pleasure and moreover, of consummating this (*jouissance*) through the act of looking. The absence of such cues and the subsequent "subordination of desire" stimulate an emphasis on others, such as the meeting of a certain group of people at a prescribed place and time for the purpose of viewing and conversation. For Debord the occasion for (passive) viewing itself can be detourned into a situation or [performance] for (active) discussion. This becomes a means toward the dialogical fulfillment of the goal _ critical education, or in its inverted, deconstructed and more politically efficacious form, education for criticism. In this post-Brechtian act of institutional subversion we should recognize another famous inversion; the graffiti slogan strategically applied to the walls of Paris in May/June 1968: "Culture is the inversion of life." For Debord the audience becomes subject. An elemental characteristic of his film theory is the didactic form and content of the (often appropriated and detourned) dialogue or *débat*, which occurs (at least is programmed to occur), between either the voices on the audio track or the author and the audience. For *In Girum Imus Nocte et consumimur igni. (We Turn in the Night Consumed by Fire* 1978), his final film, Debord placed an image of a cinema audience directly facing the live theatre audience. With a deliberate economy of means, his accompanying text incisively identifies the central problem of spectacle consumption and the alienation of both author and audience. He allows no concessions to his public. Je ne ferai, dans ce film, aucune concession au public. plusiers excellents raisons justifient, a mes yeux, une telle conduite; et je vais les dire. [35] The announcement of the film screening becomes the reason for the debate, irrespective of what is to be consumed. The objective is "authentic dialogue." With respect to Burger's theory of the avant-garde, this ultra detournement (Debord and Wolman's final category) would represent a legitimate form of sublation; a subordination of the work to the praxiological conditions of everyday life _ which would/should permit, or at the very least, actively encourage the practical exploration of Le Febvre's neo-Marxian critique of alienation under the capitalism division of labour. In the typical I.S. film project this is reinforced parodically with the narrative /dialogue, often a *dialogue des sourds* (a conversation between deaf people neither side hearing what the other has to say) as, for instance, in Debord's first film *Hurlements en Faveur de Sade* (*Screams on Behalf of de Sade* 1952).[36]

While this film (dedicated to his collaborator Gil Wolman whose own film *L'anti-concept* had appeared the year before) is technically within the Lettrist group of films, it advances many ideas that became staples of his subsequent I.S. texts and films. *Hurlements* has a powerful introduction that metaphorically establishes the proto-deconstructive fields of negation. Voix 1: "Quel printemps! Aide_memoire pour une histoire du cinema:1902 _*Voyage dans La Lune.* 1920 _*Le Cabinet du Docteur Caligari* 1924 _ *Entracte.* 1926 _*Le Cuirasse Potemkine.* 1928 *Un Chien Andalou.* Naissance de Guy_Ernest Debord. 1951 _ *Trait de bave et d'*éternite.* 1952 _ L'anti_concept. _ Hurlements en faveur de Sade.*" Voix 5: "Au moment ou la projetion allait commencer, Guy-Ernest Debord devait monter sur la scene pour prononcer quelques mot's d'introduction. Il aurait dit simplement: Il n'ya a pas de film. Le cinéma est mort. Il ne peut plus y avoir de film. Passons, si vous voulez, au débat."[37]

"Le cinéma est mort" ("Film is dead") There are no images in this film. Much of the sporadic and at times disconnected dialogue (much of it detourned) is punctuated with black leader. In fact the balance of black/silence/ to monotonal dialogue throughout the ninety minute running time is almost split in half with approximately fifty-seven minutes of darkness. The projection screen is white during sections of dialogue and black during silence. The film concludes with a 'spectacular' twenty-four minutes of darkness and silence _ the silences; the pauses of the historical avant-garde of Mallarme, Russolo, Duchamp, Becket and Cage, Greenaway, almost pale in comparison.[38]

Darkness/silence have several meanings for Debord _ the obvious symbolic and iconoclastic references to the death of cinema; and silence, that requires little elaboration today, represents the absence of stimulus from the film, which heightens the perception of the activities of the audience who become more cognizant of their own presence as a group of potential (enraged) actors. This cliche of vanguard modernism (*épater le bourgeois*) has a long and venerable history that stretches from Alfred Jarry's *Ubu Roi* to 1968 and in its institutionalized stereotypes through to the present.

Hurlements shares some of the characteristics of many of the historical prototypes of avant-garde film: including the few Futurist films, those of Dada and Surrealism and subsequently the experimental Lettrist films of Isou, Lemaitre and Wolman of the early 1950's . Beyond the history of avant-garde cinema, the literary tradition invoked and at times consciously usurped by Debord, is represented in the late nineteenth century symbolist and early twentieth century literary avant-gardes from Lautréamont, to Mallarme, Whitman and subsequently Andre Breton, the 'Pope of Surrealism'.

Debord's insertion of his own production, even his birth, into a canon of master works, may indicate a degree of role aggrandizement. It is difficult to establish whether this is pure irony or a reproduction of a typical strategy of the avant-garde, a nervous twitch representing a youthful appropriation of history, however fortuitous (or gratuitous) or naive, in order to ensure his place (with the right pedigree), in history. In this case the ego investment may be the result either of irony or a subconscious adherence to a surrealist habit. It is possible to recognize the formal innovations of Debord's first two films, in the unconventional cinematic strategies of post-Lettrist international neo-avant-garde cinema i.e. the structuralist film, aping the strategies of the *nouveau roman* _ the films of the new wave and underground film makers from the 1960's and 1970's who were fond of disclosing the cinematic apparatus, real-time-basing, chronometry (to be distinguished from chronotypy); the structuralist film maker's use of non illusionistic materialist / and phenomenologically (à la Merleau -Ponty) precise clear, white and black leader. We may recognize the humanizing and domesticating of the equipment via manual manipulations the `family' focus or some such metaphorical foils to Hollywood's corporate and hegemonic intentions. Since 1955 these formal, narrational and relational strategies signal *déju vu* -exhaustion; visual (cinematic) clichés themselves, a defeat to their intended political character through a reproduction of their decompositive and "iterative scheme." [39]

However we should not be too quick in our dismissal least we immerse the IS itself too deeply in our critique of the neo-avant-garde. It is important to acknowledge that the IS recognized the potentially redundant features of their own cinematic interventions and conventions. They were also quick to disparage those bourgeois filmmakers, Godard among them, who attempted to capitalize on their theoretical work, not because they necessarily wished to be acknowledged as originators, but because the institutional successes of the neo-avant-garde spelled the death of the debate and the entrenchment of the bourgeois status quo. For instance in an article called "Cinema and Revolution"(issue #12 of the I.S. journal), the Situationists tarred and feathered J.P. Picaper, the reviewer of the 1969 Berlin Film Festival for praising Godard for purportedly pushing "his praiseworthy self-critique to the point of projecting sequences shot in the dark or even of leaving the spectator for an almost unbearable length of time before a blank screen." The affronted Situationists were unrelenting in their admonishment both of Picaper and Godard the newly installed hero of the avant-garde. Without seeking more precisely what constitutes "an almost unbearable length of time" for this critic, we can see that Godard's work, following the latest fashions as always, is culminating in a destructive style just as belatedly plagiarized and pointless as all the rest, this negation having been expressed long before Godard had ever begun the long series of pretentious pseudo-innovations that aroused such enthusiasm among students in the previous period. [40]

After trouncing Godard for his pretensions which we can now recognize as preludes to the institutionalization of avant-garde film (the reviewer refers the reader to previous IS issue 10 and another critique of Godard: "The Role of Godard," [41] reflecting on the fact that the Cinema "as a means of revolutionary communication is not intrinsically mendacious just because Godard or Jacoppeti has touched it, any more than all political analysis is doomed to duplicity just because Stalinists have written (it)." [42] This is one of the first instances in the IS of their recognition of their own capitulation to what Raoul Vaneigem suggested in 1967 was a simple "renewing of the forms of spectacle participation and the variety of stereotypes." [43]

Godard and rhetoric aside, the Situationists did have an important role for cinema in their critique of political economy in spectacular society. In a sense they were attempting to do what Eisenstein set out to accomplish but failed to fulfill in his plan to film Marx's *Capital*.[44] In fact they wanted to go beyond *Capital*.[45] But before they could attempt this they had to reconstruct not only the experience of viewing but also the discourse of cinema itself. They wished to repudiate the bourgeois aestheticist approach to filmmaking and to return it to the praxis of life. Hence the radical deconstructive, excisionist and image taxing strategies of intervention, détournement and subversion and the Situationists' concern with context over concept, and concept over form.

Debord describes the critical process in his films, at times incisively, at times in a labored, somewhat egocentric and pretentious fashion. For instance: after a Sartrean inspired critique of the limitations of freedom and individual self emancipation in capitalist society, in his second film, a détourned documentary titled *On the passage of a few Persons Through a rather Brief Period of Time*, one of his protagonists or antagonists _ we cannot call them characters in the conventional sense _ suggests somewhat laconically...."of course we could make a film of it. But even if such a film succeeds in being fundamentally incoherent and unsatisfying as the reality it deals with, it will never be more than a recreation _ poor and false like this botched travelling shot." This speech is accompanied visually be a travelling shot past a café that is cut by a member of the public crossing the camera's field of view thus destroying its satisfactory (again in conventional cinematic terms) resolution. The film's third voice continues the critique of the cinema by attacking the authority of the auteur and the autonomy of the institution cinema itself.

> "There are people who flatter themselves that they are
> authors of films, as others are authors of novels. They
> are even more backward than the novelists because they
> are ignorant of the decomposition and exhaustion of
> individual expression in our times, ignorant of the end
> of the arts of passivity. They are praised for their
> sincerity since they dramatize, with more personal
> depth, the conventions of which their life consists.
> There is talk of the liberation of the cinema. But what
> does it matter to us if one more art is liberated through
> which Pierre or Jacques or Francois can joyously

> express their slave sentiments. The only interesting
> venture is the liberation for us of everyday life, not only
> in the perspectives of history but for us and right away.
> This entails the withering away of alienated forms of
> communication. *The cinema too has to be destroyed.*"[46]
> (Emphasis added.)

And yet Debord's primary intention, initially at least, was not simply to destroy the cinema; he wished to intervene in that institution's passive reproduction of its own conventions; its capitulation to the commodity and hence spectacle form. In committing the institution cinema to deconstruction and not simply destruction, he was allowing for its necessary redemption. Ultimately his task was reconstructive and affirmative. Negation became a means toward developing a critical process that was to be both dynamic and ongoing. The primary purpose of his interruptions and critical interventions was the reconstitution of the cinema's *raison d'être* and the roles; to use a key IS phrase, of its players.

We may recognize that Debord's general critique of the cinema carried with it an immediate contradiction for his own film making; his own position as artist/author. The legacy of surrealist thinking in his work, perhaps reveals less the debate between culture and politics, the engaged author and his audience, than the prevarication between the Janus- like author/critic. It is tempting to suggest that Debord, unable to integrate, rationalize or deconstruct the two roles to his own satisfaction, was forced into the position of forsaking one engaged project for the other, of privileging the critical project at the expense of the artist/author's. In his third film *Critique of Separation* (*Critique de la Séparation* (1960_61), the dialogue suggests that it is absolutely necessary to continue the debate even if he, the filmmaker has to become a casualty in the struggle for its continuance.

"This is a film that interrupts itself and does not come to an end. All conclusions remain to be drawn, everything has to be recalculated.
The problem continues to be posed; its expression is becoming more complicated. We have to resort to other measures.
I have scarcely begun to make you understand that *I don't intend to play the game*. (emphasis added)"

With this early indication of withdrawal that became almost totally justified by the events of 1968, Debord's theoretical questions were translated into further practical explorations of methods and techniques by others within the IS Rene Vienet's text "The Situationists and the New Forms of action Against Politics and Art" (IS #11 1967) in particular, constituted a late cultural manifesto for the IS.[47] "Up to now", Vienet wrote, "our subversion has mainly drawn on the forms and categories inherited from past revolutionary struggles, mainly those of the last century." He proposed that the IS "link up the theoretical critique of modern society with the critique of it in acts. By detourning the very propositions of the spectacle, we can explain on the spot the implications of present and future revolts."[48]Vienet concluded his broadside with a list with which we are now are totally familiar, albeit since 1967, through forms of late modernist and postmodern cultural production. To paraphrase:

1) Experimentation in the détournement of romantic photo comics (and pornographic photos). The altering of speech balloons etc.
2) The promotion of guerilla tactics in the mass media.
3) The development of Situationist comics.
4) The production of Situationist films

And in this last section of his essay, Vienet reiterated some of the strategies of détournement theorized earlier by Jorn, Debord and Wolman, adding a few more directives, including the rather idealistic requirement that each Situationist be "as capable of making a film as of writing an article." The record in fact reveals that out of the seventy I.S. members only a few of them made films and in the domain of writing less than half contributed to the IS journal, the bulk of the contributions issuing from the typewriters of Constant, Debord, Jorn, Vaneigem and Vienet. However, this did not hinder the development of some complex, relatively, coherent, persuasive and politically astute strategies for the criticism of culture and society.

Vienet's pronouncements on the strategies and role of Situationist film are remarkably contemporary. His injunction to his constituencies to appropriate modern examples of the film arts including advertisements, for détournement, is well before its time and still not fully understood as a political stratagem. Contemporary experimental artists and filmmakers are still scurrying around film archives appropriating the movies that will feed their nostalgia fetish and give them no copyright problems, this or the 'no wave' option— Baudrillard's inspired simulation. Vienet and Debord and the I.S. membership generally, understood above all, the need to be critically cognizant of one's own place, and one's own time; to quote their minor detournement of Marx's Eighteenth Brumaire "to be capable of *both* "interpreting and changing the world." Vienet continued his text with a discussion of the aims of Situationist cinema that deserves to be quoted in full.

"The cinema which is the newest and undoubtedly the most utilizable means of expression of our time has marked time for nearly three quarters of a century. To sum it up, we can say that it effectively became the 'seventh art' so dear to film buffs, film clubs and parents associations. For our purposes this age is over. (Ince, Stroheim, the one and only *L'âge d'or*, *Citizen Kane* and *My Arkadin*, the lettrist films), even if there remain a few traditional masterpieces to be unearthed in the film archives or on the shelves of foreign distributors. We should appropriate the first stammerings of this new language and above all its most consummate and modern examples, those which have escaped artistic ideology even more than American `B' movies: news reels, previews, and above all filmed advertisements. "Although it has obviously been in the service of the commodity and the spectacle, filmed advertising, in its extreme freedom of technical means has laid the foundations for what Eisenstein had an inkling of when he talked of filming *The Critique of Political Economy* or *The German Ideology*."

He concluded with the statement that opened this chapter: "Among other possibilities, the cinema lends itself particularly well to studying the present as a historical problem, to *dismantling the processes of reification*". (Emphasis added) And continued with an unfortunate metaphysical muddling of the concepts with which he began, confusing the aims of a 'revolutionary' dialectic. "To be sure, historical reality can be apprehended, known and filmed only in the course of a complicated process of mediations enabling consciousness to recognize one moment in another, its goal and its action in destiny, its destiny in its goal and action, and its own essence in that necessity."[49] What were the failures of the IS? This is properly the subject of another chapter or a book. However, we can recognize these in their critical discourse, their work and some of their actions: Debord's `failure' to reconcile the project of the social and cultural critic with the desires (will to power) of the author, (perhaps); the metaphysical Hegelian language into which Vienet departs, after a surprising Lukacsian (via Vaneigem and Debord) inspired statement about reification. This intellectual prevarication and contrariness marked so many of the IS texts— where there is Marx and Lukacs, so will follow Freud, Breton or Sartre, Hegel or Mao— and occasionally, the Marx brothers; too often, now it seems, a surrealist capitulation to the tyranny of the subject or individual ego. This last is so evident in their theory of *derive* that is evidence of pure bohemianism or *flaneury* (vintage 1830 or, 1890) and their practice of exclusion or group scission; the problems they had sustaining intellectual, political and cultural purity, or was it art political 'correctness'? The failures of the IS have been noted and discussed by others (Wilner, 1970, Gray, 1974, Bandini, 1977). They were also subjects of debate within the IS itself (Debord and Sanguinetti "La veritable scission dans L'internationale Paris 1972"). I will reiterate a few of these briefly as follows, with the knowledge that in some contexts they are still hotly contested:

1) The realization that the members of the I.S. were forced, like their historical forebears, into the position of adopting or theorizing post revolutionary utopias, of dreaming, imagining a better life i.e. after the death of cinema _ then what? After the surrealist inspired process of self-realization, of individuation is complete (Breton's "revolution of the mind"), then what? After Henri Lefebvre's critique of everyday life then what? The I.S. notion of succession, variously employed, did not fully guarantee social and cultural change, or importantly, satisfaction from this process.

2) The political events of May 1968 lead them into the adoption of the more extreme and heroic direct action, allowing the nascent anarchic positions of their critical ideologies to relegate theory to a minor position in their debates. During 1968 the IS political program was given a strong test prematurely, before it was beyond its theoretical stage what we could call loosely its laboratory period. The comparison may be difficult to sustain but perhaps we witnessed similar problems with the student democracy movement in Beijing.[50]

3) Their methods of succession/ exclusion, a result of an over zealous (Leninist derived) practice of democracy or cell purity, lead to the exclusion, the forced resignation or 'citing' of 'successful' and/or 'deviant' IS members, which resulted in the alienation of many members and a subsequent watering down of their original programs, thereby restricting the crucial terms and conditions of the debate. And this finally

resulted in the disruption and premature (in this writer's view) termination of the movement. If they had been successful in their project(s) the dissolution (withering) of the Internationale would have occurred naturally. Unfortunately this was not to be the case.
4) The realization also that they may have become too 'successful.' As Christopher Gray, one of the English members excluded (December 1967) by the SI later wrote, with some irony.

The IS..."finally received the cultural accolade it had always dreaded; it entered the heaven of the spectacle" by the scruff of the neck, and that was that."[51] And yet the Situationist project, their criticisms of monopoly capitalism and society of the spectacle (and state communism) are still current. A close reading of their texts shows them to be cognizant of the issues that still confront the culture producers of today. The I.S. text's are not too far removed from those of Burger, Jameson and others of the late 1970's and 1980's which suggest that the absorption/co-optation dynamic of consumer capitalism quickly renders most forms of autonomous avant-garde activity impotent. The failure of the Situationists to supersede the limitations of their own critique or at least their own organization, however, should not deter us from the recuperation/redemption of some aspects of their revolutionary program that are still tenable today.

By way of a conclusion: (preliminary notes toward recuperation). It is important to reflect on the historical relationships between the avant-garde projects of the I.S. and those of the other historical avant-gardes throughout the first decades of the C20th, especially as so many of their formal innovations have been absorbed (often without acknowledgement or due deference) into the strategic formations of the neo-avant-gardes which have become, via a process of institutionalization, the daily staple of academic courses, to give but one instance, in the theory and practice of so-called experimental film. Today academics are more likely to be discussing Godard's techniques than those of Isou, Lemaitre, and Debord's from which, it can be argued they derive. Similarly students of the avant-garde are more likely to read Baudrillard for a political economy of the sign (the collapsing of political economy into the sign), than they are to examine the roots of his theoretical critique in Freud, Marx, Lefebvre and Debord. There is a certain expediency _ a political unconsciousness _ in this denial of intellectual and social/political history. Many of the same issues are being hotly debated: the death of the avant-garde, the social and political efficacy of art, the cinema, the roles of the artist/author, the audience/spectator; abstraction versus materialism, experimentalism versus conventionalism; Hollywood's commercialism; the mass media, arts and the artist's autonomy etc. etc? even if today these questions have been invigorated and reformulated with feminism, phenomenology, scrubbed with semiology and psychoanalysis and polished with alternative poststructuralist theories of the subject. But perhaps the ascendancy of the subject has merely delayed the praxiological necessity of the resolution of these political questions, which in truth, may have already been answered.

It is perhaps appropriate to return to Debord for our contemporary endnote. In the final moments of his détourned documentary *On the passage of a few persons through a rather brief period of time* (1959), Voice 2 announces: "To really describe this era it would no doubt be necessary to show many other things. But what would be the point? Better to grasp the totality of what has been done and what remains to be done than to add more ruins to the old world of spectacle and of memories." [52]

---

[1]A shorter version of this chapter was first presented at the International Experimental Film Congress, Toronto, May 1989. I am indebted to two EGS Seminar/workshops in August 2003, the first lead by Dr. Siegfried Zielinski and the second by Dr. Hubertus von Amelunxen and Louis Balz for the opportunity to review the importance of Guy Debord and the International Situationists for postmodern theory and practice in film and media studies. I have also benefited from reading the work of Giorgio Agamben particularly: Agamben, Giorgio, Trans. Vincenzo Binetti and Cesare Casarino *Means Without End: Notes on Politics.* Minneapolis University of Minnesota Press. Theory Out of Bounds, V. 20. , 2000; and Agamben, G. *The Coming Community.* Minneapolis, Theory Out of Bounds, Vol. 1. University of Minnesota Press 1993.

[2]Vienet, R. "The Situationists and the New Forms of Action Against Politics and Art." in *Situationist Anthology* (ed) Knabb, Ken. Bureau of Public Secrets, Berkeley (1981) p 215

[3]Heidegger, M. *An Introduction to Metaphysics* trans Ralph Manheim New Haven London Yale University Press 1987 first published 1959 p.8

[4]Including myself.

[5] Vienet, R. in Knabb op cit p. 215

[6]Several key texts detail the history of the Situationiste Internationale. These include: Marios, J_F. *Histoire de l'internationale Situationiste.* Paris 1989; Raspaud; J_J and Voyer, J_P *L'internationale Situationiste 1958_1969* Paris Editions Champ Libre 1972; Bandini, Mirella *L'estetico, il Politico*, Rome 1977. The Raspaud/Voyer text is the semi official history of the movement. It contains the full list of the 70 members from 16 countries France (13) Germany (11), Italy (9), Holland (7), England (6), Belgium (5), Denmark (4), Sweden (4), US (3), Algeria (2), Congo, Hungary, Israel, Roumania, Tunisia and Venezuela with 1 member each. It also contains several indexes, bibliographies and a full list of the contents of the I.S. Journal.

[7]Debord withdrew his films from circulation in 1985. This protest action was taken as a result of the murder of his friend and patron Gerard Lebovici the film producer and editor of Editions Champ Libre, the publishing house for the I.S. In their reportage of the event, the Parisian press attempted to link Lebovici's death to the `associations' he and Debord purportedly had with the French urban terrorist group Action Directe. Debord refuted these allegations in his long essay "Considerations sur l'assassination de Gerard Lebovici" Paris, 1983. After his death Alice Debord his widow began to re release them and they were exhibited at the Venice Film festival in 2001 and in 2002 there was another showing in Paris. Debord's many published statements revealing his antipathy toward the institution of cinema _ "I have scarcely begun to make you understand that I don't intend to play the game"("Je commence a peine a vous faire comprehendre que je ne veux pas jouer ce jeu_la") *Critique of Separation* (1961) were carried beyond mere rhetoric. Since the early 1980's the renewed interest in the Situationists both in Europe and North America and the exhibit at the Beaubourg, the ICA in London, Boston encourage the showing of these and other key Situationist works even if their unveiling has confirmed one of their worst fears, the total absorption of the movement into the culture of capitalism. I happen to believe that this was a necessary evil; in fact since 1969 it had already been accomplished. The issue now is to review what has occurred and recuperate what may be still valuable for culture in the new millennium.

[8]The IS had some problems with the term "recuperate". The Marcusian affirmative gloss which it attained was not one which the IS wished to associate with their primary projects of negation. It is used here to acknowledge both the failures and successes of the IS project; in an attempt to restore, to recover or redeem those aspects of their project that were lost, not those which have been subsequently exhausted. In a crucial sense this reestablishes the original split within the IS membership between the cultural and the political projects which was never resolved.

[9]Gray, C. *Leaving the Twentieth Century: The Incomplete Work of the Situationiste Internationale*. London, Freefall Press Publications 1974, p 7

[10]Guy Debord, *La Société du Spectacle* Paris, Editions Champ Libre first published by Buchet- Castel 1967

[11]The influences on Debord's writings of Andre Breton, Jean-Paul Sartre, Georg Lukacs and Henri Lefebvre, particularly the texts of the last two authors mentioned: Lefebvre's *Critique de la vie quotidienne* Paris 1947 and Lukacs *History and Class Consciousness* (1922, 1960*, 1971) have been explored usefully by Peter Wollen in his essay "The Situationist International" NLR March/April 1989. Wollen also discussed the intellectual relationship between Asger Jorn and Debord. * French translation by K. Axielos and J. Bois, Paris Les editions de Minuit 1960.

[12]Agamben, G. *The Coming Community*. Minneapolis, Theory Out of Bounds, Vol. 1. University of Minnesota Press, 1993 Shekinah VIII: 1 and passim.

[13] I have previously explored this notion with respect to the theory and practice of performance. See Barber, B. "Notes Toward an adequate Interventionist [Performance] Practice The ACT Vol 1 No 1 winter/spring 1986 New York pp 14-24 and Barber, B. *Reading Rooms* Halifax, Eyelevel Gallery 1992

[14]op. cit.6 p.13 from IS No. 1, 1958 Knabb Anthology, op. cit. 1 The translation of this passage differs quite markedly in places. However, both retain the overall senses of the original. See the full series of IS journals see *International Situationiste* 1958_1969 Paris, 1975. The original essay appeared in Les Lèvres Nues #8 (May 1956) a Belgian surrealist journal

[15]op cit. 2 pp.139-163

---

[16] A recent translation of the original essay "A User's guide to Détournement" appears in the website of the Bureau of Public Secrets http://www.bopsecrets.org/SI/detourn.htm (Accessed June 2005),. This site also contains translations of all of Guy Debord's six film scripts by Ken Knabb. See Debord, Guy *The Complete Cinematic Works* forthcoming AK Press September 2005.

[17] Ibid "A User's guide Détournement" "The only historically justified tactic is extremist innovation" p.1

[18] op cit 1 pp 8-14 quote p..9

[19] The translation of *détournement* provides insights into the variety of political strategies adopted by the IS for their critical program. *"Détournement* means deflection, diversion, rerouting, distortion, misuse, misappropriation, hijacking, or otherwise turning aside from the normal course or purpose." (op cit 16 Knabb p. 6)

[20] For a general overview of deconstruction within post-structuralist theory see Dews, Peter. *The Logics of Disintegration: Post-Structuralist Thought and the Claims of Critical Theory* London, verso 1987. For a useful text on Derrida, see Norris, C. (ed) *Deconstruction and the Interests of Theory"* London, Pinter and Norman 1988 and this author's *Deconstruction, Postmodernism and the Visual Arts* London Academy Editions.

[21] Derrida, J. *Positions* London, Ahtlone Press 1987:41-3

[22] Burger, Peter. *Theory of the Avant-Garde* trans. Michael Shaw, Forward by Jochen Schulte-Sasse. Minneapolis, University of Minnesota Press 1984 p.58

[23] "Detournement as negation and prelude." This is the title of one of the texts in the I.S. journal see Knabb op cit 1 pp..55-56. Prelude alludes to a certain 'coming to consciousness', the "sublimity" of comprehension.

[24] See Derrida, J. "Fifty-two Aphorisms for a Forward" and "Jacques Derrida In Discussion with Christopher Norris" in Benjamin, A., Cooke, C., and Papadakis, A. *Deconstruction: Omnibus Volume* New York Rizzoli Academy Editions 1989 pp.67-79

[25] Knabb, pp.45-46

[26] Ibid pp.10-11

[27] The quintessential allegorist for Walter Benjamin was Charles Baudelaire (The flaneur) about whom he wrote, "Baudelaire's genius, which is nourished in melancholy, is an allegorical genius. For the first time, with Baudelaire, Paris becomes the subject of lyric poetry. This poetry is no hymn to the homeland; rather it is the gaze of the allegorist, as it falls on the city, (it) is the gaze of the alienated man" (Benjamin, W. *The Arcades Project* Expose of 1935 "Everything becomes an allegory for me - Baudelaire *Le Cygne* Boston, Harvard University Press 1999.

[28] Benjamin, W. *The Origin of the German Tragic Drama* trans J. Osbourne London New Left Books 1977 p. 166, quoted in Burger op cit. 16 p..69

[29] "Hence, for example the word *pharmakon.* In this way we hope to display in the most striking manner, the regular ordered polysemy that has, through skewing, indetermination, or over determination, but without mistranslation, permitted the rendering of the same word by "remedy", "recipe," "poison," "drug," "philter," etc. It will also be seen to what extent, the malleable unity of this concept, or rather its rules and strange logic that links it with its signifier, has been dispersed, masked, obliterated, and rendered almost unreadable not only by the imprudence or empiricism of the translators, but first and foremost by the redoubtable, irreducible difficulty of translation." "Plato's Pharmacy"in Derrida, J *Dissemination* translated with an introduction by B. Johnson Chicago, Chicago University Press 1981 pp71-2 and *passim*

[30] Knabb, p 9

---

[31] Knabb p. 12 first published by Debord and Wolman, Gil. J. in Les levres Nues #8 may 1956

[32] For a comprehensive discussion of Debord's films and his place within the Situationist International see Thomas Y. Levin's essay "Dismantling the Spectacle: The Cinema of Guy Debord' in the catalogue accompanying the Pompidou Centre retrospective exhibition of the I.S. February 21 1989_April 91989. The exhibition was subsequently shown at the ICA in London and the ICA in Boston. See other essays by Ross D., et al in *"On the passage of a few people through a rather brief period of time: The Situationist International 1957_1972.* MIT Press Cambridge Mass and London 1989

[33] The English translation will be available in September 2005.

[34] This act of insubordination to the hegemonic order of the cultural institution could be likened to several competing acts of cultural and political resistance. Politically they may be closer to Gandhi's pacifism than the more direct actions of the French Resistance during the WW II.

[35] Debord, G. *Oeuvres Cinematographiques Completes 1952_1978* p.189 Translation "I will make no concessions to the public in this film. I believe that there are several good reasons for this decision and I'm going to state them."

[36] Sometimes translated as *Howls for Sade*

[37] "Just as the projection was about to begin, Guy-Ernest Debord was supposed to step onto the stage and make a few introductory remarks. Had he done so, he would simply have said: 'There is no film. Cinema is dead. No more films are possible. If you wish we can move on to a discussion.'"

[38] Debord p.7

[39] Eco, U. *The Role of the Reader: Explorations in the Semiotics of Texts* Bloomington, Indiana University Press 1979 and Eco, U. *Semiotics and the Philosophy of Language* Bloomington, University of Indiana Press 1984

[40] Vienet p.287

[41] In their list of individuals insulted by the I.S. (Raspaud and Voyer) Godard is listed 10 times. He is described as "L'enfant de Mao et du Coca Cola, le plus con des suisses pro-chinois" Knabb p 44

[42] Vienet, pp. 297_8

[43] Vaneigem's full statement reads: "What the producers of happenings, pop art and sociodramas are now doing is concealing passivity by renewing the forms of spectacle participation and the variety of stereotypes" quoted in Willener, Alfred. *The Action Image of society: On Cultural Politicization*, London, Tavistock 1970.

[44] Vienet, R op cit 2 p33

[45] Also Marx and Engel's *The German Ideology* (1845-6) and *Outlines of a Critique of Political Economy* (1844).

[46] This text can be considered an homage/revision of Debord's seminal text "The Situationist and the new forms of action in politics or Art" first published as a pamphlet in June 1963 See *On the passage of a few people through a brief moment of time: The Situationist International* 1957-1972 Cambridge, Mass MIT Press catalogue Musée national d'art moderne, Paris, ICA London, ICA Boston. 1989-1990.

[47] Ibid p.213

[48] Ibid p.215

[49] Ibid

[50] See Giorgio Agamben's "Tiananmen" section XIX, *The Coming Community.* (1993)

[51] op. cit 2. p.15

[52] op cit 1 p33 (1959)

Postscript

"If you want to enjoy life, prepare yourself for death"
Sigmund Freud [1]

I began this book with two primary questions in mind; the first: why are there so many representations of stereotypical mad artists, particularly psychopathic killers and suicidal artists in film, when there are so few clearly documented cases of such artists within the history of art? And the second question, with two components: is there a political meaning that is able to be assigned to the proliferation of such films in contemporary society, and what does this say about the producers of such material and the consuming interest in art, death, and crime, of the cinema going public? These two preliminary questions drew upon my previous work on graphic satires (cartoons and comics) of art, and directed my research along several axes that I attempted to negotiate employing Jacques Derrida's 'four times around' deconstructive process.[2] Early on I realized that Derrida's project was at once philosophical, historical and sociological, and therefore presented a formidable challenge to any contemporary researcher of film. I was also initially somewhat skeptical that going four times around a topic would deliver "the whole story and all that was needed to know," but once I released Derrida's statement from its implicit juridical meaning –"the whole truth and nothing but the truth" – this permitted a less proscriptive and more fluid approach to be pursued in negotiating the conflation of art/crime in film. I did take seriously however, Derrida's injunction to explore the surrounds and approaches to my chosen subjects, that is to pay specific attention to "the work, frame, *passé partout* (key), title, signature, museum, archive, discourse, marketplace -- in short, wherever there is legislation by marking of the limit."[3] Thus negotiating the limit(s) provided the essential coordinates of my research into the representation of art, artists, and art history in film, enabling me to contain my study within manageable contexts that were mutually reinforcing, if not holistically comprehensive.

Each of the chapters explored beyond my two original questions and their related components, across and through – *trans/acting* – various theoretical, historical and critical fields into specific domains of philosophical and political enquiry; for example, the question of the other in the construction of social stereotypes, and the political economy of various types of humour: parody, irony and satire. Employing the post-Freudian phantasmatic models developed by Giorgio Agamben, I discussed the historical construction of various stereotypes for artists, particularly the manner in which these were ideologically inscribed into the cultural dominant, and thereby became available for reproduction, both in terms of artist's presentation of self in everyday life, and also in terms of cultural representations within the domains of mass and popular culture, specifically cinema. In several chapters I engaged in deconstructive readings of films that represented artists as homicidal and/or suicidal figures, criminals as artists, and the perfect crime, usually murder, reconstituted as a work of art. I also explored the failed artist -- artist *manqué* turned murderer, and the artist who commits suicide, as cultural stereotypes reproduced through time. I chose to research films that were closely related to my original questions but also to investigate the work of canonical directors, Alfred Hitchcock, Peter Greenaway and Guy Debord, in order to test some of my assumptions about the use of art in cinema generally, but also the presence of art and death themes in their films. I based my arguments upon the resilience of certain models circulating in the cultural domain that have a long pedigree, reaching back to the foundations of western epistemology; for example the myth of Pygmalion, the sculptor whose inert sculpture of Aphrodite (Galatea), the woman he loves, becomes alive under his embrace. In my discussion of this myth I reflected upon examples of artists who reverse its narrative trajectory by taking a live subject, killing it and then turning it into a fetish object worthy of (disinterested) aesthetic contemplation. I argued that this reversal was the perfect incarnation of the fetish character of the art object itself and a compelling reason to sustain Giorgio Agamben's phantasmatic revision of creativity to the Freudian "object of lack."[4] I also cited the importance of Thomas de Quincey's essay "On Consideration of Murder as One of the Fine Arts"(1822), and Oscar Wilde's novel *The Picture of Dorian Gray* (1890), that represent murder as a fine art, arguing that these extraordinary texts, ironic 'riffs' respectively of Emmanuel Kant's *Critique of Judgment* and Johann Wolfgang von Goethe's *Faust*, have provided strong models for various cultural reiterations through to the present.

I surmised that the shadow side of the art/crime conflation was naturally the crime of art itself, an obsession of the necrophiliacal avant-garde movements of the modernist era, that have engaged in the usurping of the symbolic authority of previous vanguards, acting out (*passages de l'acte*), an Oedipal ritualistic killing of the father in order to secure the identity and omnipotence of the son. As an artist, trained also as an art historian, who has taught in art schools for almost three decades and participated in the art world internationally, I frequently witness evidence of this 'will to power' (to provide its Nietzschean gloss), in art discourse (essays, reviews catalogues, interviews), especially in pronouncements about the supersession or 'death' of this or that art discipline – painting, film, performance art – and especially the demise of an (neo) avant-garde art movement, style or fashion. Certain artists in the media also reflect this will to power in the self-aggrandized statements and power plays. Being rather skeptical of instrumentalist rationalizations for social behavior, I have not been attracted to affirming these examples as the result of a psychological reflex, Freudian sublimation, a Lacanian or Žižekian "superego injunction," and especially not a product of evolutionary biology or psycho-biology. I was subsequently more comfortable with recognizing these behaviors, products and artifacts as results of a historically instituted process, similar to the manner in which Avital Ronell describes a "historically implanted test drive."[5]

During the course of writing this book, two artist colleagues, both males, one in the United States and the other in Germany, within twelve months of each other, committed suicide. The first was a middle-aged interdisciplinary artist based in New York who had an exceptional exhibiting career, with many solo and group exhibitions in major institutions to his credit, as well as essays, catalogues, and several major book commentaries on his work. To all intents he was an art world success and from the outside, I would have considered him very unlikely to take his own life. The German artist, almost two decades younger, but with a developing international reputation for producing intelligently ironic performances in the public sphere, someone I had met and corresponded with, I also considered unlikely to commit suicide. These two tragic events, occurring during the completion of the final chapters of the book, lead me to reflect once again upon the psychosocial dimensions of my study. Like many of my artist colleagues I pondered the reasons why these two artists took their own lives. Obituaries typically do not reveal much about the manner in which a person dies and certainly given the stigma of suicide, they do not cite the motivating factors, whatever these happen to be. An email that I received subsequently from one of the German artist's close friends in Cologne informed his friends and colleagues that he had been diagnosed as psychotic and had been hospitalized for some months before he took his own life. Not knowing either artist very well and without having access to more information regarding their lives and deaths, I had little to resolve my feelings of loss.

A question haunted me. Were the suicides of these artists the result of a psychological or physiological illness, a 'superego injunction,' as Lacan or Žižek would posit, or were both of these artists victims of manquéhood and phantasmatic ideology "the noon day demons" that I explored in chapters 3 and 4. I recalled that suicide, as philosophers from Schopenhauer to Sartre have suggested, might be the most autonomous free act that any individual can commit.[6] And yet how free, I conjectured, are one's acts if they are complicit with, or a product of ideology? I recognize that phenomenologically life – *being* – is always on the threshold, which is being with (*mitsein*) death. But if Heidegger's *dasein* is ontically construed as "a being for death," then perhaps these artists' death choice was governed by what Jean-Luc Nancy referred to as "the phantasm of metaphysics;" a function of Christian theology, in which the ego, the subject/ I, pronounces his/her own death (the Cartesian *ego sum mortuus*) and secures an 'afterlife – a transfiguration (*nachleben*). As Nancy writes: "I cannot say that it is dead, if the I disappears in effect in it's death, in the death that is precisely what is proper to it and most inalienable it's own, it is because the I is something other than a subject."[7] I assumed this to be the axiomatic crux of the phenomenological das/(s) ein, where subject hood meets the hermeneutic challenge(s) of life before an ego (I) can be (ir) rationally constituted. But what if the hermeneutic challenge precipitated questions about the value of (a) life that has been marked by frustration, however expressed – lack /failure— manquéhood? The question inevitably arises again; are artist suicides an opportunity to recognize the phantasmatic character of ideology for *magisters ludi* with suicide as the compensating (sublimating) mechanism to ameliorate failure, to transform the end into a redemptive prelude to transfiguration and apotheosis?

My natural inclination is to beware of structural functionalist and /or psychosocial and biological determinism as explanatory vehicles for my rationalizations. If the 'death drive' was at the root of their acts, why do not more artists kill themselves? I was reminded (comforted) by the Wittkowers study that demonstrated how few artists committed either suicide or homicide during the first millennium, and also by more recent sociological studies that indicate that an individual's profession, occupation, class, gender or ethnicity do not necessarily predispose him/her to suicidal motivation. The truth – such as it can be construed – I suspect now lies somewhere in between the confluence of these modalities, including the socio-historical – ideologically – determined reflex and individual psycho(path)logy – another example of the power(s) of the visible/invisible – demonstrating that the project of truth seeking is once again a Schirmachian problem alternately "concealing and revealing."[8] On one register, the deaths of these two artists only reinforced my understanding that the history of the genius /madness conflation from which we derive the manqué theory of lack; that has been and continues to be a powerful ideological force in our culture.

Sigmund Freud in *Beyond the Pleasure Principle* (1920) and some of his other works from this period (1918-1920), that were the years that he wrote on war neuroses (from which the above quote was borrowed), and completed his essay on "The 'Uncanny,'" hypothesized that the flip side of Eros – the libidinal, pleasure seeking and life affirming character of the human psyche – was another drive, which he named the Death Drive.[9] In an attempt to understand the exhibition of obsessional neuroses, compulsion and repetition, that he was observing in some of his patients, Freud was forced to reconsider his previous focus upon pleasure seeking (to satisfy the demands of the libido and desires of the ego), as prime motors of human behavior. The result of his thinking, that some commentators have suggested was somewhat of a crisis of commitment to his earlier work, Freud began to speculate about a drive, that was in effect beyond pleasure, to which he proposed the name Thanatos, after the Greek deity of death.[10] At this late stage in his work, at the conclusion of the First World War, he was attempting to provide explanatory models for crowd psychology, the repetition of social struggle and war. Freud considered that the death drive was an *ur* phenomenon, a 'primitive/archaic element beyond the pleasure principle, provided by the libido, and capable of ensuring that the subject could secure a return to the quiescence of a state beyond the womb, and prior to life itself. Freud further nominated the death drive as having the power to engage in sublimation; that in relation to the psyche's 'superego imperatives and injunctions' (to use Lacan inspired Žižekian language), is therefore associated with the most creative spheres of human activity, including religion, art, culture generally. Freud also suggested that the death drive derives its pleasure in what is disturbing and painful to the organism, hence the evidence of the urge to repeat and obsessional compulsion in the practice of everyday life. This is why confirming the existence of the death drive and understanding its effects, has become a consuming project for understanding the psychological compulsions behind evil, war and social struggle, sadism, masochism, abjection and pornography in the writings of many intellectuals: Masoch, de Sade, Lacan, Bataille, Levinas, Laplanche, Kristeva, Žižek, Butler, Agamben, Badiou, among many others.

From the perspectives addressed in this book, the existence of the death drive remains a parenthetical [question], one which if it is proven to exist, could obviate the necessity to privilege socio-historical and hence ideological explanations to the prevalence of certain stereotypical representations of mad artists, particularly psychopathic killers and suicidal artists in film. If, as I suspect, the death drive is thoroughly implicated in the existence of these phantasmatic representations, then it may also be a function of ideology, a "legitimating discourse" (after Bourdieu) that tends to operate with a great deal of complexity and contrariness. It remains the fact – a truth, perhaps – that these discourses and the institutions: art history, philosophy, psychoanalysis, cinema, from which they emanate, provide the sites within which our understanding of ideological effects, influences and power must be located. This confirms that the most successful ideological effects are the ones that have "no need of words, but only of *laissez faire* and complicitous silence.[11]

Future Possibilities

Many years ago I read Bernard Malamud's *Pictures of Fidelman*, a satirical novel that reviewed an artist's rites of passage through the styles and movements of modern art. During his passage Fidelman relocates from the United States to Italy and from being a fine artist (manqué) to becoming an artisan (glass blower). He also transfers his sexual orientation from heterosexual to homosexual. At some point in the future, I look forward to extending my research into literature. "Trans/actions: Art, Film and Death" has enabled me to scratch the surface of a large group of novels and short stories in all genres that feature narratives based upon art, artists, and art history. I have compiled (my obsessive compulsion), a new list of approximately a hundred book and short story titles, some of which have been made into films, that may tempt me into further work on this and related topics. The list includes Lise Bissonette's short story collection *Quittes et doubles: Scènes de réciprocité* that contains a story "Affairs of Art," in which a red chalk drawing of a woman's vulva (perhaps a reference to Gustave Courbet's extraordinary painting, *Origin of the World,* 1866), has remained both hidden, but also misunderstood, by generations of fetishistic art collectors. The narrative recounts how a servant who has become bewitched by the image kills the last owner of the work. And Patricia Highsmith's novel *Ripley Under Ground* (1970), that concerns Ripley the lead protagonist who masquerades as a dead painter and kills an art collector. The list also includes Somerset Maugham's *The Moon and Sixpence,* a fictionalized account of Paul Gauguin's decision to leave his middle class existence and head for the South Pacific and artist Jonathan Santlofer's novel *The Death Artist: A Novel of Suspense* (2002), which is literally that, a serial killer who stages his murders after great paintings by famous artists. A favorite author, Minette Walters is also included in my preliminary list. Walters' novel *The Sculptress* relates the story of author Rosalind Leigh who has been commissioned to write a book about Olive Martin, an obese young woman known as 'the sculptress,' who hacks up her mother and sister with an axe, and then arranges the body pieces as a work of art. In her prison cell Olive artfully carves small wax figurines, including, after their first interview, one of the author Rosalind Leigh, which to my mind, is a delicious example of the Derridian imprimatur, *sous rature.*

---

[1] Freud, S. "Thoughts for the times of war and death "in Freud, S. *The Standard Edition of the Complete Works of Sigmund Freud* trans and edited James Strachey, London Hogarth Press 1960 Vol 14: 300

[2] I have previously explored the negotiation of meaning and the symbolic contest of power with respect to the representation of modernist art in cartoons and comics. See Barber, B., *Popular Modernisms: Art, Cartoons, Comics and Cultural In/Subordination.* (Forthcoming)

[3] Derrida, J. *The Truth in Painting* Bennington, G. and McLeod, I., Trans. Chicago, University of Chicago Press, 1987:9

[4]Giorgio Agamben *Stanzas: Word and Phantasm in Western Culture* (1993), outlined the and epistemological and phantomatic origins of the fetish object *viz* "suggestively characterized as *objet de perspective (perspective object)* or *object de manque* (object of

lack), or to perceive the closeness of the fetish object to the domain of cultural creation" 33-35 and *passim*.

[5]Ronell, Avital *The Test Drive* Urbana and Chicago University of Illinois 2005 pp 86-7

[6] Schopenhauer in Schirmacher, W. (ed), *Arthur Schopenhauer. Schopenhauer: Philosophical Writings.* The German Library No. 27. The Continuum International Publishing Group. New York, London, 1994 p. 47

[7] Nancy, J-L 1991:18 Nancy, Jean-Luc, Philippe Lacoue-Labarthe and Simon Sparks (eds). *Retreating the Political.* Warwick Studies in European Philosophy. Routledge. New York, London, 1997

[8] Schirmacher, W. "Homo Generator: Media and Postmodern Technology" In Bender, G., and Druckery, T *Culture on the Brink: Ideologies of Technology* Seattle, Bay Press ,1994:73

[9] Freud, S. *Beyond the Pleasure Principle* (*Jenseits des Lustprinzips*), ed James Strachey NY Norton and company 1961 Originally published in 1922

[10] References for which appear in the Iliad and the Odyssey. Thanatos was the brother of Hypnos (Sleep) from which we derive the terms hypnosis and hypnotism

[11]Bourdieu, P. *The Logic of Practice* Stanford, Stanford University Press, 1990:133; original Paris, Les Editions de Miniut, 1980.

Appendix 1

Art, Artists, and Art History in Film[1]

AC***The Affairs of Cellini* (*The Firebrand*) (1934) Gregory La Cava. Roguish artist accused of murder in C16th Florence.

AC***After Hours* (1985) Martin Scorsese. A clever satire of the New York art world.

**The Agony and the Ecstacy*, (1958) Carol Reed. Michelangelo's epic struggle with the Pope over the painting of the Sistine Chapel Ceiling

**Alchemy* (1995) Suzanne Myers. Scenes from the life of artist Kihlstedt who makes intricate boxes for found objects.

AC**All the Vermeers in New York* (1990). Jon Jost. Drama about the New York art world set in the Metroplitan Museum which explores parallels between the art world and big business.

AC *Animal Crackers* (1930) Victor Heerman. The Marx Brothers and stolen art.

**An American in Paris* (1951) Vincent Minelli. Musical in the context of Parisian art world.

Anne Trister.(1986) Léa Poole The story of a young melcancholic artist from Switzerland sharing an apartment space with a psychologist and acting out her personal struggles on a large mural.

**Annie Hall* (1977) Woody Allen. Allen's Freudian hang-ups, existential, art and otherwise.

AC***A Perfect Murder* (1998) Andrew Davis. A remake of Hitchcock's *Dial M for Murder* with Michael Douglas, Gwyneth Paltrow and Viggo Mortenson as the artist.

AC *Appointment with Murder* (1948) Jack Bernard. The Falcon and international art thieves.

AC**Artemesia* (1997) Agnes Merlet. Dramatic chronicle of the life of the C17th artist Artemsia Gentileschi, raped by her teacher Agostino Tassi who also murdered a rival.

The Art of Love (1965) Norman Jewison. Art forgery and intrigues in Paris.

**Artists and Models* (1955) Frank Tashlin. Dean Martin and Jerry Lewis play New York bohemian artists.

Backbeat (1994) Ian Softley. The early history of the Beatles played out in the art worlds of Liverpool and Hamburg.

AC*Backtrack* (1990) Dennis Hopper. Jodie Foster (ref. Jenny Holzer) A media artist is being tracked by a killer.

**Basquiat* (1996) Julian Schnabel. Documents the trials and tribulations of Michael Basquiat the tortured genius graffiti artist directed by another artist,

AC*Batman* (1989). Tim Burton. Jack Nicholson as the joker trashes an art museum's modernist paintings and proclaims himself as the world's "first fully functioning homidical artist."

La Belle Noiseuse (The Beautiful Troublemaker, 1991) Jacques Rivette. A loose translation of Balzac's short story *The Unknown Masterpiece.*

Bell, Book and Candle (1958) Richard Quine. Kim Novak stars as a dealer in African Art.

**La Belle Noiseuse Divertimento* (1991) Jacques Rivette. A struggling painter seeks immortality.

AC**The Belly of an Architect* (1987) Peter Greenaway. An architect struggles with love, art and immortality.

The Best Age (1968) Jarolslav Papousek. Documents individual rites of passage in an art school.

A Bigger Splash (1974) Jack Hazan Stylish film about David Hockney and his friends.

AC *The Bird with Crystal Plumage, (The Phantom of Terror* 1969) Dario Argento. A 'spaghetti slasher' narrative containing a murder attempt in a gallery.

***The Birds* (1963) Alfred Hitchcock.

AC*Blackmail* (1929). Alfred Hitchcock. Murder mystery with Crewe the artist as victim.

AC*Bluebeard* (1944) Edgar G. Ulmer (Murnau's former art director and assistant). A turn of the century pathological painter and part-time puppeter engages in serial murder.

AC*Blowup* (1966) Michelangelo Antonioni. Art, murder, sex and photography.

Bon Voyage (1944) Alfred Hitchcock

The Bridge (1990) Sydney MacCartney. A dramatic story concerning a young impressionist painter and his lover.

AC*Burgler* (1987) Hugh Wilson. Includes an art theft with Whoopi Goldberg as the thief.

AC***Bucket of Blood* (1960) Richard Corman Walter Paisley a shy busboy in a beatnick café becomes an artist who engages in serial murder to make a killing in the art world.

**Camille Claudel* (1988) Bruno Nytten. A film about Rodin a tortured artist and his equally tortured lover

AC *Canvas: The Fine Art of Crime.* (1992) Alain Zaloum. A ruthless gallery dealer recruits a poverty stricken young artist into his art stealing projects.

AC**Caravaggio* (1986) Derek Jarman The Renaissance painter's art, life, loves and death

AC *Cauldron of Blood* (1967) Edward Andrew. A blind sculptor (Boris Karloff) has a psychotic wife who provides him with human skeletons as the raw material for his artwork

**Champagne* (1928) Alfred Hitchcock

AC* *La Chienne,* (1931) Jean Renoir. The film model for Fritz Lang's *Scarlet* Street featuring an amateur artist who kills his *femme fatale*.

Close to the Wind (1969) Stellen Olsson an unsuccessful sculptor who comes into conflict with his patrons.

AC *Colour Me Red* (1969) Eddie Davis. A painter decides that the re colour of his paintings is best rendered in real blood.

AC *Confessions of Boston Blackie* (1941) Edward Dmytrk. Blackie solves an art forgery crime.

AC** *The Cook, the Thief, His Wife and Her Lover* (1990) Peter Greenaway The culinary arts, adultery and murder.

**Cop and a Half* (1992) Henry Winkler. An art crime comedy starring Burt Reynolds

Corridor of Mirrors (1948) Terrance Young. Artist as collector of Renaissance Objects.

**Cousin Bette* (1997) Des McAnuff. Art, love and decadence in mid C19th Paris.

AC*Crack-up* (1946) Irving Rees. A crime story concerning art fakes.

AC**Crime Doctor's Gamble* (1947) William Castle. The crime doctor's vacation in Paris interrupted by murder and an art theft.

AC***Crime Doctor's Warning* (1945) William Castle. Doctor is involved in case where a mad artist is suspected of murdering people during blackouts.

AC *Crucible of Terror* (1972) Ted Hooker. A mad sculptor covers beautiful models with hot wax and then imprisons them in a mold of bronze.

***Daddy* (1972) Peter Whitehead. Freudian fantasy unpacking artist. Niki de St Phalle's relationship to her domineering parents.

C*The Dangerous* (1994) Robert Davi, Michael Pare. Ninja's in New Orleans. Climax in galleries and outside Museum of Art.

Dark Shadows (1966- 67) Horror TV series with art content John Sedwick, Lela Swift

AC***The Dark Side of Genius* (1994) Phedon Papamichael. An artist killer who murdered his beautiful model is paroled from prison and seeks out a new victim, a female reporter for an LA Arts weekly attempting to write about him.

AC ** *The Death Artist* (1995) Michael J. MacDonald. A gruesome remake of Roger Corman's *Bucket of Blood* (1960).

AC *The Debt Collector* (1999) Anthony Neilson. An Edinburgh loan shark who has served 17 years in prison on a murder rap becomes a celebrated sculptor and writer but when released, he seeks revenge on those he believes have wronged him

Delirious (1991) Tom Mankiewicz. A writer finds himself in the fictional world he has created.

Demolition Man (1993) Marco Brambila. Stallone and Wesley Snipes shootout in a Museum of Future.

AC***Dial M for Murder* (1953) Alfred Hitchcock references high art with the perfect crime.

**A Dog of Flanders* (1959) James B. Clark (A children's film). A young boy in C19th Flanders whose struggle to become an artist is assisted by an older painter.

Dodsworth (1936) William Wyler. Adaption of Sinclair Lewis novel. A man's struggle with high culture in Europe.

AC***The Draughtsman's Contract* (1982) Peter Greenaway. A witty chronicle of the trials and tribulations of a painter/draughtsman who is hired to draw a English country estate in C7th England. Includes the hypnotic music of Michael Nyman.

AC**Dressed to Kill* (1980) Brian de Palma. Has an opening sequence of a female victim being followed in a museum

AC**The Dying Swan* (1917) Evgenij Bauer. An intriguing story about art, dance, obsessive love, life and death in Russia around the time of the Revolution.

AC**Eddie and the Cruisers II: Eddie Lives* (1989) Jean-Claude Lord. Eddie saves his artist/girlfriend from being ripped off by an agent at her first exhibition opening.

AC***Easy Virtue* (1927) Alfred Hitchcock.

Edward Munch (1976) Peter Watkins. A remarkable biopic of the pioneer artist.

**The Eiger Sanction* (1975) Clint Eastwood. Clint Eastwood plays an art historian, collector and critic who proves that one can combine criticism with assassination. Based upon a Trevanian Novel.

**Elstree Calling* (1930) Alfred Hitchcock

**Europe After the Rain* (1978) Mick Gold. Idiosyncratic anthology of Dada and Surrealism underscored by the theories of Freud and Trotsky. Includes an inteview with Marcel Duchamp.

Every Picture tells a Story (1984) James Scott An autobiographical research by director Scott into the life and times of his father, painter William Scott.

AC**F for Fake* (1975) Orson Welles' homage to art and forgery. Art, creativity and the lies that sustain them.

**Family Plot* (1976) Alfred Hitchcock

AC***The Falls* (1980) Peter Greenaway. A documentary parody based on the atomic number 92 Uranium. A humorous meditation on art, death and immortality.

* *The Farmer's Wife* (1928) Alfred Hitchcock

Father Brown (also called *The Detective*) (1954) Robert Hamer. Father Brown in pursuit of stolen art.

Favorites of the Moon (*Les favoris de la lune*) (1984) Otar Iosseliani. A Tatisesque anarchy revolving around many lunar characters.

**Five Women around Utamaro* (1946) Kenji Mizoguchi A meditation on the status of the artist (old and new) in post-war Japan.

**Foreign Correspondent* (1940) Alfred Hitchcock.

**The Fountainhead* (1949) King Vidor. A bizarre adaptation of Ayn Rand's novel, neo Nietzschean philosophy of objectivisim represented in the life of architect and his will to power, loves and desires.

AC***Frenzy* (1972) Alfred Hitchcock

C *The Freshman* (1990). Andrew Bergman. High cult cuisine, art theft and traffic in endangered species.

**Gaslight* (1940) Thorld Dickinson and (1944) George Kukor. The art of estrangement.

Gentleman at Heart (1942) Ray McCarey. A bookie discovers more money in art forgery.

C**Genuine* (1920) Robert Wiene. Post Caligari Pygmalion plot.

AC**Ghost Busters II* (1989) Ivan Reitman. Art conservator becomes inhabited by his painting. Metropolitan like museum in New York.

The Golden Salamander (1949) Ronald Neame. An English art expert searching for some priceless antiques crosses the path of gun runners.

Good Morning Babylon (1986) Paolo Taviani. Story of two brothers, Tuscan stonemason restorers of Romanesque cathedrals who travel to America in search of their fortune.

Good Will Hunting (1991) Gus Van Sant. Matt Damon plays an angry young genius whom his psychiatrist (Robin Williams) rescues from a life of crime. Art figures prominently in their first therapy session.

Gothic (1986) Ken Russell. A sterotyped representation of a tortured genius.

The Hair Opera (1992) Yuri Obitani A first person chronicle of the life of Obitani , a trainee opera singer and aspiring film maker learns of a female artist who is exhibiting carefully mounted and dated specimens of the pubic hair of all the men she has slept with. He invites her to exchange letters with him.

The Happy Thieves (1962) George Marshall. Art Museum theft in Spain.

Horrors of the Black Museum (1959) Arthur Crabtree. Unfriendly curator.

The Horse's Mouth (1958) Ronald Neame. Documents the eccentric life of artist Gully Jimson whose paintings were executed by John Bratby, British 'kitchen sink' painter.

AC***Hour of the Wolf (Vargtimme* 1967) Ingmar Bergman. Brilliant Gothic fantasy about an artist (Max von Sydow) who has disappeared leaving only a diary. Bergmanian dark obsessions and horror.

C *How To Steal a Million* (1966) William Wyler. Forgery and museum theft.

***I Confess* (1951) Alfred Hitchcock. Murder mystery and wrong man scenario.

Icicle Thief (*Ladri de Saponette*, 1989) Marizio Nidetti. Parody of Dio Sica's *Bicycle Thief.*

I've Heard the Mermaids Singing (1987). Patricia Rozema. Extended lampoon/satire of the art world.

Imago - Meret Oppenheim (1989) Pamela Robertson-Pierce. Traces the life of surrealist artist Meret Oppenheim who produced the infamous *fur lined teacup.*

AC***Incognito* (1997) John Badham. Art forgery and murder.

Jamaica Inn (1939) Alfred Hitchcock.

Juno and the Paycock (1930) Alfred Hitchcock.

AC***Just Cause* (1995) Arne Glimcher. A diabolical murderer in prison paints his cell as a parody of an abstract expressionist painting.

Lady Ice (1973) Tom Gries. Art Thieves and the insurance business.

* *The Lady Vanishes* (1938) Alfred Hitchcock

L.A. Story (1991) Mick Jackson. Steve Martin skates through L.A. art museum

AC**Legal Eagles* (1986) Ivan Reitman. Murder art fraud, Daryl Hannah plays an artist's daughter and Winger and Redford attempt to recover stolen art.

AC**Lies* (*Kojitmal*) (1999) Jang Sun-Woo. A married sculptor has an affair with a school girl and enters into a highly changed S&M relationship which involves coprophilia and murder.

Lifeboat (1944) Alfred Hitchcock.

AC *The Lodger: A Story of the London Fog* (1926) Alfred Hitchcock.

Love is the Devil- Study for a Portrait of Francis Bacon (1998) John Maybury. The slow downward spiral of the ralationship between British painter Francis Bacon (Derek Jacobi) and George Dyer his lover, model and muse.

Loving (1970) Irvin Kershner. A screwball comedy about a misunderstood artist and those around him..

AC***Lust for Life* (1957) Vincente Minelli. Tortured genius biopic of Vincent van Gogh

Maiden Work (Chunü Zuo) Wang Guangli Story of a painter who undergoes eye surgery after a bar fight and then tries to reconstruct his relationships before the incident on film.

The Making of Judy Chicago's The Dinner Party, (1980) Johanna Demetrakus.

The Man Who Knew Too Much (1934) Alfred Hitchcock.

Man From China (1990) Zang Tielin.The experiences of an exciled Chinese painter in London.

Mannequin (1987) Michael Gottlieb. A Pygmalion narrative.

Mannequin Two: On the Move (1991) Stewart Rafill Remake of the earlier *Mannequin* (1987).

Manhattan (1979) Woody Allen . Life in New York includes a satire of the art world.

The Manxman (1928) Alfred Hitchcock.

C***Marnie* (1964) Alfred Hitchcock.

C**Melancholia* (1989) Andi Engel. Existential thriller involving figures in a complex narrative about art (Durer's *Melancholia*), angst and assassination.

**Minnie and Moskowitz* (1971) John Cassavetes. Romance between museum curator and parking lot attendant.

AC**Ministry of Fear* (1944) Fritz Lang. crime reference to a sculptor.

***The Moderns* (1988) Alan Rudolph. Ironic look at the Paris art scene of the 1920's.

The Moon and Sixpence (1942) Albert Lewin. Somerset Maugham's Gauguin inspired story about a London based broker who gives everything up to live in Paris as a painter.

**M oulin Rouge* (1952) John Huston. A Toulouse Lautrec bio pic

**Moulin Rouge* (2001) Bazz Lurhman operatic Toulouse Lautrec musical drama.

**Mr and Mrs Smith* (1941) Alfred Hitchcock.

AC***Murder!* (1930) Alfred Hitchcock.

The Mystery of Picasso (1956) Henri Georges Clouzot. Documentary about Picasso works subsequently destroyed.

**Night Gallery* (1969) Boris Sagal, Stephen Spielberg, Barry Shear. Anthology of lessons learned from paintings led to this T.V. series.

AC***New York Stories* (1989) Scorsese, Coppola, Allen,.Scorsese's Abstract expressionist artist (Nick Nolte) struggles with middle age crisis in *Life Lessons*

C***North by Northwest* (1959) Alfred Hitchcock.

Nothing Lasts Forever (1984). Tom Schiller. Comedy about an aspiring artist.

C**Notorious* (1946) Alfred Hitchcock.

**Number Seventeen* (1932) Alfred Hitchcock.

Object of Beauty Michael Lindsay-Hogg. Regarding a Henry Moore sculpture.

**One Touch of Venus* (1948) Willam A Seiter. Another Pygmalion reiteration.

**Painters Painting* (1972) Emile de Antonio.

*, *The Paradine Case* (1948) Alfred Hitchcock.

**Pecker* (1998) John Waters.

C**Peewee's Big Adventure* (1985) Tim Burton. Peewee stops in a museum in search of stolen bicycle.

AC***Performance* (1970) Nicholas Roeg and Donald Cammell. Artful thriller with Mick Jagger playing an fading pop star and artist

manqué) and Chas (James Fox) Gangland boss as "an artist...a real performer"
Pierrot le Fou, (1965) Jean-Luc Godard. High art versus low. Pop art references.
C**Pink Panther* (1964) Blake Edwards. Art and jewel thieves.
Pirosmani (1971) Georgy Shengelaya. Portrait of Pirosmani the Russian primitive artist.
**Play It Again Sam* (1972) Herbert Ross. Museum visits and world of high art as part of setting.
AC***Psycho* (1960) Alfred Hitchcock. Art crime relationships in Norman Bates' lair.
The Quince Tree Sun (*El Sol del Membrillo* 1991)Victor Erice. A story about Antonio Lopez a artist who painstakingly paints a quince tree in his garden and the social truths that result from his effort.
Pretty as a Picture: The Art of David Lynch. (1997) Toby Keller documents the making of Lynch's *Lost Highway* with an overview of the director's career as a painter and filmmaker
* *Prospero's Books* (1991) Peter Greenaway.
AC***Rear Window* (1954) Alfred Hitchcock
C***Rebecca* (1940) Alfred Hitchcock.
C** *The Rebel*(1960) Robert Day. British comedian Tony Hancock is the leader of the Infantile School of Painting. A satire on the role and behavior of the avant-garde artist.
***Rembrandt* (1936) Alexander Korda. A dramatisation of the last years of Rembrandt's life after the death of his wife Saskia and the increasing hostility to his work.
**Rich and Strange* (1932) Alfred Hitchcock.
AC***Rope* (1948) Alfred Hitchcock. Murder as high art.
C* *The Rothko Conspiracy* (1983) Paul Watson. Drama of legal battle over painter Mark Rothko's estate.
C**Sabotage* (1936) Alfred Hitchcock.
C**Saboteur* (1942) Alfred Hitchcock.
**Le Sang d'un poète* (*The Blood of the Poet*) Jean Cocteau. Agony and escstacy of the artist.
**Savage Messiah* (1972) Ken Russell. Dramatises the life of Vorticist sculptor Henri Gaudier-Brzeska.
Secret Agent (1936) Alfred Hitchcock.
AC***Scarlet Street* (1945) Fritz Lang, starring Joan Bennett, Chris Cross a quiet cashier and amateur painter falls in love with a beautiful young woman who ruins his life.

C*_Schiele in Prison_ (1980) Mick Gold documentary of artist Egon Schiele's life in WWI Vienna with regard to sex, boredom and suicide.

AC _Secret of the Whistler_ (1946) George Sherman. A wife suspects artist husband of killing her predecessor. She's next.

AC*_Shadow of a Doubt_ (1943) Alfred Hitchcock

C _The Skin Game_ (1931) Alfred Hitchcock

Some Kind of Wonderful (1987) Love story set in museum settings.

Saint Ives (1976) J. Lee Thompson. Art Theft

AC**_The Silence of the Lambs_ (1991) Jonathon Demme Dr Hannibal Lecter and Buffalo Bill two pathological serial killers display their creative talents as visual artists.

*_Sirens_ (1994) John Duigin. Art, erotica and religion.

Slaves of New York (1989) James Ivory and Ismail Merchant

Sleeper (1973) Woody Allen. Vision of museum's future.

*_Scrooged_ (1988) Richard Donner, cast Bill Murray contains two short satires of Pablo Picasso and Klein

C*_Shadows_ John Cassavetes (1957) Sequence shows a romp in the sculpture garden at the Museum of Modern Art

C*_Six Degrees of Separation_ (1994) Fred Shepsi. Art dealer in a bourgeois farce involving race, class and gender.

AC**_Still Life_ (1989) Graeme Campbell A slasher movie. Extended satire of performance art as a homicidal practice.

AC**_Spellbound_ (1945) Alfred Hitchcock.

AC**_Stage Fright_ (1950) Alfred Hitchcock.

AC**_Strangers on a Train_ (1951) Alfred Hitchcock.

Sunday in the Country (1984) Bertand Tavernier. Story about an honoured painter in later life.

Surviving Picasso (1996) James Ivory and Ismail Merchant. Anthony Hopkins as Picasso

AC**_Suspicion_ (1941) Alfred Hitchcock, cast includes Joan Fontaine Cary Grant. A satirical reference to cubist art contrasted with a naturalistic portrait of the imperious father.

AC*_Take the Money and Run_ (1969) Woody Allen. Life history of a thief including art and museum thefts.

C*_The Man Who Knew Too Much_ (1956) Alfred Hitchcock

* _The 39 Steps_ (1935) Alfred Hitchcock

*_The Party_ (1968) Blake Edwards, Peter Seller's satire of Hollywood film society and Californian hard edge abstraction.

*_To Catch a Thief_ (1954) Alfred Hitchcock.

The Tingler (1959) Willam Castle.
C**Topkapi* (1964) Jules Dassin. Museum theft movie
AC* *The Thomas Crown Affair* (1968) Art museum theft with Faye Dunnaway as the insurance agent struggling to solve the crime.
**The Train* (1965) John Frankenheimer. Art versus life question.
AC**Torn Curtain* (1966) Alfred Hitchcock.
C***Topaz* (1969) Alfred Hitchcock.
AC***The Trouble with Harry* (1955) Alfred Hitchcock.
AC *Trust Me* (1989) Bobby Houston. Satire of the art market.
C**Under Capricorn* (1949)Alfred Hitchcock.
C**Waltzes from Vienna* (1933) Alfred Hitchcock.
**The Wheeler Dealers* (1963) Arthur Hiller. Hilarious vision of art dealing in French Impressionists by crazy Texans.
**The Wolf at the Door* (1986) Henning Carlsen. Tortured genius life of Paul Gauguin
Van Gogh (1991) Maurice Pialat. A compelling account of the last three months of the painter's life.
C**Vincent: The Life and Death of Vincent van Gogh* (1987) Paul Cox. A somewhat romanticized psychological portrait of the artist.
Venice: Theme and Variation (1957) James Ivory. An extravagant view ofVenice through the work of some of the artists who have painted its citizens and architecture.
AC***Vertigo* (1958) Alfred Hitchcock. Modernist painting scene and references to art and death and the alive portrait. James Stewart and Kim Novak
* *La Vie de Boheme* (1991) Aki Kawismaki Bohemian Life and love
C**Wilde* (!997) Brian Gilbert. The life and loves and aesthetic beliefs of Oscar Wilde.
**The Wrong Man* (1956) Alfred Hitchcock
Vagabond, (1985) Agnes Varda. A bleak narrative about a young woman vagabond. References to art through postcards of paintings
**World of Gilbert and George* (1981) Autobiographical documentary of G&G by the artists.
**Young and Innocent* (1937) Alfred Hitchcock
**Yumeji* (1991) Seijun Suzuki. The ghost story about the life, loves and failures of Yumeji Takehisa (1884-1934) a real life painter and poet
AC***A Zed and Two Naughts* (1985) Peter Greenaway.

Legend:

C   Denotes films that specifically conflate art with crime and feature either homicidal or suicidal artists.

AC**Denotes films viewed and discussed in this book.

---

[1] Edited and augmented from the following sources: Craddock, J (ed) *Videohound's Golden Movie Retriever* New York, London Thomson Gale, 2005; Pym, John (ed. et al), *Time Out Film Guide* 8th Edition London, Penguin Books 2000, and *Hollywood at the Museum: A Filmography* by Patrick Butler, William Howze, Sally Shelton, David Spaulding, presented at the Museums and Popular Culture session of the AAM annual meeting Philadelphia 1995.

Appendix 2

Art, Artists and Art History in the Films of Alfred Hitchcock.[1]

The Pleasure Garden (1925) Screenplay by Eliot Stannard based on novel by Oliver Sandys. Theatre references throughout this first Hitchcock film.

The Mountain Eagle (1926) Screenplay by Eliot Stannard. A lost film for which only a brief synopsis is available.

C**The Lodger, A Story of the London Fog* (1926). Screenplay Eliot Stannard from a novel by Marie Adelaide Belloc-Lowndes. Theatre and music references, chorus girls, painted portraits of fair haired women in the lodger's rented room, one of which, an allegorical image of a woman in bondage tied to a tree, the lodger is both repulsed by and attracted to. He attempts to turn the faces of these portraits to the wall exclaiming to his landlady Mrs. Bunting and her daughter Daisy: "I'm afraid I don't like these pictures." Daisy and her mother remove the paintings from the room. Windows and doorways are used as cinematographic framing devices in this key early film which become a common Hitchcock design strategy to either produce a framed *tableau vivant* within the cinema frame, to heighten tension, signal surveillance, point of view dynamism and/or structure lighting design.

Downhill (1927) Screenplay by Eliot Stannard based on a play by Ivor Novello and Constance Collier. Stage musical, chorus girls. A mirror is used as a framing device. Star actress Julia squirts perfume at a portrait of her leading man thus animating this image in an innovative fashion.

C**Easy Virtue* (1927) Screenplay by Eliot Stannard based on a play by Noel Coward. The film's title contains an Art Deco silhouette of camera with text reading "Virtue is its own reward they say but easy virtue is society's reward for a slandered reputation." The film contains a lengthy courtroom scene of a three-way scandal between Filton versus Filton and co-respondent Claude Robson, a philandering artist who fell in love with his employer and murdered the alcoholic husband. The film contains references to painting, art models, seduction, murder, class and betrayal throughout.

The Ring (1927) Screenplay by Alfred Hitchcock from his short story. Boxing, a fairground, dancing, music, posters, mirrors and doors as framing devices feature in this film.

The Manxman (1928) Screenplay Eliot Stannard, based on the novel by Sir Hall Caine. A Faustian title perhaps interpreted through Oscar Wilde. "What should it profit a man if he gain the whole world and lose his soul."

The Farmer's Wife (1928) Screenplay Eliot Stannard based on a play by Eden Phillpotts. Doors and windows used as framing devices.

Champagne (1928) Screenplay by Eliot Stannard, Alfred Hitchcock based on a story by Walter Mycroft. Features cabaret, music, dancing, various framing devices, windows, mirrors and doors.

C**Blackmail* (1929) Screenplay Benn [W] Levy (dialogue); Alfred Hitchcock (adaptation) based on a play by Charles Bennett. Alice the young woman Crewe an artist attempts to seduce and rape accidentally kills him. Music and two portraits, "The Joker" and a collaborative caricatural portrait by Alice and Crewe figure prominently in the narrative. The film includes the British Museum with antique sculpture and other artifacts prominent in the film's penultimate chase scene.

**Juno and the Paycock* (1930). Screenplay Alma Reville and Alfred Hitchcock based on a play by Sean O'Casey. This is a romantic narrative profiling the Irish Republic struggle. A statue of Mary and Jesus figure prominently in one scene. Window and gramophone as signal framing device and as a match cut editing feature.

**Elstree Calling* (1930). Screenplay Val Valentine. A short all-star musical review as an early ironic critique of television viewing.

C**Murder!* (1930). Screenplay Alma Reville and Alfred Hitchcock, Walter Mycroft adaptation based on play and novel *Enter Sir John* by Clarence Dane and Helen Simpson. Murder mystery containing music, art and theatre references throughout especially in Sir John's soliloquies and asides. "I am only a poor actor trying to apply the technique of my art to a problem of real life" Sir John philosophizes about artists "who use life to create art and art to criticize life." Wagner and Beethoven musical inserts. Hitchcockian mirrors, windows and doors as framing devices.

C**Mary* (1931) Screenplay Alma Reville, Herbert Juttka, Dr. Georg C. Klaren, based on the play *Enter Sir John* by Clarence Dane and Helen Simpson (German version of *Murder!*). Treat as above.

The Skin Game (1931) Screenplay Alma Reville and Alfred Hitchcock based upon play by John Galsworthy. Hornblowers' potteries, Tudor Mansion, and vista views through leaded window frames. Landscape vista dissolves into photograph of poster foregrounding veracity of representation motif.

Number Seventeen (1932). Screenplay Alma Reville, Alfred Hitchcock, Rodney Ackland based on play by J. Jefferson Farjeon. Expressionist use of lighting contrasts and Hitchcock exhibits his conventional use of stairs, windows and doors as framing devices. The film contains an exquisite model train chase and spectacular crash into a ferry during the final minutes.

Rich and Strange (1932) Screenplay Alma Reville, Val Valentine with additional dialogue by Hitchcock based on a theme by Dale Colins. Character in opening sequence exclaims, "Damn the pictures (movies) I want some life". Theatre references. Photographic art and graphic cartoon represented in key scenario.

Waltzes from Vienna (1933). Screenplay Alma Reville, Guy Bolton based on a play by Dr. A.M. Willner, Heinze Reichert and Ernst Mariscka. Dialogue: "What a fool! In Germany, they worship titles; here in Vienna, artists are superior." Carved marble stairs with life sized cupids and a carved grand piano are prominent symbols. Archways and doorways employed as framing devices.

The Man Who Knew Too Much (1934). Screenplay A. Rawlinson, Edwin Greenwood, Emyln Williams (dialogue) based on subject by D.B. Wyndham Lewis and Charles Bennett Curt Courant. Frames and framing. A MacGuffin is contained in the barber's shaving brush from St Moritz to neon signs of London and the nefarious dentist Dr. Barbor. A broach picturing a skier. Church and theatre (Albert Hall) become key architectural spaces.

The 39 Steps (1935) Screenplay Charles Bennett, Ian Hay (Dialogue) based on novel *The 39 Steps* by John Buchan. A significant use of windows as framing devices. Music Hall contexts, the London Palladium with Mr. Memory as the exemplary figure with the Secret of the 39 Steps in his unconscious mind.

**Secret Agent* (1936). Screenplay Charles Bennett, Ian Hay dialogue, Jesse Lasky additional dialogue from the play by Campbell Dixon adopted from Somerset Maugham's novel *Ashendon*. Film opens with Art Deco silhouette of soldiers on a battlefield. In the opening memorial sequence a large painted portrait of a young soldier hangs on the wall and becomes object of the gaze of the one armed attendant. Organ with dead organist playing a single drone chord features in one important scene. Mirrors, windows, doors and a telescope employed as framing devices. Art Deco silhouette of three dead soldiers in a closing sequence.

Sabotage (1936) Screenplay Charles Bennett, Alma Reville (adaption) Helen Simpson (dialogue from Joseph Conrad's novel *The Secret Agent*. The Bijou Cinema becomes a key symbolic space for projection and construction of suspense. The early animation film "Who killed Cock Robin?" becomes a film within a film, ironically framing suspenseful situation. This animated film may also be the origin for references to Cock Robin in Greenaway's mixed media drawing with the same title, *A Walk Through H* (1978) and *The Falls* (1980). An aquarium window and bus windows become important framing devices. Bird shop contains many artifacts.

Young and Innocent (1937) Screenplay Charles Bennett, Edwin Greenwood, Anthony Armstrong, Gerald Savory (dialogue) based upon the novel *Shilling for Candles* by Josephine Tey. Art Deco graphic appears in opening credits. Use of cobwebbed windows for framing. A stone statue figures prominently in two sequences. Band music, drumming (the drummer) perform important narrative functions.

The Lady Vanishes (1938) Screenplay Sidney Gilliat, Frank Launder, from novel *The Wheel Spins* by Ethel Lina White. Train windows used as important framing devices.

**Jamaica Inn* (1939) Screenplay Sydney Gilliat, Joan Harrison, J.B. Priestley (additional dialogue) from Daphne Du Maurier novel. Exquisite sculptural figurine produced into discussion about the nature of beauty by Sir Humphrey who receives the response "but it's not alive" from one of his guests. Sunburst floor tile pattern, wrought iron railing and a large painted portrait figure are prominent in two sequences.

C**Rebecca* (1940) Screenplay by Robert Sherwood, Joan Harrison, Philip MacDonald (adaptation with Michael Hogan) from the novel by Daphne du Maurier. The Manderley mansion becomes a primary animated architectural protagonist. X, the new Mrs. de Winter's recently deceased father was an artist (a painter). X is also an amateur painter. She sketches Mr. de Winter in an early courting sequence. After marriage X breaks Rebecca's priceless ceramic cherub and hides it in a drawer. A full length portrait of Lady Caroline de Winter dressed in white described as "Maxim's favorite" by Mrs. Danvers is used to intimidate X. who is dressed similarly. Windows and doors, mirrors, and curtains figure prominently in many scenes, as do a fashion magazine and a film projector.

Foreign Correspondent (1940) Screenplay by Charles Bennett, Joan Harrison, James Hilton (dialogue) Robert Benchley (dialogue). A gun is camouflaged as a camera to assassinate Van Meer. Westminster cathedral is a key architectural space.

Mr. and Mrs. Smith (1941) Screenplay by Norman Krasna. Window used as surveillance frame.

C**Suspicion* (1941). Screenplay by Samson Raphaelson, Joan Harrison, Alma Reville from novel *Before the Fact* by Francis Iles (Anthony Berkeley).   Art references include Picassoesque still life that twice attracts the attention of detective Benson and an animated three quarter length realist portrait of General McLaidlaw casts his imperious gaze over the relationship between Johnnie and Lina.

Saboteur (1942) Screenplay Piter Viertel, Joan Harrison, Dorothy Parker based upon original subject by Alfred Hitchcock. A group of circus entertainers (freaks) play significant role. Telescope as framing/surveillance device. Jewelry figures in one scene. Movie theatre sequence provides venue for the real life shoot out as the denouement.

C**_Shadow of a Doubt_ (1943) Screenplay Thornton Wilder, Alma Reville and Sally Benson from a story by Gordon McDonnell. Montage of dancers (_Merry Widows Waltz_) opens this important narrative detailing the complex relationship between two Charlies - "like twins." The photograph of Charlie and his sister Emma as children and the friendship ring given to young Charlie are important signifiers. Humorous debates between neighbours Herb and Joe about the perfect (aesthetic) murder according to the Thomas de Quincey prescription. A press photographer scene engages the ethics of unsolicited documentary photography. Windows, doors, curtains used as framing devices.

*_Lifeboat_ (1944) Screenplay Jo Zwerling based on original subject by John Steinbeck. The film contains numerous references to documentary filmmaking, fashion, and writing. (Connie Porter). Music and art figure as class signifiers. Close-up of Kovac's chest tattoo, a heart with the letters BM. Hitchcock's inventive cameo in a "Reduco" advertisement.

Bon Voyage (1944) Screenplay J Orton, Angus McPhail, based on original subject by Arthur Calder-Marshall. Opening scene in French Deuxieme Bureau shows large portrait of General Charles de Gaulle. A British Ministry of Information (propaganda) film.

Adventure Malagache (1944) British Ministry of Information war time film production. No writers listed. Mirror and poster described in synopsis (Sloan, 1995:198)

C**_Spellbound_ (1945) Screenplay Ben Hecht, Angus McPhail suggested by _The House of Dr. Edweardes_ by Francis Beeding (Hilary St. George Saunders and John Palmer).This film contains the famous dream sequence designed by surrealist painter Salvador Dali. Hitchcock expressed a wish to "break with the traditional way of handling dream sequences through a blurred and hazy screen." He discussed with Truffaut his reasons for contracting the Surrealist painter. "I asked Selznick if he could get Dali to work with us and he agreed, though I think he didn't really understand my reasons for wanting Dali. He probably thought I wanted his collaboration for publicity purposes. "The real reason" Hitchcock disclosed "was that I wanted to convey the dreams with great visual sharpness and clarity, sharper than the film itself. I wanted Dali because of the sharpness of his work. (De) Chirico has the same quality, you know, the long shadows, the infinity of distance, and the converging lines of perspective" He later admitted that "he didn't care for the scenario" (Truffaut, 1966:118). Doors, windows, mirrors figure prominently. John Ballantine's fixation is on drawn lines, napkin, paper, bedspread and snow.

Notorious (1946) Screenplay Ben Hecht based on a subject by Alfred Hitchcock. Opening close-up shot of a hand holding a camera and panning over group of photographers and reporters outside a courthouse. Contemporary art works adorn Alicia's house. Sebastian's mansion also contains equestrian paintings.

The Paradine Case (1947) Screenplay David O Selznick, Alma Reville (adaption) from novel by Robert Hitchens. Hitchcock's art training reinforced his meticulous control of set details and he often used these to provide key signifiers to the action. In the first sequence Mrs. Paradine stares at a life size painting of a uniformed gentleman. In a key dramatic scene in T*he Paradine Case* a fat woman is shown munching on an apple to the side of a mid shot of the central protagonists in the film. Discussing this with Truffaut he said "... what I am trying to bring out is that these elaborate details are generally overlooked by the public because all the attention is focused on the major characters in the scene. Therefore you put them in for your own satisfaction, and of course for the sake of enriching the film."[2] A huge oval portrait of Mrs. Paradine is embedded in the headboard of her bed and becomes the object of attention of a driver in one scene in the film. Windows, doors used as framing devices. Hitchcock does his cameo as a man leaving the train and Cumberland Station carrying a cello.

C**Rope* (1948) Screenplay Arthur Laurents, Hume Cronyn from the play by Patrick Hamilton. Framed printed image or drawing is closely examined by woman. A few references to art and culture in the dialogue set against a beautifully painted and changing cityscape backdrop. Windows key framing devices, as is a large painting of grey hooded figures near the Cassone containing the body of David. The murder constructed as a perfect orgasmic work of art by Phillip and Brandon Nietzschean 'supermen' c.w. Thomas de Quincey's aesthetics of murder.

C**Under Capricorn* (1949) James Bridie, Hume Cronyn based on a novel by Helen Simpson. Art reference provided in Wood, *Hitchcock's Films Revisited*. "The famous moment when Adare persuades Henrietta to look at herself in the mirror he improvises by holding up his coat behind a pane of glass. It is swiftly followed by his gift of a real mirror, asking her whom she sees in it, and answering for her "Lady Henrietta Considine" thereby eliminating Frisky and the marriage. The image "is the first artwork I've done."[3] Close-ups of "still life" dessert fruit on dining room table and the penultimate shrunken head.

Stage Fright (1950) Screenplay Whitfield Cook, Alma Reville (adaption) from novel by Selwyn Jepson. Theatre references throughout. The final "bringing down of the curtain" that kills Jonathon provides a suitably ironic and artfully dramatic ending. Doors and windows as framing devices.

**Strangers on a Train* (1951) Novel by Patricia Highsmith with screen adaptation by Raymond Chandler, Czenzi Ormonde, Whitfield Cook. Bruno's mother shows him her wonderfully gross expressionistic portrait of his father that occasions great hilarity. The perfect murder concocted by Bruno for him to be rid of his father and Guy Haines, his wife. Hitchcock's cameo shows him struggling on board a train with his cello.

I Confess (1951) Screenplay George Tabori, William Archibald adapted from the play *Nos Deux Consciences* by Paul Anthelme. Father Paul paints the rectory anteroom wall. His superior Father Milet asks him how long it will take to finish and if he knows any "paints that do not smell." Religious relics, paintings and sculptures adorn the church. Quebec City and Chateau Frontenac; door frames and windows figure prominently.

C**Dial M for Murder* (1953) Screenplay Frederick Knott. Grace Kelly's icy beauty and diaphanous dress in *Dial M for Murder* connote to be looked-at-ness and the strangling scene itself is a tightly choreographed aestheticisation of violence providing, like so many of Hitchcock's other film murders, an example of his high art. Hitchcock's meticulous attention to detail is very evident in this film. He chose two prints by Rosa Bonheur, Wedgewood and Staffordshire figurines, oriental Buddhas, teacups and tennis trophies for the mantelpiece of the Wendice apartment in Maida Vale, a tony district of London. After the first take of the famous scissors scene in which Grace Kelly stabs her assailant in the back Hitchcock reportedly said: "This is nicely done but there wasn't enough gleam to the scissors, and murder without gleaming scissors is like asparagus without a hollandaise sauce."[4] How like Hitchcock to link murder with food; but of course, he also linked murder with sex and art, the latter providing a neat squaring of the circle. For Hitchcock the art of murder rather than being a source of cheap entertainment should and could be compared to the transcendent perfection idealized in the work of the great artists - masters - within the art historical canon. And if a few artists had to be murdered in the quest to achieve immortality, so be it. As the camera pans over the body it moves back to quickly take in a pile of three large art books - monographs on Giovanni Bellini, Leonardo Da Vinci and the third an indecipherable monograph but possibly the other key figure from the Italian renaissance, Michelangelo.

**Rear Window* (1954). Screenplay John Michael Hayes based on short story by Cornell Woolrich. Signal references throughout to the lively arts: photography, sculpture, painting, design, music (opera, jazz, popular music), dance, gourmet food and fashion. Windows, doors, telescope and a camera figure as important surveillance and framing devices.

To Catch a Thief (1954) Screenplay by John Michael Hayes based on a novel by David Dodge. Posters, windows and doors employed as framing devices. Narrative focus is upon the jewelry theft by cat burglar John Robie (Cary Grant). A Watteau like *fête gallant* in final sequences of party guests in eighteenth century costumes and masks.

C***The Trouble with Harry* (1955) Screenplay John Michael Hayes based on a novel by John Trevor Story. Sam Marlow a young artist struggling with his 'aesthetic identity' and Harry a dead man who can't be gotten rid of. Finally Sam is discovered by a critic and a millionaire who claim his paintings as "works of genius." Art and art history references throughout with a specific emphasis on abstraction.

The Man Who Knew Too Much (1956) Screenplay by John Michael Hayes, based upon a story by Charles Bennett and D.B. Wynham-Lewis. Ambrose Chappell taxidermy shop contains many exotic animal skins. Albert Hall, and a play within a play with percussive music performance as primary opening and closing sequences.

The Wrong Man (1956) Screenplay Maxwell Anderson, Angus McPhail based on *The true story of Emmanuel Balestrero* by Anderson. In a final sequence 'wrong man' jazz musician Manny stares fixedly at a picture of the Sacred Heart. His reflection is double exposed with his doppelgänger walking down a street. Windows, doors, shadowy hallway and stairs are used as key framing devices throughout.

C**Vertigo* (1957) Screenplay Alec Oppel, Samuel Taylor based on novel *D'entre les Morts* by Pierre Boileau and Thomas Narcejac. Saul Bass produced the dizzying spirals with juxtaposed eyes Lissajous' spirals invented by the French mathematician to express mathematical formulas (McGilligan, 561). Paintings by Midge and her studio apartment contain many modernist *objets d'art*. Her studio apartment also features large picture windows. Madeleine frequents the enigmatic three quarter length oil portrait of Carlotta Valdez in the museum (Palace of the Legion of Honour). Midge imbricates her own image upon her copy of the painting in order to shock Scottie into paying her more attention. Scottie represents his image (memory) of Madeleine in Judy thus turning her into a fetish object. San Francisco architecture references throughout.

***North by Northwest* (1959) Screenplay Ernest Lehman. Glen Cove estate contains many artworks on the wall, mostly innocuous landscapes and equestrian paintings. United Nations building conference room contains large wall maps. Palimpsest (magic note pad) provides Roger with address destination of Eve Kendall. Grand Central Station figures prominently and a major action sequence occurs in a Sotheby's like art auction with Roger bidding extravagantly on several art objects. Mount Rushmore sculptures (reconstructed) provide final suspense filled moments as Eve and Roger escape their pursuers.

C***Psycho* (1960) screenplay Joseph Stephano based on a novel by Robert Bloch. A reproduction of a version of the painting *Susannah surprised at her bath by the Elders* and in Norman's anteroom covers a hole through which he surveys Janet Leigh. Another painting an allegorical rape scene adorns the wall of the room which also contains many stuffed animals and birds revealing Norman's hobby - taxidermy. The film also contains doors, windows, mirrors, sunglasses, and curtains as important framing devices. Norman's/ mother's house also contains significant allegorical paintings and figurines.

***The Birds* (1963) Screenplay Evan Hunter from the short story by Daphne Du Maurier The house of Mitch's mother contains original art, framed prints and the Bodega Bay café has reproductions of landscape and seascapes on its walls. Frames and windows as framing devices but not much else in this very artfully constructed film!

**Marnie* (1964) Screenplay Jay Presson Allen from Winston Graham's novel. Marnie's mother's home contains some innocuous class accented images on the wall. Mark Rutland's luxurious office contains many examples of pre-Columbian art. Storm causes tree branch to crash through the window thus revealing a small vitrine full of ethnological artifacts. The colour red in various contexts (example: the large red (modernist) dots on the jockey's clothing) stimulates Marnie's childhood neurosis.

Torn Curtain (1966) Screenplay Brian Moore. Elaborate maze like geometric floor and empty galleries in East Berlin Museum. Ballet performance provides exciting finale. Windows and doors serve as important framing devices.

**Topaz* (1969) Screenplay Samuel Taylor based on a novel by Leon Uris. Kusenov's are trying to exit Moscow and enter a factory involved in the manufacture of porcelain figurines. Close-up of a figurine of kissing couple is broken by Tamara. Juanita's house in Cuba has artwork distributed throughout. Francois sketches Henri in an important scene before he is killed.

C**Frenzy* (1972) Screenplay Anthony Shaffer based on the novel *Goodbye Piccadilly, Hello Leicester Square* by Arthur La Bern. An Hitchcockian auteur film à *la lettre*, with Hitchcock riffing on Hitchcock throughout. References to: wrong man themes, food (French *cordon bleu* gourmet versus standard English fare, especially breakfast of sausages, (bangers) bacon, fried bread and tomatoes, jails, blondes, mother, shot through with favorite little Hitch apothegms, proverbs, stock phrases hackneyed sayings, ironic slogans, catchwords. "Bob's yer uncle" :I'm alright Jack and pull up the ladder" you know what they say "virtue is its own reward" and "everybody expects a bad penny to turn up sooner of later." Frenzy includes two whistling scenes and each significant space for the interior scenes: apartments, pub bars, hotel room have specially chosen art works on the wall providing some accent to the character of the protagonists or to the diegesis. Example: Bob Rusk's walk-up apartment near Covent Garden has two famously mass reproduced popular prints of 'factory paintings' of beautiful Eurasian women and a cheap reproduction of a group of flamenco dancers to emphasize his bachelorhood and low brow working class (low competency in Bourdieu's sense) status. The upscale apartment of Hetty and Johnny, who provide refuge for Dicko Blaney, contains several modernist popular landscape prints and one painting of a game bird (pheasant). Brenda Blaney's Club contains an imperious looking eighteenth century sculpture of a male bust and an oval framed romantic English landscape painting in rear of restaurant framing respectively Brenda and Dick as they discuss Blaney's hard luck. The dining room and kitchen of the Inspector's house contains black and white photographs on the wall and an unidentified standing figure (approx 2' h) in the kitchen. Coburg Road Hotel where Babs and Blaney spend a night in the cupid room has a long rectangular reproduction over the queen-sized bed of a generic reclining nude (possibly a reproduction of a Joshua Reynolds' painting).

Family Plot (1976) Screenplay Ernest Lehman based upon novel *The Rainbird Pattern* by Victor Canning. Julia Rainbird's mansion contains many framed images revealing her collecting habits. Psychic's glass ball, beaded curtain, chandelier and wind chimes are prominent signifiers. Reference to "the perfect murder" in the Gothic Cathedral. Doors, windows, sunglasses, and artful hair colours!

 *Denotes implicit references to cultural production, with some references to art, artists and/or art history
** Denotes explicit references to art, artists and/or art history
C** Denotes art/crime conflation

---

[1]This list has been compiled from viewing the films in my Hitchcock collection and others that were available through local video rental stores. I am also indebted to Sloan, J. *Alfred Hitchcock: The Definitive Bibliography* Berkeley, Los Angeles University of California Press 1999; Spoto, D. *The Dark Side of Genius: The Life of Alfred Hitchcock* New York: Ballantine Books, 1983, and McGilligan, P *Alfred Hitchcock: A Life in Darkness and Light.* New York, Regan Books Harper Collins, 2003
[2]Truffaut, F., with Scott, H.G. *Hitchcock* New York: Simon and Schuster 1967: 154
[3]Robin Wood's *Hitchcock's Films Revisited* p.332
[4] Spoto, D. *The Dark Side of Genius: the Life of Alfred Hitchcock* New York: Ballantine Books, 1983:.368

Bibliography

Adamson, W. *Hegemony and Revolution: A Study of Antonio Gramsci's Political and Cultural Theory* Berkeley, University of California Press 1980

Adorno, T. *Negative Dialectics* New York, Seabury 1973

Adorno, T. *Introduction to the Sociology of Music* New York, Seabury 1976

Agamben, G, *Potentialities: Collected Essays in Philosophy.* Trans. Daniel Heller-Roazen Stanford University Press. Stanford, 2000

Agamben, G, *Means without End: Notes on Politics.* Trans. Vincenzo Binetti and Cesare Casarino. Minneapolis, University of Minnesota Press. Theory Out of Bounds, V. 20, 2000

Agamben, G. *The Man without Content.* Trans. Georgia Albert Stanford University Press. Stanford, 1999

Agamben, G. *The Coming Community.* Minneapolis, Theory Out of Bounds, Vol. 1. University of Minnesota Press, 1993

Agamben, Giorgio, *Remnants of Auschwitz.* Trans. Daniel Heller-Roazen New York, Zone Books. 1999

Agamben, Giorgio, *Stanzas: Word and Phantasm in Western Culture.* Trans. Ronald L. Martinez Theory and History of Literature, Vol. 69. Minneapolis, University of Minnesota Press. 1993

Allen R. and Gonzales S. I. *Alfred Hitchcock: Centenary Essays* London British Film Institute 1999

Allen, R. "Critical Theory and the Paradox of Modernist Discourse" Postmodern *Screen* Issue 28, 2: 69-85 1987

Allen, C.C. *Are You Fed Up with Modern Art?* Tulsa, Rainbow Press 1952

Althusser, L. *For Marx* trans. B. Brewster London N.L. Books 1977

Althusser, L. *Lenin and Philosophy and Other Essays.* Trans B. Brewster London N.L. Books 1971

Anderson, P. *Considerations on Western Marxism* London NLR Books 1976

Andrew, D. *Concepts in Film Theory* Oxford, New York Oxford University Press 1984

Arac, J. *Postmodernism and Politics* Manchester, Manchester University Press 1986

Arac, J. *Genealogies: Historical Situations for Post-Modern Literary Studies* New York Columbia University Press 1987

Arato, A. & Gebhardt E., *The Essential Frankfurt School Reader* Intro. P. Piccone New York, Urizen Books 1978

The Armory Show: International Exhibition of Modern Art 1913 New York Arno Press 1972

Aronowitz, S. *How Class Works: Power and Social Movements* New Haven, Yale University Press 2003

Auiler, D., *Hitchcock's Notebooks* London Avon Books 1999

Badiou, Alain. *Ethics: An Essay on the Understanding of Evil.* Verso Books. New York, 2001

Badiou, Alain, Trans. Jorge Jauregui *Art and Philosophy. Lacanian ink* 17. The Wooster Press. Fall 2000

Badiou, Alain,. "The Political as a Procedure of Truth." Trans. Barbara P. Fulks *Lacanian Ink* 19. The Wooster Press. Fall 2001,

Bakhtin, M. *Rabelais and His World*, Trans. Herlene Iswolsky Boston, MIT Press 1965.

Bakhtin, M. *The Dialogic Imagination* Trans. Caryl Emerson and Michael Holquist, Austin, U of Texas 1981

Barber, B. *Reading Rooms* Halifax, N.S. Eyelevel Gallery 1992

Barber, B., Guilbaut, S. and O'Brian, J. *Voices of Fire: Art, Rage, Power and the State.* Toronto, University of Toronto Press 1996

Barber, B. *Performance [Performance] Performers: Essays and Conversations* edited Marc Léger Toronto, YYZ Press 2008

Barber, B. (Ed) *Condé+Beveridge: Class Works* Halifax, NSCAD Press 2008

Barker, F. *The Politics of Theory*, Colchester: University of Essex Press, 1983

Barthes, R. *Writing Degree Zero* London, Cape 1967

Barthes, R. *Mythologies* London, Cape 1972

Barthes, R. *The Pleasure of the Text* Trans R. Miller, New York Hill and Wang 1975

Barthes. R. *Image Music Text* Trans. Stephen Heath New York, Hill and Wang 1985

Baudrillard, J. *Oublier Foucault* Paris Editions Galilee 1987

Baudrillard, J. *For a Critique of the Political Economy of the Sign* St Louis, Montana 1986

Baudrillard, J. *The Mirror of Production* trans. M. Poster St. Louis, Telos Press 1975

Baudelaire, C. *Art in Paris 1845-1862 Reviews of Salons and other Exhibitions* Trans. and ed. J.Mayne London New York Phaidon 1965

Baudelaire, C. *Selected Writings on Art and Artists* trans. with Intro P.E Charvet, Harmondsworth Penguin 1972

Bauman, Z. *Legislators and Interpreters: On Modernity, Post-Modernity and Intellectuals* Ithaca N.Y. Cornell U Press 1987

Baxandall, L. *Marxism and History Proceedings of the Marxist Caucus*, College Art Association Meeting 1972

Bazin A. *What is Cinema?* Trans. and ed. Hugh Gray, 2 vols. Berkeley and Los Angeles, University of California Press 1967-71

Benjamin, W. *Illuminations* edited with an introduction by Hannah Arendt, H. Zohn Trans. N Y Schocken Books 1969

Benjamin, W. *The Arcades Project* trans. Howard Eiland and Kevin McLaughlin. Cambridge Mass., and London Harvard University Press 1999

Bennett, T., Martin, G., Mercer, C. & Woollacott, J.(eds) *Culture, Ideology and Social Process: A Reader* London, Open University Press 1981

Ben-Porat, Z. "Method in Madness: Notes on the Structure of Parody, Based on MAD TV Satires" *Poetics Today* 1

Bergson, H., *Laughter: An Essay on the Meaning of the Comic* Trans. Brereton and Rothwell, London, Macmillan 1911

Bernstein, R (Ed) *Habermas and Modernity* Cambridge, Mass. MIT Press 1985

Bhabha, H.K. *The Location of Culture* New York, Routledge 1994

Bhaskar, R. *Scientific Realism and Human Emancipation* London, Verso 1986

Black, J.*The Aesthetics of Murder: A Study in Romantic Literature and Contemporary Culture* Baltimore, The John Hopkins University Press 1991

Bocock, R. *Hegemony* The Open University Key Ideas Series, Chichester, London, Ellis Harwood/Tavistock Publishers 1986

Bois, Y-A *Reinhardt* San Francisco MOCA catalogue 1991

Bois, Y-A, Krauss, R., et al (eds). *October: The Second Decade, 1986-1996.* October Books Cambridge, Mass., MIT Press. 1998

Bois, Y-A. "Barnett Newman's Sublime = Tragedy." In *Negotiating Rapture.* Exhibition catalogue. Chicago, Museum of Contemporary Art 1996

Bois Y-A. *Formless: A User's Guide.* New York Zone Books. 1997

Bolton, R. (Ed) *Culture Wars: Documents from the Recent Controversies in the Arts* New York, The New Press 1992

Booth, W. A *Rhetoric of Irony* Chicago and London Chicago U Press 1974

Bordwell, D., Staiger, J., and Thompson, K., *The Classical Hollywood Cinema: Film, Style and Mode of Production to 1960* New York, Columbia University Press 1985

Bourdieu, P & Darbel, A. *L'amour de l'art: Les Musees et leur public* Paris Editions de Minuit 1966

Bourdieu, P. and Passeron, J.C. *Reproduction in Education, Society and Culture* Trans. Richard Nice London, Beverly Hills, Sage Publications 1977

Bourdieu, P. *Outline of a Theory of Practice* Cambridge, Trans R. Nice, London, New York, Cambridge U Press 1977

Bourdieu, P. *Distinction: A Social Critique of the Judgement of Taste* Translated by Richard Nice, Cambridge Mass. Harvard University Press 1984

Bourdieu, P. *The Logic of Practice* Stanford, Stanford University Press 1990, original Paris, Les Editions de Miniut 1980

Bozovic, Miran and Slavoj Žižek. *An Utterly Dark Spot: Gaze and Body in Early Modern Philosophy (The Body, in Theory: Histories of Cultural Materialism).* University of Michigan Press. June 2000

Brantlinger, P. *Crusoe's Footprints: Cultural Studies in Britain and America* New York Routledge 1990

Brennan, T and Jay, M. *Vision in Context: Historical and Contemporary Perspectives on Sight* New York, Routledge 1996

Brunette, P and Wills, D., *Screen/Play: Derrida and Film Theory* Princeton, N.J Princeton University Press 1989

Buck-Morss, S. *The Dialectics of Seeing: Walter Benjamin and the Arcades Project* Cambridge MA MIT Press 1990

Buchloh, B., Guilbaut, S., and Solkind, D., *Modernism and Modernity: The Proceedings from the Vancouver Conference.* Halifax, NSCAD and NYU Press 1983, 2004

Burawoy, M. *The Politics of Production* London Verso 1985

Burch, N. *Theory of Film Practice*, trans. Helen R. Lane New York: Praeger, 1973

Bürger, P. *Theory of the Avant-Garde*, Minneapolis, University of Minnesota Theory and History of Literature Vol 4 1984

Butler, Judith, Ernesto Laclau and Slavoj Žižek. *Contingency, Hegemony, Universality: Contemporary Dialogues on the Left.* London, New York,, Verso Books. 2000,

Calinescu, M. *Faces of Modernity* Bloomington, Indiana University Press 1977

Callinicos, A. *Marxism and Philosophy* London, Oxford University Press 1985

Castoriadis, C. *World in Fragments: Writings on Politics, Society, Psychoanalysis, and the Imagination* Stanford, California Stanford University Press 1997

Chabrol, C. & Rohmer, Eric. *Hitchcock: the First Forty-Four Films*, Trans. Stanley Hochman, New York, Frederick Ungar, 1979

Cheetham, M. *The Rhetoric of Purity: Essentialist theory and the Advent of Abstract Painting'* Cambridge, Cambridge University Press 1991

Clark, T.J. *The Absolute Bourgeois: Art & Politics in France 1848-1851* New York and London 1973

Clark, T.J. *Image of the People Gustave Courbet and the Second French Republic 1848-1851* New York and London 1973

Cohen, P M *Alfred Hitchcock: The Legacy of Victorianism* Lexington, Kentucky: University Press of Kentucky, 1995.

Copjec, Joan, Slavoj Žižek and Alain Badiou. *Umbr(a): Science and Truth.* Center for Psychoanalysis and Culture.2000.

Copjec, J (ed) *Supposing the Subject* New York Routledge 1994

Coward, R. and Ellis, J. *Language and Materialism: Developments in Semiology and the Theory of the Signifier* London, Routledge & Kegan Paul, 1975

Crow, T., *Modern Art in the Common Culture* New Haven and London, Yale University Press 1996

Crystal, David *The Cambridge Encyclopedia of the English Language* Cambridge University 1995

Dane, J. *Parody: Critical Concepts versus Literary Practices,* Aristophanes to Sterne Norman and London, U of Oklahoma Press 1988

Dane, J. *The Critical Mythology of Irony* Athens Georgia and London, the University of Georgia Press 1991

De Quincey T. *Confessions of an Opium Eater* Edinburgh, Adam and Charles Black 1822

De Quincey, T *On Murder Considered as one of the Fine Arts* Edinburgh, Adam and Charles Black 1827

De Quincey, T. *Published and Unpublished Works 1853 -1860* Edinburgh, Adam and Charles Black (14 Volumes)

de Certeau, M. *Ecriture de l'histoire* Paris, Gallimand 1975

De Duve, T. *Att nom de l'art* Paris, Editions Minuit 1989

De Duve, T. *Resonnance du readymade* Paris, Jaqueline Chambon 1989

De Lauretis T. and Heath, S. *The Cinematic Apparatus*, (ed.) London St. Martins Press 1980

De Lauretis, T. *Feminist Studies/Critical Studies* Bloomington Ind., Indiana University Press. 1986

De Man, P. *Resistance to Theory* Minneapolis University of Minnesota Press 1986

De Man, P. *Allegories of Reading: Figural Language in Rousseau, Nietzsche, Rilke and Proust* New Haven, Yale University Press 1979

Denzin, N. K. *The Cinematic Society: The Voyeur's Gaze* London, Sage 1995

Derrida, J. *The Truth in Painting* Trans. Bennington, G. and McLeod, I., Chicago, University of Chicago Press, 1987

Derrida, J. *Writing and Difference* Trans. A Bass, London, Routledge Kegan Paul 1978

Derrida, J. *The Post-card: From Socrates to Freud and Beyond* Trans. A. Bass Chicago, University of Chicago Press 1987

Derrida, J. *Of Grammatology* Trans. G. Spivak Baltimore, John Hopkins University Press 1976

Derrida, J. *Dissemination* translated with an introduction by B. Johnson Chicago, Chicago University Press 1981

Dewey J. *Art as Experience* New York G.P Putnum & Sons 1934

Dews, P. *Logics of Disintegration: Post-Structuralist Thought and the Claims of Critical Theory* London Verso 1987

Dunlap, I. *The Shock of the New*. St. Louis, San Francisco, American Heritage Press 1972

During, S. (Ed) *The Cultural Studies Reader* London and New York Routledge 1993

Eagleton, T. "Capitalism, Modernism and Post-Modernism" New Left Review 152:60-73 1984

Eagleton, T. *The Ideology of the Aesthetic* London, Basil Blackwell 1989

Eco, U. *The Role of the Reader: Explorations in the Semiotics of Texts* Bloomington, Indiana University Press 1979

Eco, U. *Semiotics and the Philosophy of Language* Bloomington, University of Indiana Press 1984

Eco, U. *Interpretation and Over Interpretation* Cambridge, New York, Cambridge University Press 1992

Elliot, B., and Purdy, A. *Peter Greenaway, Architecture Allegory* London: Academy Editions 1997

Ellis, J. et al *Screen Reader I Cinema Ideology Politics* London, The Society for Education in Film and Television 1977

Estren, M.J. A *History of Underground Comics* Berkeley Straight Arrow Books 1974, 1987

Feinberg, L. *Introduction to Satire* Ames, Iowa, the Iowa State University Press 1967.

Fokkema, D and Bertens, H (Eds) *Approaching Postmodernism* Amsterdam, Philadelphia, John Benjamins 1986

Foster, H.(ed) *The Anti-Aesthetic: Essays on Post-Modern Culture.* Port Townsend, Washington 1983

Foucault, M., *The Order of Things*: *An Archeology of the Human Sciences* New York, Random House 1971

Foucault, M. *The History of Sexuality Volume I:* An Intro. Trans R. Hurley New York Vintage Books, Random House 1978

Foucault, M. *The Archeology of Knowledge* Trans A.M. Sheridan-Smith New York, Harper and Row 1972

Foucault, M. *Language, Counter-memory, Practice* Trans. Bouchard and Simon Ithaca N.Y. Cornell University Press 1977

Freud, S. *Wit and its Relation to the Unconscious.* Trans. and Intro A.A. Brill, London, Kegan Paul, Trench, Trubner & Co 1926

Freud, S. *The Standard Edition of the Complete Works of Sigmund Freud* London, Hogarth Press 1960

Freud, S. *Leonardo da Vinci and a Memory of His Childhood* New York, Norton 1964

Freud, S, *Moses and Monotheism,* New York, Knopf 1939

Fried, M. *Realism, Writing Disfiguration: On Thomas Eakins and Stephen Crane* Chicago, University of Chicago Press 1987

Fry, R. *Vision and Design* London, Chatto and Windus 1921

Fussell, P. *Class: A Guide through the American Status system* New York, Touchstone 1983

Gagnier R. (Ed) *Critical Essays on Oscar Wilde* Toronto, Macmillan 1991

Gaillie D. *Social Inequality and Class Radicalism in France and Britain* Cambridge, Cambridge University Press 1983

Gans, H. *Popular Culture and High Culture* New York, Basic Books 1974

Garvin, R. (Ed) *Romanticism, Modernism, Postmodernism* Lewisberg, Pa., Bucknell University Press; London Associated University Press 1980

Giddens A. *The Class Structure of Advanced Societies*, London 1973

Giddens A. "Modernism and Post-Modernism" New German Critique 22 15-18 1981

Gitlin, T. *Years of Hope, Days of Rage* New York, Bantam Books 1988

Goldstein, J & McGhee P. (Eds) *The Psychology of Humour: Theoretical Perspectives and Empirical Issues*, New York and London, Academic Press 1972

Gramsci, A. *Selections from the Prison Notebooks of Antonio Gramsci.* Edited and trans. Q. Hoare and G. Nowell Smith, London, Lawrence and Wishart 1971 a selection from the original Italian Edition: A Gramsci *Quaderni del Carere* (1928-1935) (ed) V. Gerratana, Turin, Einaudi, 1948-51

Gramsci, A. *Selections from Political Writings Vol. I 1910-1920* and *Vol. II 1921-1926* ed and translations Hoare, Q. and Mathews London, Lawrence and Wishart 1977, 1978

Grossberg, L., Nelson, C & Treichler, P. (Eds) *Cultural Studies* New York London Routledge 1992

Greenberg, C. *Art and Culture* Boston, Beacon 1962

Grosz, E. (ed) *Space, Time and Perversion: Essays on the Politics of Bodies* London and New York Routledge (1995)

Guilbaut, S. *How New York Stole the Idea of Modern Art* Chicago, University of Chicago Press 1983

Guilbaut, S.(ed) *Reconstructing Modernism* Cambridge Mass., MIT Press 1990

Gurevitch, M., Bennett, T., Curran J. and Woollacott, J.,(Eds) Culture, Society and the Media London, Methuen 1982

Habermas, J. *Knowledge and Human Interests* Trans. J. Shapiro London, Heinemann 1972

Habermas, J. *"Modernity: An Incomplete Project"* Trans. S. Ben-Habib, in H. Foster (ed.), *Postmodern Culture. London: Pluto Press.* 1983

Habermas, J. *The Philosophical Discourse of Modernity* Oxford University Press 1987

Hadjinicoloau, N. *Art History and Class Struggle.* Trans. Louis Asmal, London, Pluto Press 1978

Hall, S., Clarke, J., Jefferson, T., & Roberts, B., (Eds) *Resistance Through Rituals: Youth Subcultures in Postwar Britain* London, Hutchinson 1976ʹ

Hall, S. "Cultural Studies: Two Paradigms" in R. Collins et. al. *Media Culture and Society a Critical Reader* London, Sage 1986

Hammerton, J.A. *Punch Library of Humour Stage and Studio* London Educational Book Co c. 1863

Handwerk, G. *Irony and Ethics in Narrative: From Schlegel to Lacan* New Haven and London, Yale University Press 1985

Hanninen, S., and Paldan, L.(eds) *Rethinking Ideology* Paris International General IMMRC 1982

Hardt, M., and Negri, A. *Empire* Cambridge MA Harvard University Press 2000

Hassan, I. *The Dismemberment of Orpheus: Toward a Post-Modern Literature* New York Oxford University Press 1971Hassan, I. *Paracriticisms: Seven Speculations of the Times* Urbana, Ill. 1975

Hassan, I. "The Culture of Postmodernism". Theory Culture and Society 2 (3), 119-32 1985

Haug, W.F. *Commodity Aesthetics, Ideology and Culture.* New York and Bagnolet International General 1987

Hebdige, D., *Subculture: The Meaning of Style* London, Methuen 1979

Heidegger, M. *An Introduction to Metaphysics* trans. Ralph Manheim New Haven London, Yale University Press 1987 (first published 1959).

Hesse, H. *Magister Ludi (The Glass Bead Game)* New York, Bantam Books 1970, originally under the title *Das Glasperlenspiel* Fretz &Wesmuth Ag Zurich 1943

Highet, G. *The Anatomy of Satire* Princeton New Jersey, Princeton University Press 1962

Hirschkop, K & Sheperd D.(eds) *Bahktin and Cultural Theory* Manchester, Manchester University Press 1989

Hobbes, T. *Leviathan* London, Fontana 1962

Hobsbawm, E. and Ranger, Terence (Eds) *The Invention of Tradition* Cambridge University Press 1984

Holt, E.G.(ed) *The Triumph of Art For the Public: The Emerging Role of Exhibitions and Critics* New York Anchor Press Doubleday 1979

Hutcheon, L. *A Theory of Parody: The Teachings of Twentieth Century Art Forms* London and New York Methuen 1985

Hutcheon, L. *A Poetics of Postmodernism: History Theory Fiction* New York, London Routledge Kegan Paul 1988

Hutcheon, L. *The Politics of Post-Modernism* London, N.Y., Routledge 1989

Hutcheon, L. *Splitting Images: Contemporary Canadian Ironies* Oxford, Toronto Oxford University Press 1991

Hutcheon, L. *Irony's Edge: The Theory and Politics of Irony* London, New York Routledge 1994

Huyssen, A. *After The Great Divide: Modernism, Mass Culture, Post-Modernism* Bloomington, Indiana University Press 1986

Jacobs, F. *The Mad World of William M. Gaines* New York Bantam Books 1973

Jameson, F. *Postmodernism* Durham Duke University Press 1991

Johnston, R. D. "The Staging of the Bourgeois Imaginary in *The Cook, The Thief, His Wife and her Lover* (1990). *Cinema Journal* 41:2 winter 2002

Kaplan, E A. (Ed) *Postmodernism and its Discontents: Theories, Practices.* London, New York Verso 1988

Kapsis, R. *Hitchcock: the Making of a Reputation* Chicago: University of Chicago Press, 1992

Kennedy, E. *A Philosophe in the Age of Revolution: Destutt de Tracy and the Origins of Ideology* Philadelphia, The American Philosophical Society 1978

Kermode, F. *The Sense of an Ending* London and New York Oxford University Press 1967

Klein, M. *Developments in Psychoanalysis* New York, Da Capo Press 1983

Knott, F. *Dial "M" for Murder* New York, Random House, 1953.

Kracauer, S. *Theory of Film: The redemption of Physical Reality* New York Oxford University Press 1965 (1956)

Krauss, R. *The Originality of the Avant-Garde and Other Modernist Myths* Cambridge Mass and London MIT Press 1985

Kris, E. *Psychoanalytic Explorations in Art* New York, International Universities Press 1952

Kristeva, J. *Desire in Language* New York, University of Columbia Press 1980

Kristeva, J. *Powers of Horror: An Essay on Abjection* trans. Leon S. Roudiez New York Columbia University Press 1982

Kristeva, J. *Strangers to Ourselves* New York: Harvester Wheatsheaf 1991

Kuhn, A. *The Power of the Image: Essays on Representation and Sexuality* London Routledge, Kegan Paul 1985

Lacan, J. *Ecrits: A Selection* Trans A Sheridan-Smith London, Tavistock 1977

Lacan, J. *The Four Fundamental Concepts of Psycho-Analysis* edited Miller trans A Sheridan New York ,W.W. Norton 1977

Laclau, E and Mouffe, C. *Hegemony and Socialist Strategy* London Verso 1985

Lakatos K. and Musgrave, L. *Criticism and the Growth of Knowledge, International Colloquium in the Philosophy of Science* Vol 4, Cambridge, Cambridge University Press 1965

Lapsley, R and Westlake M. (eds.) *Film Theory an Introduction* Manchester, Manchester University Press, 1988.

Lasch, C. *The Culture of Narcissism: American Life in the Age of Diminishing Expectations* New York Norton 1978

Lawrence, Amy *The Films of Peter Greenaway* Cambridge University Press 1997

Leavis, F.R and Thompson D. *Culture and Environment*, London, Chatto and Windus 1937

Lebel, J-P. *Cinema et idéologie* Paris: Editions Sociales, 1971

Lee, R. "Ut Pictura Poesis, The Humanistic Theory of Painting" Art Bulletin 22:4 1940

Leyton, E. *Hunting Humans: The Rise of the Modern Multiple Murderer* London Blake Publishing 2001

Lowenthal, L. "Historical Perspectives of Popular Culture" American Journal of Sociology Vol. 55 1950

Lowenthal, L. *Literature Popular Culture, and Society* Englewood Cliffs New Jersey Prentice Hall 1961

Lutz, C. A and Collins J. L *Reading National Geographic* Chicago and London, University of Chicago Press 1993

Lyotard, J-F. *The Postmodern Condition: A Report on Knowledge* Minneapolis, the University of Minnesota Press 1984

Mahon, D., *Studies in Seicento Art & Theory* London, Greenwood 1947

Malamud, B. *Pictures of Fidelman: An Exhibition* New York, Farrar, Strauss, Giroux 1969

Marcus, G. *Lipstick Traces: A Secret History of The 20th Century* Cambridge, Mass Harvard University Press 1989

Marx, K., *The German Ideology* (Ed) C.J. Arthur, London, Lawrence and Wishart

Marx, K., *Preface to a Contribution to a Critique of Political Economy in Karl Marx and Frederick Engels*, Selected Works London, Lawrence and Wishart 1968

Matejka, L. & Pomorska, *Readings in Russian Poetics (Formalist and Structuralist Views)* Cambridge Mass. M.I.T. Press 1971

McCabe, C. *Theory/ Low Culture: Analysing Popular Television and High Film.* Manchester, Manchester University Press 1986

McGilligan, P *Alfred Hitchcock: A Life in Darkness and Light.* New York, Regan Books Harper Collins 2003

McNall, S., Levine, R., and Fantasia, R. (Eds) *Bringing Class Back In Contemporary and Historical Perspectives Boulder*, San Francisco, Oxford Westview 1991

Melia, P and Woods A, *Peter Greenaway Artworks 63-98* Manchester University Press

Metz, C. *Film Language* New York: Oxford University Press, 1974, and

Metz, C. *Language and Cinema* trans. D. Umikerseboek The Hague: Mouton, 1974

Michelson, A., Krauss, R. Crimp, D. and Copjec J. Eds *October: The First Decade 1976-1986* Cambridge Mass, London MIT Press

Mitchell, W.J.T *Iconology: Image, Text, Ideology* Chicago, Illinois University of Chicago Press 1986

Modleski, T. *The Women Who Knew Too Much: Hitchcock and Feminist theory* New York, London Methuen 1988

Moore, B. *Space, Text and Gender* Cambridge, Cambridge University Press 1986

Murray, T. *Like a Film: Ideological Fantasy on Screen, Camera and Canvas* London: Routledge 1993

Mulvey, L. *Visual and Other Pleasures* Bloomington Indiana University Press 1989

Nancy, Jean-Luc, Philippe Lacoue-Labarthe and Simon Sparks (Eds). *Retreating the Political.* Warwick studies in European Philosophy. Routledge. New York, London, 1997

Nelson, C. and Grossberg L (Eds) *Marxism and the Interpretation of Culture* Urbana Ill 1988

Nietzsche, Friedrich *Beyond Good and Evil: Prelude to a Philosophy of the Future* Translated by R.J. Hollingdale with an introduction by Michael Tanner London, Penguin Books, 1973

Norris, C. *Derrida* London, Fontana and Cambridge, Mass Harvard University Press 1987

Norris, C.(ed) *Deconstruction and the Interests of Theory* London Pinter & Norman; Oklahoma Press 1988

Norris, C. *Deconstruction, Postmodernism and the Visual Arts* London Academy Editions 1988

Norris, C. *What's Wrong With Postmodernism: Critical Theory and the Ends of Philosophy* Baltimore, John Hopkins University Press 1990

O'Neill, J.P. (Ed) *Barnett Newman: Selected Writings and Interviews.* New York, Alfred A. Knopf 1993

Pahl, R.E (Ed). On Work: Historical, Comparative and Theoretical Approaches Oxford Basil Blackwell 1992

Pally, Marcia "Cinema as a Total Art Form: An Interview with Peter Greenaway" *Cineaste* 18:3 1991

Parker, R & Pollock, G. *Old Mistresses: Women, Art and Ideology* New York Pantheon 1981

Pascoe, D. *Peter Greenaway: Museums and Moving Images* London Reaktion Books 1997

Pelles, G. *Art Artists and Society: Origins of a Modern Dilemma: Painting in France and England 1750-1850* New Jersey, Englewood Cliffs, Prentice Hall 1963

Pinsky, L.E. *Realism of the Renaissance* Goslitizdat 1962

Peucker, B. *Incorporating Images: Film and the Rival Arts* Princeton, Princeton University Press 1996

Poggioli, R. *The Theory of the Avant-Garde* Cambridge University Press 1968

Poster, M. (Ed) *Baudrillard: Selected Writings.* Cambridge Polity 1988

Powell, C and Paton, G. *Humour in Society: Resistance and Control* Houndmills, Basingstoke, Hampshire, Macmillan Press 1988

Preziosi, D. *Rethinking Art History: Meditations of a Coy Science.* New Haven Yale University Press 1989:72-3

Quart, L "The Cook, The Thief, His Wife and Her Lover" Cineaste 18 No 1 (1990)

Radway, J. *Reading the Romance* Chapel Hill University of North Carolina Press 1984

Rees, A.L and Borzello, (Eds.) *The New Art History* London Camden Press 1989

Resnick, S. and Wolff, R., *Knowledge and Class: A Marxian Critique of Political Economy* Chicago: University of Chicago Press, 1987

Roberts, J. *Postmodernism, Politics and Art* Manchester, Manchester University Press 1990

Rohmer, E and Chabrol, C. trans. Hochman, S. *Hitchcock: The First Forty-Four Films* New York: Ungar Publishing, 1979

Rollins, N "Greenaway-Gaultier: Old Masters, Fashion, Slaves" Cinema Journal 35 No 1 Fall 1995

Rosenberg, B. and White, D. M. *Mass Culture* N.Y. The Free Press 1957

Rosenberg, B & White, D. M. *Mass Culture Revisited* New York Van Nostrand Rheinholt, 1971

Roszak, T. *The Making of a Counterculture: Reflections on the Technocratic Society and Its Youthful Opposition.* New York Doubleday and Co 1968

Ryall, T. *Alfred Hitchcock and the British Cinema* Urbana and Chicago: University of Illinois Press 1986

Schirmacher, Wolfgang, Sven Nebelung (eds). *German Essays On Psychology.* The German Library 62. The Continuum International Publishing Group. New York, London, 2000

Schirmacher, Wolfgang (ed). *German 20th Century Philosophy: The Frankfurt School.* The German Library 78. The Continuum International Publishing Group. New York, London, 2000

Schirmacher, Wolfgang (ed), *Arthur Schopenhauer. Schopenhauer: Philosophical Writings.* The German Library No. 27. The Continuum International Publishing Group. New York, London, 1994

Sennett, R. and Cobb, J. *The Hidden Injuries of Class* New York, Vintage Books 1973

Shikes R. E. and Heller, S. *The Art of Satire. Painters as Caricaturists and Cartoonists from Delacroix to Picasso.* New York Pratt Graphics Centre and Horizon Press 1984

Shusterman, R. (ed) *Bourdieu: A Critical Reader* Oxford Blackwell Publishers 1999

Sklar, R., and Musser, C., *Resisting Images: Essays on Cinema and history* Philadelphia Temple University Press 1990

Sloan, J.E. *Alfred Hitchcock: The Definitive Filmography* Berkeley, Los Angeles: University of California Press 1993

Spoto *The Art of Alfred Hitchcock: Fifty Years of His Films* New York: Doubleday 1979Spoto, D. *The Dark Side of Genius: the Life of Alfred Hitchcock* New York: Ballantine Books, 1983

Spotts, F. *Hitler and the Power of Aesthetics* Woodstock, NY Overlook Press 2003

Stam, R., Burgoyne, R., Flitterman-Lewis, *S. New Vocabularies in Film Semiotics: Structuralism Post-Structuralism and Beyond* London, New York, Routledge 1992

Stephenson, R.M. "Conflict and Control Functions of Humour." American Journal of Sociology 56 1951 569-574

Sterritt, D. *The Films of Alfred Hitchcock* Cambridge: Cambridge University Press, 1993

Steinmetz, L and Greenaway P. *The World of Peter Greenaway* Boston, Journey Editions 1995

Tagg, J. *Grounds of Dispute: Art History, Cultural Politics and the Discursive Field* Minneapolis, University of Minnesota Press

The Block Reader in Visual Culture London and New York Routledge 1996

Thewelweit, K. *Male Fantasies* Vol I&2 Translation Carter, E and Turner, C. Forward, Rabinowich, A and Benjamin, J., Minneapolis University of Minnesota Press 1989

Thompson, E.P, *The Making of the English Working Class* Harmondsworth, Penguin Books 1980

Thompson, J.B *Ideology and Modern Culture* Stanford California, Stanford University Press 1990

Truffaut, F., with Scott, H.G. *Hitchcock* New York: Simon and Schuster, 1967

Van Wert, W. F. "The Cook, the Thief, his Wife and her Lover" Film Quarterly 44:2 winter 1990-91

Voloshinov, V.N. *Marxism and The Philosophy of Language.* L. Matejka and I.R. Titunic, Cambridge Harvard U P 1973

Walker, J.A. *Art and Artists on Screen* Manchester and New York, Manchester University Press 1993

Wilde, A. *Horizons of Assent: Modernism, Postmodernism and the Ironic Imagination* Baltimore Md., John Hopkins University Press 1981

Wilde, O. *The Artist as Critic: Critical Writings of Oscar Wilde* edited by Richard Ellmann New York, Vintage Books, Random House 1968,

Willis, P. *Learning to Labour*, London, Gower 1977

Willis, P. with Simon Jones, Joyce Canaan and Geoff Hurd *Common Culture: Symbolic Work at Play in the Everyday Cultures of the Young* Boulder and San Francisco Westview Press 1990

Williams, G. A "Gramsci's Concept of Egemonia" Journal of the History of Ideas 21:4 pp 586-99

Williams, R. *Culture and Society 1780-1950* London Chatto and Windus 1958

Williams, R. *Keywords: A Vocabulary of Culture and Society* London, Fontana 1976

Williams, R. *Problems in Materialism and Culture: Selected Essays* London Verso 1980

Williams, R. *Towards 2000* London Chatto and Windus, New York Pantheon 1985

Williams, R. *Raymond Williams on Television: Selected Writings* London New York Routledge 1989

Williams, R. *The Politics of Modernism* London, Verso 1989

Willoquet-Maricondi, P., and Alemany-Galway, M.. *Peter Greenaway's Postmodern/ Poststructuralist Cinema* Lanham, Maryland and London, The Scarecrow Press

Wittkower, R.& M. *Born Under Saturn, The Character and Conduct of Artists. A Documented History from Antiquity to the French Revolution* New York, Norton Random House 1963

Wittkower, R "Individualism in Art and Artists: A Renaissance Problem" *Journal of The History of Ideas* Vol 22 pp 285-302 1961

Wittgenstein, L. *Philosophical Investigations Philosophical Investigations*, translated by G.E.M. Anscombe Oxford, Basil Blackwell, 1963

Wittgenstein, L. *Tractatus Logico-Philosophicus* 1 translated by D.F. Pears and B.F. McGuiness London, (Routledge and Kegan Paul, 1961

Wolfe, J. *The Social Production of Art* London, Macmillan 1981

Woods, Alan *Being Naked and Playing Dead* Manchester, New York Manchester University Press, 1996

Wood, R. *Hitchcock's Films Revisited* London and Boston, Faber and Faber, 1989

Woodiwiss, A.*Social Theory after Post-modernism* London, Pluto Press, 1990

Wright, E. (Ed) *Feminism and Psychoanalysis: A Critical Dictionary* Oxford, Blackwell, 1992

Wright, E.R. *Class Counts* Cambridge, Cambridge University Press, 2000

Žižek, S., (ed) *Everything You Always Wanted to Know About Lacan (But were Afraid to ask Hitchcock)* London, Verso 1992

Žižek, S. *The Fright of Real Tears, Kieslowski and The Future.* Bloomington, Indiana University Press. 2001

Žižek, S. (Ed). *The Fright of Real Tears: The Uses and Misuses of Lacan in Film Theory.* Bloomington Indiana University Press. 2000,

Žižek, S., *Did Someone Say Totalitarianism? Four Interventions in the Misuse of a Notion.* London, New York, Verso Books. 2001,

Lukacs, G, John Rees (Translator), Slavoj Žižek and Esther Leslie. *A Defense of History and Class Consciousness.* London, New York, Verso Books. 2000,

Žižek, S., *The Art of the Ridiculous Sublime: On David Lynch's "Lost Highway" Occasional Papers* (Walter Chapin Simpson Center for the Humanities), University of Washington Press. 2000,

Žižek S., *Enjoy Your Symptom! Jacques Lacan in Hollywood and Out.* London and New York, Routledge 2000,

Žižek, S., *The Ticklish Subject: The Absent Centre of Political Ontology (Wo Es War).* London, New York, Verso Books. 1999

Žižek, S., Elizabeth Wright (Editor) and Edmond Wright (Ed). *The Zizek Reader (Blackwell Readers).* London Blackwell 1999,

Zupancic, A. and Žižek, S., *Ethics of the Real: Kant and Lacan (Wo Es War).* London, New York, Verso Books. February 2000

9 780974 853437